Jan Constantin
**Epistemic Defeat**

# Epistemic Studies

―

Philosophy of Science, Cognition and Mind

Edited by
Michael Esfeld, Stephan Hartmann and Albert Newen

Editorial Advisory Board:
Katalin Balog, Claus Beisbart, Craig Callender, Tim Crane, Katja Crone,
Ophelia Deroy, Mauro Dorato, Alison Fernandes, Jens Harbecke,
Vera Hoffmann-Kolss, Max Kistler, Beate Krickel, Anna Marmodoro,
Alyssa Ney, Hans Rott, Wolfgang Spohn, Gottfried Vosgerau

# Volume 47

Jan Constantin
# Epistemic Defeat

A Treatment of Defeat
as an Independent Phenomenon

DE GRUYTER

The dissertation "Epistemic Defeat – A Treatment of Defeat as an Independent Phenomenon" was written to fulfill the graduate requirements for the PhD program of the a.r.t.e.s Graduate School for the Humanities at the University of Cologne (Albertus-Magnus-Platz, 50923 Cologne, Germany). The research was conducted at the University of Cologne's philosophy department as part of the project "Dissense in der Philosophie. Semantische und epistemologische Grundlagen", funded by the Deutsche Forschungsgesellschaft under the grant number 283100111.

ISBN 978-3-11-126999-3
e-ISBN (PDF) 978-3-11-073054-8
e-ISBN (EPUB) 978-3-11-073068-5
ISSN 2512-5168

**Library of Congress Control Number:** 2021937868

**Bibliographic information published by the Deutsche Nationalbibliothek**
The Deutsche Nationalbibliothek lists this publication in the Deutsche Nationalbibliografie; detailed bibliographic data are available on the Internet at http://dnb.dnb.de.

© 2023 Walter de Gruyter GmbH, Berlin/Boston
This volume is text- and page-identical with the hardback published in 2021.
Printing and binding: CPI books GmbH, Leck

www.degruyter.com

# Preface

The dissertation "Epistemic Defeat – A Treatment of Defeat as an Independent Phenomenon" was written to fulfill the graduate requirements for the PhD program of the a.r.t.e.s Graduate School for the Humanities at the University of Cologne, Germany (Albertus-Magnus-Platz, 50923 Cologne, Germany). I was engaged in researching and writing this dissertation from 2015 to 2019.

The research was conducted at the University of Cologne's philosophy department as part of the project "Dissense in der Philosophie. Semantische und epistemologische Grundlagen", funded by the *Deutsche Forschungsgesellschaft* under the grant number 283100111.

I want to thank my supervisor, Prof. Dr. Thomas Grundmann, for years of guidance, cooperation, friendship and spirited debate. He inspired and challenged me to do all of my best work and had a huge positive influence on my professional and personal development. I could not have asked for a better mentor.

My thanks also go to Prof. Dr. Sven Bernecker for his insightful comments and for his extensive feedback that helped me improve my work considerably. Prof. Dr. Anne Burkard also deserves my heartfelt thanks for her careful review of the finished manuscript and for highly interesting suggestions concerning possible didactic applications of the work.

I also want to thank my colleagues and dear friends Dominik Balg and Steffen Koch for their daily readiness to discuss ideas and for generally being the best office mates I could have wished for. Further thanks go to Karolin Meinert, Chris Ranalli, Jakob Ohlhost, Carina Schleeweit and Peer Schittenhelm. All of you made the workplace into a place to have fun at. I will miss our lunches together.

Finally, I would like to thank my family for their continued love and support. My wife Julia Ida Constantin and my parents Ewald and Doris Wieben deserve special notes of thanks for keeping me motivated and listening to my strange ideas. I am also grateful to Gerd Wieben, Anja Wieben-James and Henry James for proof-reading some of my work and for showing interest in the things I am passionate about. I fully realize how fortunate I am to have all of you in my life.

# Contents

**Introduction —— 1**

**1 Defeaters, Functional Profiles and Deep Distinctions —— 7**
1.1 Terminology —— 7
1.2 Deep and Superficial Distinctions —— 14
1.3 A Preliminary Theory and Taxonomy of Defeat —— 22

**2 Rebutting Defeat —— 28**
2.1 Rebutting Defeaters —— 28
2.1.1 Partial, Successful and Perfect Rebuttal and Relative Concentrations of Input —— 31
2.1.2 Degrees of Rebuttal and an Account of Rebutting Defeat —— 40
2.2 The Epistemic Status of Defeaters —— 42
2.2.1 Rebutting Defeat and the Defeater-Justifier-Symmetry —— 43
2.2.2 The Inclusive Thesis: Defeaters Need Not Have Positive Epistemic Status —— 49
2.2.3 The Exclusive Thesis: Defeaters Do Need to Have Positive Epistemic Status —— 54

**3 Undercutting Defeat —— 60**
3.1 The Naïve Higher-Order Account —— 62
3.1.1 Pollock's View —— 62
3.1.2 The Milk-Taster Case and the Naïve Higher-Order Account —— 65
3.1.3 Worries about the Naïve Higher-Order Account of Undercutting Defeat —— 71
3.2 The Suspension Account —— 76
3.2.1 Undercutting Defeat and Suspension of Judgment —— 77
3.2.2 First Objection: The Source-Sensitivity of Undercutting Defeaters —— 84
3.2.3 Second Objection: Undercutting Defeaters and Higher-order Support —— 85
3.2.4 Third Objection: Undercutting Defeaters and the Weighing of Support —— 87
3.2.5 A Summary of the Arguments and an Extension to the Account of Rebutting Defeat —— 89

| | | |
|---|---|---|
| 3.3 | | The Commitment-based Higher-Order Account —— 92 |
| 3.3.1 | | Actual and Apparent Commitments: A First Stab at the Concept —— 93 |
| 3.3.2 | | The Nature of Epistemic Commitments: Getting the Account off the Ground —— 96 |
| 3.3.3 | | Arguments against Commitment-based Higher-Order Accounts of Undercutting Defeat —— 101 |
| 3.3.4 | | The Demandingness-Trilemma as the Central Problem Facing Accounts of Undercutting Defeat —— 105 |
| 3.4 | | The Rebasing Account —— 106 |
| 3.4.1 | | The Re-evaluation of Doxastic Attitudes and the Concept of Rebasing —— 108 |
| 3.4.2 | | The Re-evaluation of Doxastic Attitudes and Higher-order Rebutting Defeat —— 115 |
| 3.4.3 | | Formulating the Unpacked Version Rebasing Account of Undercutting Defeat —— 122 |
| 3.4.4 | | Simplifying the Rebasing Account of Undercutting Defeat —— 128 |
| 3.4.5 | | Accounting for the Key Features of Undercutting Defeat —— 131 |
| 3.5 | | Some Objections —— 136 |
| 3.5.1 | | First Objection: The Rebasing Account Can't Deal with Counterexamples Any Better than its Rivals —— 136 |
| 3.5.2 | | Second Objection: The Rebasing Account Does Not Allow Undercutting Defeat for Unreflective Subjects —— 139 |
| 3.5.3 | | Third Objection: The Rebasing Account Does Not Allow Undercutting Defeat for Cognitively Unsophisticated Subjects —— 143 |
| | | |
| **4** | | **Putting Things Together —— 147** |
| 4.1 | | The Extended Account of Rebutting Defeat —— 147 |
| 4.2 | | A Defense of Causal Accounts of Defeat —— 152 |
| 4.2.1 | | Attempting to Account for Double-Agent Cases, While Preserving Theoretical Unity —— 153 |
| 4.2.2 | | Against the Reasons-Against-Belief Theory of Defeat —— 160 |
| 4.3 | | The Rebasing Account of Undercutting Defeat in its Final Form —— 165 |
| | | |
| **5** | | **Defeat and Epistemic Justification —— 169** |
| 5.1 | | Defeat and Epistemic Norms —— 172 |
| 5.1.1 | | Type-1 Obligations: Obligations to Re-evaluate —— 174 |

| 5.1.2 | Type-2 Obligations: Obligations to Re-evaluate in a Certain Way —— 176 |
|---|---|
| 5.2 | Defeat and Internalism —— 182 |
| 5.2.1 | Introducing a Simple Internalist Picture —— 183 |
| 5.2.2 | An Internalist Accommodation of Epistemic Defeat —— 187 |
| 5.2.3 | A Problem for Moderately Internalist Versions of Evidentialism —— 193 |
| 5.3 | Defeat and Externalism —— 196 |
| 5.3.1 | Simple Reliabilism —— 196 |
| 5.3.2 | Reliabilism's Trouble with Defeat —— 198 |
| 5.3.3 | Reliabilism and the Rebasing Account of Undercutting Defeat —— 203 |
| 5.3.4 | Testing the Reliabilist Accommodation of the Rebasing Account: Rebasing and Chaining —— 206 |
| 5.3.5 | Testing the Reliabilist Accommodation of the Rebasing Account: Active and Passive Ignorance —— 210 |
| 5.4 | Normative Defeaters —— 214 |
| 5.4.1 | Assessing the Case for the Possibility of Normative Defeat —— 215 |
| 5.4.2 | Remaining Motivations to Accept the Possibility of Normative Defeat: The Example of Goldberg's View —— 226 |
| 5.4.3 | The Rebasing Account and Normative Defeat: Passively Ignored Defeaters as Normative Defeaters? —— 228 |
| **6** | **Defeat and Disagreement —— 233** |
| 6.1 | Disagreement —— 235 |
| 6.1.1 | Examples and Basic Terminology —— 235 |
| 6.1.2 | Disagreement as a Defeater: Strong and Weak Versions of Conciliationism —— 238 |
| 6.2 | A Theory-driven Argument for Strong Conciliationism —— 242 |
| 6.2.1 | Source-neutral and Source-sensitive Support and Defeat —— 243 |
| 6.2.2 | The Argument for Strong Conciliationism —— 247 |
| 6.3 | The Rebasing Account of Higher-Order Defeat —— 258 |
| 6.3.1 | Higher-order Defeaters and Undercutting Defeaters —— 258 |
| 6.3.2 | Complex and Simple Cases of Higher-Order Defeat —— 262 |
| 6.3.3 | Persistent, Fleeting and Infectious Higher-Order Defeaters —— 266 |
| 6.3.4 | Peer-Disagreement and Higher-Order Defeat —— 268 |

**Conclusion —— 271**

**Bibliography —— 274**

**Index – Definitions and Examples —— 284**

**Index – Names —— 287**

# Introduction

When we judge whether or not something is the case, we want the resulting attitude to be epistemically *justified*. This means that we want to form and hold it in a way that makes it *well supported* by good reasons, evidence or some other basis that renders it likely to be adequate. When I wonder whether my neighbor is breaking a law when he annoyingly washes his car on a Sunday and for the fifth time this week, I might ask myself whether the truth of the proposition that he is breaking a law is well supported by my evidence. If I distinctly remember a friend of mine, who is a law-student, mention that washing your car five times a week in your own backyard is not permitted, it seems that it is indeed well supported. I may then judge and consequently form the belief that my neighbor is breaking the law on the basis of that memory of her testimony and my current impressions, which ideally makes it a justified belief. Had I instead formed the belief on the basis of my wish that it be true that any activity that is this obnoxious is against the law, the belief would have been epistemically *un*justified.

If everything is going well for us, epistemically, we have many justified and few unjustified beliefs. Some of them may even be so well formed or obvious that very few, if any, new realizations can or should convince us of their falsity. It is hard to envision a situation in which one has reason to doubt one's own name or belief in one's own existence. Most of the support for our beliefs is not that good, however. It is almost always realistically possible for it to be counterbalanced or called into question by new information. My lawyer-friend's opinion may *for now* sufficiently support my belief about the lack of lawfulness of my neighbor's car-washing habit to make it justified, but it is certainly possible that this changes. I may find out that my friend was drunk that evening or that many lawyers disagree with her. That kind of information neutralizes the justifying power of my friend's opinion and renders it inappropriate for me to continue to believe that the long arm of the law may yet put an end to my neighbor's nefarious practices. Support that is sufficient *in this sense*, namely, support that is good enough for justification, *for now* or *as long as nothing messes up its justifying power*, can give our beliefs "prima facie" justification (Pollock 1974, p. 42). It should be rather obvious that the absolute majority of our justified beliefs enjoy at least prima facie justification. Equally clear is the significance of justification-removing information for the extent to which we are doing well with respect to the truth and what beliefs it might be OK for us to hold. Such information is called a "defeater" (Pollock 1974, p. 42).

The idea behind epistemic defeat is quite intuitive. A defeater is a piece of information obtained by a subject that renders a belief held by that subject unjustified by shedding doubt on that belief. Intuitively, this results in a state where it would be *irrational* for the subject to hold on to the belief in the face of the defeater. In the example above, the information that my lawyer-friend was drunk that night is a defeater for my belief that my neighbor is breaking the law: It sheds doubt on the support that my friend's testimony offers for my belief and it makes it irrational for me to continue to believe that my neighbor is breaking the law. I will call the belief that my neighbor is breaking the law in this example and analogous attitudes in similar cases the "target-attitude" of the defeater and speak of it being *defeated*. The reason why I will not call it "target-belief" is that, as I will show later, attitudes other than beliefs can be the target of defeaters.

The idea of a defeater removing the justification of its target-attitude is intuitively straightforward but, as will become clear, fully explaining what it means in the more specialized vocabulary of epistemology opens up a number of difficult questions. One of the arising tasks is the following: The information that my lawyer-friend was drunk does not indicate that my belief about my neighbor's unlawful behavior is false. It rather shows that there is something wrong with the *basis* for my belief. This needs to be modelled in a way that respects constraints that arise from widely accepted features of epistemic justification.

A second task concerns the integration of a theory of defeat with broader frameworks. Since defeaters interfere with epistemic justification, how they are best characterized and categorized depends on the theory of epistemic justification that is accepted.[1] For instance, Internalists claim, roughly, that justification is wholly internal or accessible to the subject, whereas externalists think that it consists in an objective fact about the world, like an objectively reliable process (cf. Pappas 2014). Accordingly, what it means for a defeater to remove a belief's justification might mean different things for internalists, externalists and others. Since the possibility of defeat is intuitively very plausible and widely accepted in epistemology (e. g. Pryor 2004; Bergmann 2006; Lackey 2008; Grundmann 2011; Goldman 2012), the phenomenon must be accommodated by any theory of justification. One of the main goals of this book is the development of a theory of defeat that is neutral with respect to the different theories of justification and that can then be integrated with a broad plethora of such theories. What this means is that the phenomenon of epistemic defeat will not be treated as

---

[1] For the purposes of this book, whenever I mention the term "justification", I will refer to *epistemic* justification, unless otherwise indicated.

a mere test-case for theories of justification, but as an interesting phenomenon in its own right. What this does not mean is that the theory of defeat will be developed completely independently of the features of justification. This would clearly be impossible since defeat targets justification and the structure of the latter must therefore fit the structure of the former.

Achieving the goal of a universal theory of defeat will require answers to a number of related questions about the different forms that defeaters can take and about their broader features. What kinds of states can be defeaters (Pollock and Cruz 1999)? Do defeaters need to be justified themselves in order to have their destructive effect or is "mere" belief enough (cf. Pryor 2004; Alexander 2017)? Is a subject's belief also defeated, if there exists a fact that somehow speaks against that belief and that the subject is not aware of, but that she *ought* to be aware of (e.g. Harman 1973, 1980)? These and other questions will be addressed along the way. They illustrate why the easily accessible idea of epistemic defeat is by no means easy to forge into a comprehensive account.

A secondary goal of this book is to provide a theory of defeat that can be fruitfully applied to more specialized debates. One older example where defeater theory is used to shed light on a different issue is the epistemology of religious belief. It seems that science, certain bits of philosophy and other sources provide defeaters for the belief that there is a god and for the claims of the Bible (e.g. Quinn 1985). Some hold against this that those defeaters can themselves be defeated. Alvin Plantinga even argues that naturalism, the view that only objects and properties observable by science exist, is self-defeating (e.g. Plantinga 1994, 2000; Jäger 2005). The participants of this debate realized that such claims must ultimately depend on a proper understanding of what a defeater is and what it does (Beilby 2002). But there are also more recent debates that gain in size and relevance and where the application of defeater theory is both fruitful and slow in developing. The application that will be conducted in this book concerns the analysis of peer-disagreement. When someone disagrees with us, whom we judge to be just as likely as ourselves to be right about the contentious issue, it seems that this fact has a negative impact on the justificatory status of what we believe. (e.g. Christensen 2007; Elga 2007; Feldman 2007) This is exactly what a defeater does and thus it would seem that disagreement is relevant to justification because it constitutes a defeater (see also Matheson 2009; Thune 2010; Grundmann 2013; Goldberg 2013). But what kind of defeater does it give us and what difference does it make, whether it gives us one kind, rather than the other? Since the epistemology of disagreement is highly relevant in contemporary philosophy and has far-reaching implications in many aspects of life, I will conduct an application of the theory of defeat developed here to this field in order to illustrate its versatility and the practical relevance of theories of defeat. It will be shown that, while the way in which disagreement defeats depends on the details of the case, this dependency is clearly structured in accordance with the functions of different kinds of defeaters, as laid out by the theory. This will also allow a verdict in favor of one of the competing accounts of peer-disagreement.

Next, the structure of this book will be introduced in more detail. First, two general assumptions must be made visible: In the first four chapters, I will be exclusively concerned with *doxastic* defeaters,[2] that is, with defeaters that are in some sense part of the subject's system of doxastic attitudes, either by being an attitude like belief, disbelief or suspension of judgment themselves, or by being otherwise available to or registered by the subject in some sense. This approach will be broadened in the fifth chapter, when the possibility of normative defeat will be investigated. In addition, I will start my analysis from a broadly causal picture of defeat, that is, from a picture, according to which defeaters characteristically cause loss of justification. This assumption will be defended in chapter four. To get an overview, I will quickly go through the chapters, before moving on.

In the first chapter, I argue that defeaters must be individuated by the function they perform with respect to the surrounding doxastic structure of their target-attitudes. I will identify at least two "deep" functions that correspond to the two best-known kinds of defeaters and suggest that they can therefore be regarded as the most fundamental kinds, with most other kinds being derivatives. Furthermore, preliminary accounts of the fundamental kinds of defeaters will be established, which will form the starting point for further discussion.

The second and third chapters will in many ways be the centerpiece of this book. Each of them will develop one of the preliminary accounts from the first chapter into full-fledged analyses of the ways in which defeaters defeat and relate them to existing work.

The fourth chapter will feature extensive arguments that are supposed to illustrate the superiority of the developed account – the Rebasing Account of Defeat – over existing rivals and answer many of the questions that arise along the way. In addition, the causal picture of defeat presupposed up until this point will be dealt with and defended against a promising alternative (Loughrist 2015) in light of the discussion so far.

In the fifth chapter, it will be shown how different theories of epistemic justification can cash out the Rebasing Account, which will complete the answer to the question how defeaters remove *justification*. I will also deal with the issue of *ignoring* defeaters. The question whether there are non-doxastic defeaters will

---

[2] This label is taken from Lackey 1999.

also be revisited. Some think that information that is not part of the doxastic system, but is such that the subject doesn't possess it but *ought* to possess it, can defeat knowledge (e.g. Harman 1973, 1980; Pollock and Cruz 1999; Baehr 2009; Axtell 2011; Goldberg 2017a forthcoming) or even justification (e.g. Kornblith 1983; Lackey 1999, 2005b; Gibbons 2006). I will turn to the question whether there are such *normative* defeaters[3] in the last section of the fifth chapter and also investigate under what circumstances, if ever, defeaters that *are* part of the subject's doxastic system would nevertheless have to be counted as normative defeaters.

Chapter six will then conclude the book. It will deal with the epistemology of disagreement from a defeater-based approach. Specifically, I will investigate both *whether* various kinds of disagreement structurally correspond to cases of defeat and therefore generate defeaters and *what kinds* of defeater may be generated by what kinds of disagreement. For example, if it can be shown that the information that one disagrees about the truth of the putative target-attitude with someone whom one judges to be equally likely to be right as oneself makes the target-attitude at least somewhat less justified, it seems that such information acts at least as a partial defeater (e.g. Thune 2010). However, there is still much room for debate about the extent of this defeat, which in turn seems to depend on the exact nature of the defeater (see Matheson 2009; Christensen 2010a; Kelly 2011; Thune 2010). Clarification on how the circumstances of the disagreement (like the relative levels of competence of the opponents and other factors) relate to the conditions relevant to different types of defeaters in general will clearly be highly relevant here. I will agree with the view that certain kinds of disagreement provide a kind of undermining defeat and supplement this view with arguments from analogous cases and characteristic features of such defeaters, as established in previous chapters.

In general, this book aims to give an extensive account of defeat as a broader epistemic principle that can be applied to all kinds of issues, many of which I can only name or gloss over. It may therefore seem at times as though I am ignoring the more important issues and focus on a theoretical detail. However, I hope to show that a correct understanding of such supposed details has very wide implications and can lead to great progress in the application areas, simply by providing weighty theoretical reasons for or against certain positions. The more general thought here is that, while intuitive judgments on key cases certainly are an important source of philosophical evidence, at least in some areas too little work is done to supplement them with premises from broader

---

[3] Again, the label is taken from Lackey 1999.

principles. What we often find instead is the development of highly local principles from case-judgments that are entirely dependent on the prospects of finding counterexamples, where that prospect is pretty good, precisely because they apply only to a narrowly delineated topic. Examples include the independence principle in the debate around peer-disagreement (cf. Christensen 2011, pp. 1–2) and the preemption principle for epistemic authority (cf. Zagzebski 2012). Principles can be made less vulnerable to counterexamples, if they can be derived from broad and widely accepted epistemic principles. This is helpful because it shows that the discovery of applying broader principles in a debate can stabilize positions and further consensus on them. The principle of defeat is both especially fruitful in that regard, as my discussion of the issue of disagreement will show, and somewhat underexplored. Philosophers tend to take it for granted that there are defeaters and that they work broadly as their discoverers describe them to work. Even when they take center stage, their effect is not so much analyzed or explained as it is merely described.[4] This is why the topic of defeat is not just a theoretical detail, but an issue that, if properly explored, can significantly further the project of epistemology. In this context, I want to give substantial room to theoretical arguments that connect the analysis of defeaters to other theories and principles. That said, thought-experiments and case analysis will still occur frequently and play an important role. In fact, I aim to take the results very seriously. These cases may also serve to illustrate that defeat on its own is more interesting than meets the eye. In this regard, it is my hope that I will manage to convey to the reader the sense of academic curiosity that gripped me when I started thinking about this book's topic.

---

[4] A notable exception is Loughrist's (2015) account. He also notes the near-absence of a detailed and comprehensive theory of defeat, in spite of numerous mentions and working definitions in the papers of epistemologists and makes an excellent attempt at rectifying the situation. The fruitfulness of an application to fields where much narrower principles are in use, such as peer-disagreement, serves as an argument for the need for a good theory as well (cf. Loughrist 2015, pp. 11 ff).

# 1 Defeaters, Functional Profiles and Deep Distinctions

To get started, I will give and to some extent defend criteria for distinguishing fundamental from non-fundamental kinds of defeaters and take a first stab at analyzing the fundamental kinds. First, I will introduce and define the terminology I will be using throughout the book. This will also provide a framework for evaluating strategies to distinguish between types of defeaters by function. Second, I will look at cases of defeat and use the framework to describe structural differences between them. It will be argued that the manners in which defeaters defeat can be distinguished in "deep" and "superficial" ways, where only the former are constitutive of the most basic kinds of defeaters: rebutting and undercutting defeaters. The explicit goal of this exercise is to narrow down defeater-classes to a few fundamental ones. For this, I will partly rely on initially plausible hypotheses that can be discussed at a later point and partly on more clear-cut arguments from case-analysis and the general structure of epistemic justification. This will lay the groundwork for analyzing the fundamental classes of defeaters in detail. Third, a preliminary account of rebutting and undercutting defeat will be introduced, which will serve as a starting point for a more thorough analysis in the next chapters.

## 1.1 Terminology

When dealing with defeaters, talk about justification, epistemic support, basing and the like will be inevitable. Importantly, I want to give an account of defeat that is neutral with respect to theories of justification and so I want to phrase such talk in a vocabulary that does not commit me to any one such theory. To make it clearer why such vocabulary is needed for what I have in mind, let me quickly go over the plan: In the picture I will be working with, defeaters characteristically remove or weaken the justification of their target-attitudes. They therefore stand in relation to some aspect of what makes those beliefs prima facie justified and so the concept of justification is relevant to an account of defeat. Now, as any epistemologist will know, the question of how to properly conceive of epistemic justification is not even remotely settled and a significant number of accounts can be identified. In order to stay as neutral as possible, the task must therefore be to find a theory of defeat that can be shown to be not only compatible, but integrable (in a more substantial sense) with as many of these accounts as possible.

In order to at least approximately achieve this goal, accounts of justification can be conceived of as arranged on two spectra between two pairs of "pure" views: On the one hand, a spectrum exists between a staunchly access-internalist view according to which justification is exclusively a matter of the subject's accessible psychology and a staunchly externalist view, according to which justification can be only a matter of facts outside of the subject's ken. On the other hand, a spectrum exists between a deontological view of justification, according to which justification is essentially a matter of normative rule-fulfillment, and the aforementioned staunchly externalist view, according to which justification is a purely descriptive concept. All three views will be developed in much greater detail in chapter 4. The general idea, however, can already be seen: If the account of defeat I am attempting to develop can be integrated with all of these simple views, it can be expected to be integrable with all other views on the spectra (provided that the characteristics that define the spectra are sufficiently relevant to the mechanics of defeat). This will only work if the theory of defeat can be spelled out in terms that are neutral with respect to the three pure views, that is, in terms that can be cashed out in the terms of each view. Phrasing the goal here in slightly different terms, the terminology to be developed is merely a way to attach easily recognizable names or labels to important joints of the doxastic structure that defeaters characteristically interact with. I take it that the relevance of these joints to epistemic justification is the bare minimum that one has to accept, if one hopes to accommodate the phenomenon of defeat and the fact that they are an inherent component of any theory of justification. What theorists disagree over is rather what exactly plays the role of the joints. It seems that deontologism is something of an exception to this, since it can stay relatively neutral about how these roles are filled, as long as it is ensured that the resulting attitudes can be evaluated through normative rules. Thus, while it is a point of disagreement between internalist and externalist theories whether what makes an attitude justified can be external to one's conscious grasp, a deontologist could accept either position, as long as the subject can be held responsible for responding properly to these factors. Therefore, I will assume that, for the terms to be introduced, neutrality between internalism and externalism amounts to neutrality between all three positions.

Generally, defeaters must be explained against the background of what I call the "surrounding doxastic structure" of target- attitudes. That is, defeaters defeat by interacting with whatever ordering of stuff makes it the case that the defeated attitude starts out justified. Whether this stuff has to be *cognitive* stuff can be left open. The ordering of the surrounding doxastic structure of a doxastic attitude can be configured in a number of ways that determine the epistemic status of that attitude. It can, for example, be such that the attitude is *justified*; merely *supported* to some (possibly insufficient) degree by some item it is based on; *not supported* at all but held on the basis of something unsuited; *supported by, but not held on the basis of* some item, and so on. Whatever is relevant to these matters is part of the surrounding doxastic structure. Thus, the structure will include that which makes it the case that the relevant attitude has a certain epistemic status, but it will not include *unrelated* facts about the wishes and dreams of the subject, their other *unconnected* beliefs, tastes, or other characteristics. Filling in the details of what is or can be part of the structure mostly belongs to the project of analyzing justification and need not be done here in full. For my purposes, it is enough to establish *surrounding doxastic structure* as a label for everything that is relevant to the epistemic status of an attitude and therefore a candidate for being interacted with by a defeater, and to add only uncontroversial, functional descriptions of key parts of the structure that are required in order to capture important patterns and differences in these interactions. Neutrality is thus preserved in the sense that the descriptions can be fulfilled by various items, depending on one's favorite theory of justification. In what follows, I will provide these descriptions and attach labels to the relevant functional profiles.

The first term is that of "input".

*Input: i* is a piece of input, iff a subject *S* is in possession of *i* and there is a doxastic attitude *b* for *S*, such that it is possible that *b* is *doxastically based* on *i*.

Input is what is available to a subject for basing a doxastic attitude on, *independently on the effect it may have on the so-based attitude*.[1] That is, input can support a given attitude, but it need not do so, as attitudes can, in principle, be based on items that are epistemically irrelevant, such as wishes or dreams. The specifics of a given theory of justification may amount to restrictions on this very liberal picture, as such theories differ often precisely with respect to what kinds of things typically form the basis of doxastic attitudes. For example, for internalism this may be mental states like experiences or beliefs or even external states, depending on what version of the view is adopted (cf. e.g. Conee and Feldman 2004b; Kelly 2016). In contrast, some externalists will want to say that input is whatever belief-formation processes work on or start from to produce beliefs. This could mean mental states, like beliefs, but also experiences or external facts (cf. Goldman 2012; Goldman and Beddor 2016). These differences will presumably also ground different constraints on what it means that

---

[1] Plantinga 1994 employs the term of "doxastic input" in a similar way.

input is "possessed" or "available" for basing, as mental states will likely be present in these modes in a different sense than external facts. Suffice it to say that there is agreement among different theories of justification that subjects can be in a position such that there is something available to them that can be the basis of a doxastic attitude and that, if it is made the basis of an attitude, makes a difference to the epistemic status of that attitude. That *something* is what I call "input".

Importantly, input does not necessarily have to have a potentially *positive* impact on the epistemic status of the doxastic attitude that can be based on it. This is why I will distinguish between *positive, neutral or negative* input for a given attitude. Let me illustrate the general idea with respect to positive input, as it is often the most relevant with respect to the justification of beliefs: A piece of input is positive input for a belief when it would improve a belief's epistemic status, if the belief was based on it (in the sense of a counterfactual). Thus, $i'$ is a piece of positive input for the belief $b$, iff $i'$ is a piece of input of a subject $S$, such that, if $S$ based $b$ on $i'$, $b$'s epistemic status would improve (it would become justified to a higher degree) (cf. Korcz 2000, pp. 525–526). There is a sense in which input epistemically *supports* an attitude that it can have a positive impact on, whether or not the relevant attitude is actually based on it. This kind of support is *propositional support*.[2] A fairly close notion might be that of *evidence*, but the idea of positive input can also be fleshed out in externalist terms, such as those of reliabilism: A piece of positive input for a belief $b$ is something that a reliable process available to the subject can process and that has $b$ as its output. Input can also be neutral. I take it that we can base beliefs and other attitudes, at least in principle, on a great many different things, possibly including wishful thinking, external instructions, mantra-like conditioning or epiphanies. The vast majority of these things won't make the attitude better or worse off, either because they are intrinsically unsuited (completely unrelated to correctness of the attitude) or because we lack the capacities to process them in the relevant way.[3] I *can* base the belief that it will rain tomorrow on the realization that there is a car outside my window. Having observed the car is thus input for the belief that it will rain tomorrow, but it is neutral in that it does not pertain in any relevant sense to whether it will rain. Also, being sometimes blatantly irrational, one might base a doxastic attitude on a piece of input that one knows to fail to epistemically support the belief. I

---

2 For an example of this term in use, see Kvanvig 1996, pp. 285–288. See also Turri 2010.
3 One may think that input should be less liberally constrained, but since one would have to argue for this and nothing hangs on it for me here, I will assume the most liberal option with the understanding that more limited conceptions work just as well.

might base the belief that my crush likes me on wishful thinking, fully knowing that wishful thinking doesn't make the belief any better or worse off. Finally, input can also be *negative input* for a doxastic attitude, if it would make the attitude *worse* off, if it were based on the input. As we will see later, rebutting defeaters are negative input, but the details of this are somewhat more complicated and there is a lot of groundwork to be put into place first, so I will not go into more detail here.

The second term to be introduced is that of a doxastic attitude "being based on" some piece of input or the input "basing" a doxastic attitude.

> *Basing:* A doxastic attitude *b* is based on a piece of input *i*, iff *i* is part of the cause of the formation of *b*.

The idea is that in order for an attitude to be justified in the sense we mostly care about, not only must one have the right kind of input for the attitude, but the attitude must also be *related* to the input in the right way. There must not just be positive input, but the attitude must also be held *on the basis of* that input. To illustrate this better, consider the following well-known case: Raco is a racist who believes on the basis of his prejudices that people of a certain ethnicity are especially susceptible to a disease. He then becomes a doctor and acquires a lot of excellent medical evidence that this is indeed true. However, he does not employ his new knowledge as the basis for his belief, but continues to hold it on the basis of his prejudices (cf. Lehrer 2000, pp. 196–197). Since it is intuitively extremely plausible that Raco's belief is not justified, in spite of his excellent medical evidence, the view that the relevant attitude must be based on the relevant input in order to achieve justification is widely held in epistemology (e.g. Pollock and Cruz 1999, pp. 35–36; Korcz 2000, pp. 525–526; Kvanvig 2003, section B1; See also Turri 2010).

The basing-relation is standardly conceived of as a causal relation.[4] Thus, very roughly, an attitude *b* is based on a piece of input *i precisely* if holding *b* is an effect of possessing or acquiring *i*.[5] Proper basing or "well-foundedness" (Conee and Feldman 1985, p. 24; Feldman 2002b, p. 46) is crucial to *doxastic* justification, which can be contrasted with *propositional* justification, which results

---

[4] See, however, the somewhat more nuanced, dispositional approach proposed by Turri (2010). I will not go into these debates here. It should become apparent that something like Turri's conception can be applied to the account I develop in later chapters.

[5] Not much hangs on how to spell this out exactly. Let me just note that I will assume basing to be a causal relation and that my definition here is controversial, but not deeply relevant for my purposes. For an overview of causal theories, see Korcz 1997. For objections and discussion, see e.g. Plantinga 1993a; Lehrer 2000; Korcz 2000.

from sufficient propositional support. The notion of propositional justification, unlike doxastic justification, concerns only the weight and direction of support of the input available, leaving basing aside. Due to the structural features of specific defeater-types, there is reason to think that some defeaters characteristically remove doxastic justification, which explains the relevance of the basing relation to their analysis. All of these issues and notions will be addressed in much greater detail later. Note that the presence of the basing-relation is what turns mere input into input relevant to doxastic justification. The definitions of input and basing thus supplement each other in explaining the relationship between mere input and relevant input in this sense. Since it will be useful to quickly refer to either kind, additional labels will be given to them.

The third term is therefore that of a "doxastic base".

*Doxastic Base:* $j$ is a doxastic base, iff $j$ is a piece of input of a subject $s$, such that $S$ has a doxastic attitude $b$ and $b$ is based on $j$ (or $j$ bases $b$).

As noted above, a doxastic base is a piece of input that *actually* stands in relation to an attitude, such that it is relevant to the status of the attitude with respect to doxastic justification. Importantly, parallel to distinctions between positive, neutral and negative input, we can also distinguish between *positive, neutral and negative doxastic bases:* A positive doxastic base for an attitude is a piece of positive input that stands in the basing relation to that attitude. The kind of epistemic support that an attitude enjoys in virtue of having a positive doxastic base will be called "doxastic support". Thus, an attitude that is doxastically supported to a sufficient degree is doxastically justified. Correspondingly, a neutral or a negative doxastic base for an attitude would be a neutral or negative piece of input, respectively, that the attitude is based on with corresponding effects on doxastic justification (no change for neutral bases, negative impact for negative bases).

It is in principle possible to have more than one doxastic base for a doxastic attitude, since any attitude can in principle be based on more than one piece of input. This possibility is compatible with different theories of justification. For evidentialism as a version of internalism, for example, a belief might be based on several pieces of evidence at once, while in an externalist theory like reliabilism, a process or method may have more than one starting point in the formation or sustenance of an attitude. When referring to the set of all doxastic bases for a belief, I will be speaking of its "total doxastic base".

Finally, the fourth term is that of a "justifier".

*Justifier:* $j'$ is a justifier, iff $j'$ is a total doxastic base for a doxastic attitude $b$ of a subject $S$, such that $b$ is epistemically justified.

A justifier is the total doxastic base of a doxastically justified attitude. Having a label for this will make it easier to quickly refer to a target-attitude's bases. Note that a justifier is a *total* doxastic base, which means that several doxastic bases can be aggregated into a justifier. Thus, it might be that only several pieces of positive input together suffice to imbue the attitude that is based on them with a sufficiently positive epistemic status for it to count as justified. Of course, sometimes a single doxastic base is enough.

Another import of this definition of a justifier is the fact that it allows for a justified attitude to be based *not only on positive* doxastic bases, but also on neutral or even negative ones. As long as the total doxastic base, that is, the set of all input that forms the base of the attitude, is sufficiently supportive of the attitude (if it is, on balance, sufficiently positive), it will be justified. For example, I might base my belief that it will rain tomorrow on watching the weather forecast *and* on seeing a child play in front of my window. That belief is justified because the weather forecast is a very weighty positive doxastic base, while seeing the child is neutral and thus offers no doxastic support at all. Nevertheless, seeing the child is a doxastic base for the belief, because I base my belief on it and it is therefore also part of the belief's justifier. This idea can be extended not only to doxastic justification, but also propositional justification: If one possesses a set of pieces of input $r$ for an attitude $b$, such that if one held $b$ on the basis of $r$, $b$ would be doxastically justified, then $b$ is propositionally justified.[6] This idea will be critically revisited in the last chapter. It appears that there are cases where one can have sufficiently positive input for propositional but still be barred from doxastic justification because one has made or will make some mistake within the process of basing one's attitude on it (Turri 2010, pp. 315–316; cf. Silva 2017, pp. 315–318). Such cases seem to show that doxastic justification goes beyond basing an attitude on a set of input that is sufficiently supportive.

---

**6** This may sound a bit too reliabilist-friendly to be completely neutral. Effectively, this characterization of propositional justification corresponds to a way for a reliabilist to spell out the notion, namely, as derivative of doxastic justification (cf. Comesaña 2010, p. 585). However, I am not suggesting that an attitude is propositionally justified by a set of input r, *in virtue of* it being true that if the subject based the attitude on r, it would be doxastically justified. Theories like evidentialism are free to extend the notion of input and have it do the lion's share of the analytical work, while reliabilism is free to do the same with the basing relation, since I did not put any restraints on what could play the role of input. I simply take it that any theory of justification must be able to accommodate doxastic justification and that this requires that it comes out true that there is input for an attitude that, if used as a base, renders it more justified and that there is input that does not. The input that does is what propositionally justifies. This should be acceptable to most people.

This concludes the review of the terminology I will be using. Now that we have names for the relevant joints of the surrounding doxastic structure of a given doxastic attitude, we can clarify the idea behind defeaters and the development of a preliminary categorization and analysis.

## 1.2 Deep and Superficial Distinctions

Consider the following examples:

> LEAVE: Marla is the manager of a department in a big company. She has read the regulations and is now certain that her employee, Frank, is not entitled to any more paid leave this year. He has already taken 24 days and Marla believes that to be the maximum. She is determined to repel any further requests from him in that regard. On the way to her office, she overhears the company lawyer tell a colleague that all employees are entitled to 30 days of paid leave this year. Marla now believes that the lawyer believes that Frank has a right to 6 more days of paid leave.

> LAW: Carina is a judge and believes that Jack has committed a serious crime at the zoo. Tim, a witness, claims that he saw Jack do it and Carina believes him. Now, Tom appears before the judge and testifies that he saw Tim water his roses at his home at the time of the crime. Since she judges him to be honest, Carina forms the belief that Tom saw Tim water his roses at his home at the time of the crime.

> SCHOOL: James believes that his daughter Lara is skipping school today. He thinks this because she was especially unwilling to go there this morning and he just saw someone that looked like her enter the coffee shop. Upon approaching the coffee shop, he meets Thomas. Thomas tells him that he is also looking for his daughter, Maude, who is well known for skipping school frequently and who admires Lara and often dresses just like her. James forms the belief that someone who is dressed like his daughter, but who is not his daughter, is skipping school in the area today.

A few general observations about these cases are in order: Plausibly, Marla, Carina and James all lose justification for their initial convictions. They each obtain a new piece of information that defeats their previously held beliefs. Let us assume for now that the new beliefs they form in response to the new information fills the role of a defeater in these cases. It can easily be seen that the relevant beliefs are not relevantly different from one another. However, the *manner* in which the three defeaters remove justification differs greatly in the three scenarios. It stands to reason that comparing the cases will yield some inkling as to what characterizes the three different ways of defeating.

In LEAVE, the information that the lawyer believes that Frank is entitled to 6 more days of paid leave heavily counts against the *truth* of the belief that he has no more leave. Since the lawyer is significantly more competent with respect to employment laws and company regulations than Marla, his judgement that Frank is due more leave offers excellent propositional support for that proposition and against Marla's belief that he is not (the defeater's target-attitude). What is more, the lawyer's belief seems to *outweigh* Marla's original justifier (having read the regulations). What this means, exactly, will be spelled out in the next chapter but should be intuitive enough for now. In this situation, it would be inappropriate for Marla to hang on to the target-attitude. A defeater like the one in LEAVE, which defeats justification by being directed against the truth or accuracy of the target-attitude, is called a "rebutting" defeater (e.g. Pollock 1974, p. 42; Bergmann 2005, p. 424, 2006, p. 159; Grundmann 2011, p. 158).

In LAW, the information that Tim was watering the roses at home at the same time at which Jack supposedly committed a crime at the zoo constitutes the defeater. Notably, it does *not* count against the truth of the target-attitude (Carina's belief that Jack committed the crime), since it is neutral with respect to the relevant proposition. Rather, it counts against the *justifier* (in this case, a further belief) of the target-attitude. Specifically, it is directed against the truth of Carina's belief that Tim saw Jack do it, in the same way that the rebutting defeater in LEAVE is directed against Marla's belief about Frank's leave. Thereby, it also threatens the target-attitude: The defeater (Tom's testimony) indicates that Tim did not see Jack commit the crime. Since Carina's belief that Jack did it is solely based on her belief that Tim saw him do it, the target-attitude's single doxastic base is rendered unjustified by the defeater. Thus, it is also no longer sufficiently supportive with respect to the target-attitude to justify it. It would be inappropriate for Carina to believe that Jack did it, given that she believes this only because Tim reported seeing Jack and that Tom's testimony suggests that this couldn't have been true. The defeater in LAW thus defeats justification by being directed against the truth of the doxastic bases of the target-attitude. LAW is an example of a "reason-defeating" defeater (Grundmann 2011, p. 158; Melis 2014, p. 438), also sometimes called a "no-reason defeater" (Sudduth 2008).

In SCHOOL, the defeating is done by the information that someone who looks like James' daughter Lara, namely Maude, is likely to be in the area. Unlike the other two cases, the defeater does not indicate that any of James' beliefs are false. Instead, it suggests that it is unwise of him to rely on his doxastic base in this situation because it doesn't support his belief. After all, given what Thomas tells him, it could easily be Maude and not Lara he saw and so a Lara-like visual impression is unlikely to be a solid base for the target-attitude. Both the truth of the target-attitude that Lara is skipping school and the accuracy of the impression it is based on remain unchallenged, but the epistemic connection between the two does not. It seems that the defeater in SCHOOL indicates that the *target-attitude's total doxastic base does not sufficiently support that belief.*

SCHOOL is an example of an "undercutting" defeater (e.g. Pollock 1974, p. 42; Bergmann 2005, p. 424, 2006, p. 159).

Again, two premises about the cases should be uncontroversial: a) there is a difference between the three types of defeater and b) that difference is not due to a difference between the categorical properties of the defeating items (they are all ordinary beliefs), but rather to a difference in the function of those items, i.e., the way in which they defeat. What the comparison of the cases shows is that each defeater is directed against a different part of the target-attitude's surrounding doxastic structure: Rebutting defeaters are directed against the target-attitude itself, reason-defeating defeaters are directed against the justifier of the target-attitude, and undercutting defeaters are directed against the epistemic connection between the base and the target-attitude. Thus, it seems that for every part of the surrounding doxastic structure of the target-attitude that is relevant to its justification, it is possible to obtain a defeater that challenges it. Furthermore, it seems that rebutting, undercutting and reason-defeating defeat cover all available points of attack. This suggests that these three kinds of defeaters exhaust the fundamental ways in which new information can render a target-attitude unjustified, since there is no further part of the surrounding doxastic structure that can be uniquely attacked by some other type of defeater.[7] It is therefore likely that such other kinds of defeaters that are sometimes mentioned in the literature (possible examples include Pryor 2004, pp. 352–353; Kotzen 2008; Plantinga 1994) are merely subcategories of these three. This point will not be investigated in detail, but the cases and observations about the target-attitudes' surrounding doxastic structures offer enough initial support for it to serve as a rational assumption at this point.

What I want to show now is that it is possible to draw an even deeper distinction between types of defeaters that does not just rely on what part of the surrounding doxastic structure the defeater is directed against, but on what *kind* of part. Compared to rebutting and reason-defeating defeaters, undercutting defeaters are special in that they are not directed against the truth of any attitude or other truth-capable part of the surrounding doxastic structure, but rather against an *epistemic relation* between such components.[8] This points to a similarity be-

---

[7] An exception may be that of higher-order defeaters, which are discussed in the last chapter in the context of disagreement. They appeal to the competence of the act of basing one's attitude. However, they differ from undercutting defeaters only to a limited degree.
[8] The general parallel between rebutting and reason-defeating defeaters suggested here is only plausible under the assumption that the bases of attitudes consist of truth-apt items, such as other attitudes or experiences and the like. Fortunately, if this assumption should turn out to be false, not much is lost, since there couldn't be any reason-defeating defeaters for attitudes

tween rebutting and reason-defeating defeaters: They both *indicate that something is false*, which is nevertheless taken by the subject to be true. Is this similarity enough to make one a special case of the other and leave us with only, say, rebutting and undercutting defeat as the fundamental types of defeater?

The kinds of defeat illustrated by the examples are naturally characterized with respect to a target. This can be phrased in two different ways. One would be to say that the protagonists obtain defeaters for the *reasons* or justifiers they have for their beliefs. Alternatively, one can say that they obtain a defeater for the specific *beliefs* they hold (the target-attitudes). Both ways of phrasing facts about defeat have been used:

> DEFINITION: If $M$ is a reason for $S$ to believe $Q$, a state $M^*$ is a *defeater* for this reason if and only if the combined state consisting of being in both the state $M$ and the state $M^*$ at the same time is not a reason for $S$ to believe $Q$. (Pollock and Cruz 1999, p. 195)

> DI: $d$ is a defeater at $t$ for $S$'s belief $b$ iff (i) $d$ is an experience or propositional attitude or combination thereof; (ii) $S$ comes to have $d$ at $t$; (iii) as a result of $S$'s coming to have $d$ at $t$, $b$ ceases to be justified. (Bergmann 2005, p. 422)

Contrary to Bergmann's claim (Bergmann 2006, pp. 159–162), these two formulations are not equivalent. It seems to be possible to find cases where DEFINITION is fulfilled because the putative defeater negatively influences the support provided by a justifying basis, while obtaining the putative defeater does not result in even a partial loss of justification, thereby failing DI (cf. Loughrist 2015, pp. 57–62). This is because the input whose support is removed by the putative defeater can be replaced by a new piece of positive input with equal weight at the same time. The question is, then, whether new information by which a former reason (here understood as a supportive doxastic base) ceases to be a reason, but which makes no difference at all to the justificatory status of the belief one holds on the basis of that former reason, should be called a "defeater". If one leans for a positive answer, one prefers a reasons-based (e.g. Loughrist 2015) or "front-door" (Kvanvig 2007, p. 107) approach. If one opts for a negative answer, one prefers a "causal" (Loughrist 2015, p. 8) or "backdoor" (Kvanvig 2007, p. 107) approach. Throughout this book, I will pursue a project that, following authors like Bergmann (2005, 2006) or Plantinga (1994, 2000), aims at a causal account of defeat, according to which a defeater is defined by its justifi-

---

based on non-truth-apt items in the first place. Thus, the parallel would hold for all cases where both defeater-types are an option.

cation-diminishing effect on the target-attitude. At this point, the commitment to a causal account has to remain a theoretical posit, but the approach will be further defended in chapter 4. This is because the account I will have developed by then will itself provide theoretical support for the general project. Accordingly, for now I will assume something like Bergmann's formulation in DI as a working hypothesis.

Thus, the defeaters from the three cases can be defined as such with respect to specific target-attitudes: Marla's belief that the lawyer thinks that Frank is entitled to more leave is a rebutting defeater *for her belief that he is not entitled to any more leave*. Carina's belief that Tom saw Tim water his roses is a reason-defeating defeater *for her belief that Jack committed the crime*. With specific target-attitudes in mind, the three manners of defeat from the examples can be easily distinguished: Rebutting defeaters target the belief itself, reason-defeating defeaters target the attitudes that form its base, and undercutting defeaters target its connection to the base. But, as I want to argue now, it is also possible to find more fundamental differences between defeater-kinds that are *independent of a specified target-attitude*. It can be shown that the difference in function between rebutting and reason-defeating defeaters solely depends on what belief is pragmatically designated as the target-attitude. The difference between rebutting and reason-defeating defeaters on the one hand and undercutting defeaters on the other hand runs much deeper, and depends on true functional characteristics of the involved defeaters.

In Leave and Law, the protagonists are described as having (at least) two explicit beliefs, one of which justifies the other: The beliefs Marla obtained from reading the regulations prima facie justify her belief about Frank's entitlements. Carina's belief that Tim saw Jack commit the crime prima facie justifies her belief that Jack did commit it. As already pointed out, the rebutting defeater in Leave directly challenges the truth of Marla's belief about Frank's entitlements, whereas the reason-defeating defeater in Law challenges the truth of Carina's belief that Tim saw Jack commit the crime. Thus, both rebutting and reason-defeating defeaters can be named "truth-attacking" defeaters. Since there is no categorical difference between the truth-attacked attitudes in the two cases, the differences between the defeaters depend wholly on which of the subject's attitudes, namely the justifier or the justified attitude, is picked out as the target-attitude.[9]

To make things easier, I will call the supporting input the "justifier", like before, and the justified attitude the "justifiee". The reason why the defeater in Law

---

[9] The differences arise from the fact that the defeated beliefs play different roles within the surrounding doxastic structure of the target-belief.

is a reason-defeating defeater and not a rebutting defeater is that it truth-attacks the belief that Tim saw Jack commit the crime (the justifier), rather than the belief that Jack committed the crime (the justifiee), and in this case we are interested in the justificatory status of Carina's belief that Jack committed the crime. We want to say that the defeater is reason-defeating because it truth-attacks the reason for the attitude that we are interested in and that we take to be the target-attitude of the defeater. However, from the perspective of the justifier, the truth-attacking defeater works exactly like (and really just is) a rebutting defeater. Only if evaluated from the perspective of the justifiee, the truth-attacking defeater becomes a reason-defeating defeater.

Whether the justifier or the justifiee is of interest in the relevant case and is thus taken to be the target-attitude (and therefore from which perspective the defeater is identified) depends to a large extent on the description of the case and on pragmatic considerations. It therefore seems as though distinctions between defeater-types relying on which belief is taken to be the target-attitude don't run very deep. Even more significantly, since all cases of reason-defeating defeat can be reformulated as special cases of rebutting defeat, but not vice versa, reason-defeating defeaters appear to be derivative of rebutting defeaters. Let me illustrate: In LEAVE, the defeater truth-attacks the belief that Frank is due more leave (the justifiee), rather than the information obtained from the regulations (the justifier) and is therefore a rebutting defeater from the perspective of the justifiee, while being no defeater at all from the perspective of the justifier. This means that LEAVE is a "pure" case of rebutting defeat: As long as no further attitudes are based on the truth-attacked belief, no attitudes suffer reason-defeating defeat. Generally, then, a truth-attacking defeater can be a rebutting defeater, without being a reason-defeating defeater. But, obviously, it cannot be a reason-defeating defeater without being a rebutting defeater. This is because there is no "pure" case of reason-defeating defeat: Having a reason-defeating defeater implies that, in addition to the target-attitude, there is a reason, that is to say a doxastic base that acts as justifier for that attitude which is truth-attacked. Redesignation of target-attitudeship to the attitude based on that base is then possible, which would transform the case into a case of rebutting defeat. Given the structure that is necessary for reason-defeating defeat, this will be possible in all cases.

Since rebutting defeat is thus the broader category, reason-defeating defeaters are special instances of rebutting defeaters.[10] However, one should not make

---

[10] It must be noted that the example used here makes this verdict particularly tempting, as it involves two potential truth-attack-targets in the form of full-fledged doxastic attitudes. It thus

too much of this hierarchy. Any attitude can potentially act as both a justifier and a justifiee, and thus any truth-attacking defeater can potentially act both as a rebutting and as a reason-defeating defeater. For example, if Marla in LEAVE, after overhearing the lawyer, formed the belief that Frank will not go on holiday for the rest of the year, based on her belief that he is due no more leave, that belief would be unjustified. The lawyer's opinion, which until this point was a pure rebutting defeater, would act as a reason-defeating defeater for it. In addition, we would *think* of this version as a case of reason-defeating defeat as well, because focusing on the holiday-belief makes us designate it as the target-attitude. All of this shows that the fundamental characteristic of these defeaters is that they are truth-attacking, i.e. directed against target-attitudes and bases and not the relations between them. This is why they belong in the same category.

To sum up, whether a rebutting defeater is thought of as a reason-defeating defeater depends on whether the rebutted attitude acts as justifier for a further attitude and whether the justifier or the justifiee is of more interest in a given scenario. Of course, which attitude is of more interest can be epistemically extremely important, for example when we want to know how far a newly acquired piece of information threatens the justificatory status of our previously held doxastic system. It may be relevant to know which attitudes would be rendered unjustified and whether this is because the new information shows them to be false or whether it takes away their support by rebutting our reasons for them, especially since reason-defeating defeaters are likely harder to detect than rebutting defeaters. The difference between rebutting and reason-defeating defeaters is therefore not irrelevant and is best captured by what I call a "superficial" distinction. It is superficial in that it depends on a (pragmatic) designation of one of the involved attitudes as the target-attitude. As we have seen, when the focus of interest lies on the general manner in which defeaters remove justification in distinctive ways, it is helpful to abstract away from their effect on a specified attitude and look at the points of the target-attitude's surrounding doxastic structure that they interact with.

From this perspective, I now want to compare rebutting defeaters to undercutting defeaters, where the latter are exemplified in SCHOOL. James' justifier in

---

remains an open question whether there can be reason-defeating defeaters in this sense in cases where the reason is not such an attitude, but, for example, an experience or some other non-doxastic state. This is because it is an open question whether there can be truth-attacking defeaters for non-doxastic states, such states not necessarily being of the right kind to even be justified. I suspect that the relevant apparent reason-defeating defeaters are actually undercutting defeaters. I will not go into this here, but it should become apparent in later chapters that they can be dealt with easily within my rebasing framework.

SCHOOL is the observation that someone who looks like Lara entered the coffee shop, and his justifiee is the belief that Lara is skipping school. Both states might well be true/accurate in light of the information that someone else who looks like Lara, but isn't Lara, is skipping school in the vicinity. Still, the defeater seems to render the belief that Lara is skipping school unjustified. Consequently, it must be directed against some other part of the surrounding doxastic structure and, as already noted – and since it indicates that the justifier does not offer sufficient support for the justifiee (or that it is not sufficiently positive) – the best candidate is the *relation* between them (cf. Pollock 1974, pp. 42–43). Importantly, which attitude is the target-attitude of such a defeater does not depend on pragmatic considerations or case-description: It will always be the attitude that stands at the output-end of the attacked support relation. There are no two defeated attitudes to choose between, like in cases of reason-defeating defeat, unless more than one attitude stands in the same kind of basing relation to the relevant set of input (and in such cases, there is no question that one is dealing with only one kind of defeater). Thus, because undercutting defeaters are directed against a substantially different part of the target-attitude's surrounding doxastic structure from both rebutting and reason-defeating defeaters, the functional difference between undercutting and rebutting defeaters runs much deeper than the superficial difference between rebutting and reason-defeating defeaters. I will therefore call it a "deep distinction". It will be revealed later that this distinction doesn't go all that deep after all, but it can be taken to run significantly deeper than what I have labelled superficial distinctions.

The import of these considerations is that there are two ways of distinguishing and categorizing defeaters. The first is 1) by their function with respect to a designated target-attitude; this concerns the way they interact with different *parts* of the surrounding doxastic structure of the *designated* target-attitude. The second is 2) by their function, full stop. This concerns the way they interact with different *kinds of parts* of the surrounding doxastic structure of *any* target-attitude. Pairs of defeater-types that can be distinguished only according to 1) are only *superficially distinguishable*, while pairs of types that can be individuated according to 2) are *deeply distinguishable*. Defeater categories that are subcategories of other categories they are only superficially distinguishable from, such as the group of reason-defeating defeaters with respect to rebutting defeaters, are *superficial categories*. All other defeater categories are *deep categories* (rebutting and undercutting defeaters). I can now start constructing accounts of the two deep categories of defeat.

## 1.3 A Preliminary Theory and Taxonomy of Defeat

In this section, I will take a first stab at giving a (causal) account of rebutting and undercutting defeat. First, it is worthwhile to take a look at traditional characterizations, both because I expect similarities between them to further support the provisional limitation of my taxonomy to rebutting and undercutting defeat, and because it gives an overview of different ways of spelling out the more coarse-grained observations in the previous section. John Pollock's view is probably the best-known account, which has been adopted and modified, in one way or another, by many philosophers following him. Terminology varies slightly: Rebutting defeaters are sometimes called "overriding defeaters" or "overriders", while undercutting defeaters are occasionally referred to as "undermining defeaters" or "underminers". I will stick to "rebutting" and "undercutting" defeat here, assuming that the other terms are synonymous. Here, then, are some existing accounts and remarks, starting with Pollock's original distinction between Type I (rebutting) and Type II (undercutting) defeaters:

> John Pollock:
> First, if $P$ is a prima facie reason for $S$ to believe that $Q$, then any reason for $S$ to believe that $Q$ is false (even though $P$ is true) is a defeater. Such a defeater defeats the conditional truth- functionally. Let us call these *type I* defeaters. (Pollock 1974, p. 42)

> The second kind of defeater attacks the connection between $P$ and $Q$ rather than attacking $Q$ directly. [...] This second kind of defeater is, roughly speaking, a reason for thinking that, under these circumstances, knowing-that-$P$ is not a good way to find out whether $Q$. [...] Let us call these *type II* defeaters. A type II defeater is any reason for believing that $\neg (P => Q)$ which is not also a reason for believing that $\neg Q$. (Pollock 1974, pp. 42–43)

> R is a *rebutting* defeater for P as a prima facie reason for Q if and only if R is a defeater and R is a reason for believing ¬Q. (Pollock 1987, p. 485)

> R is an *undercutting* defeater for P as a prima facie reason for S to believe Q if and only if R is a defeater and R is a reason for denying that P wouldn't be true unless Q were true. (Pollock 1987, p. 485)

> Michael Bergmann:
> D 2. $d$ is a *rebutting* defeater for $b$ iff $d$ is a defeater for $b$ which is (or is an epistemically appropriate basis for) the belief that $b$ is false.

D 3. *d* is an *undercutting* defeater for *b* iff d is a defeater for *b* which is (or is an epistemically appropriate basis for) the belief that one's actual ground or reason for *b* is not indicative of *b*'s truth. (Bergmann 2005, p. 424)

Albert Casullo:
Overriding defeaters, however, are *source neutral*. If S's justified$_d$ belief that not-*p* defeats the justification$_k$ conferred on S's belief that *p* by source *A*, then it also defeats the justification$_k$ conferred on S's belief that *p* by *any other* source. (Casullo 2003, p. 46)

...undermining defeaters for S's justified belief that *p* are *source sensitive*. They defeat by providing evidence that the alleged source of justification is not likely to generate true beliefs. Typical undermining defeaters show either that the source itself is defective in some way [...] or that the source is operating in an environment for which it is not well adapted... (Casullo 2003, p. 45)

Giacomo Melis:
Let *p* be a previously justified proposition (for a subject *S* at a time *t*): while overriders overtly suggest that not-*p*, underminers don't. (Melis 2014, p. 434)

Underminers suggest that something was wrong with the source of justification or with the justificatory process, and they operate their defeat by appealing to the higher-order commitment that the belief in question was based on that source or that process. If the suggestion is that the process, rather than the source, was defective, the defectiveness is to be understood as the occurrence of a mistake or some other disturbing event. (Melis 2014, p. 438)

...the way in which underminers and overriders suggest that the justificatory process was defective is different. Overriders merely suggest that the justificatory process failed to lead to truth, underminers suggest that a disturbing event (like a mistake in the proof) has caused the process to fail. The former suggestion is perfectly compatible with the justificatory process having been executed impeccably, and having being delivered by a reliable source working in good circumstances; the latter is not. (Melis 2014, p. 437)

The similarities between the various accounts are supposed to lend some further plausibility to the claim that rebutting defeaters defeat by *supporting the negation of the proposition embedded in the target-attitude*, while undercutting defeaters defeat by *suggesting that there is something epistemically problematic about the epistemic relation between justifier and target-attitude*. On these relatively coarse descriptions, all accounts mentioned hereagree. They diverge, among other things, on the correct way to spell out undercutting defeat in more detail: Pollock states that undercutting defeaters suggest that a counterfactual relation between the justifier and the target-attitude does not hold (Pollock 1987, p. 485), Bergmann takes them to challenge the propriety of the basing relation between justifier and target-attitude (Bergmann 2005, p. 424), and Melis and Casullo think that undercutters indicate that something went wrong in the process leading from the justifier to the formation of the target-attitude (Casullo 2003, p. 45; Melis 2014, p. 437). The views don't always fully explain how these observations lead to a loss of justification on the part of the target-attitude and they differ with respect to the broader pictures of justification they commit to. These issues will be addressed in detail in the next two chapters. Adapting parts of these existing views, I will now try to formulate the working account that will be used to conduct that investigation.

Let me first give a preliminary account of defeaters in general that loosely follows Bergmann's DI:

Def-1:

$d$ is a defeater, iff

1. $d$ is a piece of information for a subject $S$ that is acquired at time $t$
2. there is a doxastic attitude about the proposition $p$, $A(p)$, that is held by $S$ at $t$ and at $t$-$1$, such that

    2.1 $A(p)$ is justified at $t$-$1$ and unjustified at $t$ as a result of $S$'s acquiring $d$ at $t$.

Let me quickly point out the key difference compared to Bergmann's DI. As I remarked, DI explains under which circumstances something is a defeater *for a specified attitude*, in that case the belief $b$. In contrast, Def-1 explains under which circumstances something is a defeater in and of itself. While Bergmann explains what *being a defeater for a specified target-attitude* consists of via *the function of the defeater with respect to that attitude*, my account explains what *being a defeater* consists of in terms of *the function of the defeater in general*. Since, as was argued earlier, building specified target-attitudes into the analysis blurs the lines between deeply and superficially distinguishable kinds of defeaters, my account is better positioned to accommodate the relevant distinctions. It also puts defeat itself, rather than the defeasibility of target-attitudes, squarely at the center of attention. This will help to illustrate the versatility of defeat when applied to other topics later. Furthermore, the references to belief in Bergmann's account have been replaced by the more neutral terms of "doxastic attitude" and "information". These will be filled in in detail later and represent my working hypothesis that things other than beliefs can defeat things other than beliefs.

The reason why Def-1 is closely modelled on DI in the first place is that, unlike Pollock and Cruz' proposal, DEFINITION DI (and thus Def-1) is neutral with respect to theories of justification. Reference to "reasons", as well as other weighted terms in epistemology, like "evidence", "reliable" and so on are avoided. Def-1 merely states that $b$ is rendered unjustified *as a result* of the acquisition of $d$. This leaves it somewhat mysterious how that result is achieved by the defeater, but that vagueness is a desirable feature at this point, as the details of defeat will depend on the kind of defeater at play. The more precise meaning of "as a result of" also depends on the relevant theory of justification at play, given that what is supposed to be lost must stand in an influence-relation with the structure of the cause of the loss. Thus, the phrase must remain vague until the integration with the three central theories is conducted (though significant clarification will have been achieved in the meantime).

With Def-1 in place, we can now turn to rebutting and undercutting defeat:

Rebut-1:

$d$ is a rebutting defeater, iff

1. $d$ is a defeater:

    1.1 $d$ is a piece of information for a subject $S$ that is acquired at time $t$

    1.2 there is a doxastic attitude about the proposition $p$, $A(p)$, that is held by $S$ on the basis of the justifier $r$ at $t$ and at $t$-$1$, such that

       1.2.1 $A(p)$ is justified at $t$-$1$ and unjustified at $t$ as a result of $S$'s acquiring $d$ at $t$.

2. $d$ suggests that $A(p)$ is incorrect.

Undercut-1:

$d$ is an undercutting defeater, iff

1. $d$ is a defeater:

1.1 *d* is a piece of information for a subject *S* that is acquired at time *t*

1.2 there is a doxastic attitude about the proposition *p*, *A(p)*, that is held by *S* on the basis of the justifier *r* at *t* and at *t-1*, such that

    1.2.1 *A(p)* is justified at *t-1* and unjustified at *t* as a result of *S*'s acquiring *d* at *t*.

2. *d* suggests that *r* does not sufficiently support *A(p)*.

The concept of a defeater "suggesting" that the target-attitude is incorrect (in case of rebutting defeat) or not sufficiently supported (in case of undercutting defeat) is taken from the passages by Mellis (2014, p. 434, 437, 438) quoted above. It fits Pollock's original definition in the passage quoted above (Pollock 1987, p. 485), as well as Bergmann's "D 2" (Bergmann 2005, p. 424), although it is a deal less precise (a situation that will be rectified in the next chapter). This general idea behind rebutting defeat has been accepted by most philosophers.[11] It is also intuitively plausible: Say, I believe that it will rain tomorrow for no reason at all. If I then hear the forecaster say that it will be sunny, I am in a situation where I believe that it will rain, but new information suggests to me that it will not rain. In that situation, I should stop believing that it will rain. What characterizes an undercutting defeater, according to Undercut-1, is that it does not suggest anything about the correctness of the target-attitude, but that it suggests instead that the target-belief is not sufficiently supported by its total doxastic base, which is close to what Bergmann says in D 3 in the quoted passage (Bergmann 2005, p. 424). Again, this makes sense, since it would be inappropriate to believe something which one has reason to deem unsupported. I will argue at length for an analysis that takes this thought seriously in the third chapter. Note that, so far, Rebut-1 and Undercut-1 serve more as a characterization than a full account.

It is glaringly clear that all this talk of a defeater "suggesting" something is far too imprecise. The project of formulating a full account of defeat is in no small part defined by an attempt to fill in terms such as this one. Still, while the formulation is generally too vague, it already captures the idea that rebutting and undercutting defeaters are distinguished with respect to the differences between the parts of the surrounding doxastic structure that they are directed against. As an outlook of what is to come and in order to make the working account proposed here not seem completely hopeless, I can already hint at what

---

[11] See also Plantinga 1994; Casullo 2003; Grundmann 2009b; Sturgeon 2014; Melis 2014.

"suggesting" comes down to: Defeaters can be thought of as suggesting that there is something wrong with the target-attitude by propositionally supporting belief in the proposition that the target-attitude is incorrect or that it is not well-based. More on this later.

This concludes both the first chapter and the introduction of the preliminary account of defeat, Defeat-1, with the attached accounts of rebutting and undercutting defeaters, Rebut-1 and Undercut-1, as working hypotheses. I argued that a satisfactory account of defeat must construe the phenomenon independently of specified target-beliefs and with focus on the defeater itself, which is what the preliminary account does. Furthermore, I have shown that the best candidates for the most fundamental kinds of defeat are rebutting and undercutting defeaters, since they are deeply distinguishable. Finally, I have located the characteristics that distinguish these two kinds of defeat in the content of the suggestions they make with respect to the target-attitude, which captures the thought that they are distinguished on the basis of differences between the parts of the surrounding doxastic structure they are directed against.

# 2 Rebutting Defeat

The goal of this chapter is the development of accounts of rebutting and undercutting defeat that can then be bundled into the Rebasing Account of Defeat. Building on the preliminary account from chapter 1, I will first look at rebutting defeaters, which defeat by generating a logical incompatibility between the proposition embedded in the defeater and the one embedded in the target-attitude. This allows for a distinction between different types of rebutting defeaters and corresponding degrees of rebuttal, making room for *partial* defeat. Next, I will rely on these results to generate a theoretically motivated argument for the thesis that defeaters themselves need to be supported, in order to have their defeating effect. In addition, I will provide some additional support for existing arguments for this position.

## 2.1 Rebutting Defeaters

Recall the example of rebutting defeat from the previous chapter:

> LEAVE: Marla is the manager of a department in a big company. She has read the regulations and is now certain that her employee, Frank, is not entitled to any more paid leave this year. He has already taken 24 days and Marla believes that to be the maximum. She is determined to repel any further requests from him in that respect. On the way to her office, she overhears the company lawyer tell a colleague that all employees are entitled to 30 days of paid leave this year. Marla now believes that the lawyer believes that Frank has a right to 6 more days of paid leave.

Initially, we can ask what it is, exactly, that does the defeating in this example. Several candidates come to mind: First, it might be *Marla's hearing* the lawyer saying that all employees are entitled to 30 days of leave. Second, the defeater might also be *the belief* that she forms in response to it, namely the belief that the lawyer believes that all employees are entitled to 30 days of leave. Third, it might be the *fact* that the lawyer believes as he does that constitutes the defeater.[1]

---

[1] Importantly, that fact can only play the role of defeater that I am interested in here, *insofar as it is registered and processed* by Marla. This may be different for other kinds of defeaters, but I take it that doxastic defeaters must somehow be or be represented in the subject's doxastic system. Unlike Bergmann (2006, pp. 154–160) however, who takes doxastic defeaters to be mental

There is a fourth option: in the previous chapter, I followed Pollock, Bergmann and others in proposing that rebutting defeaters defeat by suggesting that the target-attitude is incorrect.[2] Looking at the present case, we can put this in more precise terms: The lawyer's statement suggests that it is false *that Frank is due no more leave*. Thus, it suggests that that proposition is false. Accordingly, to suggest that the target-attitude is incorrect seems to amount to suggesting that the target-proposition (the proposition that the target-attitude is about) is false. Furthermore, it can be seen what it means to "suggest" that the target-proposition is false: The lawyer's statements suggests that the proposition that Frank is due no more leave is false because it provides positive input for and thus propositionally supports the negation of that proposition (it propositionally supports the proposition that Frank is due more leave). It does this not directly, but by propositionally supporting a belief in the proposition that all employees are due 30 days of leave, which implies that the employee Frank, who has taken only 24 days so far, *is* due more leave. And, of course, this implies that it is false that Frank is due no more leave.

This picture of support-relationships as a chain is what makes the fourth option visible: Assuming that a belief in the intermediate proposition that it is not true that Frank is due no more leave is adopted by Marla while she *at the same time* believes that Frank is due no more leave on the basis of her earlier investigations, *that* new belief might also serve as the defeater in the example.[3] In that situation, the defeater doesn't just support the negation of the target-proposition, but rather *is about* that negation. Sometimes, this is explicitly so, as suggested by the passage by Albert Casullo from the previous chapter: "If $S$'s justified$_d$ belief that not-$p$ defeats the justification$_k$ conferred on $S$'s belief that $p$..." (Casullo 2003, p. 45).

I will assume that all four options are plausible candidates for being the realizer of the defeater in LEAVE. The latter can be conceived of as a piece of input in the form of a sense-impression, as a belief formed in response to that input, as a fact that the subject has access to or has a belief in the negation of the target-proposition. Importantly, all options have in common that they propositionally support (or directly assert) not-p, where $p$ is the target-proposition held to be

---

states, I am open and even sympathetic to the idea that they can be external states that are mentally represented.
2 See for example, Pollock (1987, p. 485) and Bergmann's D 2 (Bergmann 2005, p. 424).
3 We can imagine that Marla has stored the target-attitude and is not currently thinking about it. In that case, it may well be that she adopts a new belief that is incoherent with it, before she has had a chance to drop the old one.

true.⁴ This generates what one might metaphorically call "rational pressure" to give up the target-attitude. That pressure derives from the fact that the proposition $p$ is *logically contradictory* to the proposition that the defeater supports belief in, namely *not-p*, and it is *paradigmatically irrational* to believe a contradiction (cf. Sturgeon 2014, p. 112). The way I understand paradigmatic irrationality here is that, whatever one wants to say about irrational states, believing a contradiction should come out as irrational and it requires no explanation as to why it is irrational that goes beyond what it is for two propositions to be contradictory. This should be plausible enough.⁵ We can also say that rational pressure is exerted by the rebutting defeater because it is positive input for a proposition (the negation of the target-proposition) that is contradictory to the proposition initially held to be true.

So far, I have adopted and illustrated the predominant view on rebutting defeat⁶ and offered some additional defense for it.⁷ The thought that rebutters defeat by supporting what amounts to a logical contradiction with the target-proposition can be integrated with Defeat-1 and Rebut-1 in the following way:

Def-2:

$d$ is a defeater, iff

1. $d$ is a belief that $q$ or a piece of positive input for belief that $q$ of a subject $S$ that is acquired by $S$ at time $t$

2. there is a doxastic attitude about the proposition $p$, $A(p)$, that is held by $S$ at $t$ and at $t$-$1$, such that

---

4 Or, in the case of the fourth option, the defeater directly creates the paradigmatically irrational state of believing contradictory things.
5 Doubt could be cast on this assumption, if one holds some variant of dialetheism, according to which both a proposition and its negation can be true, as proposed by Priest 2006. I will not discuss this here, but it should be kept in mind that proponents of such views may either want to deny the possibility of rebutting defeat, at least for some propositions, or come up with a different fundamental explanation.
6 As mentioned in the previous chapter, the first to adopt it was Pollock (1974, 1987), but it has found broad acceptance since then.
7 I will show later that the view is slightly too strong, as rebutting defeaters can also provide neutral input to the relevant proposition to the same effect. However, since this has little bearing on the principles governing rebutting defeaters, I will for now assume that they always support belief in the negation of the target-proposition. On this assumption, rebutting defeaters constitute what one may call "negative" input.

2.1.  $A(p)$ is justified at $t$-$1$ and unjustified at $t$ as a result of $S$'s acquiring $d$ at $t$.

Rebut-2:

$d$ is a rebutting defeater, iff

1. $d$ is a defeater:
    1.1.  $d$ is a belief that $q$ or a piece of positive input for belief that $q$ of a subject $S$ that is acquired at time $t$
    1.2.  there is a doxastic attitude about the proposition $p$, $A(p)$, that is held by $S$ at $t$ and at $t$-$1$, such that
        1.2.1.  $A(p)$ is justified at $t$-$1$ and unjustified at $t$ as a result of $S$'s acquiring $d$ at $t$.
2. $q$ is the negation of $p$.

Given the different epistemic items that have been identified as possible fillers of the defeater-role, these definitions can do away with the slightly vague notion of "information" used in the previous versions. Defeaters are either beliefs or positive input for beliefs. As a result, a certain amount of flexibility has been introduced into the theory that derives from the flexibility of the notion of *input*. Note that this conception does not yet fully explain how and why rebutting defeaters remove *justification*. It merely explains why holding the target-attitude in the face of the defeater is paradigmatically irrational. But not every theory of justification regards rationality as a condition for justification. How Rebut-2 can nevertheless be integrated with such views will be shown in chapter 4. At this point, more needs to be said in order to build a complete account of rebutting defeat.

### 2.1.1 Partial, Successful and Perfect Rebuttal and Relative Concentrations of Input

Since, according to the view expressed so far, rebutters often consist in propositional support for a proposition that is contradictory to the target-proposition, they leave the original justifier for the target-attitude intact. Therefore, cases of rebutting defeat are cases where one has two opposing sources of positive input, each of which supports belief in a proposition that is incompatible with the other. What is of particular interest is that the weight or strength of the input on the defeater's side, relative to the weight of the justifier, determines the epistemic effect of the rebutter. Three outcomes are possible.

First, if the justifier is much weightier than the potential defeater in terms of propositional support, it seems that there is nothing wrong with continuing to hold the target-attitude justifiedly. Thus, the putative rebutter only manages to *remove justification* for the target-attitude, if the support that the rebutting defeater offers to the negation of the target-proposition *is weighty enough*, compared to the support provided by the justifier.[8] Second, it is possible that the defeater outweighs the original justifier to such an extent that the subject is not only no longer justified holding on to her attitude about the target-proposition, but is now also propositionally justified to *believe its negation* instead. Third, even if the defeater is not weighty enough to *remove* justification, it may still have an impact by *lowering the degree of justification* of the target-attitude (Thune 2010). For an illustration of the three effects, compare the following cases:

> LEAVE-FULL: Marla is the manager of a department in a big company. She has read the regulations and is now certain that her employee, Frank, is not entitled to any more paid leave this year. He has already taken 24 days and Marla believes that to be the maximum. She is determined to repel any further requests from him in that respect. On the way to her office, she overhears the company lawyer tell a colleague with great confidence that 6 of the 10 employees in Marla's department are being granted extra leave this year.

> LEAVE-PERFECT: Marla is the manager of a department in a big company. She has read the regulations and is now certain that her employee, Frank, is not entitled to any more paid leave this year. He has already taken 24 days and Marla believes that to be the maximum. She is determined to repel any further requests from him in that respect. On the way to her office, she overhears the company lawyer with great confidence tell a colleague that all employees are entitled to 30 days of paid leave this year.

> LEAVE-PART: Marla is the manager of a department in a big company. She has read the regulations and is now certain that her employee, Frank, is not entitled to any more paid leave this year. He has already taken 24 days and Marla believes that to be the maximum. She is determined to repel any further requests from him in that respect. On the way to her office, she overhears the company lawyer tell a colleague that there is some, though not much, evidence that some legal obscurity allows the employees at the company 30 days of paid leave this year.

LEAVE-FULL is a modified version of LEAVE, in which overhearing the lawyer gives Marla some positive input for the proposition that it is not true that Frank is due

---

[8] This point is made in Pollock (2010), where Pollock puts it in terms of degrees of justification. See also Thune (2010).

no more leave, which is enough to remove the justification of the target-attitude, but not enough to justify belief in the negation of the target-proposition. The information from the lawyer indicating that six of her ten employees are due more leave makes it somewhat likely, from Marla's perspective, that Frank is among them. Thus, Marla's belief that Frank is due no more leave is not likely to be true and can no longer be justifiedly held by her. At the same time, the new information does not sufficiently support the proposition that Frank *is* due more leave, and thus that it is not true that Frank is due no more leave, to justify belief in it. The fact that it becomes somewhat likely that Frank is among the lucky employees does not make it justified to believe that he is. The defeater at play provides positive input for the negation of the target-proposition that sufficiently counterbalances but does not completely swamp the justifier. Thus, the defeater renders the target-attitude unjustified, but does not itself justify the corresponding disbelief. I will call this kind of case a case of "Successful Rebuttal".

Things are different in LEAVE-PERFECT. The case is basically the same as LEAVE. Here, the lawyer's statement intuitively not only renders Marla's belief that Frank is due no more leave unjustified, but also justifies the contrary belief that he is due more leave. It does so by providing positive input for the negation of the target-proposition that is much more weighty than the justifier (Marla's reading of the regulations) and completely swamps it. Thus, the defeater in LEAVE-PERFECT removes the justification for the target-attitude and swamps the justifier to a degree that makes belief in the negation of the target-proposition justified. I will call this kind of case a case of "Perfect Rebuttal".

If Perfect Rebuttal is at one end of the spectrum of severity of a rebutter's effect, the rebutter at play in LEAVE-PART is at the other end of that spectrum. Intuitively, the lawyer's statement does not render Marla's belief that Frank is due no more leave unjustified. If she continued to hold it, there would be nothing wrong with that. So, one might think that the lawyer's statement in LEAVE-PART is no defeater at all, which is also what Def-2 would predict. However, it seems that there is a difference between LEAVE-PART and a situation in which Marla does not hear the lawyer at all and receives no new information with respect to whether Frank is due more leave. After all, before overhearing the lawyer, she had no indication whatsoever that her belief is false, while the lawyer's judgment on the possibility of legal obscurities seems to give at least some indication that it is. How can this difference be cashed out? It appears that what one wants to say is that information that counts against the truth of the target-belief, but does not remove justification for the belief, at least *diminishes* its justification (cf. Pollock 2010, p. 12). Rebutting defeaters that diminish, but don't remove, justification can be called "partial rebutters" (see Plantinga 1994, 2000, 2000, p. 362; Bergmann 2006, p. 155; Thune 2010; Kotzen 2008).

In order to fully grasp what it means for a rebutter to diminish justification, one must first understand justification as coming in degrees: Not only can we say that an attitude is either justified or not, but also that it is well justified, barely justified, sufficiently justified and so on. It just seems to be a "plain fact" (Leplin 2009, p. 91) that justification is not an all-or-nothing phenomenon and the thesis that it comes in degrees is widely accepted (e.g. Plantinga 1986, pp. 3–12; Pollock 2001a; BonJour 2010, pp. 58–59; Betz 2013; Pritchard and Turri 2014). For example, I both justifiedly believe that the King's German Legion fought at Waterloo and that I had a bagel for breakfast today. However, the second belief is much better justified than the first one, as my memory of eating a bagel for breakfast offers much better support for the corresponding belief than the information from historical novels and cursory research that I base the first belief on.

This suggests the following picture of degrees of justification and epistemic support (in my terminology): Roughly, the degree of doxastic justification that an attitude enjoys depends on the degree to which its total doxastic base is positive with respect to it.[9] Accordingly, doxastic attitudes can be *doxastically supported to varying degrees* in that the total doxastic base for an attitude can be larger or smaller and have higher or lower percentages of positive input with differing weights. The more extensive the set, the bigger the percentage of positive (as opposed to neutral or negative) input in it, and the more relative weight[10] key pieces of positive input have, the more doxastic support that base offers its attitude and the better it is justified (if it is, indeed, justified). I will be using the term "relative concentration of positive input" as an umbrella term for these matters. Thus, the higher the relative concentration of positive input for an attitude A(p) in the total doxastic base of A(p), the better A(p) is doxastically supported and, if A(p) is well enough supported to be justified, the higher the degree of justification that A(p) enjoys.

---

**9** The caveat here is that this rests on the assumption that propositional and doxastic justification are this straightforwardly related. This need not be correct (see e.g. Turri 2010; Silva 2017). Since I do not wish to go into the details of this issue here, however, I will make that assumption for now. Note that it makes no difference to the matter of rebutting defeat: A rebutting defeater changes the composition of the available input. This will always result in loss of doxastic justification. The issue with the direct relationship concerns a case where justification is lost in *other* ways (see Silva 2017).

**10** I am assuming here that input has "weight", which is a scale on which the support a given piece of input can be compared to other pieces. The exact nature of the scale does not matter here, but it is intuitively extremely plausible that some piece of positive input, like a visual impression, can offer more support to a given attitude than another, like a rumor.

Correspondingly, the *degree of propositional support* that an attitude enjoys can be spelled out in terms of the relative concentration of positive input. The difference to doxastic support is that the degree of propositional support depends not only on that concentration in the total doxastic base of the attitude in question, but on *all available* input. Thus, the higher the relative concentration of positive input for an attitude A(p) in the entire doxastic system of the subject, the better A(p) is propositionally supported.

Importantly, while both propositional or doxastic support and justification come in degrees, those degrees do not coincide. An attitude only counts as *justified* once its doxastic support reaches a certain threshold and gets better justified, if the support increases *further*.[11] The reason for this is that it is clearly possible to hold a somewhat supported, but not justified attitude. For example, when one jumps conclusions, one forms attitudes on the basis of positive input that is overestimated and does not suffice to justify those attitudes.

With this framework in place, partial rebuttal can be explained easily. A partial rebutter neutralizes part of the support for the target-belief in that it adds positive input for belief in the negation of the target-proposition to the surrounding doxastic structure. Because that input is positive with respect to a proposition that is contradictory to the target-proposition, it acts as *negative* input for the target-attitude and changes the composition of the available input, such that now the relative concentration of positive input for the target-attitude is lower than it was before. As a result, the propositional support for the target-attitude is diminished. Another way to put this is that partial rebutting defeaters introduce input that *neutralizes* part of the previously possessed support for the target-attitude by counterbalancing it with support for a conflicting attitude.[12]

Interpreted straightforwardly, this counterbalancing affects *propositional* rather than doxastic support, since a newly acquired rebutting defeater is not itself (yet) part of the target-attitude's total doxastic base. Yet, in cases like LEAVE, one also gets the impression that there is something wrong with Marla's belief that Frank is due no more leave in the sense that it lacks some of its previous *doxastic* justification as well. Intuitively, it is not like Marla could acknowledge that her overall information does not support her belief but still rationally con-

---

**11** For such a threshold view on justification, see e.g. Smith 2016, ch. 5.2 A threshold conception with regards to knowledge is discussed in Rothschild and Spectre (2018).

**12** It seems that this does not happen in cases where the putative rebutting defeater is pitched against conclusive support (see Grundmann 2019). This is surprising, since it suggests that conclusive support is special indeed. Still, as I will show in chapter 6.3, there can be defeaters against it, albeit under very specific circumstances.

tinue holding it, merely because she chooses not to base it on most of that information, including, specifically, the part that contradicts her belief. This points to a more general feature of doxastic justification: There must be more to that concept than what has been suggested so far. Specifically, doxastic justification must be capable of being affected by changes *outside* of the relevant attitude's total doxastic base, such as the acquisition of a rebutting defeater.

I will present two principled ways in which a rebutting defeater can defeat doxastic justification: Either rebutting defeaters typically *become part of* the target-belief's total doxastic base, for example, as a result of some monitoring mechanism or reflex kicking in, and can only defeat doxastic justification, if they do. In that case, rebutting defeaters, contrary to the idea tacitly assumed so far, do not defeat only in virtue of providing *propositional* support against the target-belief, but must provide *doxastic* support. Alternatively, there may be connective principles included in the concept of doxastic justification that regulate when and in what manner input from outside of the total doxastic base can be relevant to the belief's epistemic status with respect to doxastic justification. Prime candidates for such principles are possible normative features of justification. For example, a rebutting defeater may be said to defeat doxastic justification, not in case it *is* part of the total doxastic base, but in case it *ought to* be. Which of the two solutions is possible and which is preferable is highly dependent on the theory of justification one adopts and on broader considerations concerning epistemic normativity. I will discuss the relationship between theories of justification and the analysis of defeat at length in chapter 4.

Interpreting rebutting defeaters as counterbalancing input accounts for the intuitive difference between LEAVE-PART and a situation without any counter-information: In LEAVE-PART, overhearing the lawyer gives Marla input that counterbalances the support for her belief that Frank is due no more leave to a degree *where the remaining support is enough to allow justification, but still less than before and therefore not enough to allow justification to the same degree as before.* Partial rebutters can be defined as follows:

Partial Rebuttal:

$d$ is a partial rebutter for its target-attitude about $p$, $B(p)$, iff

1. $d$ is a rebutting defeater and
2. taking into account both the degree of propositional support that $d$ offers against $B(p)$ and the degree of propositional support offered by $B(p)$'s total doxastic base, $B(p)$ ends up with a degree of propositional support that still suffices for propositional justification.

Plausibly, it is not just partial rebuttal that is best understood in terms of degrees of support and justification, but also successful and perfect rebuttal. Where a partial rebutter neutralizes only a small fraction of the original justifier's support for the target-belief without thereby diminishing it enough for the removal of justification, successful rebutters are best seen as neutralizing the justifier to a degree where a threshold is reached and justification is removed entirely. Correspondingly, perfect rebutters provide so much positive input for belief in the negation of the target-proposition that they not only neutralize *all* of the support provided by the original justifier, but in addition (even taking into account the degree of *their* support that is neutralized by the justifier) change the composition of the available input in a way that *leaves belief in the negation of the target-proposition propositionally justified* instead. Partial, successful and perfect rebuttal therefore mark theoretically interesting points on a spectrum of degrees of support-neutralization. Successful and perfect rebuttal can be spelled out as follows:

Successful Rebuttal:

$d$ is a successful rebutter for its target-attitude about $p$, $B(p)$, iff

1. $d$ is a rebutting defeater and
2. taking into account both the degree of propositional support that $d$ offers against $B(p)$ and the degree of propositional support offered by $B(p)$'s total doxastic base, $B(p)$ ends up with a degree of propositional support that suffices neither for propositional justification, nor for propositional justification for the belief that *not-p*.

Perfect Rebuttal:

$d$ is a perfect rebutter for its target-attitude about $p$, $B(p)$, iff

1. $d$ is a rebutting defeater and
2. taking into account both the degree of propositional support that $d$ offers against $B(p)$ and the degree of propositional support offered by $B(p)$'s total doxastic base, $B(p)$ ends up with a degree of propositional support that does not suffice for propositional and that suffices for propositional justification for the belief that *not-p*.[13]

---

[13] In this, I disagree with Plantinga (1994), who holds that defeaters require the subject to suspend judgment.

So far, we have looked at examples to distinguish these three types of rebutters. However, since they mark points on a spectrum, one may ask whether more can be said about the relations between these points. Specifically, it may be suspected that the degree to which a rebutting defeater has to propositionally support the negation of the target-proposition in order to constitute at least a successful rebutter is related to the degree of support that the justifier offers in a systematic and obvious way. Casullo makes a straightforward suggestion in this direction:

> One suggestion is that $S$'s justified belief that $p$ is defeated by $S$'s justified belief that not-$p$ if and only if $S$'s belief that not-$p$ is justified to at least the same degree as $S$'s justified belief that $p$. (Casullo 2003, p. 44)[14]

I take it that, according to this thesis, a rebutter must propositionally support the negation of the target-proposition at least to the same degree as the justifier doxastically supports the target-proposition and thus fully counterbalance the justifier in order to be a successful rebutter. The thesis in the background here is that it must do so in virtue of being supported to such a degree itself and thus that a defeater, in order to defeat, must be doxastically supported or even justified and that it inherits its weight from its own justifier. That thesis is itself controversial and will be investigated and defended in the next chapter. Here, I will assume it for the sake of argument, as it paves the way for an instructive discussion of the suggestion considered by Casullo.

At first glance, that suggestion looks plausible enough. A rebutter that fully counterbalances the original justifier is surely a successful rebutter, since it leaves the target-attitude utterly unsupported. Furthermore, since its support for the negation of the target-proposition is, in such cases, itself fully counterbalanced by the original justifier, it is not a perfect rebutter.

However, as plausible as the idea may look, it can easily be seen that it is wrong. As we have seen, a rebutter is successful iff it neutralizes *enough of the justifier to reach the threshold where justification is removed*. That threshold is unlikely to be the point where nothing of the justifier is left, since, as seen above, it is clearly possible to have some support for an attitude, without it being enough for justification. Correspondingly, in order for a rebutter to neutralize "enough" of the justifier, it is not necessary that it neutralize *the entire* justifier, which would be the case if the defeater provided the same degree of support against the target-attitude as the justifier does for it, as Casullo suggests. To understand this better, consider the following case:

---

[14] This suggestion is summarised by Casullo from Plantinga (1993a). While Casullo expresses some doubts about it, he also seems to generally endorse it (Casullo 2003, p. 60, 70–71, 76).

LEAVE-ENOUGH: Marla is the manager of a department in a big company. She has read the regulations and is now certain that her employee, Frank, is not entitled to any more paid leave this year. He has already taken 24 days and Marla believes that to be the maximum. She is determined to repel any further requests from him in that respect. Marla's reading of the regulations provides just enough doxastic support for Marla's belief that Frank is due no more leave for that belief to barely count as justified. On the way to her office, she overhears the company lawyer tell a colleague that there is some, though not much, evidence that some legal obscurity allows the employees at the company 30 days of paid leave this year. Given the trustworthiness of the lawyer and the degree of certainty in his voice, the lawyer's statement provides half as much propositional support for the belief that Frank is due more leave as Marla's reading of the regulations provides doxastic support for the belief that he is not.

In LEAVE-ENOUGH, the rebutting defeater does not offer the same degree of support as the justifier, but less, neutralizing only half of the justifier's doxastic support. According to Casullo's suggestion, it should therefore be a case of partial and not successful rebuttal. Yet, since the justifier (Marla's reading of the regulations) was only barely sufficient to justify the target-attitude in the form of the belief that Frank is due no more leave, any weakening of its doxastic support must result in the loss of justification for that belief.[15] Since the rebutter neutralizes half of the positive input contained in the justifier, half of its support is lost, rendering LEAVE-ENOUGH a case of successful rebuttal and therefore a counterexample to the thesis that rebutters must fully neutralize the original justifier in order to be successful. They simply must neutralize enough of it, and in a case where the originally available support just barely suffices for justification, "enough" can mean any proportion above zero.

Naturally, in cases where the justifier is stronger, a higher degree of support on the side of the rebutting defeater is required to successfully rebut the target-attitude. This also shows that the necessary degree to which a rebutter must support the negation of its target-proposition in order to count as a successful rebutter depends on the degree of support that the original justifier provides and on the degree of support that is minimally required for justification. The first variable depends on the details of a given case of rebuttal, while the second depends on the answer to a separate, more general epistemological question. I thus follow Casullo's route out of the conundrum and note that "the conditions under

---

**15** Of course, any rebutter results in a loss of some degree of justification, as explained above. In this case, what is meant is that any weakening of support must result in the target-belief *no longer counting as justified at all*. I have been assuming that, while justification comes in degrees, those degrees do not coincide with degrees of support, again, because an attitude can be supported, but not justified.

which [a rebutting defeater successfully] defeats $S$'s justification for the belief that $p$ is a function of the relative degree of justification each enjoys" (Casullo 2003, p. 45).

This discussion shows that there is clearly something right about the thought that obtaining information that indicates that our belief is false can't be simply dismissed, even in cases where it shouldn't sway us. Specifically, it appears to be possible to suffer epistemic defeat, without thereby losing justification entirely (for this point, see Thune 2010; and Loughrist 2015). The orthodox view, held by Pollock, Bergmann and others, that defeaters characteristically *remove* justification therefore turns out to be false. However, what has been said so far is friendly to the closely related thesis that defeaters cause a gradual *loss of support*. This is plausible for rebutting defeat but must be re-evaluated in light of the characteristics of undercutting defeat, which will be done in the next chapter. Furthermore, it has become apparent that rebutting defeaters can have a variety of distinguishable effects on the target-belief's epistemic status and the rational requirements that the subject is under, as the comparison between partial, successful and perfect rebuttal shows.

### 2.1.2 Degrees of Rebuttal and an Account of Rebutting Defeat

The last point to be addressed is the question how all of this structure is to be integrated into an account of rebutting defeat and defeat in general. Def-2 (and Bergmann's DI), as it stands, will not do. According to this account, defeaters *by definition* destroy their target's justification. Thus, its defender has to say that failed rebutters are no defeaters and that there is no partial rebuttal.[16] This is at odds with intuitive verdicts in cases like LEAVE-PART and it disassociates partly neutralizing information from defeat on a mere technicality. Also, as long as defeat concerns only the categorical loss of justification, there is no room for the spectrum of effects that rebutters in particular can have on the epistemic status of their targets. A straightforward solution would be to modify Def-2, such that it depicts defeaters as lowering the degree of justification of their target-beliefs, instead of necessarily removing it entirely. Here is my suggestion:

Def-3:

---

[16] Bergmann seems to be aware of partial defeaters, as he mentions them in "Justification and Awareness" (2006, p. 178). However, he explicitly ignores them there and it is not clear what he thinks the relation between defeaters and justification is supposed to be like.

*d* is a defeater, iff

1. *d* is a belief that *q* or a piece of positive input for belief that *q* of a subject *S* that is acquired by *S* at time *t*
2. there is a doxastic attitude about *p*, *A(p)*, that is held by *S* at *t* and at *t-1*, such that

    2.1. *A(p)* is supported to degree *x* at *t-1* and to degree *y* at *t*, such that

    2.1.1. $x > y$ and

    2.1.2. the change from *x* to *y* is a result of *S*'s acquiring *d* at *t*.

Rebut-3:

*d* is a rebutting defeater, iff

1. *d* is a defeater:

    1.1. *d* is a belief that *q* or a piece of positive input for belief that *q* of a subject *S* that is acquired by *S* at time *t*

    1.2. there is a doxastic attitude about *p*, *A(p)*, that is held by *S* at *t* and at *t-1*, such that

    1.2.1. *A(p)* is supported to degree *x* at *t-1* and to degree *y* at *t*, such that

    1.2.1.1. $x > y$ and

    1.2.1.2. the change from *x* to *y* is a result of *S*'s acquiring *d* at *t*.

2. *q* is the negation of *p*.[17]

---

**17** Note that issues arising from the relationship between rebutting defeat and the target-attitude's total doxastic base *do not invalidate* Rebut-3. The analysis still gives us the conditions under which rebutting defeaters are obtained and distinguishes it from other kinds of defeat. It also sheds light on its defining characteristics. Rather, they show that Rebut-3 does not contain the full *explanation* of the phenomenon of rebutting defeat. That explanation will include parts that are tailored to different theories of justification, as they connect with Rebut-3. I will explore these connections in chapter 4.

In paradigmatic cases of defeat, like LEAVE, LAW and SCHOOL, the degree of justification brought about by obtaining the defeater, $y$, will be so low that $A(p)$ is no longer justified because $y$ lies below the threshold for justification. In cases of partial rebuttal, $y$ is still high enough to permit justification, but lower than the original degree of justification, $x$. Thus, Def-3 and Rebut-3 accommodate the phenomenon of partial defeat and a spectrum of possible effects of rebuttal, as well as the plausible thesis that rebutting defeaters support belief in the negation of the proposition embedded in their target. For the time being, they therefore form an adequate analysis of rebutting defeat. Further modification for theoretical reasons will be required later, but it will be independent of case judgments.

Understanding rebutting defeaters as counterbalancing justifiers brings with it a commitment to the idea that defeaters have some epistemic weight themselves. There are different ways of spelling out what this comes down to. One might straightforwardly assume that rebutting defeaters have weight in the same way that justifiers do: By either being epistemically supported themselves or by having positive epistemic status in some basic way. However, precisely this symmetry between defeaters and justifiers has been denied by several influential philosophers. In the next section, I will elaborate on this matter and use the results of this section to construct a theoretical argument in favor of the thesis that defeaters need to enjoy positive epistemic status in order to defeat.

## 2.2 The Epistemic Status of Defeaters

Defeaters can themselves be defeated. Recall the LEAVE-case: Marla checks the regulations and believes that Frank is due no more leave. She then overhears the lawyer saying that all employees are due more leave than Marla thought. Clearly, the new information that the lawyer believes this is a successful rebutting defeater (call it D1), and Marla's belief, if retained, is unjustified. Now, imagine that, right after she overhears the lawyer, Marla sees that the lawyer is, in fact, talking to Mary (call this piece of information D2). Marla knows that the lawyer hates Mary and will do everything in his power to mislead her. In this situation, it seems that D2 undermines D1, such that Marla would now again be justified in believing that Frank is due no more leave. Such defeater-defeaters have often been remarked upon in the literature (cf. e.g. Plantinga 1993b, pp. 231–237, 1993a, pp. 216–221, 1986; Pollock and Cruz 1999, pp. 45–58, 1999, pp. 37–38; Jäger 2005; Grundmann 2011, pp. 161–162; Lackey 2008, p. 46).

## 2.2.1 Rebutting Defeat and the Defeater-Justifier-Symmetry

Rebutting defeat and defeater-defeat are closely related. If a rebutting defeater is a piece of input that supports belief in the negation of the target-proposition, it follows that positive input for the target-attitude can also act as a rebutting defeater for that first rebutting defeater: Say, you go to the fridge, open it and get the visual impression that there is milk in it, which you subsequently believe. Five minutes later, your sister opens the fridge, looks carefully and starts complaining that there is no milk left. Your sister's complaints provide you with at least a partial defeater for your belief that there is milk in the fridge. After all, her eyesight is no worse than yours and you may have confused yoghurt with milk or misjudged the color of some liquid, however unlikely that may be. At the same time, the fact that you had the clear impression that there is milk in the fridge supports belief in the proposition that your sister does not truly believe that there is no milk in the fridge but does not want fridge-cold milk or is pulling your leg. So, it seems that, depending on background information about your sister's proneness to pranks and the like, there is a certain symmetry inherent in that situation: Sure, the clearer it is to you that your sister justifiedly believes that there is no milk, the worse off is your milk belief, but it is also true that the clearer your milk-impression was and the more carefully you looked, the less likely it is that your sister really believes that there is no milk in the fridge. The justifier for your belief that there is milk acts as a (partial) defeater for the defeater you get from your sister.

This suggests that the weighing and comparing of support that rebutting defeaters engender could generally be described in terms of defeat-defeat. As discussed in the previous section, rebutting defeat can be seen as an expansion of one's total set of input relevant to the target-proposition. If the original justifier, taken together with the defeater, still propositionally supports the target-attitude to a sufficient degree, the defeater is only partial, if it sufficiently supports neither the target-attitude nor its negation, it is successful and if it supports belief in the negation of the target-proposition, it is perfect. Connecting these observations to defeater-defeat, one could also say that this is due to the defeater and the target-attitude (or its justifier) being defeaters for each other, or at least for very closely related attitudes: A perfect defeater outweighs the original justifier for its target-attitude to an extent that allows it to justifiedly put in place a belief in the negation of the target-proposition.[18] At the same time, this defeater-based

---

18 In case the defeater is itself a belief in this negation, it is to be distinguished from the belief that is propositionally justified in a case of perfect rebuttal in a gradual way: The defeater may

belief is not as well supported as it would have been, had there not also been the target-attitude/its justifier. So, the presence of the target-attitude/its justifier lowers the degree of propositional support that the defeater-based belief in the negation of the target-proposition enjoys and thus acts as at least a potential partial rebutting defeater itself.

Importantly, the degree of symmetry between defeater and target-attitude this reveals depends on whether the rebutting defeater is itself the belief in the negation of the target-proposition. If it is, there will be perfect symmetry between it and the target-attitude. However, it is quite implausible that rebutting defeaters are standardly such beliefs. Even if one finds it plausible that people can hold a belief in a proposition as the target-attitude, while simultaneously believing its negation, it is easy to craft examples where defeat occurs, but the negation-belief is not formed. LEAVE, for example, will evoke the defeat-intuition, regardless of the fact that it does not (explicitly or implicitly) have Marla believe that Frank is due more leave or that it is not true that he is due no more leave. So, in normal cases of rebuttal, there will usually be a certain asymmetry: While the rebutter, as a piece of input *supporting* belief in the negation of the target-proposition, is an actual defeater for the target-attitude, the target-attitude is only a potential defeater for a belief in the negation of the target-proposition in that *it would be an actual defeater, if that belief were formed*. Still, there is a high degree of structural symmetry in rebutting defeat that comes out when considering partial and perfect rebuttal in light of the phenomenon of defeater-defeat.

This symmetry is highly relevant to a small, but important controversy about defeaters, surrounding the following question: Does the defeater itself need to be justified? To see this, the controversy and the positions must first be laid out in some detail. In what follows, I will argue that a defeater does not necessarily need to be justified but needs to have some positive epistemic status in order to defeat. I will first address the opposing view and argue against it, taking into account arguments given in its defense in the literature. Afterwards, I will discuss arguments that speak in favor of requiring support for defeaters and show that the plausibility of defeater-defeat provides a powerful motivation for this view.

---

be a belief to degree 0.8 in the negation of the target-proposition, for example, but due to the original justifier of the target-attitude, belief in the negation of the target-proposition, all things considered, is only supported to a degree of 0.6. So, the belief that is propositionally justified in a case of perfect rebuttal is not the same as the defeating belief. I don't want to endorse the defeater-as-belief thesis in general, but merely point out that this phenomenon can be accommodated under its assumption.

In the cases discussed so far, the defeating information always has a positive epistemic status: For example, Marla in LEAVE and James in SCHOOL receive their defeaters from testifiers (the company lawyer and a fellow father) they have no reason to mistrust and every reason to trust. Under regular circumstances, believing on the basis of testimony from these people would be perfectly justified, in the sense of being at least propositionally justified for the hearer. One question now is what would happen to the intuition that justification of the target-attitude is lost in such cases, if the defeating input is not so justified. LEAVE can be modified to highlight this:

> LEAVE-WISH: Marla reads the regulations and believes on the basis of this that Frank is due no more leave. However, she likes Frank and really wants him to have more leave. Over the span of a few hours, this wish subconsciously coalesces into a belief that conflicts with her original belief.[19]

Is Marla now no longer justified in believing that Frank is due no more leave? The answer is not at all clear to me.[20] However, maybe one can get a grip on it by considering two neighboring questions. First, clearly her epistemic situation becomes worse, but in what way, exactly? Her wish-belief takes her to a state where she is clearly irrational (cf. Pryor 2004, pp. 364–366). Not only should she not hold the unsupported belief that Frank is due more leave, but she especially shouldn't do so in the face of her original belief that this is false. Also, more generally, she should not hold attitudes that she realizes to be conflicting (or, possibly, she should hold no conflicting attitudes at all). It is only this last, general point that potentially affects the epistemic status of the target-attitude. However, it is far from clear that the irrationality of holding defeating belief and target-attitude at the same time suffices to conclude that it is irrational to

---

**19** If one finds it implausible that Marla could have two such blatantly conflicting beliefs, one can also think of the defeater (her wishful thinking) as a kind of impression that Frank is due more leave that stands in tension with the target-belief, or maybe have her form the belief that Frank can have as many days of leave as he wishes, which conflicts somewhat less directly with it. It seems that wishful thinking consists in some form of "putting a belief on the table" that one really wants to be true and I find it plausible that such a state is at least prima facie a candidate for defeat. Again, if one is unhappy with this, the example can again be modified. Imagine instead that Marla's boyfriend, who knows nothing about the regulations, testifies that Frank is due more leave.
**20** On Pollock's original view, defeaters need not have positive status. He argues for this by way of similar cases (cf. Pollock 1974, pp. 43–44). However, I do not share his apparently clear intuition that in such cases, the target-attitude is defeated. Since I am not alone in this (cf. Loughrist 2015, pp. 120–121), further argument on the part of Pollock's position is required.

hold the target-attitude. After all, there is more than one way of escaping the irrationality here.

This leads to the second question: Is Marla required to give up the target-attitude? According to the position adopted by William Alston, she is not (see for this point Alston 2002, pp. 196–201) and I agree that this is the intuitive verdict. The target-attitude enjoys independent support, while the defeater is the result of wishful thinking and giving up the defeater would get Marla out of her irrational state just as well. So, how could an epistemic requirement to give up the target-attitude in this situation possibly be motivated? Plantinga (Plantinga 1993a, 1994, 2000, 2002) defines defeaters solely with respect to how one rationally ought change one's noetic system (one's system of doxastic attitudes, experiences etc.), *given* that one has acquired a potential defeater (Plantinga 2002, p. 275; see also Lackey 2008, p. 260; Pollock 1974, pp. 43–44, 1974, pp. 43–44). Accordingly, assuming that Marla fixedly holds the new belief from wishful thinking, her only option is to give up the belief that Frank is due no more leave (the target-attitude) and this option seems to be, in some sense, rational (in Plantinga's (2000, p. 365) terms, it is "internally rational"). So, in Plantiga's view, defeaterhood is independent of the question whether, all things considered, the target-attitude must be given up. He considers a piece of information that, if it is fixed in the noetic system, requires giving up the target-attitude to be a "perfectly respectable and epistemically relevant kind of defeater" (Plantinga 2002, p. 275). This may be the case, but it sheds some doubt on whether the notion of defeat Plantinga discusses is the same notion that I and most other philosophers who have written on the topic are after. It seems that what Plantinga is describing is more properly labelled a *potential* defeater in that it would require the dropping of the target-attitude, if fixed in the doxastic/noetic system (see also Kvanvig 2007). I will return to this discussion shortly.

Of course, one could always claim that the whole question concerning which attitude should be given up and which one retained is beside the point. Requirements to form or give up doxastic attitudes may be completely independent of their justificatory status, so that the target-attitude, while rendered unjustified by the defeater, need (or should) not be given up (this line is taken by Bergmann 2006, pp. 164–166). This is an impressive theoretical commitment as it divorces justification from epistemic normativity. It would result in a large number of cases in which belief in a proposition, for example, is somehow permitted, even though that belief is not justified. Examples are cases like LEAVE-WISH, where one obtains an unsupported defeater, but also cases in which one holds an unsupported belief that then renders *any conflicting newly adopted attitudes or other input* unjustified, even though their adoption is permitted or may even be required. So, in order to avoid Alston's objection, one would have to bite the bullet in all of these cases and take an unconventional stance on justification and epistemic normativity, which would certainly raise the suspicion that this move is wildly ad hoc. Given how demanding and plainly odd this result is, it is surprising how many philosophers have subscribed to the thesis that unsupported defeaters are possible (e.g. Plantinga 2000; Pryor 2004; Bergmann 2006; Pollock 1974).

I want to get a bit clearer on the issue. To ask whether a defeater itself needs to be *justified* brings some theoretical baggage with it. For example, if "justified" is taken to mean "formed via a reliable process", one may be able to find much clearer examples of unsupported defeat. To understand this better, imagine that Fred has a chemistry teacher who teaches him to employ testing method M, in order to determine whether a fluid is acidic. Normally, the teacher is a highly reliable testifier, but in this instance, she has made an unlikely, albeit grave mistake when preparing her lesson: In fact, M is a completely unreliable testing method for acidity. Still, in trusting his teacher, Fred employs an extremely reliable second-order method. So, Fred uses a reliable method to acquire an unreliable method. Later in life, Fred hears from a reliable chemist that fluid F is acidic and believes this. He then double-checks this using M, but this yields the result that F is not acidic. Does this defeat his belief that F is acidic? Intuitively, it clearly does, but according to the simple version of reliabilism under consideration, the putative defeater at play here is not justified. At the same time, the case is different from LEAVE-WISH because an argument can be made that Fred's trust in the result of an application of M is at least *rational*, whereas Marla's wishful thinking is not. This illustrates again that defeat-intuitions are mostly driven by our concept of rationality and so, as soon as rationality and justification come apart, one will find examples of defeat that are, to some extent, independent of justification.[21] This presents a problem for theories of justification that do not hold that justification involves rationality and yet still wish to accommodate defeaters. I will return to this issue in the fourth chapter when discussing reliabilism's difficult relationship with defeat.

---

[21] Here, I understand being "rational" as basing one's beliefs or other attitudes on all easily *accessible* input one possesses that is relevant to the proposition in a way that employs the best basing methods *one is capable of*. This is meant to have a somewhat internalist tint because I do think that rationality is normative and that it is a staple of at least "pure" externalist theories of justification that they conceptually divorce justification from rationality (see Kiesewetter 2017, ch. 7, 8). I am aware that there are conceptions of rationality that are more in line with externalism, but I do not think that they are fit to explain intuitions in cases of defeat. Such intuitions are best explained by a "guiding" conception of rationality (see Gibbons 2013, pp. 119–191).

For now, the matter can be simplified by distinguishing three questions that can be asked about defeaters: 1) Do defeaters need to be justified? 2) Do defeaters need to be rational (to hold)? 3) Do defeaters need to have some positive epistemic status? The third question is broader than the first two because it is guaranteed to cover potential cases of *both* unjustified defeaters and irrational defeaters, should those two come apart. Thus, for a theory of justification that does not deem being rational a positive epistemic status, for example, question 2) is pointless, but question 3) still hits the mark. Furthermore, it is quite plausible that defeaters can be states that are not even of the right kind to be either candidates for justification or for rationality. They may, for example, be experiences or perceptions (cf. e.g. Pollock and Cruz 1999, pp. 191–197; Bergmann 2006, pp. 154–157). In addition, a distinction can be made between types of any such states that are epistemically good and types that are epistemically bad (e.g. perceptions vs. illusions). Unlike the first two questions, question 3) covers all relevant states because it does not specify what the distinction between being epistemically good and being epistemically bad amounts to. This is helpful because the question concerning the epistemic status of defeaters is mostly discussed with reference to defeaters that have no positive epistemic status at all, whatever that may come down to. For instance, Plantinga discusses an example where what he deems a defeating belief is formed through paranoid depression (cf. Plantinga 2000, p. 365) and Lackey, also a defender of the view that defeaters don't need to have a positive epistemic status, presents a case where a student is vulnerable to epistemic peer pressure by the highly irrational members of a cult (cf. Lackey 2008, pp. 257–259). So, the question that I will discuss in the remainder of this chapter is question 3).[22]

Finally, I turn to the debate itself. First, some terminology is in order. When I speak of a defeater having positive epistemic status, I mean that it either 1) is justified or at least rational (if the two come apart) or that it 2) is such that by default and without any further support it makes the associated attitude justified or rational. The second way of having positive status is supposed to allow for defeating experiences etc. When a putative defeater lacks positive status, I call it "non-positive". Non-positive defeaters simply fulfill neither 1) nor 2). Examples are doxastic attitudes one has no sufficiently positive basis for,[23] or that one even has reason to take to be false or inadequate, or experiences one has reason to doubt. "Non-positive" can accordingly refer to either the lack of a proper basis

---

[22] For a similar clarification, albeit with a different focus, see Loughrist (2015, pp. 118–119).
[23] Leaving open whether this basis would have to be accessible or not. More on this in Chapter 4.

or the presence of a defeater-defeater for the putative defeater. The question at issue here can thus also be phrased in the following way: Can non-positive pieces of input be defeaters?

### 2.2.2 The Inclusive Thesis: Defeaters Need Not Have Positive Epistemic Status

The main argument for the thesis that there are non-positive defeaters (I will call this the "Inclusive Thesis") has already been touched upon. The idea here, defended by Plantinga, is that holding on to a putative defeater makes it, "downstream from" the assumption of that putative defeater, irrational to hold on to the target-attitude. Lackey (2008) and Pryor (2004) also hold versions of this view. Clearly, this stance depends on a very specific understanding of rationality that Plantinga calls "internal" rationality. Roughly, one is internally rational if one responds to one's experiences in a way that keeps one's doxastic or noetic system coherent, where these experiences include phenomenal imagery from the senses and so-called "doxastic experience", which is the experience that some proposition seems correct (cf. Plantinga 2000, pp. 110–113). Thus, according to this view, if it seems correct to Marla that Frank is due more leave, however ill-formed this seeming might be, this experience (or the belief formed on its basis) can defeat her belief that he is not because it rationally conflicts with that belief, and holding both would render the doxastic system incoherent. I will not discuss the view in depth, as this has already been done (Alston 2002; Merricks 2002; Talbott 2002). However, one important point can be added and it pays to lay it out in some detail.

Assuming that one is internally rational only if one believes in accordance with all of one's seemings and if they conflict, it is not rational to believe in accordance with either conflicting seeming. Thus, if one has formed two incompatible doxastic attitudes and experienced the doxastic seeming that both seem right, both are irrational. The Inclusive Thesis would follow. However, it is intuitively false that in cases of conflicting seemings both relevant attitudes are irrational, as the following case illustrates:

> RECALCITRANT: Donald has a recalcitrant belief that his child is smarter than the average child. This means that he is psychologically incapable of shaking this belief, even if it turns out to be false. Donald is now presented with a host of good evidence that shows that his child is of average intelligence. Because Donald is generally a very rational guy, he admits the weight of this evidence and adopts the belief that his child is averagely smart (he agrees with teachers who tell him this and refrains from signing up his child for programs designed for precocious students etc.). However, he still also holds the recalcitrant belief

that his child is smarter than average and when he doesn't pay attention he slips easily into the associated behavioral patterns.

To be sure, it is irrational for Donald to continue to hold both of his beliefs about his child simultaneously, but it doesn't follow that *each belief, separately*, is irrational for him to hold. He may be in an overall bad epistemic state but it is not at all plausible that this state also afflicts all of the individual beliefs contributing to it (cf. Loughrist 2015, pp. 122–125). Specifically, it seems that, while his belief that his child is smarter than average is not rational to hold, his adopting the belief that his child is averagely smart on the basis of excellent evidence is rationally commendable. The example thus suggests that, in cases where only one of two beliefs is non-positive, that belief will be the one that is rendered irrational.[24] Furthermore, it suggests that, *even if one of the incompatible beliefs is held fixed*, which, in the literature, is mostly supposed to be the case for the non-positive, putative defeater,[25] it doesn't follow that *the other* belief is irrational. If the belief held fixed is the non-positive one, the other belief may remain rational or justified. It merely follows that the subject now has an irrational noetic system containing a recognized incompatibility. As Loughrist puts it, "to move immediately from the claim that the conjunction of beliefs is unjustified to the claim that each belief is unjustified is to commit the fallacy of division" (Loughrist 2015, p. 122).

To emphasize: The reasoning behind the Inclusive Thesis comes down to the observation that the addition of non-positive attitudes that conflict with already held attitudes render the subject's *entire doxastic system* irrational. It does not follow that the originally held attitude involved in the conflict is thereby rendered irrational (and thus, in Plantinga's view anyway, unjustified). What does follow is that, *given that the non-positive attitude is held fixed*, the only way to move to a coherent doxastic system is to give up the attitude conflicting with it. But note that this is not necessarily due to the fact that that particular attitude is now unjustified and/or irrational. In fact, the whole point amounts to the observation that *defeaters and their target-attitudes stand in rational conflict*. This observation is not trivial and it is certainly a respectable phenomenon of episte-

---

**24** This kind of case can also motivate the more general idea within the relevant field that the mere avoidance of overall epistemic states that contain an incoherence cannot be all there is to rationality (cf. Ewing 1953, pp. 144–145; Bratman 1981; Kiesewetter 2017, ch. 4). For an extensive discussion of several positions and a defense of the view that rationality doesn't consist in such structural adequacy conditions at all, see Kiesewetter 2017.

**25** Recall that the fixing of belief is expressed by the locution "given that I have come to believe…" (Plantinga 1994, p. 23, fn 33)

mic interest. But moving from it to the Inclusive Thesis is an implausibly big leap. At best, the stance under consideration here captures why a new piece of information has defeating *potential:* It would, if kept, get us into rational trouble because we hold a certain other attitude. But the phenomenon is not, or at least not fully, the effect that interests us in cases like LEAVE, SCHOOL etc. If we want to fully analyze why the protagonists in these cases lose support for the target-attitude, the option to resist forming a conflicting attitude or dismissing the relevant seeming should not be screened off and, even more importantly, we must explain why the putative target-attitude *itself* is weakened, not why it is part of the reason that we now have an irrationality in the whole of our doxastic system. The Inclusive Thesis is very much a symptom of thinking about defeat exclusively in terms of noetic systems, but for the reasons given here I strongly doubt that this is enough.

Before moving on to the other side of the debate, I will quickly address two slightly different ways of arguing for the Inclusive Thesis. First, Jim Pryor takes a position that allows him to concede that non-positive attitudes do not defeat, but instead *rationally obstruct* the subject from having certain doxastic attitudes. In his view, attitudes like beliefs bring with them certain rational commitments, where commitments are "hypothetical relations between your beliefs" (Pryor 2004, p. 364) in the following sense: Belief $a$ may commit you to belief $b$ in that, if you have justification for $a$, you also have justification for $b$ and if you hold $a$, but not $b$, you exhibit a rational failing (cf. Pryor 2004, p. 364). Accordingly, if Marla forms the belief that Frank is due more leave (or, if one finds the possibility of holding directly contradicting beliefs strange, that Frank is due as much leave as he likes), this commits her to the falsity of the belief that he is not. If she holds that latter belief anyway, she is clearly irrational. In this sense, this belief is rationally obstructed by the former belief. In many ways, this is simply a different way of spelling out Plantinga's position without accepting the necessity of rationality for justification and so, the same arguments concerning that view seem to apply here. However, it is worthwhile to note that Pryor does *not* take a belief to be rational, just in case it fits the subject's phenomenal and doxastic experience, as Plantinga does for internal rationality, but that he calls a belief rational iff it is not rationally obstructed (or opposed) by any other belief the subject holds. This is why he divorces rationality from justification. However, even from this rather limited view on rationality, it follows that Fred's belief that his child is smarter than average in RECALCITRANT is on a par, epistemically speaking, with his belief that his child is averagely smart. After all, both beliefs are rationally obstructed.

It seems that this is clearly the wrong result. In addition to committing one to a problematic verdict on cases like RECALCITRANT, it is highly doubtful that this extremely narrow account of rationality that equates rationality with coherence is fit to underpin the intuitions we generally have in cases of defeat. What Plantinga and Pryor themselves wish to explain is the phenomenon that a subject that holds a justified belief receives some new information, which renders the belief irrational. Rational obstruction can only explain this if the new information comes with rational commitments. However, there is no reason to think that it always does. It is plausible that rational commitments arise from the doxastic attitudes one forms, but it is far from clear that they also arise from more fundamental types of input. The problem is that such fundamental types, like experiences or, depending on one's theory, even (accessed) external facts, can plausibly be defeaters, but do not commit one to anything. Imagine that Marla in LEAVE hears the lawyer's statement and thus has a contentful auditory experience. The mere having of this experience does not commit her to anything. Therefore, by Pryor's lights, it is possible for her to refuse to take the lawyer's word because she knows that her belief that Frank is due no more leave rationally obstructs the belief that he is due more leave for her. Since she thereby avoids commitments that may obstruct the belief about Frank's leave, Pryor would have to say that there is no defeater for Marla's belief and that she is rational/justified in holding on to it to the same degree as before, but this is clearly false. This demonstrates that defeat is richer than rational obstruction, even though rational obstruction is, again, a legitimate epistemic phenomenon. It simply is not the one we are after.

The second line of argument comes from Michael Bergmann, who claims that non-positive attitudes can defeat putative target-attitudes incompatible with them, even though they may not require the subject to give up those target-attitudes (cf. Bergmann 2006, pp. 165–168). His reasoning is that it is not primarily due to a lack of coherence induced by the new attitude that defeat occurs, but to the fact that holding the new attitude and the incompatible target-attitude simultaneously is not an appropriate *response to the evidence* that is available after having acquired the new attitude. Bracketing the question how one should rationally change one's attitudes in reaction to a defeater,[26] he follows the other defenders of the Inclusive Thesis in focusing on situations in which one holds both a non-positive new attitude and a previously justified belief that is incompatible with it and asks whether the latter remains justified. His argument for a

---

[26] Bergmann thinks that justification is disconnected from questions concerning rational changes in one's noetic system. He remains neutral with respect to Alston's (2002) criticism of Plantinga's view, which Bergmann calls the "Rational Change Objection" (Bergmann 2006, p. 164, 165). As I stated earlier, Bergmann seems to underestimate the theoretical commitment to a divorce of justification from epistemic normativity that this move brings with it.

negative answer to the question rests on the posit that the non-positive new attitude is added to the subject's evidence, such that, while the original evidence may have justified the putative target-attitude, the new evidence that includes the new attitude no longer allows justifiedly holding it. One of his examples that are supposed to make this intuitively plausible is a case where a subject believes on the basis of her experience that she has hands and then, for no good reason, becomes convinced that she is a brain in a vat. In such a case, Bergmann argues that, while her perception may have allowed the justified hand-belief, her experience, *together with her belief that she is a brain in a vat,* does not (cf. Bergmann 2006, p. 165).[27]

In response, it must first be noted that a lot depends on the notion of *evidence* at play here. That notion appears to be extremely liberal, given that *merely believing something*, no matter how crazy or irrational, already constitutes evidence that occupies the same status as, say, trustworthy testimony or visual perception. Such a conception of evidence has extremely problematic consequences: There are many people who quite firmly believe that non-white people lack cognitive capacities and are by nature weaker and less entitled to basic human rights than whites. This is typically held together with a whole host of similar racist beliefs that stand in propositional relations to one another (for example, specific racist beliefs are inferred from a general xenophobic belief etc.). These beliefs are held without any good reason and are paradigmatic examples of unjustified irrational attitudes. In the conception of evidence suggested by Bergmann, however, the racist holding these belief systems must be said to have quite a bit of evidence for any given racist belief, simply in virtue of holding a large number of other racist beliefs that imply or otherwise conditionally support them. While Bergmann could still maintain that this doesn't mean that the racist's beliefs are *justified*, since there will likely be even more evidence that speaks against them, he cannot guarantee this result and neither can he agree to the intuitively correct explanation for the racist's epistemic shortcomings: The racist's beliefs are unjustified precisely because there is *no* evidence for them and the subject only holds them because of irrational bias. Clearly, the point generalizes, because a belief that belongs to any web of interrelated beliefs will necessarily be supported by some evidence in the form of the other beliefs. Even more dramatically, it follows that we can justify *any* belief in the complete absence of what can plausibly count as good reasons (and possibly even in the presence of well supported counter-reasons), merely by somehow bringing our-

---

[27] For an argument that Bergmann, by his own lights, may not even be able to coherently make this claim, see Loughrist (2015, pp. 130–131).

selves to believe as many related propositions as possible, which is an absurd consequence. At the very least, at this point the burden of proof has been handed back to Bergmann and the other proponents of the Inclusive Thesis. If the reason for accepting that thesis is supposed to be that a non-positive attitude is part of the subject's new total evidence, much more work must be done to convince the reader of the notion of evidence at play here and its relation to defeaters.[28] As things stand, Bergmann delivers no reason for one to be convinced of the Inclusive Thesis.

### 2.2.3 The Exclusive Thesis: Defeaters Do Need to Have Positive Epistemic Status

Of course, the plausibility of the Inclusive Thesis to some extent depends on the plausibility of its opponent, which I will call the "Exclusive Thesis". It states that a defeater needs to have some positive epistemic status. In other words: There are no non-positive defeaters. Given that the Inclusive Thesis is the more venerable view, arguments for the Exclusive Thesis mostly take the form of objections against it. One of those arguments has already been discussed in the form of Alston's observation that non-positive pieces of input do not require the subject to give up the target-attitude. There is a second argument against the Inclusive Thesis that is even more pressing because it cannot be evaded by divorcing requirements to hold or drop beliefs from matters of justification: The Arbitrariness Objection (Bergmann 2006, p. 166; Alexander 2017, p. 896). The idea behind this

---

[28] It isn't clear to me why Bergmann espouses this extremely liberal view on evidence. After all, as part of his overall view, he sees "connectors", that is, strong, felt inclinations that connect basic evidence to belief-responses, as part of a subject's total evidence (cf. Bergmann 2006, pp. 114–118). However, he states that not all connectors make a response fit the evidence and proceeds to exclude those that are not learned from an observed correlation (cf. Bergmann 2006, p. 117 ff). So, in order to hold the Inclusive Position, he would need to say that the connector between the part of the evidence containing the unsupported defeater and the retained target-belief is (paradigmatically) faulty. But why would a connector that is responsible for holding on to beliefs in the face of *unsupported* new evidence be one of those "bad" connectors? Conversely, someone who systematically fails to respond to unsupported defeaters apparently has a "disconnector", the negative version of a connector, for such evidence (cf. Bergmann 2006, p. 115). Why isn't that disconnector perfectly fine? At the very least, Bergmann doesn't say nearly enough about why the subject's total evidence in cases of unsupported defeat no longer supports the target-belief. Given that whether this is so depends on the connectors contained in that total evidence, this will, by his own lights, depend on what kinds of connectors are plausibly present. It is dubious at best that this is enough to establish the Inclusive Thesis.

argument is that it would be arbitrary to draw fundamental distinctions between reasons to believe (positive input) and defeaters, which often appear to be reasons not to believe (negative input). Since it is uncontroversial that reasons to believe must themselves have positive epistemic status, at least when they act as premises for inferences, it would be arbitrary to hold that defeaters, on the other hand, do not need to have positive status in order to defeat. This objection is quite powerful, because the assumption that there is some parallel between positive input /reasons and defeaters is not just pre-theoretically likely, but receives further motivation from theoretical considerations (see also Loughrist 2015, pp. 135–138).

In fact, I want to argue that it is mostly due to the structural features of defeat and support that the Arbitrariness Objection suffices to establish the Exclusive Thesis. In order to make the parallel between positive input/reasons and defeat clearer, it is instructive to look at a counterargument by Bergmann (cf. 2006, pp. 166–167). He argues against the Arbitrariness Objection that the motivation for thinking that reasons need positive epistemic status in order to support derives from their function in inferences. Non-positive premises cannot establish the truth of conclusions. This suggests a picture in which reasons *transmit* their epistemic status to beliefs derived from them. Defeaters, he argues, do not fit into the same picture because defeat can hardly be understood as the transmission of "unjustifiedness" or some other negative status (cf. Alexander 2017, p. 896). Bergmann concludes that defeaters are not like reasons, after all. In response, David Alexander (2017, pp. 893–896) points out that the fact that the parallel between reasons and defeaters does not consist in both of them transmitting their epistemic status does not mean that there is no parallel. He claims that a proponent of the Arbitrariness Objection would not be moved by the idea that defeaters defeat by transmission in the first place. Rather, they would assent to the thesis that, just as the degree of justification of a conclusion is limited by the degrees of support of the premises in an inference, the degree to which a defeater renders a belief *un*justified is limited by the *degree of support* the defeater enjoys. So, defeaters are similar to reasons in that their effect depends on their own status. Bergmann's objection has no force against this thesis, which, if true, does reveal a significant structural similarity between reasons and defeaters. It can be added to this point that whether this fact can be couched in terms of "transmission" presumably depends on whether this terminology refers to a real epistemic relation or is, in fact, metaphorical. After all, reasons don't physically "give" conclusions justification, but merely limit the conclusion's total degree of justification. It seems, then, that there is some merit to drawing a parallel between reasons and defeaters and thus to argue for the arbitrariness of the Inclusive Thesis.[29]

Admittedly, the above line of argument will hardly convince a proponent of the Inclusive Thesis, for much the same reasons why Bergmann's point should not make a proponent of the Inclusive Thesis waver: Just as Bergmann thinks it independently plausible, without much argument, that non-positive attitudes are evidence, the Arbitrariness objection merely assumes a parallel between reasons and defeaters. While Alexander's arguments lend some support to that assumption by moving the focus from the transmission picture to a more plausible background thesis, it does not suffice to clearly establish the parallel.[30] This can be remedied by looking at the observations about partial defeat and defeater-defeat made in the last section and in the beginning of this section.

Virtually everybody accepts or should accept the possibility of defeater-defeat. If it is further accepted that defeaters characteristically diminish justification, it is hard to understand how they are supposed to interact with attitudes that are not justified. Even leaving justification aside, they also clearly seem to adversely affect other epistemic properties of their targets, e.g., by rendering them less rational or by making reasons for them unavailable or unsupportive. They do this characteristically, that is, they do it either in all or in paradigmatic cases.[31] How, then, could there be defeater-defeaters for (potential) defeaters that have no positive status at all? Acquiring a non-positive potential defeater and a defeater-defeater simultaneously, for example, will introduce incoherencies in the same way that Plantinga describes the effect of a defeater, so, in his view, a defeater-defeater cannot save you from a defeater (unless one counts its effect on which attitudes are to be given up and which are to be kept, but then Alston's objection applies in any case). Of course, one could hold that there simply are no defeater-defeaters for non-positive, potential defeaters, but only for positive potential defeaters. While this would render the position coherent, it has the strange consequence that non-positive defeaters have a much more stable adverse effect on the status of their targets than positive defeaters do, because one could not restore the status of a target-attitude affected by a non-positive defeater by doing further research. But acquiring one non-positive attitude that conflicts with some other attitude one holds should not mean game over for

---

[29] While I accept that there is some such parallel sufficient to refute Bergmann's view, I do not wish to say that defeaters are just reasons. This is because I propose a causal account of defeat that rejects a full structural parallel between reasonas and defeaters. More on this later.
[30] Indeed, Alexander himself seems to doubt it (cf. Alexander 2017, pp. 903–911).
[31] I, of course, want to say that this happens in all cases, but this commitment is not necessary here.

## 2.2 The Epistemic Status of Defeaters — 57

the entire epistemic project surrounding the issue. A subject that is irrational in only one instance seems to be able to redeem herself by continuing her inquiries diligently in the future, especially if those inquiries lead to a disproof of her earlier irrational attitude. This much is intuitively plausible to me, but unlike Bergmann and, to a degree, Alexander, this by no means universally evoked intuition is not the only reason I can give to accept the Exclusive Thesis.

The differences between partial, successful and perfect rebutting defeat are well supported by a host of clearly structured cases, paradigmatic instances of which have been given in the previous section. They reveal a systematic and consequently explicable framework. The picture of rebutting defeat as input that can be weighed against the original justifier with scalable effects that range from a miniscule reduction of the total supportiveness of the available input to a massive swamping of the original justifier is a highly plausible one that systematically explains a large range of cases. Now, a proponent of the Inclusive Thesis must either hold that rebutting defeaters can also be non-positive or provide an independent argument for the thesis that *only* undercutting defeaters can be non-positive. In the absence of any discernible attempt to do the latter, it must be assumed that the Inclusive Thesis is supposed to hold for both kinds of defeaters (which is also the prima facie more plausible option). The problem is then that non-positive rebutting defeaters do not fit into the framework that best explains their effect. A non-positive rebutting defeater, by hypothesis, has no weight to be compared to the original justifier, even if it can be counted as "evidence", as Bergmann proposes. It therefore cannot change the relative weight (or "degree of positivity", in my terminology) of the total available input toward the negation of the target-proposition. As a result, a case of non-positive rebutting defeat is equivalent to a case of no defeat at all because the propositional support provided by the totally available input remains unchanged. A proponent of the Inclusive Thesis may now argue that this begs the question because they want to make the claim that non-positive defeaters *do* have weight.

It is at this point that the lack of foundation of the Inclusive Thesis becomes clear: First, if non-positive pieces of input (which non-positive defeaters minimally are) have weight, it is absolutely unclear how much weight they are supposed to have and how this is supposed to be established. A common test to get a feeling for the weight of a piece of input is to weigh it against an opposing piece, but this test will surely suggest that non-positive pieces have no weight, for what other systematic result is to be expected when independently supported attitudes or self-supporting experiences are weighed against baseless claims? The burden of proof is clearly on the proponent of the Inclusive Thesis at this point.

Second, a piece of input having "weight" is merely a different expression of the concept of propositional support. A more weighty piece of input provides more significant propositional support for a suitable attitude concerning a specific proposition. Propositional support is at least part of the foundation of justification. Roughly, having enough propositional support (i.e. positive input) for belief in proposition $p$ amounts to being in a state where believing that $p$ on the basis of that support (absent defeaters) would be justified in all relevant respects.[32]

In light of the differences between partial, successful and perfect rebutting defeat, this is why it makes sense to understand rebutting defeaters as pieces of input that have weight/provide propositional support with respect to the negation of the target-proposition. Accordingly, if the proponent of the Inclusive Thesis wants to claim that non-positive potential defeaters have weight, they must claim that they can propositionally support something and are suited to partake in the justification of other attitudes. But if they accept *that* they run straight into the basic assumption behind the Arbitrariness Objection, namely, that non-positive states cannot justify. The general point here is important: There is not just a parallel between rebutting defeaters and reasons. Rebutting defeaters *are* reasons of a certain kind, or at least they are input. A rebutting defeater does not simply mysteriously confer the negative property of unjustifiedness to its target, but renders it less well supported by counterbalancing its basis of support and it can only do that because it propositionally supports and can even fully justify another attitude. For now, this has only been argued for the case of rebutting defeat. However, this is enough to make trouble for the Inclusive Thesis, because it forces its proponents to make a substantial distinction between rebutting and undercutting defeaters with respect to their epistemic status, which is something they have thus far neglected to do. Furthermore, I will argue in the next chapter that undercutting defeat comes down to higher-order rebutting defeat. If this is found convincing, that distinction cannot be made because undercutting defeat then adheres to similar rules as rebutting defeat, which would fully establish the Exclusive Thesis. At this point, however, it should be clear enough that there is little reason to accept the Inclusive Thesis without further argument and that such further argument would be difficult enough to provide.

The conclusion of this chapter is the first part of a bigger picture I intend to build. I have introduced and analyzed rebutting defeaters. Their mechanics are straightforward and allow the accommodation of a range of effects for a rebutter

---

[32] Given that the basing of the belief is a competent one. More on this later.

that is scalable between minimal variants of partial and perfect defeat. I have also argued that there are a number of reasons, including theoretical ones, for rejecting the Inclusive Thesis for rebutting defeat. Rebutting defeaters thus necessarily have positive epistemic status, which means that they are either justified or rational, or the kind of input that has positive status without requiring further support. In the next chapter, it will turn out that undercutting defeaters lack the elegant structure of rebutters, mostly because they involve relatively complex cognitive operations. However, I will attempt to capture undercutting defeat in a way that has at its base the very same mechanism revolving around the contradiction between a proposition and its negation that lies at the heart of rebutting defeat. On the one hand, this will give us a complete explanation of undercutting defeat, as opposed to several rival accounts. On the other hand, and more to the point, it will mean that many revelations about rebutting defeat will carry over to undercutting defeat, including the appliance of the Exclusive Thesis. Thus, ultimately, both kinds of defeaters necessarily have positive epistemic status. Still, this does not exhaust the bigger picture. The discussion of undercutting defeaters will show that the focus on propositional support that is perhaps most natural to the examination of rebutting defeat is unwarranted. Undercutting defeaters are best explained by taking into account the basing relation and the structure of the re-evaluation of doxastic attitudes. Reconsidering rebutting defeat along the same lines will turn out to be surprisingly fruitful.

# 3 Undercutting Defeat

In this chapter, I will turn to undercutting defeaters. A discussion of Pollock's original account of undercutting defeat will be traced and the thesis that higher-order beliefs must play a significant role in its analysis will be examined. I agree that undercutting defeaters must somehow appeal to higher-order attitudes but I will also raise a problem for this "naïve" higher-order account. In fact, it incurs a high theoretical cost by leading to higher-order conditions for justification. I will then consider a way to avoid this cost by avoiding higher-order components in an account of undercutting defeat altogether: the Suspension Account. This hypothetical view states that undercutting defeaters defeat by supporting suspension of judgment, which is non-cotenable with the target-attitude, that is, it cannot be rationally held at the same time (cf. MacFarlane 2014). I will argue against the Suspension Account, showing that this relatively simple view is unable to accommodate a number of plausible structural features of undercutting defeat and to adequately distinguish it from rebutting defeat. A more developed alternative will then be examined in the form of the more sophisticated commitment-based version of the higher-order account. The problems I raise for this view organically lead to the groundwork for the Rebasing Account of Undercutting defeat (my own view), which I will develop in the final step. The general idea is that, since processing a defeater constitutes an act of *reasoning*, the theoretical cost of a higher-order account can be sidestepped by having the defeater *prompt the formation of the relevant higher-order attitude and make it relevant to justification* during the processing of an undercutting defeater. The idea is that undercutting defeaters produce incompatibilities, which prompt re-evaluation processes which in turn involve the subject to *rebasing* the target-attitude to such a re-evaluation. The attitude then depends on it, instead of its original justifier for its epistemic status. Good reasoning in cases of defeat will lead to a justified dropping of the target-attitude, while bad reasoning may leave it in place, but render it unjustified. Thus, higher-order conditions on justification in general are avoided by restricting them to cases of undercutting defeat. Throughout the chapter, I will keep track of all the moves by continuously making modifications to Defeat-1, Rebut-1 and Undercut-1, thereby tracing the argument-based development that leads to the Rebasing Account.

At the heart of an understanding of undercutting defeat lies the question what exactly undercutting defeaters appeal to and how they interact with the surrounding doxastic structure of their target-beliefs. This is reflected in the relatively recent views of Sturgeon (2014) and Melis (2014, 2016), who argue that undercutting defeat can only be fully explained by bringing higher-order beliefs or commitments into the picture. Higher-order beliefs are beliefs about other (first-order) beliefs, the connections between them or their epistemic status. For example, my belief that my shoes are brown is a *first-order belief*, while my belief that I hold the belief that my shoes are brown on the basis of my visual impression that they are is a *higher-order belief*. The idea is that undercutting defeaters defeat much like rebutting defeaters, except that instead of providing support for a first-order attitude, like belief in the negation of the target-proposition, they support a higher-order attitude about the connection between the target-belief and its total doxastic base. I agree with Sturgeon and Melis that such higher-order beliefs must play a role in any satisfactory account of undercutting defeat, but I will also show that integrating them is difficult and that their proposals don't quite manage to do this in a satisfactory way. Ultimately, an account of undercutting defeat should be such that it a) fully explains the phenomenon and b) is neutral with respect to different theories of justification. I will argue that neither Sturgeon's nor Melis' view satisfies both of them. In response, I will then lay out my own proposal for an account of undercutting defeat that does.

I will, again, start by looking at Pollock's original view. In particular, Scott Sturgeon's explication and criticism of Pollock's account with respect to how and why an undercutter removes justification will be discussed in some detail, which will show that a deeper explanation of undercutting defeat is required. Furthermore, it will become apparent why appealing to higher-order attitudes is an attractive way to provide such an explanation. Next, I will back up Sturgeon's thesis by investigating and criticizing a hypothetical alternative to such a "Higher-Order Account" of undercutting defeat, which attempts to explain undercutting defeat without reference to higher-order attitudes: the "Suspension Account". The Suspension Account can be shown to be incapable of accommodating important structural features of undercutting defeat, which will be established as constraints on any account of undercutting defeat. In a third step, I will then examine some arguments raised against Sturgeon's view and add a few worries of my own that show that the view is at least incomplete, thereby demonstrating it to fail to respect constraint a). Melis' version of the Higher-Order Account does better in this respect, but it will be shown both that it has serious problems of its own, which have to do with the status and function of epistemic commitments. These get it into trouble with certain views on justification and thus with constraint b). Based on the lessons that can be drawn from this discussion, I will finally introduce my own account of undercutting defeat – the "Rebasing Account". It can be shown to avoid the problems of its rivals and to bring considerable explanatory power to the table.

## 3.1 The Naïve Higher-Order Account

### 3.1.1 Pollock's View

In order to understand what motivates the idea that undercutting defeaters appeal to higher-order attitudes, one must first understand why an account that does without such attitudes seems unsatisfactory. One such account is Pollock's original view (Pollock 1974, 1987; Pollock and Cruz 1999). Let me start with a reminder of SCHOOL as a case of undercutting defeat:

> SCHOOL: James believes that his daughter Lara is skipping school today. He thinks this because she was especially unwilling to go there this morning and he just saw someone that looked like her enter the coffee shop. Upon approaching the coffee shop, he meets Thomas. Thomas tells him that he is also looking for his daughter, Maude, who is well known for skipping school frequently and who admires Lara and often dresses just like her. James forms the belief that someone who is dressed like his daughter is skipping school in the area today.

I noted that the information that someone who looks just like Lara is skipping school in the vicinity defeats James' belief that Lara is skipping school *in virtue of being directed against the relation between James' total doxastic base for the target-attitude and the attitude itself.* This is also what Pollock says in his original account, where he talks about an undercutting defeater "attacking" the relation between the target-attitude and the reason it is based on (Pollock 1974, p. 42). The question is how to interpret the metaphors "being directed against" and "attacking" here. Pollock attempts to clarify this with the claim that a defeater is a reason, such that it, together with the original reason for the target-attitude is not a reason to hold the target-attitude:

> DEFINITION: If $M$ is a reason for $S$ to believe $Q$, a state $M^*$ is a *defeater* for this reason if and only if the combined state consisting of being in both the state $M$ and the state $M^*$ at the same time is not a reason for $S$ to believe $Q$. (Pollock and Cruz 1999, p. 195)

A reason for a belief that $p$, according to Pollock, is a state $m$, such that it is logically possible for the (fitting) belief that $p$ to be justified on the basis of $m$ (Pollock 1987, p. 484; Pollock and Cruz 1999, p. 195). I take it that Pollock would agree to extend this to the thesis that a state $m$ of a subject $S$ is a reason for the belief that $p$, $B(p)$, iff, if $S$ was in $m$ and had no other reasons for or against anything,

$B(p)$ would be justified for $S$, if she formed it based on $m$.[1] In my terminology, a reason for the belief $B(p)$ is a set of input for subject $S$, such that that set would be a justifier for $B(p)$, if it were the total doxastic base for $B(p)$. A defeater, according to Pollock, is a reason such that the conjunction of it and the original reason for the target-attitude is *not* a reason for that attitude: $d$ is a defeater for the belief $B(p)$, iff $d$ is a reason, such that $B(p)$ is exclusively based on the reason or sets of reasons $m$ and the conjunction of $d$ and $m$ is not a reason for $B(p)$. According to Sturgeon, the idea is that "defeaters do their work because they are reasons to believe something which cannot be rationally believed while also believing the claim for which the defeated reason is a reason" (Sturgeon 2014, p. 112).

Pollock's account so far does not distinguish between different types of defeaters. This is done by two different explanations as to why the original reason, together with the defeater, is conjunctively not a reason for the target-attitude, which further enriches the picture. In the case of rebutting defeat, the explanation is that the defeater on its own is a reason for belief in the negation of the target-proposition and thus generates an inconsistency and therefore a paradigmatically irrational state (Pollock 1974, p. 42, 1987; Pollock and Cruz 1999, p. 196; Sturgeon 2014, pp. 110–112). Leaving aside issues of partial rebutters that do not amount to full reasons in Pollock's sense, my account (like pretty much all other accounts) shares this feature, as explained in the previous section. Thus, $d$ is a rebutting defeater for the belief that $p$, $B(p,)$ iff $d$ is a reason, such that $B(p)$ is based on the reason $m$ and the conjunction of $d$ and $m$ is not a reason for $B(p)$, because $m$ and $d$ support belief in $p$ and not-$p$, respectively.

Pollock's explanation of undercutting defeat is more troublesome. According to Pollock, an undercutting defeater is not a reason for the negation of the target-proposition, but rather a reason to think that it *is not true that if the target-proposition were not true, one would not have reason to believe that it is* (Pollock 1987, p. 486; Pollock and Cruz 1999, p. 196; Sturgeon 2014, pp. 107–109). Consider an example: I look at an assembly line producing widgets that look red to me and form the belief that the widgets are red on the basis of that impression. Now, a trustworthy person tells me that the widgets are illuminated by a red light, which defeats my belief that they are red.[2] Why? The information that the widgets are illuminated by a red light indicates that *it is not true that the widgets would not have appeared red to me if they were not red*. If they were white, for example,

---

[1] This assumption is based on remarks in Pollock 1974, p. 33, 34 and Pollock and Cruz 1999, pp. 36–38.
[2] The example is based on one found in Pollock (1974).

they would still *look* red in the red light.[3] I will follow Sturgeon and formalize the proposition that *it is not true that if the target-proposition were not true, one would not have reason to believe that it is* as "¬ (m ⊖ p)", where m is the reason and p is the target-proposition (Sturgeon 2014, p. 110). The symbol "⊖" functions as a placeholder for the (otherwise formally complicated) idea that there is an existential relationship between the truth of target-attitudes and reasons. Thus, "x ⊖ y" can be expressed as "if y were not true, there would be no x", where x is the reason and y the attitude it supports. On Pollock's view, undercutting defeaters defeat by (propositionally) supporting ¬ (m ⊖ p).

Sturgeon argues that this explanation does not fit as smoothly into Pollock's framework as the one for rebutting defeat and, in fact, runs into counterexample. In order to explain rebutting defeat, it is stated that it is logically impossible to rationally, and therefore justifiedly, believe that p on the basis of m and d because m and d support both p and *not-p*, and it is impossible to rationally and justifiedly believe the contradiction (cf. Sturgeon 2014).[4] Why does Sturgeon think that Pollock cannot just rely on the same principles for his explanation of undercutting defeat? Because in case of undercutting defeat, m and d support p and ¬ (m ⊖ p), respectively, and it *is* logically possible to justifiedly believe that p and that ¬ (m ⊖ p). To illustrate: In certain variants of the widgets-case, I can justifiedly believe both that the widgets are red and that it is not true that they wouldn't look red, unless they were red (cf. Sturgeon 2014, pp. 112–113). For example, I might believe that vision is not a good indicator of the widget's redness in this situation on the basis of the trustworthy person's testimony, and at the same time I might nevertheless believe with justification that the widgets are red on the basis of having read the specifications for the widgets, according to which they must be red. Given this special feature of undercutting defeat, there must be more to the explanation of undercutting defeat.

Sturgeon offers a more satisfying answer on behalf of Pollock: While it might be logically possible to believe that p and that ¬ (m ⊖ p), it is not logically possible to believe that p and that ¬ (m ⊖ p) *on the basis of m and d*, conjunctively

---

[3] Another way to look at this is that the visual impression of red widgets can only justify the belief that the widgets are red provided that, under the present circumstances, if something looks red, it probably is red. The trustworthy person's testimony challenges just that provision, which is an idea that is already sympathetic to the view that higher-order attitudes play a role here.

[4] I take the assumptions in the background to be that *rationality is necessary for justification* and that *believing contradictions is paradigmatically irrational*. From now on, I will adopt the second assumption, presuming that it needs no further explanation. The first assumption was already discussed to some extent and will be left open.

(Sturgeon 2014, p. 113). The reason why this variant of the widgets-case is not a case of undercutting defeat is that the belief that the widgets are red is based on reading the specifications ($m^*$) and not on them appearing red ($m$). The information that there is a red light ($d$) is a defeater for the belief that the widgets are red ($B(p)$), only insofar as that belief depends on a red-impression ($m$). This is why Pollock speaks of defeaters as defeaters for reasons, not for target-attitudes: Based on $d$ and $m$, it is impossible to justifiedly believe that $p$, whereas based on $d$ and $m^*$, it is possible. Nevertheless, it is also perfectly possible to say that $d$ is an undercutting defeater for $B(p)$, just in case the reason it appeals to also acts as (part of) $B(p)$'s total doxastic base, as I would do.

What is important at this stage is that this sensitivity to what acts as the doxastic base of the target-attitude is peculiar to undercutting defeat, but not to rebutting defeat. While the widgets-case demonstrates that undercutting defeaters are sensitive in this way, it is clear that rebutting defeaters are not. Since rebutting defeaters support belief in something contradicting the target-proposition on their own, it does not matter what the target-attitude containing that proposition is based on. Sturgeon thus argues that this "source sensitivity" (Casullo 2003, p. 45) is captured by Pollock's account, once we take into account the basing-relation, which renders it cogent (Sturgeon 2014, p. 114). He seems to think that the account reaches explanatory "bedrock" (Sturgeon 2014, p. 111) under these conditions. While I agree that the observation of the importance of the basing-relation goes some way to fully explain why undercutting defeaters diminish their targets' degree of justification, I will argue later in this chapter that it nevertheless leaves explanatorily relevant structure within the details of undercutting defeat in the dark. It does not, after all, reach *explanatory bedrock*. For now, however, let us accept Sturgeon's conclusions for the sake of argument and examine the problems he nevertheless sees with Pollock's conception.

### 3.1.2 The Milk-Taster Case and the Naïve Higher-Order Account

Sturgeon claims that "undercutting defeaters do their work in tandem with other mental states, by joining forces with higher-order commitment about the basing of lower-order belief" (Sturgeon 2014, p. 117). To establish this, he presents a counterexample to Pollock's account:

> MILK: Subject $S$ tastes a bit of milk to see if it's gone off. Being a normal milk taster, $S$ is unaware that her view of the milk is based on smell as much as taste. Indeed, she believes her view of the milk is not based on smell, not even in part. When she tastes the milk, however, $S$ has a certain complex gustatory and olfactory experience; and she comes to believe

on its basis that the milk is o.k. But *S* is unaware that she is basing her view of the milk on smell. We may even suppose that *S* would deny this is true were she to consider the matter. Suppose the milk taster is then told, by someone she trusts, that her nose is bunged up, that she is subject to random olfactory hallucination. This leads her, after a bit of reflection, to deny that she wouldn't have had her overall gustatory and olfactory experience of the milk unless the milk were o.k. After all, she realizes that her overall gustatory and olfactory experience of the milk includes the olfactory part of that experience; and she believes herself to be subject to random olfactory hallucination. Nevertheless, her new information does not, and should not, lead her to change her view of the milk. She continues rationally to believe that the milk is o.k. on the basis of her complex gustatory and olfactory experience. (Sturgeon 2014, pp. 114–115)

*S* believes that the milk is drinkable (*p*) on the basis of a complex experience (*m*) and then acquires a Pollockian reason to believe that it is not the case that she wouldn't have had that experience, if the milk wasn't drinkable (*d*). The case thus satisfies Pollock's conditions for undercutting defeat, especially given that the defeater appeals to *m*, that is, to the doxastic base of the target-attitude, thereby satisfying the criterion of source-sensitivity. Nevertheless, it seems that *S* is intuitively perfectly rational in continuing to believe that the milk is drinkable.

Sturgeon explains this by appealing to the fact that the milk taster lacks the higher-order belief required for undercutting. So, it seems that, only if the milk taster had also believed that her belief about the milk is partly based on smell, it would have been undercut by the information that her nose is bunged up.[5] Sturgeon concludes that undercutting defeaters defeat by appealing to higher-order "commitments" and that such commitments are therefore a necessary condition on undercutting defeat. This thesis is included in the following formulation of his position: "Belief in U undercuts belief in Φ exactly when you are committed to their being a strong link between your belief in Φ and source of information S" (Sturgeon 2014, p. 117).

This brings up a problem: Sturgeon does not explain what a commitment is, exactly. He seems reluctant to phrase his view in terms of higher-order beliefs and presumably wants something weaker on the higher-level to play their role. This is a bit surprising, since the milk taster in MILK might be said to be committed to the higher-order proposition that her complex sensory experience supports the belief that the milk is OK, in virtue of *de facto* basing her belief on smell. The reason why she does not suffer undercutting defeat appears to be the absence of a *belief*. So, why is MILK not also a counterexample to the view that

---

5 This verdict is not based on a single case, but gets further support from another variant of the case where the subject has false, but *justified* higher-order beliefs that intuitively shield her from undercutting defeaters (Sturgeon 2014, p. 115).

undercutting defeaters appeal to commitments, whatever they may be? To avoid confusion here, let me simplify the issue by starting directly from the case verdict. MILK appears to teach us that undercutting defeaters appeal to higher-order *beliefs*. Let's call this account the "naïve" Higher-Order Account.[6]

In light of the discussion so far, an undercutter's "appealing to" higher-order beliefs can be spelled out further: Since the milk taster believes her milk-belief to depend solely on taste and not on the complex gustatory and olfactory experience, the information that her nose is bunged up does not provide her with a *higher-order rebutting defeater*.[7] Had she instead believed that her belief is based on the complex experience, such that the experience sufficiently supports the belief, the new information would intuitively have defeated her belief that the milk is OK.[8] Plausibly, this is because the information that her nose is bunged up suggests (in the sense of propositionally supporting) that it is false that the complex experience sufficiently supports the belief that the milk is OK and this contradicts her higher-order belief that it does. Thus, in such a case, the undercutting defeater generates the same kind of incompatibility *between the defeater and the higher-order belief that the target-attitude's total doxastic base is sufficiently supportive (positive) of the target-attitude* that a rebutting defeater generates *between the defeater and the target-attitude*. Thus, if what makes or breaks MILK as a case of undercutting defeat is the presence or absence of the relevant higher-order belief, it seems that the deciding factor is whether the potential undercutting defeater constitutes a higher-order rebutter in this sense. Ac-

---

[6] Importantly, I do not claim that Sturgeon holds the naïve Higher-Order Account, although this is how Casullo interprets him (Casullo 2016, p. 5). Since Sturgeon phrases his view in terms of commitments, I am dubious of this interpretation, but I also don't want to go too deep into Sturgeon exegesis. So, I will simply remain neutral and discuss the naïve Higher-Order Account on its own merits.

[7] This idea is adapted from Giacomo Melis, who talks about the undercutter "challenging" a higher-order commitment (Melis 2016, p. 273, 274). His characterization of the content of such a commitment (Melis 2016, p. 276), I take it that he has something like rebuttal in mind, even though he, like Sturgeon, doesn't tell us much about the exact way a defeater is supposed to interact with a commitment. However, he also talks about an undercutter's appeal to commitments that are realized as full-fledged higher-order attitudes (Melis 2016, p. 273), where it is quite plausible that he means higher-order rebuttal. Here, it also becomes clear why talk of "commitments" isn't helpful at this point in my discussion. It seems that an explanation of undercutting defeat via higher-order rebuttal is what a Higher-Order Account is going for, but it is far less clear how one can even have a rebutting defeater for a commitment than it is how one can have such a defeater for a belief. I will return to this question when I discuss Melis' view in more detail.

[8] This also fits with Sturgeon's view, since believing something presumably commits one to its truth, whatever a commitment turns out to be.

cordingly, in the Higher-Order Account of undercutting defeat, undercutters are simply higher-order rebutters for higher-order beliefs about the doxastic support that their target-attitudes enjoy (cf. Melis 2014, 2016). As Casullo (2016, pp. 5–6) shows, this picture is only coherent if it is furthermore supposed that the relevant higher-order belief is at least *justified*. Otherwise, merely forming certain higher-order beliefs about one's doxastic bases will generate outlandish defeaters or implausibly protect one from others.[9] This should be clear enough, as one could otherwise dogmatically believe that one's beliefs are based on, say, infallible divine revelation, and thus implausibly never receive an undercutting defeater.

The resulting account can be stated as follows:

HOUD:

$d$ is an undercutting defeater, iff

1. $d$ is a defeater:

    1.1. $d$ is a belief that $q$ or a piece of positive input for belief that $q$ of a subject $S$ that is acquired by $S$ at time $t$

    1.2. there is a doxastic attitude about $p$, $A(p)$, that is held by $S$ at $t$ and at $t$-$1$, such that

    1.2.1. $A(p)$ is supported to degree $x$ at $t$-$1$ and to degree $y$ at $t$, such that

    1.2.1.1. $x > y$ and

    1.2.1.2. the change from $x$ to $y$ is a result of $S$'s acquiring $d$ at $t$.

2. $S$ holds the justified higher-order belief $B(j,s,p)$ that $A(p)$ is doxastically based on the set of input $j$, such that $j$ sufficiently supports $A(p)$.

3. $q$ is the negation of the proposition $B(j,s,p)$ is about.

---

[9] To see this, consider Casullo's Visualist-case, where the subject simply believes that all her beliefs are based on sight, comes to believe that there is a dog by hearing it bark and is then told that sight is unreliable. If higher-order beliefs wouldn't need to be at least justified, she would thus have obtained an undercutting defeater, but this is implausible. Higher-Order dogmatism would similarly protect the Visualist from undercutters that appeal to sources that the subject is justified to believe that she is using but vehemently disbelieves to be using (Casullo 2016, pp. 5–6).

This is in line with the expectation that both kinds of defeaters fundamentally rely on the same mechanism.[10] Accordingly, it can also be expected that undercutting defeaters need to have positive epistemic status for mostly the same reasons that rebutting defeaters do. They are supposed to lower the degree of support that a higher-order proposition enjoys that is relevant to the status of the target-belief. As laid out in the previous chapter, this only makes sense if they are supported themselves. Thus, it appears that the Exclusive Thesis holds for both types of defeater, which lends more theoretical unity to defeat than previously expected. This hypothesis will receive further support when the Rebasing Account of undercutting defeat is developed. Furthermore, HOUD has the additional benefit of depicting undercutters as supporting an attitude (belief in $q$), the content of which is contradictory to the content of a belief of the subject ($B(j,s,p)$), so that the subject holding on to her original beliefs, in addition to the defeater, would result in a paradigmatically irrational state, just like in the case of rebutting defeaters. This feature ties into an important point of motivation for the Higher-Order Account in general that goes beyond the accommodation of cases like MILK.

This point also puts us in a position to explain why, in spite of the clarifications suggested by Sturgeon, Pollock's original view is not explanatorily adequate, on top of failing to account for cases like MILK. Pollock's explanation as to why an undercutting defeater renders a target-attitude in the form of a belief that $p$, $B(p)$, unjustified is that 1) undercutting defeaters suggest that it is not true that if the target-proposition were not true, one would not have reason to believe that it is ($\neg\,(m \ominus p)$) and 2) that it is impossible to rationally hold both $B(p)$ and believe that $\neg\,(m \ominus p)$, given that the belief that $p$ is based on $m$.[11]

While I agree that it is *intuitively* clearly irrational to both believe that $p$ on the basis of $m$ and that $\neg\,(m \ominus p)$, it does not seem to be *paradigmatically* irrational. Recall that what forms the explanatory foundation of standard accounts

---

10 Importantly, the realization that undercutting defeaters are really higher-order rebutters dismantles the deep distinction I advocated in the first chapter to some extent. The fundamental mechanics of the two defeater-types are ultimately the same. However, the distinction still remains deeper than the one between rebutting and reason-defeating defeaters because, while those types do their work entirely on the same level as the target-belief, undercutting defeaters manage to affect the target-belief on the first level by doing the same work on a higher level. Explaining the latter phenomenon requires more complex epistemic scaffolding than explaining the first one does, as will become clear. Accordingly, it still makes sense to distinguish rebutting from undercutting defeaters. However, we should also expect the two to be similar in every respect that does not touch upon this scaffolding.
11 I leave aside for now whether requiring rationality for justification is still neutral with respect to theories of justification.

of rebutting defeat, including Pollock's own view, is the *contradiction* between the proposition believed and the one propositionally supported by the defeater. There is no such contradiction in the case of undercutting defeat on Pollock's account. For contradictory attitudes, there is nothing more to be said as to why this is irrational than that $p$ and $\neg\, p$ are contradictory. In contrast, one must say a lot more about why believing that $p$ on the basis of $m$ and believing that $\neg\,(m \ominus p)$ is irrational and there is more than one potential explanation. For example, one might say that the fact that $\neg\,(m \ominus p)$ obtains amounts to sensitivity of the reason $m$ to the truth of $p$ and this sensitivity is required for epistemic justification on the basis of $m$. Together with the hypothesis that it is impossible to rationally believe something while simultaneously having reason to believe that one is not rational in doing so, this would give us a deeper explanation. Alternatively, one could say that the truth of $\neg\,(m \ominus p)$ establishes that believing on the basis of m does not reliably lead to the truth about $p$ and that this, together with the hypothesis that epistemic rationality is truth-oriented, would explain why it is irrational to believe that $p$ on the basis of $m$ in the face of $\neg\,(m \ominus p)$. The point is that, compared to these options, Pollock's account of undercutting defeat remains at the explanatory surface and surely does not reach bedrock. At the very least, it does not reach the same depth of explanation as standard accounts of rebutting defeat.

The naïve Higher-Order Account, on the other hand, has all the resources needed to reach bedrock, since its explanation of the phenomenon turns on rebuttal on a higher level. It can explain undercutting defeat *via* rebutting defeat. To illustrate, here is an explanation of undercutting defeat in the SCHOOL-case: Thomas' testimony about Maude skipping school in the area propositionally supports belief in the proposition that [having seen someone looking like Lara enter the coffee shop does not really support the belief that Lara is skipping school today]. James generally believes that seeing someone looking like Lara somewhere supports the belief that she is there and, consequently, that seeing someone looking like her enter the coffee shop is a good basis for his belief that she is skipping school. The proposition suggested by the defeater in the form of Thomas' testimony, [having seen someone looking like Lara enter the coffee shop does not really support the belief that Lara is skipping school today], logically contradicts the higher-order proposition believed by James, namely that [having seen someone looking like Lara enter the coffee shop does support the belief that Lara is skipping school today].[12] What is more, Thomas' testimony provides

---

**12** It is possible (and a lot more plausible) to spell this out in terms of higher-order commitments, as Sturgeon presumably would prefer. I will turn to a commitment-based Higher-Order

propositional support that outweighs the doxastic support that James may have for his higher-order belief. The result is that James is now propositionally justified to believe that his belief that Lara is skipping school today is not supported by anything and this makes it impossible to continue to rationally hold it. The intuition that there would be something irrational about James continuing to believe that Lara is skipping school stems from the fact that he would thereby accept a contradiction and that is paradigmatically irrational. The Higher-Order Account, unlike Pollock's view, can thus explain *why* it is irrational to believe on the basis of a set of input, while one also has information that questions its supportive qualities. I therefore disagree with Sturgeon that taking the basing relation into account gives Pollock's view the depth it needs to be fully satisfactory (see Sturgeon 2014, p. 113, 114). If this is correct, it provides further motivation to adopt the Higher-Order Account (or other extended accounts) that is independent of counterexamples.

### 3.1.3 Worries about the Naïve Higher-Order Account of Undercutting Defeat

The naïve Higher-Order Account clearly comes with downsides, and they have been recognized. I will discuss two objections here, one of which is unsuccessful, while the other can be regarded as the fundamental problem faced by the Higher-Order Account of undercutting defeat. Let me start with the argument that I don't take to be successful.

Besides the thesis that undercutters defeat by appealing to higher-order beliefs, the proponent of the naïve Higher-Order Account claims that it is precisely this feature that distinguishes undercutting defeaters from rebutting defeaters. Sturgeon makes this claim when he contends that, while undercutting defeaters must work in tandem with higher-order beliefs, rebutting defeaters do their work in isolation (Sturgeon 2014, p. 117). Against this, Albert Casullo presents the following consideration: For any rebutter, there is a certain degree $q$ to which it needs to be supported in order to be a successful rebutter, where $q$ depends on the target-attitude's degree of justification. Why wouldn't the subject in cases of rebutting defeat also need to believe both that the defeater is supported to degree $q$ and that $q$ is enough to neutralize a sufficient portion of the target-attitude's support, if that kind of higher-order awareness is required in cases of undercutting defeat (Casullo 2016, pp. 7–10)? Why is access to higher-order in-

---

Account later; now I'll only demonstrate the explanatory advantage of a Higher-Order Account over Pollock's original view.

formation required in one case, but not the other? In the absence of a principled distinction, the two should be treated alike. This results in two problems: First, it seems implausible to posit higher-order requirements for rebutting defeat, and so there may be no reason to go with the highly demanding naïve Higher-Order Account for undercutting defeat. Second, whatever the overall status of higher-order requirements, such requirements cannot serve to *distinguish* the two types of defeaters from one another.

The problem with this argument is that it ignores the possibility of partial rebuttal and a difference in function of higher-order information. An explanation of defeat is an explanation that points out what is epistemically problematic about holding the target-attitude (with the same certainty as before) in the face of a defeater. In case of rebutting defeat, *that* explanation requires no reference to higher-order beliefs: A rebutting defeater generates an incompatibility by supporting an attitude that conflicts with the target-attitude. Paradigmatically, the attitude supported by the defeater is belief in a proposition that is inconsistent with the target-proposition. Holding both the target-attitude and the defeater is therefore paradigmatically irrational. This is also true in cases of merely partial rebuttal, where it becomes problematic to hold on to the target-attitude with the same conviction as before, due to its loss of support. Assuming that every rebutter is at least a partial rebutter, it can therefore be explained why holding on to a defeated belief in the same manner as before is epistemically problematic without mentioning higher-order beliefs.[13] Things are different for undercutting defeat. The MILK-case, as well as the general need to find an explanation of undercutting defeat at the same depth as the one for rebutting defeat and the discussion of the Suspension Account, show that what has been said about an undercutting defeater's impact on the level of first-order beliefs is not enough to fully explain why it is epistemically problematic to hold on to the target-attitude in the face of the defeater. In the next section, I will discuss an attempt to handle undercutting defeaters only on the first level. Foreshadowing a bit, it will be discovered that bringing higher-order beliefs into the picture potentially closes that gap and takes care of counterexamples. So, there is good reason to think that higher-order belief plays a role in an account of undercutting defeat, but not of rebutting defeat.

While Casullo's argument against the thesis that appeals to higher-order beliefs may serve to distinguish the two types of defeaters is thus not convincing,

---

[13] Higher-order beliefs about the relative weight of the defeater may become relevant in a second step, when we consider what a rational reaction to rebutting defeat may be. Plausibly, one weighs support and treats the target-belief in accordance with the result, which may require the formation of attitudes about the degrees of support that the defeater and the target-belief enjoy.

his second point gets to the heart of Higher-Order Accounts of undercutting defeat. He presents an example that is supposed to establish that higher-order beliefs are *never* necessary for undercutting defeat and that thus potentially rules out any version of the view that included higher-order beliefs. He argues that the problem with prerequisite higher-order beliefs is that they make it too easy to shield oneself against undercutting defeaters and, consequently, make it too hard for normal epistemic subjects to obtain such defeaters. The subject can simply refrain from having any beliefs about the doxastic bases of her beliefs:

> Consider the case of *The Unreflective Cognizer:* Suppose that *S* is a normal cognizer who has a wide range of prima facie justified beliefs based on diverse sources such as visual perception, auditory perception and memory. *S*, however, is unreflective about the sources of his beliefs and, as a consequence, forms no beliefs about the source of his beliefs. (Casullo 2016, p. 7)

The Unreflective Cognizer seems to be completely immune to undercutting defeaters on the modified naïve Higher-Order Account, due to his lack of higher-order beliefs, justified or otherwise. This is highly implausible, not only because we would expect the Unreflective Cognizer himself to be a potential object of undercutting defeat, but because we expect *ourselves* to be vulnerable to undercutting defeaters. Most of us are in the same situation as the Unreflective Cognizer with respect to many of our everyday beliefs, however, in that we very often have no higher-order beliefs concerning their basis, let alone justified higher-order beliefs. Since undercutting defeat is supposed to be a common phenomenon, such beliefs cannot be required to suffer it. They are only considered and formed occasionally by normal epistemic subjects. This issue lies at the heart of the problems with the Higher-Order Account and deserves further investigation.

Casullo's point can be extended: According to the naïve Higher-Order Account, a subject is required to hold a (justified) higher-order belief about the surrounding doxastic structure of her lower-order belief, in order for that lower-order belief to be undercut. Specifically, an undercutting defeater is supposed to render the lower-order belief *unjustified* by appealing to a justified *higher-order belief* about it. I stress this to illustrate that there is reason to be worried that the naïve Higher-Order Account commits its defender to higher-order conditions on epistemic justification *in general*. The worry stems from the fact that a defeater cannot remove justification by attacking a higher-order belief about the corresponding first-order belief's doxastic bases, if that higher-order belief is not relevant to justification. But if it *is* relevant to justification, this would have to be because justification itself requires justified higher-order beliefs about the justified belief's bases and that is a highly demanding condition (see e.g. Alston 1986; Pollock and Cruz 1999, pp. 63–65; Pollock 2001b, p. 43;

Bergmann 2005, pp. 430–431). The point underlying Casullo's Unreflective-Cognizer case may thus go beyond merely being a counterexample.

In order to hold a plausible view, the defender of the naïve Higher-Order Account ought to subscribe to the following claims:
1) Defeaters essentially remove their target-attitude's justification.
2) Undercutting defeaters remove justification by appealing to justified higher-order beliefs about the target-attitude's doxastic bases.
3) Defeasible doxastic attitudes can be justified on the basis of given pieces of input, even though the subject has no higher-order belief about that input or the basing-relation.

The first claim is a corollary of assuming a causal account of defeat, as I have been doing thus far: A defeater is a defeater in virtue of being such that its acquisition causes the target-attitude to lose justification.[14]

The second claim is the thesis of the naïve Higher-Order Account of undercutting defeat, and the third claim is something most current epistemologists adhere to in order to avoid overly demanding conditions on justification. For example, it is inherent in Sturgeon's description of the milk taster, who is justified in believing that the milk is OK in part on the basis of smell, even though she does not believe that her belief is so based (cf. Sturgeon 2014, pp. 114–115).

The big problem here is that there seems to be tension between those three claims: 3) states that what is relevant to undercutting defeat, according to 2), namely justified higher-order beliefs, is generally irrelevant to justification. This, in turn, stands in tension with 1), namely the idea that defeaters characteristically remove justification.

This tension can be diagnosed in MILK, as well. According to the case description, the milk taster can be justified on the basis of smell, even though she has no belief about the bases of her belief. It seems that this implies that higher-order beliefs are not relevant to epistemic justification. How, then, can it be consistently claimed that the reason why the potential undercutting defeater, the information that the milk taster's nose is bunged up, is not a defeater and therefore does not remove justification *because* no higher-order belief is present? This tension appears to put a proponent of the naïve Higher-Order Account in an uncomfortable position, since she can seemingly only hold on to her account if she gives up 3), that is, if she accepts the thesis that justified higher-order beliefs are required for epistemic justification. That, however, is not a good option.

---

[14] It can be suspected that the claim is a corollary of *any* account of defeat. I will return to this point in chapter 4.

Higher-order requirements for justification would result in most of us not having many justified beliefs, because normal subject do not hold higher-order beliefs in most cases (as argued by e. g. Casullo 2016; compare also Pollock and Cruz 1999, pp. 60–65). They also may exacerbate the internalist regress problem, if it turns out, depending on the success of attempts of dealing with the regress, that the justification of the higher-order belief requires a further justified higher-order belief on every higher level of abstraction, of which there are potentially infinitely many (cf. e.g. Alston 1985, 1986; Klein 2005). It thus appears that access to the explanatory power of the naïve Higher-Order Account comes with very high theoretical costs, since it allows for the accommodation of undercutting defeat only for implausibly demanding theories of justification.

However, it seems that the naïve Higher-Order Account in the form of HOUD need not fall prey to the implausibility of higher-order conditions on justification in general. Note that, while it does state that a justified higher-order belief needs to be present and relevant to the justification of the related lower-order belief, in order for the lower-order belief to be *undercut*, it does not follow that the higher-order belief needs to be present and relevant in this way, in order for the lower-order belief to be generally justified. There is a way in which justified higher-order beliefs can be added to the picture without incurring such commitments. If we just want to capture the thesis that a good number of our ordinary beliefs are justified, the naïve Higher-Order Account need not accept that suitable higher-order beliefs are *always* relevant to lower-order justification, in order to make the idea that undercutting defeaters appeal to higher-order beliefs work, but only that they are *in case there is an undercutting defeater present*. So, it may be that, normally, no higher-order beliefs are necessary for lower-order justification and thus, normal subjects can be justified without holding such beliefs. But *if* a suitable higher-order belief is present, it is relevant to lower-order justification, and if a potential undercutting defeater is obtained, whether it actually defeats may then depend on whether such a higher-order belief is, in fact, present.

Admittedly, this solution is not much more satisfactory than the original view, since one may reasonably object that, while we don't want all of our beliefs to depend on justified higher-order beliefs for their justification, we do want most of them to be *undercuttable*, that is, we want most of them to be potential subjects to undercutting defeat. After all, in cases like SCHOOL, one need not specifically mention any higher-order beliefs on the part of the subject in order to make it intuitively plausible that the new information defeats. The only way to ensure that suitable higher-order beliefs are present exactly when needed is to suppose that undercutting defeaters somehow *bring with them* higher-order beliefs that then automatically *become* relevant to lower-order justification. This would ensure that most beliefs are undercuttable, that they don't generally require higher-order beliefs for their justification, and that undercutting defeaters nevertheless appeal to higher-order beliefs. However, at this point this sounds like an implausible ad hoc solution and is not in line with the lessons we drew from the MILK case, where it is exactly the contingent absence of a higher-order belief that is decisive for the question whether the information that the milk taster's nose is bunged up is an undercutting defeater.

So, is a Higher-Order Account generally no longer feasible? As it stands, it doesn't look like there are any non-ad hoc ways that secure both justification and undercuttability for many of a normal subject's beliefs and that avoid higher-order requirements for justification. At the very least, the view's (presumed) proponent, Scott Sturgeon, does not give us any (based on Sturgeon 2014). But discarding the view just yet seems premature. In the next section, I will show that it makes sense of a number of structural characteristics of this kind of defeat and is superior to possible contenders that may be able to do without higher-order requirements. In order to show this, I will introduce a hypothetical, pure first-order contender, which I call the "Suspension Account". designed to be as undemanding as possible. The discussion of this view which, to my knowledge, is held by no one, is supposed to show that we cannot do without appeal to higher-order attitudes or commitments, if we want a comprehensive account of undercutting defeat. This can be illustrated both in the ways in which the Suspension Account fails and in the ways in which the naïve Higher-Order Account provides straightforward explanations of various phenomena. Once it is established that some higher-order stuff is needed, I will consider a more sophisticated Higher-Order Account.

## 3.2 The Suspension Account

According to the Suspension Account, an undercutting defeater is a piece of input that propositionally supports suspension of judgment in the target-proposition and defeats the target-attitude in virtue of the doxastic attitude of suspension of judgment being incompatible with the target-attitude (typically belief). Undercutting defeaters, in this view, differ from rebutting defeaters only insofar as rebutting defeaters do not recommend suspension of judgment, but belief in the negation of the target-proposition.

In order to motivate this idea, let me look at a somewhat abstract rendition of an instance of undercutting defeat:

S believes that *p* on the basis of some justifier *j*. Now S obtains a new piece of information *d* that tells her that, in S's current situation, relying on a certain kind of input that *j* happens to belong to generally leads to false beliefs. This leads S to realize that her belief that *p* is problematic because it is not sufficiently supported by *j*. Consequently, S gives up her belief that *p*.

I want to begin by making two important observations about this story. First, S's rational reaction to the defeater is to give up the belief that *p* and to suspend judgment about *p*. What I want to draw attention to is that undercutting defeaters support more than the mere giving up of an attitude. They support the cognitive attitude of *suspension of judgement* (cf. Lasonen-Aarnio 2014, p. 328). The second observation is that, in most cases, *d* is not the proposition that a specific attitude of S's, like the belief that *p*, is problematic. Rather, it is typically a piece of more general information about the current epistemic situation that amounts to reason to believe that certain kinds of input, to which *j* happens to belong, are not to be trusted.[15] In SCHOOL, for example, the defeating is not done by the realization that James' particular impression of someone looking like Lara entering the coffee shop, but rather that, in the area and at the present time, it is easily possible to have *such impressions* incorrectly, due to the presence of Maude. These two points can be combined to motivate the Suspension Account. To see how, more must be said, both about suspension of judgment as a doxastic attitude and about how it can be supported by new information.

### 3.2.1 Undercutting Defeat and Suspension of Judgment

Few conclusions have been drawn from the nature of suspension of judgment for the analysis and explanation of undercutting defeaters until now. Maybe the reason is that suspension of judgement is often regarded as identical to absence of belief. But as Jane Friedman convincingly argues, this is too weak (Friedman 2013b, 2015). There are infinite propositions that I have never thought about or that I would not even understand (if they contain concepts that I don't have). It would be clearly false to say that I suspend judgement about all of them, even though I clearly hold no beliefs about them. For example, I have (until

---

[15] Of course, it is possible that undercutting defeaters concern very specific attitudes of the subject, in which case this explanation will not work. I ignore this shortcoming here, as the Suspension Account serves more as a testing ground for objection than a serious account of undercutting defeat, but I will come back to it in the last section.

now) never considered whether my best friend's sister's dog likes pinecones. That does not mean that I suspend judgment about this matter (cf. Friedman 2013b, pp. 167–169). It would be obviously inappropriate for my best friend's sister to say: "I wonder whether my dog likes pinecones. Well, I know that Jan suspends judgement about it. He doesn't even know that I have a dog, after all!". Suspension of judgement must thus be more than the mere absence of belief.

Some philosophers take the plausible stance that suspension of judgement is a full-fledged doxastic attitude to a proposition, just like belief or disbelief (e.g. Bergmann 2005, pp. 420–421; Friedman 2013b, pp. 177–180, 2015, pp. 2–3, 2013a, 2015, pp. 1–3). Friedman (2013b) argues further that it is a *sui generis* attitude, but, since I cannot go into detail about her argumentation here, I will leave open whether it is reasonable to go that far and about what kind of doxastic attitude it is. What is of more relevance for my purposes is that, as a full-fledged doxastic attitude, suspension of judgement can be recommended by the available input and even be justified, just like belief. For example, you read in a reliable newspaper that 10,000 refugees crossed the border today. This propositionally supports belief in the proposition that 10,000 refugees crossed the border today and thus you can (and in such cases often spontaneously do) now justifiedly believe that this is so on this basis. If you suspend judgment on the basis of the available information, on the other hand, that attitude would be inadequate, since it is not supported by the newspaper. It is plausible to treat inadequately suspending judgement in this sense as on a par with unjustifiedly believing or disbelieving. By the same token, if you read in one newspaper that 10,000 refugees crossed the border today and in another, equally reliable newspaper that no refugees did, you can (and in such cases often spontaneously do) adequately and *justifiedly* suspend judgement about whether immigrants crossed the border today on the basis of both newspaper reports.[16]

Generally, I take it to be plausible that suspension of judgment is an attitude that is appropriate to take up in the face of input that is insufficient or too well balanced for belief or disbelief. That is, I take it that one is propositionally justified to suspend judgment in cases where either the available positive or negative input is, by itself, not weighty enough to propositionally justify belief or disbelief in the relevant proposition, or where both the available positive and negative input are each counterbalanced by the other to a degree that leaves not enough of it to justify belief or disbelief. Basing an attitude of suspension

---

[16] I take it to be highly plausible that suspension of judgment can be justified, as the example suggests. Depending on the exact relation between suspending judgment and actively withholding belief, I may disagree with Plantinga (1994) on this.

of judgment on an instance of either kind of input-configuration will typically result (absent defeaters) in it being doxastically justified.[17]

Friedman also stresses the following important feature of suspension of judgment: While suspension of judgment may be said to be appropriate as a *result* of some form of inquiry and reflection, it is also appropriate *during* such an activity (Friedman 2015, p. 12). Without discussing Friedman's entire account, we can say that, plausibly, one is justified to suspend judgment *as a consequence* of the realization that one does not possess the right input-configuration for belief or disbelief, but one is also justified and even required to suspend judgment *as long as one reflects on what input is available and during other kinds of inquiries and re-evaluations into such matters*. The latter kind of suspension might be relevantly different from the first, as it is less clear that it is a full-fledged doxastic attitude. This reflects that belief or disbelief can be both *unjustified*, given the possessed input, and *premature*, if the input has not yet been processed. To make things easier, I will call the kind of suspension of judgment that is appropriate during input-processing (in the form of e.g. reflection or re-evaluation) "uncommitted suspension of judgment" and the fully formed attitude "committed suspension of judgment". For the discussion of the Suspension Account, it is enough to focus on committed suspension of judgment as a potentially supported or justified attitude, leaving uncommitted suspension aside for now.

Assuming that suspension of judgement is a respectable doxastic attitude in its own right, one might reconsider the way in which an undercutting defeater supports it. In HOUD, this is supposed to happen by way of rebutting a higher-order belief about the doxastic bases of the target-attitude. Given what was said about suspension of judgment, there is an alternative: The defeater may propositionally support suspension of judgment about the target-proposition directly. The tension between the undercutting defeater and the target-attitude would then stem from a tension between the target-attitude and suspension of judgement and not between two higher-order attitudes. Let me elaborate this idea.

---

**17** While I am generally skeptical about Friedman's (2015) view, according to which suspension is closely tied to inquiry and question-directed states of mind, my minimal justification-conditions for suspension of judgment are compatible with much of what she says. Thus, one may be propositionally justified to suspend judgment about some matter $p$, without actually taking up that attitude. Then, one may consider whether $p$ and suspend judgment about it, first before having processed the already available input on the basis of no input, and later on the basis of the possessed, inconclusive input. Whether continuing to suspend judgment afterwards requires an "interrogative attitude" (Friedman 2015, p. 8) can be left open.

Why would we think that the rational response in cases of undercutting defeat is suspension of judgment? Recall that in typical cases, undercutting defeaters consist in general information about a given situation. For example, learning that my surroundings are illuminated by red lights gives me good reason to be suspicious about my perceptually based attitudes about the colors of the objects around me. It seems that, when I then have the impression of a red wall before me, I am justified in suspending judgment about its color because of the defeating information. Having the impression directs my attention to the color of the wall and, together with what I have learned about the lighting conditions and certain background principles, provides justification for suspension of judgment. Why? Because these pieces of input suggest that, even when I have the impression of a red wall, I have no reason to think that the wall is or is not red. Thereby not having positive or negative input for belief of disbelief in a proposition propositionally justifies suspension of judgment about it, as I suggested above. Note that this step has absolutely nothing to do with any beliefs about the doxastic bases of other beliefs. It is the same kind of step we take when we form attitudes in response to processing new input.

This idea is very close to Pollock's account, which also stated that something is a defeater, just in case it, together with the original justifier, is not a reason to hold the target-attitude (see the previous section). However, it goes one step further in that it explains why this is so and utilizes suspension of judgment as a full-fledged attitude to do so. According to the Suspension Account, the defeater, together with the justifier, not only fails to be a reason for the target-attitude but is also a reason for suspension of judgment. This leads to a number or differences, one of which lies in the explanation as to why defeater and justifier support suspension of judgment. The Suspension Account, however, has more of a burden to bear, as it postulates that defeater and justifier do not only *not* justify something, but also do justify a full-blown doxastic attitude. Notably, this burden is not yet borne: The information that there is a red light shining on everything around me, together with the impression of a red wall, does not by itself show that I have no positive or negative input for belief or disbelief in the proposition that the wall is red. I mentioned that "certain background principles" are also required. In order to properly motivate the Suspension Account, these must be made explicit.

There is often a "typical" way of getting at certain truths in one's surroundings. For example, when we form beliefs about the color of things, we typically rely on perception (our own or that of others), since in normal situations that is the only way for us to assess colors. This allows the following helpful speculation: Generally, given our physiology and the features of normal situations in which we form beliefs, it makes sense for us to operate under the assumption that the only available and reliable way to form a correct attitude about things of some kind $a$ is the way $w$, that is, under the circumstances typical for $a$.[18] For example, when we are awake during the day and on planet Earth, we plausibly operate under the assumption that the only reliable way to find out the color of things is through perception. Other reliable ways, like the examination of the surfaces of objects with a microscope, are typically not available and therefore not typical ways. If they *were* typically available tomorrow, we would likely have a hard time getting rid of our well-entrenched expectation of having to find out about color through perception. As a result, when we learn that $w$ as a typical way to find out about $a$ is currently not trustworthy, we obtain reason to think that we have no positive or negative input for belief or disbelief in $a$-matters and therefore propositional support for suspension of judgment on $a$-matters.[19]

Note again that this support is independent of any higher-order beliefs about the specific bases of the subject's attitudes and stems from more general factors. This picture provides an easy, hopefully not too cognitively demanding way for us to appreciate undercutting information, without having to have direct access to the bases of our beliefs. While it might be a speculation and would have to be investigated empirically, it is both helpful in explaining the intuition that undercutting defeaters suggest suspension of judgment, and plausible, as it describes an evolutionarily beneficial mechanism: It is beneficial, insofar as creatures that behave in the described way will be sensitive to highly relevant information and thus avoid false beliefs without needing to possess the ability to correctly assess the total doxastic bases of their own attitudes in a matter of seconds. It is therefore plausible at this point to assume that undercutting defeaters, at least in the form of *general* information about one's current situation, directly support suspension of judgment.

So, an alternative to HOUD is the Suspension Account as a view that characterizes undercutting defeaters in terms of the kind of attitude they support, instead of the level of abstraction they appeal to. To rehearse the parallel between

---

**18** This could also be spelled out in terms of common epistemic practices under normal conditions (cf. Willaschek 2007, pp. 263–266). However, I prefer the picture of evolutionarily developed higher-order operating principles, commitments or beliefs for a limited but pervasive group of methods of attitude formation. It has the benefit that no implications for the general structure of justification are guaranteed. I don't want to firmly commit to any of this, however, with the exception of the thesis that there are higher-order attitudes that are propositionally justified for normal subjects in *some* way. I will return to this later.
**19** Plausibly, such background assumptions are part of the background information that plays a role in defeat. Unlike Plantinga (1994), I want to limit the relevant background to such operating principles, instead of entire noetic systems.

rebutting and undercutting defeaters on the Suspension Account: Undercutting defeaters generate incompatibilities by supporting attitudes that conflict with other attitudes already held, just like rebutting defeaters do. Since one cannot at the same time rationally or even consciously believe that $p$ and suspend judgement about whether $p$, there is an incompatibility between the defeated belief and the suspension of judgment as recommended by the defeater (cf. Friedman 2015, pp. 9–10). Call this kind of incompatibility "*doxastic incompatibility*".[20] The main difference between the two is that, while rebutting defeaters produce incompatibilities that consist in beliefs in logically contradictory propositions, undercutting defeaters produce incompatibilities that consist in support for attitudes that are doxastically incompatible. Here is the modified account:

Def-4:

$d$ is a defeater, iff

1. $d$ is a doxastic attitude or a piece of positive input for a doxastic attitude $A^*(q)$ about a proposition $q$ for a subject $S$ that is acquired by $S$ at time $t$

2. there is a doxastic attitude about $p$, $A(p)$, that is held by $S$ at $t$ and at $t$-1, such that

    2.1. $A(p)$ is supported to degree $x$ at $t$-1 and to degree $y$ at $t$, such that

    2.1.1. $x > y$ and

    2.1.2. the change from $x$ to $y$ is a result of $S$'s acquiring $d$ at $t$.

Undercut -2:

$d$ is an undercutting defeater, iff

1. $d$ is a defeater:

---

[20] Concerning this point, see also e.g. Kölbel (2014); MacFarlane (2014). I am not entirely convinced that rationality or some other kind of normativity is required to spell out doxastic incompatibility. Alternatively, we might say that suspending judgment includes a disposition to resist believing or disbelieving the relevant proposition (cf. Bergmann 2005, p. 421) or that two attitudes are doxastically incompatible iff it is not possible to, at the same time, *consciously* believe that p and *consciously* suspend judgment about p. Not much hangs on this here, but it is worthwhile to point out that there are ways to make sense of doxastic incompatibility without infusing normativity into the theory, in order to preserve theory-neutrality for what I am saying here.

1.1. $d$ is a doxastic attitude or a piece of positive input for a doxastic attitude $A^*(q)$ about a proposition $q$ for a subject $S$ that is acquired by $S$ at time $t$

1.2. there is a doxastic attitude about $p$, $A(p)$, that is held by $S$ at $t$ and at $t\text{-}1$, such that

    1.2.1. $A(p)$ is supported to degree x at $t\text{-}1$ and to degree y at $t$, such that

        1.2.1.1. $x > y$ and

        1.2.1.2. the change from $x$ to $y$ is a result of $S$'s acquiring $d$ at $t$.

2. $A^*(q)$ is suspension of judgement about $q$.

3. $q$ is identical with $p$.

Def-4 and Undercut-2 feature doxastic attitudes, rather than only beliefs in the role of *defeaters*, so that the possibility that an undercutting defeater is itself an attitude of suspension of judgment can be accommodated. The account seems to reach explanatory bedrock, as long as it is assumed that the standard account of rebutting defeat does: Sticking to the target-attitude in the face of an undercutting defeater would be unjustified for the same reason that doing so in the face of a rebutting defeater would be. It would amount to accepting a pair of incompatible attitudes, which is paradigmatically irrational.[21]

So, it seems that the Suspension Account is marked by an attractive simplicity and appears to be a straightforward application of the lessons drawn from the analysis of rebutting defeat. However, this is precisely why it fails to accommodate a number of structural features that undercutting defeaters plausibly have. In what follows, I will present those features and level objections based on them against the Suspension Account. The view will be shown to give the wrong verdicts in corresponding examples. At the same time, it will be explained why the naïve Higher-Order Account has no problem integrating the relevant structural features, motivating it further. The results of this discussion will also be used in the final section of this chapter as a testing ground for my own theory.

---

[21] Depending on possible awareness-restrictions on such requirements of rationality (e.g. Lord 2015; Kiesewetter 2017, ch. 7) or on defeaters, this can be modified, such that sticking to the target-attitude in the face of defeat amounts to accepting a pair of incompatible attitudes one has *good reason* to take to be incompatible or to *knowingly* accepting such a pair.

### 3.2.2 First Objection: The Source-Sensitivity of Undercutting Defeaters

First, as we have already seen, undercutting defeaters are *source sensitive* (Casullo 2003, p. 45; cf. Melis 2014, p. 435). There are two ways of understanding an undercutter's source-sensitivity: Whether it defeats can depend either on the *actual* doxastic base of the target-attitude, or on a set of input that *the subject believes or has justification to believe* to be the doxastic base of the target-attitude. Call these two interpretations the *objective* and the *subjective* conception of source-sensitivity, respectively. Cases like MILK lend some weight to the subjective conception of source-sensitivity, which leads the proponent of the naïve Higher-Order Account to propose a higher-order belief as a condition on undercutting defeat. Since this is the starting point for this discussion, I will assume the subjective interpretation for the criterion of source-sensitivity, unless otherwise indicated.

Now, what generates a particularly dire problem for the Suspension Account of undercutting defeat, is the fact that it has undercutting defeaters fail the criterion of source-sensitivity *on both interpretations* because it contains no conditions concerning doxastic bases at all. Take the following example:

> MICRO: Ewald is a biologist and is hiking out in the mountains. He looks at a rare flower and has the impression that it is red. Since the hue seems remarkable to him, he takes the flower to his truck and puts it under a microscope, which tells him that the reflectance properties of the surface indeed correspond to a pattern associated with redness. Because his microscopic analysis has had a perfect track record so far, Ewald purposefully and successfully bases his belief that the flower is red on the microscopic examination, instead of his visual impression. He then learns from a reliable source that all the flowers around him are illuminated by a red light.

Intuitively, MICRO is not a case of undercutting defeat. The explanation for this is that the potential defeater does not appeal *either* to the input Ewald actually bases his belief on, or to the input he believes himself or has justification to believe himself to base his belief about the color of the flower on. That is, the new information that all flowers around him are illuminated red does not at all call into question the epistemic connection between his microscopic examination and his belief that the flowers are red. Instead, it does call into question the connection between his visual impressions and his belief, but he neither actually bases, nor believes or has justification to believe himself to be basing his belief about the flower's color on those visual impressions.[22] However, Ewald is in a

---

22 Note that, while Ewald may not have *justification*, he may well have some support for this

situation (outside, using perception) in which color perception is a *typical way* of getting at the truth about the color of a flower. What he hears about the red light does shed doubt on the trustworthiness of this way under the given circumstances. Therefore, the red-light information, together with the impression of a red flower and the relevant operating principle, propositionally supports suspension of judgment about the color of the flower.

According to Undercut-2, this is all it takes for the red-light information to be an undercutting defeater for Ewald's belief that the flower is red. It therefore gives the wrong verdict for the case. This illustrates a general disadvantage of the Suspension Account compared to the Higher-Order Account. The latter can avoid the wrong verdict for MICRO by pointing out that Ewald neither believes, nor is justified to believe, nor is committed to the stance that his target-attitude rests on the source that is undercut by the defeater. In fact, given his presumably clear memory of the procedure, he is at least propositionally justified to believe that his belief that the flower is red does *not* depend on his visual impression of its color. Because the relevant higher-order propositions concern specific sources or justifiers for the target-attitude, Higher-Order Accounts can thus straightforwardly account for the source-sensitivity of undercutting defeaters, whereas the Suspension Account is bound to what counts as a typical way to get to the truth about certain matters and therefore cannot do so. It will often give the wrong verdict in cases where the target-attitude is formed in non-typical ways, such as MICRO. Pure first-level accounts, like the Suspension Account, depict undercutters as too similar to rebutters in this regard.

### 3.2.3 Second Objection: Undercutting Defeaters and Higher-order Support

The second problem with the Suspension Account is that it cannot adequately explain the epistemic value of *higher-order support*. The general idea comes from Michael Bergmann, who states that higher-order support is epistemically valuable, at least because its makes it harder for us to obtain undercutting defeaters (Bergmann 2005, p. 427).

Take the following example:

> THEORY: Gerrit formulates a theory on some complicated subject matter. He collects evidence and then does his best to apply the methods of the field to it. He thereby arrives at a new theory, which he then writes a paper about. His supervisor starts reading the

---

higher-order belief. This support can, for example, be derived from the fact that vision is the typical way to get colour beliefs under his circumstances.

paper but doesn't have the time to finish it and read Gerrit's conclusions. She only reads the sections where Gerrit evaluates the evidence he compiled. Gerrit then meets his supervisor on the way to the canteen and asks her what she thinks. The supervisor replies that Gerrit has done an excellent job in collecting and evaluating the evidence. The methods he used are reliable and ably applied.

Intuitively, the information that Gerrit's conclusions are well supported by his evidence is epistemically relevant to the epistemic status of his belief in them. However, he seems to have gained no new information with direct regard to the correctness of his theory. The supervisor's statement does not directly provide support for the relevant first-order attitude, but propositionally supports the associated higher-order belief that his evidence actually supports his conclusions. An explanation as to how this may help the epistemic status of the relevant first-order attitude is then required.

Higher-Order Accounts offer an excellent explanation: On the level of higher-order attitudes, undercutting defeaters have the same features as rebutting defeaters, namely, they can be perfect, successful or failed/partial higher-order rebutters. In normal cases of undercutting defeat, the occurring higher-order rebuttal is at least successful, since we rarely have very weighty special support for the higher-order beliefs attached to our first-order beliefs. In SCHOOL, James has no explicit, positive reason to believe that observations of people dressed like Lara who enter coffee shops indicate that Lara is skipping school. He simply seems to assume that he is in a normal situation and that, in normal situations, such observations do support his target-attitude. This assumption is plausibly legitimate, unless challenged on good grounds. We can say that it is defeasibly justified *by default*.[23] Because it is a fairly regular state of affairs that we rely on default assumptions about the reliability of the methods we employ when forming attitudes, it seems to us as though undercutting defeaters involve no weighing of support. After all, there rarely is anything of note to weigh them against. Rebutting defeaters are different in that we very often do have some support for the

---

23 I don't mean to advocate a general default-challenge schema for justification, in the sense of, e. g. Wright (2004) here (see also Williams 2001 for such a view). However, I find it plausible that there are conditions that render beliefs justified by default. I cannot discuss the details of such a view here, but it should be plausible enough that a higher-order operating principle, commitment or belief on the reliability of perception in normal cases satisfies the relevant conditions, whatever they are (for more details on such a view and the relevant conditions, see Willaschek 2007). As already mentioned, I do want to commit to the thesis that there are higher-order attitudes that are propositionally justified for normal subjects in *some* way. I will explain later why this justification is constituted either by default or because we typically possess positive input for them.

first-order belief that they are directed against. Thus, because first-order beliefs are not justified by default, but most often have some independent support, rationally reacting to *first-order* rebutting defeaters involves the weighing of support much more often than *higher-order* rebutters which, on this picture, are undercutting defeaters.

This is why cases of higher-order support, like THEORY, are noteworthy: They feature additional support for the higher-order attitude that undercutting defeaters rebut and therefore can potentially be cases of unsuccessful undercutting defeat. This is because additional support can make the difference between a successful higher-order rebutter and an unsuccessful one. The supervisor's judgement makes it much harder for Gerrit to obtain a successful higher-order rebutting defeater and thereby weakens the impact of any potential undercutting defeater. The fact that, with it, Gerrit is pretty well justified in believing that the connection between his supporting base and the target-attitude is in good order *protects* him in this sense against defeaters that target just that connection. For example, if a trustworthy colleague told Gerrit that, at the beginning of his studies, he has been given a drug that leads to highly unreliable evaluations of evidence on the subject, that testimony can be confidently ignored by Gerrit, since the supervisor's judgement outbalances the support it provides for doubt about Gerrit's actual evaluation of the evidence, leaving the relevant higher-order belief justified (albeit somewhat less well than before).

There is certainly a lot to this kind of explanation of the value of higher-order support. Since it crucially relies on higher-order beliefs whose support can be compared to that of an undercutting defeater, however, it is not available on the Suspension Account. In Undercut-2, undercutting defeat cannot be construed as higher-order rebuttal, since it locates the incompatibility that is crucial for undercutting defeat not on the level of the relevant higher-order attitudes, but on the basic level, between the target-attitude and suspension of judgement. This move systematically bars the Suspension Account from employing the Higher-Order Account's straightforward explanation of the value of higher-order support and makes it very difficult to accommodate cases like THEORY. Given the plausibility of the idea that higher-order support protects against undercutting defeaters, this bullet is too big to bite for the Suspension Account.

### 3.2.4 Third Objection: Undercutting Defeaters and the Weighing of Support

A third and final problem with the Suspension Account is that it allows the support offered by undercutting defeaters to be *weighed against* the justifier, which is a typical feature of rebutting defeat, but implausible in standard cases of undercutting defeat. This is another way in which the two types are depicted as too similar.

To see this, consider the following case:

DEVICE: Conrad is the proud owner of a device that tells him which doxastic attitude he should take up in any given situation. From past experience, he knows that the device is highly reliable. Thus, when he considers whether $p$ and the device says "believe that $p!$", it is likely that belief is the adequate doxastic attitude in the current situation. The device's reliability is due to its wireless access to lots of data and its high information processing capability. Thus, the device's recommendation is a weighty piece of positive input for taking up the recommended attitude. In that respect, it functions like any other source of propositional support: When Conrad enters a room, immediately looks at the device and it says "believe that there is a door in the opposite wall!" and he subsequently believes on the basis of the device's recommendation that there is a door in the opposite wall, that belief is well founded (for example, because the device has access to the building's floor plan). However, exactly *how* the device comes to its recommendations, what and how much data it has access to and whether it is more or less reliable at making such recommendations than Conrad himself is, is a complete mystery to him. All that Conrad knows is that the device is reliable and its recommendations are good. One day, he reads a biology book that states that whales are mammals. He comes to believe on that basis that whales are mammals and that belief, being based on trustworthy literature, is justified. But then the device chimes and says "suspend judgement about whether whales are mammals!".

Intuitively, after learning about the device's recommendation, Conrad's belief that whales are mammals is no longer justified. This is because the device provides support for suspension of judgment about whether whales are mammals, and that doxastic attitude is incompatible with the – also well supported – belief that whales are mammals. It thus acts as a defeater for his belief that whales are mammals. So far, Undercut-2 is able to capture what we want to say about the case. The crucial question is, however, what kind of defeater the device's recommendation is. Since the defeater propositionally supports suspension of judgement about its target-proposition, Undercut-2 categorizes it as an undercutting defeater, but that result is wrong. The support that the device's recommendation provides for suspension of judgement is *independent of the support* that reading the biology book provides for the target-attitude in the same way that the lawyer's opinion in LEAVE is independent of Marla's reading of the regulations. Nothing about the device's recommendation suggests that there is anything wrong with basing one's beliefs on reading the perfectly normal biology book or that there is no support for belief in the target-proposition. The way in which it supports suspension of judgement is therefore relevantly different from the way in which undercutting defeaters paradigmatically do.

As already noted, undercutting defeaters are source sensitive. The device's recommendation in its role as defeater is not source sensitive. It supports suspension of judgment, no matter what Conrad's target-attitude that whales are mammals is based on. For example, had Conrad's belief been based on the trustworthy testimony of his sister, it would still have been rendered unjustified by the device. The device's recommendation therefore does not *undercut* the justification of the target-attitude, but rather counterbalances it. This is further supported by the following consideration: When a rebutting defeater is obtained, the subject may characteristically weigh and compare the epistemic support for and provided by the defeater with the support for the target-proposition. This is not so in cases of undercutting defeat, as SCHOOL illustrates. In DEVICE, it would intuitively be perfectly legitimate for Conrad to weigh and compare the support that the biology book provides for his belief with the support that the device provides for suspension of judgement. Since it thus seems to behave exactly like a paradigmatic rebutting defeater and not like a paradigmatic undercutting defeater, DEVICE should be categorized as a case of rebutting, rather than undercutting defeat. It can therefore be concluded that DEVICE shows that the Suspension Account fails to adequately discriminate between rebutting and undercutting defeat, since it falsely categorizes the case as a case of undercutting defeat.

### 3.2.5 A Summary of the Arguments and an Extension to the Account of Rebutting Defeat

The three arguments presented here establish the Higher-Order Account's superiority over the Suspension Account by showing that the latter cannot accommodate important characteristics of undercutting defeaters that the former is specifically designed to recognize. They can be summarized as follows:

**Table 1.**

| Feature of UD/View | HOUD | Suspension Account | Case in point |
|---|---|---|---|
| *Source-sensitive* | Yes | No | Micro |
| *Neutralized by higher-order support* | Yes | No | Theory |
| *Cannot rationally be weighed against justifier* | Yes | No | Device |

Before leaving the Suspension Account behind, it makes sense to take a small detour. The third example discussed here, DEVICE, teaches us something remarkable about rebutting defeat: Input that supports suspension of judgment, or *any* doxastic attitude that is incompatible with the target-attitude, can be a rebutting defeater. Rebut-3 so far only allows rebutters to support disbelief and must be modified to accommodate this. What really distinguishes rebutting from undercutting defeaters is that the support they provide for an incompatible attitude is *independent* of the support provided by the justifier and that the two measures of support are both relevant to the ultimate status of the target-attitude and can be rationally weighed against each other. This suggests the following modifications:

> Def-5:
>
> d is a defeater, iff
>
> 1. d is a doxastic attitude or a piece of positive input for a doxastic attitude $A(q)$ about a proposition $q$ for a subject $S$ that is acquired by $S$ at time $t$
> 2. there is a doxastic attitude about $p$, $B(p)$, that is held by $S$ at $t$ and at $t$-1, such that
>
>    2.1. $B(p)$ is supported to degree $x$ at $t$-1 and to degree $y$ at $t$, such that
>
>    2.1.1. $x > y$ and
>
>    2.1.2. the change from $x$ to $y$ is a result of $S$'s acquiring $d$ at $t$.
>
> Rebut-4:
>
> d is a rebutting defeater, iff
>
> 1. d is a defeater:
>
>    1.1. d is a doxastic attitude or a piece of positive input for a doxastic attitude $A(q)$ about a proposition $q$ for a subject $S$ that is acquired by $S$ at time $t$
>
>    1.2. there is a doxastic attitude about $p$, $B(p)$, that is held by $S$ at $t$ and at $t$-1, such that
>
>    1.2.1. $B(p)$ is supported to degree $x$ at $t$-1 and to degree $y$ at $t$, such that
>
>    1.2.1.1. $x > y$ and
>
>    1.2.1.2. the change from $x$ to $y$ is a result of $S$'s acquiring $d$ at $t$.

2. $A(q)$ is either

   2.1. the belief that $q$ and $q$ is the negation of $p$

   or

   2.2. suspension of judgement about $q$ and $q$ is identical with $p$.

3. The propositional support for $A(q)$ is independent of the doxastic support for $B(p)$.

Let us quickly go through the new features of note.

For Def-5: In order to account for the possibility of input for suspension of judgment playing the defeater-role, as exemplified by DEVICE, the account now states in condition 1. that a defeater is input for a *doxastic attitude* (or is that attitude), rather than a belief. It may seem that the change renders the definition inadequate because it does not state that $A(q)$ and $B(p)$ are incompatible. Note, however, that the incompatibility between $A(q)$ and $B(p)$ that is necessary for defeat *need* not be explicitly stated because it is implicit in the definition of the defeater in general: If one suspends judgment about $p$ and then receives input supporting that very same attitude (such that there is no conflict), one's original suspension does not lose, but rather gain justifiedness. It thus fails the definition of defeat and does not amount to a defeater of any kind. If the attitude supported by the new input and the target-attitude differ, on the other hand, we are dealing with a defeater, where it is then further specified by the conditions specific to rebutting or undercutting defeat, such as 2. and 3. in Rebut-4.

The changes made to Rebut-4 are only slightly more extensive: Condition 2.2 states that a rebutting defeater can not only recommend belief in the negation of the target-proposition, but also support suspension of judgement about it. This is supposed to capture the results from DEVICE. Furthermore, Rebut-4 allows for the possibility that the attitude of suspension of judgement is adopted quickly and can itself act as a rebutter. To elaborate a bit: We are able to hold at the same time two beliefs in contradictory propositions that rebut one another. This happens, for example, when we don't immediately notice the connection or when we simply don't change one of them fast enough. We are also generally able to hold contrary beliefs over longer periods of time, however irrational this may be. If this is true of beliefs, it is plausibly also true of suspension of judgment. Therefore, we should be able to hold at the same time two *doxastically incompatible* attitudes toward *the same* proposition that rebut one another (cf. Friedman 2015, p. 4). For example, I might not currently think about one of my beliefs, but automatically suspend judgement in the proposition that it is about in response to new information. This doesn't mean that I no longer have the stored belief, but rather that I now hold incompatible attitudes, one of which must be given up if I want the other one to be justified.[24]

Condition 3. is also new and in need of some elaboration. It is supposed to keep Rebut-4 from becoming equivalent to Def-5 and to distinguish rebutting from undercutting defeaters. I will go into more detail of what it means for the defeater's support to be "independent" of the target-attitude's support when I present my final version of Undercut. The general idea, however, is this: A rebutting defeater's support (or the support it provides) is independent from the target-attitude's justifier, just in case it is rationally permissible for the subject to weigh the former against the latter. This is the case when the defeater defeats but does not appeal to the total doxastic base of the target-attitude and is therefore not source-sensitive, but "source-neutral". In other words, the defeater's support is independent in the relevant sense when it doesn't matter to its defeating power what the target-attitude is based on.

This concludes my discussion of the Suspension Account. The offered counterarguments establish three things: 1) the Suspension Account is not an adequate analysis of undercutting defeat. It cannot accommodate characteristic features of undercutting defeat, namely, source sensitivity, lack of independence between support relations and relation to higher-order support. 2) In order to give such an analysis, taking suspension of judgement seriously is a good idea. 3) Undercutting defeaters appear to involve higher-order attitudes. Accepting higher-order attitudes or commitments into the picture provides straightforward ways to accommodate all the features of undercutting defeat the Suspension Account cannot deal with. In light of this, the present discussion provides further motivation for Higher-Order Accounts of undercutting defeat.

## 3.3 The Commitment-based Higher-Order Account

The Suspension Account was an attempt to account for undercutting defeat in the least demanding way possible. This resulted in a lack of complexity that didn't allow the account to properly capture the phenomenon. The naïve Higher-Order Account does better but it is also unacceptably demanding, as was shown in section 3.1. In this section, I will examine a more modest version of

---

[24] In cases of rebutting defeat, I also must lower my credence with respect to the attitude I keep. Rebutting defeaters are symmetric and even if one is weaker than the other, it still partially defeats.

the Higher-Order Account: the Commitment-based Higher-Order Account. I will motivate it from the failures of its contenders and then argue that it also fails, thereby unearthing another interesting feature of undercutting defeaters, namely, their sensitivity to what the subject has reason to believe about the target-attitude's bases and their support for it.

At the end of section 3.1, one can get the impression that Higher-Order Accounts of undercutting defeat are, by nature, too demanding. Higher-order attitudes are not commonly held about defeasible attitudes, they are cognitively complex and incur high theoretical costs. Still, this impression is misleading. After all, Higher-Order Accounts need not share the naïve Higher-Order Account's focus on higher-order *beliefs* as the touchstone for undercutting defeaters. It is time to discuss the notion of a "commitment". Several proponents of Higher-Order Accounts have claimed that undercutting defeaters appeal not to beliefs, but to higher-order commitments:

> [...] undercutting defeaters generate their distinctive kind of pressure only in concert with higher-order commitment about the basing of lower-order belief. (Sturgeon 2014, p. 117)

> Underminers suggest that something was wrong with the source of justification or with the justificatory process, and they operate their defeat by appealing to the higher-order commitment that the belief in question was based on that source or that process. If the suggestion is that the process, rather than the source, was defective, the defectiveness is to be understood as the occurrence of a mistake or some other disturbing event. (Melis 2014, p. 438)

I'll call such a view a "commitment-based Higher-Order Account" or, in short, "C-based Higher-Order Account". Whether C-based Higher-Order Accounts fare better than the naïve Higher-Order Account clearly depends to a large extent on the notion of *commitment* and on what it means for an undercutting defeater to *work in tandem* with or *appeal* to a commitment. I will start with an attempt to spell out these ideas in terms of mere co-instantiation and show that the resulting view suffers from various shortcomings. Next, I will look at a more substantial reading of appealing and argue that it, too, does not yield an adequate C-based account of undercutting defeat.

### 3.3.1 Actual and Apparent Commitments: A First Stab at the Concept

According to Sturgeon, "[...] undercutting defeaters function as non-dogmatists insist that perceptual experience works [...] in tandem with background commitment about the basing of lower-order belief" (Sturgeon 2014, p. 118). Based on a straightforward reading of this passage, for an undercutter to *work in tandem with* a commitment is for it to somehow *be in place* together with the commitment or to be co-instantiated with it. Adding the relevant requirement to Pollock's account would allow for two ways to spell out Sturgeon's view. In the first version of an extended Pollockian account, $d$ is an undercutting defeater for the reason $m$ for the attitude $b$, iff it is logically impossible for the subject to rationally hold both $b$ and $d$ on the basis of $m$ and the subject is committed to $b$ being properly based on $m$.

The problem with this view is that Sturgeon provides no reason why MILK shouldn't be a counterexample against it, just as it is against Pollock's original view. Intuitively, one would think, after all, that the milk taster, in virtue of basing her belief partly on smell, is committed to her belief being properly based partly on smell, whether or not she explicitly believes this (Lam 2012). Thus, the first version of the extended Pollockian view is unattractive.

Maybe this suggests that Sturgeon has something more demanding in mind when he states that undercutters work "in tandem with" background commitments. What might be meant is that the undercutter must *be part of the available input, together with* a higher-order commitment. This is a second version of the extended Pollockian view: $d$ is an undercutting defeater for reason $m$ for the attitude $a$, iff it is logically impossible for the subject to rationally hold both $a$ and $d$ on the basis of $m$ and it is a piece of input for the subject that it is committed to $a$ being properly based on $m$. The point of note is that this version of the account no longer states that higher-order states themselves are required for undercutting defeat, but that they are somehow available (in the sense that input is available) to the subject.

While it could in principle be argued that this condition is *not* met for the milk taster with respect to the relevance of smell to her belief, this is far less clear than it is for the higher-order belief-condition of the naïve Higher-Order Account: The milk taster clearly does not have the relevant belief, but it is not obvious that the fact that she is committed to $a$ being properly based on M. Thus, this version of the extended Pollockian account may still be too weak. Even more worryingly, there is another way in which it is too strong: One may have misleading justification for thinking that one is committed to one's attitude being properly based on input $m^*$, while it is actually based on input $m$ where $m$ and $m^*$ are not identical. In that case, it seems that one is committed to the belief being properly based on $m$, but that commitment is not available for basing attitudes on and thus not part of one's input (input, after all, is not necessarily factive). In turn, while one may have justification for thinking that the belief in question is based on $m^*$, one is not actually committed to the belief being based on $m^*$. In this case, there is no (fitting) actual commitment that is part of one's input, since, ex hypothesi, the only actual commitment (the attitude being based on

m) is not available, due to misleading justification. At the same time, it is plausible that potential defeaters that concern the justified, though false, proposition that the belief is based on $m^*$ would intuitively amount to genuine undercutting defeaters, which fits well with further examples Sturgeon gives (cf. Sturgeon 2014, p. 115ff).

This, however, shows that *actual* higher-order commitments do not have to be part of the available input, in order for undercutting defeat to occur. Some other higher-order state, like a *merely apparent* commitment, seems to do the work here. While this is a problem for the specific view currently under consideration, it generally seems that the idea that undercutters appeal to higher-order propositions that are somehow part of one's input, here attributed to Sturgeon, is on the right track. These propositions apparently don't need to be the content of actual commitments, but as contents of apparent commitments, that is, of commitments *one has reason to take oneself to be subject* to, they seem to be relevant. Thus, this version of Sturgeon's view at least very generally points in the right direction. However, it must be noted that de facto co-instantiation of undercutting defeater and actual higher-order commitments as parts of the available input turns out to be unnecessary for undercutting defeat, which spells trouble for the relevant view. Finally, even if these problems could be solved and it turned out that actual higher-order commitments must be co-instantiated with the undercutting defeater, either generally or as part of the input, this would still not fully explain how undercutting defeat works. Merely pointing to a correlation here is not enough. A commitment-based bedrock explanation of undercutting defeat can be expected to contain an account of the relationship between the defeater and the commitment, as well as the relationship between the commitment and the target-attitude that helps us to understand how the undercutter removes the target-attitude's justification via the commitment. In order to pave the way for such an account, more must be said about the nature and content of the right commitments and their relation to justification. Thus, pointing out that undercutting defeaters work "in tandem with" higher-order commitments does not amount to a satisfactory C-based Higher-Order Account.[25]

---

[25] Melis uses a potentially more substantial term when he talks about the defeater "appealing" to a commitment: "[...] in general, an underminer $d$ appeals to some higher-order commitment $c$ when $d$ could not do its defeating job, unless $c$ was in place [...]." Melis 2016, fn. 8. However, as it stands, this basically repeats Sturgeon's thesis about undercutting defeaters in that it merely claims that undercutting defeaters characteristically require the simultaneous presence of a higher-order commitment. The view thus inherits the problem of lacking a bedrock explanation because it does not shed light on the exact relationship between the defeater, the commitment and the target-attitude. This is especially surprising, as the *appealing* relation has the potential

### 3.3.2 The Nature of Epistemic Commitments: Getting the Account off the Ground

Since the propositional content of undercutting defeaters concerns the doxastic bases of the target-attitude, it makes sense that the content of the higher-order commitment that Sturgeon and also Melis have in mind specifically concerns those bases. The most straightforward way for the defeater to appeal to the commitment is thus the following: For a defeater to appeal to a higher-order commitment is for it to stand in a relation to the commitment that is analogous to rebutting defeat. Since commitments need not be justified beliefs and can thus not suffer genuine rebutting defeat, I will call this rebuttal-analogous relation "quasi-rebuttal". Accordingly, the defeater would need to contain a proposition that is logically incompatible with the proposition that the target-attitude commits to. Of course, this means that, on C-based Higher-Order Accounts, undercutting defeaters amount to higher-order quasi-rebutting defeaters. This delivers the following account:

> C-based Undercut:
>
> $d$ is an undercutting defeater for a subject $S$'s doxastic attitude about $p$, $S(p)$, held on the basis of input $b$ iff
>
> 1) $d$ is a defeater,
>
> 2) In virtue of holding $S(p)$, $S$ is subject to a higher-order commitment $c$, according to which $b$ sufficiently supports $S(p)$ and
>
> 3) $d$ is a quasi-rebutter for $c$.

In order to turn this into a full account of undercutting defeat, one would now need to clarify the relationship between the quasi-rebuttal of a higher-order commitment and the justificatory status of the attitude that is the source of that commitment. Specifically, one would need to motivate the "Commitment-Justification Link" or "C-J Link":

---

to yield more theoretical substance than mere co-instantiation. Of course, it is possible that Sturgeon and Melis generally take *working in tandem with* and *appealing to* to express relations that are more substantial than mere co-instantiation and simply don't say much more about them because they rely on our natural understanding of the relevant terms. But for the evaluation of C-based Higher-Order Accounts, it is a worthwhile endeavor to explicate such an understanding for the appeal to higher-order commitments. I will focus on *appealing* here, because I take it to be the more accessible formulation.

C-J Link:
A subject $S$'s doxastic attitude about $p$, $S(p)$, is justified, only if there is no commitment $c$ that $S$ is subject to in virtue of holding $S(p)$, such that $S$ possesses a quasi-rebutter for $c$.

A C-based Higher-Order Account needs the C-J Link to hold because it needs to account for a defeater's capacity to remove justification. Before this account can be properly evaluated, the key concept of a *commitment* must be spelled out.

Generally, I will understand an epistemic commitment as a proposition, the truth of which one is somehow epistemically responsible for in virtue of holding a specific doxastic attitude on the basis of a specific set of input. Thus, the milk taster is committed to her taste and smell faculties working properly in virtue of believing that the milk is OK on the basis of taste and smell. Further elaboration is in order. First of all, the higher-order commitments at issue here are what Shpall calls "rational commitments", as opposed to "normative commitments" (Shpall 2014, p. 146). One is subject to a rational commitment in virtue of holding certain doxastic attitudes, practicing certain ways of belief-formation or making certain normative evaluations of such ways (cf. Lam 2012, pp. 556–560). In contrast, one is subject to a normative commitment in virtue of performing certain acts, such as, for example, making a promise (cf. Shpall 2014, p. 148). In what follows, I will set normative commitments to the side and focus exclusively on the rational commitments, which are much more relevant in a purely epistemic context.

Rational commitments play an important role in dialectical inquiry. A common argument against a philosophical view, for example, is that the view commits its proponents to a number of highly implausible consequences (cf. Lam 2012, p. 550). One may argue against Lewis' modal realism for instance, that it commits one to an unduly bloated ontology. In the same way, people are sometimes convinced of the falsity of their moral beliefs when it is drawn to their attention that these beliefs commit them to approving murder or other atrocities. This highlights three important features of rational commitments. First, what commitments one is subject to depends on the actual state of one's noetic system. They are thus *subject-dependent* (cf. Lam 2012, p. 554; Shpall 2013, p. 730, 2014, p. 154) or, more precisely, dependent on systems of doxastic attitudes and other epistemically relevant states.

Second, commitments are *objective*, in that one being committed to the truth of certain propositions in virtue of holding a certain attitude in a certain way does not depend on one believing that one is so committed or on one having justification for believing that one is so committed (Lam 2012, p. 554, 555). It seems that the mere fact that those propositions stand in the appropriate relation to the held attitude is sufficient, at least in paradigmatic cases like logical implication. This is illustrated by the possibility of learning about one's commitments through the objections of others, as well as the intuitiveness of the idea that the milk taster commits herself to the adequacy of her sense of smell by using it to determine the status of the milk. In the former case, the relation is propositional, in the latter one might call it "procedural". I will not take a stance on what constitutes an "appropriate" relation here and simply assume that, besides strict logical relations, epistemic relations, either propositional or procedural, are also candidates.

Third, commitments are, in some sense, *binding* (cf. Shpall 2013, p. 729, 2014, p. 153). When you learn that you are committed to the existence of Santa Claus and also firmly and justifiedly believe that he does not exist, you are required to change something in your noetic system. If your belief that Santa Claus does not exist is well supported, you would standardly fulfill this requirement by *escaping the commitment* (cf. Shpall 2013, p. 729, 730, 2014, p. 153, 154). A commitment can be escaped by abandoning its source, that is, by giving up on the doxastic attitude or way of forming certain attitudes that commits one to whatever turns out to be false.[26] This looks promising for the idea of understanding undercutting defeaters as quasi-rebutters for commitments: A conflict between new information and a commitment one has in virtue of the attitudes one holds often appears to require that one revise one's attitudes. Whether this is enough to motivate the CJ-link, however, depends on both the exact sense in which commitments are binding and on certain assumptions about justification. In what follows, I will argue that the link does not hold for mere commitments. I will suggest, however, that the link plausibly holds for commitments that are *doxastically accessible* for the subject. While such commitments are still not quite the right requisite for a full analysis of undercutting defeat, the point ties into the observation made about merely apparent commitments as part of the available input during the discussion of Sturgeon's account. I will attempt to show that, while C-based Higher-Order Accounts ultimately fail, there is some-

---

[26] While Shpall (2013, 2014) only looks at commitments generated by doxastic attitudes, Lam (2012) gives a broader account of commitments as being generated by a range of epistemic items, including ways to form attitudes. I find it plausible that forming beliefs in a certain way commits one to that way being truth-conducive, but it is not clear to me how exactly one would escape such a commitment. If the way or method is sufficiently basic, skepticism presumably threatens, in which case it might be practically impossible to escape the relevant commitments. Here, it is less plausible that one is rationally required to escape the relevant commitment (for a discussion, see Lynch 2013). However, for the sake of argument, I will assume that these cases can be resolved satisfactorily.

thing right about the idea that undercutting defeaters trade on the features of commitments. I will try to bring this out in more detail in this section.

What does it mean, exactly, that commitments are binding? Perhaps, a more illuminating way of phrasing this question would be: Given that one is committed to $c$, how is one to epistemically behave as a result? First, the kind of normativity here is derived from considerations of rationality. Being subject to a rational commitment puts constraints on rational ways of forming or dropping doxastic attitudes related to it. Thus, any requirement that arises from a rational commitment is a rational requirement.

Second, the things one is committed to are propositions, in the sense that one is committed to *the truth* of certain *propositions* (cf. Lam 2012, p. 551). If I believe that the window broke because a rock hit it, I am not necessarily committed to *believing* that it is not true that someone only made it look as though that is what happened (I wouldn't usually believe this and it seems hard to fault me for that), but I am committed to this *being true* and it thus seems to hold epistemic significance for me.[27] A commitment doesn't necessarily have a built-in instruction concerning the formation or dropping of an attitude, but it does somehow hold us responsible when the propositions we commit ourselves to turn out to be false.

This leads to the third important observation about the normativity of commitments: Being *committed to c* is not the same thing as being *rationally required to believe that c* (cf. Shpall 2013, p. 728, 2014, p. 148, 149; Lam 2012, p. 551). Unlike being subject to a rational requirement, which would impose immediate compliance,[28] being subject to a commitment doesn't have any immediate normative consequences. First, even assuming for a moment that commitments exert some normative force to adopt belief in their content, they may still be outweighed by other considerations and thus not necessarily amount to all-things-considered requirements. Second, *pace* Shpall, it is even implausible to think that one is rationally required to believe what one is committed to in *any sense*. Take a simple case: I am a very simple epistemic subject and hold only three, perfectly consistent beliefs; x, y, and z (thus, there would be no outweighing reason to not believe the content of all the commitments derived from these three beliefs).

---

[27] This idea, taken from Lam (2012), conflicts with Shpall's view, which takes commitments to concern attitudes like belief (cf. Shpall 2013, p. 728). In Shpall's account, commitments turn out to have (some) unconditional normative force (I will get to this point shortly), which rules out cases of faultless discovery of commitments. I will argue that such cases are highly plausible, which is why I accept Lam's view here.

[28] When I speak of a "rational requirement", I always mean an all-things-considered requirement (see e.g. Shpall 2013).

Each belief has potentially infinitely many logical implications $x_n$, $y_n$ and $z_n$. Since what I believe implies every $x_n$, $y_n$ and $z_n$, I am committed to the truth of them all. But besides countless, often barely distinct and for the most part highly irrelevant propositions, there will be many $x_n$, $y_n$ and $z_n$ that only follow from x, y and z via incredibly long and complex inferences that are often beyond my cognitive capacities and may not even be intelligible to me. It would be completely crazy to hold that, in such a case, I am rationally required to believe all of these irrelevant or far removed implications of my three beliefs (cf. e.g. Kiesewetter 2017, ch 7.7). Furthermore, if commitments amounted to requirements to believe, one would have to conclude that I am highly irrational, given the incredibly huge amount of beliefs I should have, but fail to have. This, too, looks clearly false. Also, remember that this is only a very simple case where I only hold three consistent beliefs. The real belief systems of real people are far bigger and more complex, so that real people are committed to many more truths and consequently fail even more rational requirements. The result would be that everybody is completely irrational, no matter how well-maintained their belief system is, which also looks absurd. It can therefore be safely concluded that being committed to *c* does not constitute any kind of normative reason to believe that *c*.

So far, I have said only a few positive things about the binding character of commitments. This is because it is a topic of disagreement between me and, presumably, defenders of the relevant C-based Higher-Order Account. Before discussing the available options, however, I want to point out that what has been said so far already unveils one of the disadvantages of such an account, at least insofar as it trades on the nature of commitments. The idea is that an undercutting defeater quasi-rebuts a commitment that arises from the defeated belief. The CJ-link must then be explained via the normative force of the commitment in that the quasi-rebuttal of the commitments rationally requires the subject to escape the commitment by giving up the defeated belief. In this picture, the CJ-link is thus established on the condition that structural irrationality, that is, irrationality due to logical incompatibilities, is incompatible with justification and, accordingly, that such rationality is necessary for justification. This condition is, admittedly, one that many would agree with, but it is nevertheless not fully neutral with respect to theories of justification. In some views, structural rationality simply isn't necessary for justification: The belief that *p* may be reliably formed, even though one already reliably believes that *q* where *p* and *q* are logically incompatible. According to simple process reliabilism, both attitudes nevertheless seem to turn out to be justified.[29] I will go into more detail about this in the fifth

---

[29] This point will be picked up and defended in chapter 5.

chapter, but, very broadly, a plausible account of undercutting defeat should be compatible with a view that takes epistemic justification to be purely a matter of objective facts, like reliability, and that does not assume structural rationality as a condition on justification. A C-based Higher-Order Account that explains undercutting defeat via epistemic normativity through structural irrationality is unable to ensure that undercutters can remove justification on such an account and is therefore not fully neutral with respect to theories of justification.

A defender of C-based Higher-Order Accounts may be tempted to simply bite this bullet or even insist that the phenomenon of undercutting defeat further *supports* the view that structural rationality is, in fact, necessary for justification. However, there are other reasons to think that commitments do not have the right normative character to capture undercutting defeat. For the relevant C-based Higher-Order Account to get off the ground, a quasi-rebutter for a rational commitment, absent defeater-defeaters, must rationally require the subject to escape the commitment by dropping its source (the target-attitude). This is only secured if it is supposed that commitments exert at least pro tanto normative force on their own. That is, merely being committed to $c$ must rationally require one to "track" $c$, in the sense of being sensitive to its truth or falsity (cf. Lam 2012). In turn, this must mean that one does something wrong if one does not escape any commitment that commits to a proposition one has reason to take to be false. Assuming that rationality is necessary for justification, this then establishes the CJ-link. In what follows, I will raise numerous arguments against several versions of the C-based Higher-Order Account that show that the CJ-link cannot plausibly be established.

### 3.3.3 Arguments against Commitment-based Higher-Order Accounts of Undercutting Defeat

The first problem arises from tying rational commitments too closely to the justification of doxastic attitudes.

First, consider a view according to which an attitude is only rational to hold if one is sensitive to the truth of all commitments arising from it. In this "extreme view" then, an attitude is only rational if one properly tracks all the rational commitments that have it as their source. Clearly, the extreme view is sufficient to establish the CJ-link. As long as justification implies rationality, the extreme view ensures that tracking all of one's commitments is necessary for justification. If so, undercutting defeaters mark changes in the epistemic statuses of commitments that must be tracked, such that they result in changes in the epistemic status of the source of those commitments – the target-attitude.

Unsurprisingly, however, the extreme view is unattractive because it entails that normal human beings are almost never rational in holding any doxastic attitude. It is implausible for reasons that are very similar to those that lead us to reject the idea that commitments always need to be beliefs: They put too heavy a burden on the average epistemic agent. Let us plausibly assume that, in virtue of believing that $p$ on the basis of some input $r$, one is committed to the truth of $p$, as well as to the truth of all propositions implied by $p$. In addition, one is committed to the truth of higher-order propositions about the epistemic relationship between belief that $p$ and $r$, such as the proposition that $r$ sufficiently supports belief in $p$, as well as all of that higher-order proposition's implications. This is plausible enough, as an argument that would show the subject holding the belief that any of those implications is both false and, in fact, an implication of her attitude and the way she holds it would put rational pressure on her to revise her belief. Now, the implications of the believed proposition, *any* believed proposition, and the higher-order proposition will be both infinitely many and infinitely complex. This alone makes it cognitively impossible for a normal human to comprehend them all, let alone track them (cf. e.g. Kiesewetter 2017, p. 182ff). Thus, while it is plausible that an argument showing the subject that it is not true that $r$ sufficiently supports her belief that $p$ will pressure her to revise her belief, it is *not* plausible that an argument showing that the extremely complex proposition $q$ that follows from $p$ is false will do the same. In addition, most normal humans will not even *remember* many of the sets of input they relied on in forming their current attitudes. While they are still plausibly committed to the quality of that input, they cannot be expected to track what they can't remember. To drive this point home: Even if one is in principle inclined to hold normal humans to the standard of rational omniscience when it comes to tracking commitments, doing so will lead to skepticism. All of our doxastic attitudes incur infinitely many, infinitely complex commitments that we are incapable of tracking, due to cognitive limitations and imperfect memory. If this is incompatible with justification, it follows that none of our doxastic attitudes are justified.

A straightforward way to escape such skeptical consequences is to weaken the tracking-requirement so that it no longer covers *all* of one's commitments. After all, there are more moderate positions with less demanding standards for rationality (Nottelmann 2010). Melis, for example, restricts the set of relevant commitments to those that the "relevant" subject would track:

> The propositions towards which the *relevant agent* is committed are such that she would take them to be true (or just warranted) on reflection—at least for as long as she stands by the related piece of justification. (Melis 2016, p. 273)

The idea seems to be that the tracking requirement applies to those commitments of which it is true that a *rationally ideal* version of the subject would believe their content upon reflection. Let us assume that a rationally ideal version of a normal human shares their cognitive and physical limitations, but has as much insight into the available input, the structure of their noetic system and into their rational commitments as is possible within those limitations. The CJ-link could then be postulated to hold only for commitments of the normal human that the rationally ideal version would form beliefs in upon reflection.

The problem with this approach is that it can't get just those cases right that motivated Higher-Order Accounts in the first place. Consider again MILK: In virtue of holding her belief on the basis of both taste and smell, the milk taster surely is committed to her sense of smell functioning properly. Also, a rationally ideal version of the milk taster, having insight into the bases of her attitudes, would be disposed to believe that her belief is partly based on smell. When she then learns that her nose is bunged up, the milk taster acquires a quasi-rebutter for that commitment. Accordingly, the account under scrutiny will yield the verdict that this new information acts as a defeater and removes her justification for the milk-belief (cf. Melis 2016, p. 276). This conflicts with the intuitive verdict on the case. The same holds in cases where the subject holds a reasonable, but false belief. Sturgeon discusses a modified version of MILK, in which the milk taster has a justified belief that her milk belief does not depend on smell at all (and thus presumably that it only depends on taste (cf. Sturgeon 2014, p. 115), based on the reliable testimony of her teacher. Again, it seems like her milk-belief is not defeated by the information that her nose is bunged up and she can justifiedly continue to hold it, even though the milk taster is de facto committed to the proposition that smell supports beliefs about the milk's freshness and a rationally ideal version of her would be disposed to believe so. This version of the case is of additional note in that the milk taster's basis for her false higher-order belief should already constitute an undercutting defeater on the view presently under consideration, all by itself. After all, it supports a higher-order proposition that may act as a quasi-rebutter against the higher-order proposition concerning the support offered by her *actual* base: The teacher's testimony supports belief in the proposition that her belief is supported solely by smell, which is incompatible with the proposition that her belief is supported by a complex gustatory and olfactory experience (taste and smell). Accordingly, in this view, any false but justified belief about the bases of one's beliefs will automatically count as an undercutter and render the relevant first-order beliefs unjustified. A die-hard externalist might be driven to accept these consequences and explain away such cases,[30] but when evaluated in terms of an overall satisfactory theory of defeat this is not a comfortable position to be in. Again, the CJ-link cannot be established because commitments that are only part of an ideally rational being's input are too far removed.

At this point, one may be tempted to further weaken the relevance-condition on the commitments until it fits the bill and the CJ-link can be established. Here is a good candidate: Only those commitments must be justification-relevantly tracked that are such that, if the subject considered the truth of their content-propositions, she would take them to be true. While the commitments that turn out to be relevant to justification in this view are not too far removed to establish the CJ-link, it is not as plausible as it first seemed that commitments in general are the right target for higher-order rebuttal.

To see this, consider another modification of MILK: The milk taster believes that the milk is OK, based on smell and taste. She falsely, but justifiedly believes, however, that she holds her belief on the basis of *sight*. Now, the milk taster receives the believable information that her sense of sight is temporarily impaired. Intuitively, her belief that the milk is OK is undercut by this new information. How could a C-based Higher-Order Account accommodate this, given that the target-attitude in the case, being based not on sight, but on smell and taste, does not give rise to a commitment that is incompatible with the defeater? The only incompatibility arises between the defeating new information and a commitment to the truth of the proposition that [the milk taster's belief is based on sight] that arises from her believing just that proposition, such that *that* higher-order belief is rebutted. But, by hypothesis, the higher-order belief is not part of the target-attitude's total doxastic base. So, there is no commitment in this case, the quasi-rebuttal of which would ensure undercutting defeat on the C-based Higher-Order Account, as it stands.

More can be said on this issue and I will show in the next section that this weakest version of the C-based Higher-Order Account is generally on the right track here. Still, its focus on commitments does not quite get to the heart of the issue. As the example shows, the question is not what commitments the subject has, but whether the higher-order attitude that is rebutted is part of the tar-

---

[30] Melis (2016, pp. 276–277) thinks that such a view is well suited for an externalist about justification, while adding some sort of awareness-requirement to a C-based Higher-Order Account is supposed to be more attractive for an internalist. However, I believe that even an externalist should not find herself driven to the acceptance of the extremely counterintuitive consequences described here. She would have to deny almost all of the intuitive attraction that fist drove people to think about defeat in the first place. In the next chapter, I will show that externalists have a much more plausible account of defeat at their disposal.

get-attitude's total doxastic base. Thus, even if in all plausible cases of undercutting defeat a quasi-rebutted commitment can be found, this still doesn't give a satisfactory account of undercutting defeat because the relevant commitment cannot be ensured to be properly related to the target-attitude. This is indicated by cases where the subject has a false, but justified belief about what the bases of their attitude are. No amount of weakening the relevance-condition on commitments for the CJ-link can fix this problem. Thus, the C-based Higher-Order Account, while faring much better than both its naïve counterpart and the Suspension Account, is either implausibly demanding or cannot account for important variations of the cases that motivated it in the first place. Therefore, I hold that it ultimately fails as well.

### 3.3.4 The Demandingness-Trilemma as the Central Problem Facing Accounts of Undercutting Defeat

So far, I have examined and rejected three initially promising accounts of undercutting defeat: the naïve Higher-Order Account, the Suspension Account and the C-based Higher-Order Account. Their flaws were, in order: 1) the postulation of implausibly demanding higher-order conditions on justification (specifically, justified higher-order beliefs); 2) insensitivity toward deeper structure of undercutting defeat, specifically, toward the phenomena of source-sensitivity, the impossibility of weighing against the justifier and the possibility of protection against defeat through higher-order support; 3) a failure to account for undercutting defeat's sensitivity toward what the subject believes or is propositionally justified to believe about the bases of the target-attitude and their support.

Before proposing my own account, I want to make a few general remarks. As seen earlier, adopting some version of the Higher-Order Account commits one to certain conditions for justification. If I want to say that undercutting defeaters remove justification by appealing to higher-order attitudes, at least in cases where this happens, justification must depend on those higher-order attitudes. The challenge is then to explain how this is possible, if one does not simultaneously want to accept that higher-order attitudes are necessary for justification. This becomes more difficult when it is considered that cases like MILK and the problems with higher-order commitments suggest that no relation to higher-order propositions that is independent of the subject's epistemic perspective will do. There seems to be some epistemic relation between a subject holding a target-attitude and a higher-order proposition that is required for undercutting defeat and that lies somewhere between believing the higher-order proposition and being objectively committed to it.

Otherwise, it seems that we are left with what can be called the "Demandingness Trilemma":

Either, 1) we agree that undercutting defeaters appeal to higher-order attitudes and, since defeaters remove justification, accept the consequence that there seems to be a higher-order condition on justification. This provides a full explanation of undercutting defeat via the Higher-Order Account but commits to highly demanding higher-order conditions on justification and therefore fails to give us the theory-neutrality that we want in an account of undercutting defeat.

Or 2) we avoid such a commitment and adopt something like the Suspension Account that restricts undercutting defeat to the basic level. This, however, leaves it mysterious how undercutting defeaters remove justification, since appealing to higher-order beliefs is part of what it means for a defeater to *undercut* and fails to explain defeat-protection via higher-order support.

Or else 3) we accept that undercutters appeal to some objective relation to a higher-order proposition, like a commitment. This entails biting the bullet on the cases discussed in the previous paragraph.

The Demandingness Trilemma is the main problem with formulating a satisfactory account of undercutting defeat. In what follows, I will present a view on undercutting defeat that can avoid it by employing higher-order attitudes and higher-order rebuttal to explain undercutting defeat, while holding that such attitudes are only relevant to epistemic justification *in cases of undercutting defeat, but not in general.*

## 3.4 The Rebasing Account

For my solution, I will investigate the idea that undercutting defeaters bring higher-order attitudes with them. If a solid position could be constructed from this thought, it would allow one to accept that undercutting is done by appealing to higher-order attitudes, while still being able to allow for lower-order doxastic attitudes to be justified independently of such higher-order attitudes. Let me explain.

It does not follow from the fact that all justified lower-order attitudes can potentially be undercut and that undercutting requires them to be justified partly in virtue of higher-order attitudes that all justified lower-order attitudes are justified partly in virtue of higher-order attitudes. It merely follows that they are justified partly in virtue of higher-order attitudes, *in case they are undercut*. Thus, general higher-order conditions on justification can be avoided, if obtaining a defeater somehow makes it the case that the target-attitude relies for its justification in part on a higher-order attitude, where this was not true before. This move seems arbitrary at first, but there is independent motivation for thinking that defeaters have this effect. I will show that this result is by no means ad hoc, but rather flows naturally from plausible principles about belief re-evaluation and reasoning. My account will benefit from Casullo's insights in several ways. He proposes the view that $S$'s belief that [$r$ does not really support that $p$] is an undercutting defeater for $S$'s belief that $p$, iff $S$ has *some support* for the proposition that $p$ is based on $r$ (cf. Casullo 2016, p. 7). I will pick up the idea that whether one has support for the relevant higher-order proposition is relevant to undercutting defeat. Casullo's suggestion here is a useful one that goes a long way to explain how higher-order beliefs are attached to undercutting defeaters.

For both rebutting and undercutting defeaters, an important observation was that they generate incompatibilities in the subject's noetic system. Rebutting defeaters typically produce logical incompatibilities with the target-proposition or doxastic incompatibility with the target-attitude, both at the basic level. Undercutting defeaters also generate lower-order doxastic incompatibilities by supporting suspension of judgement (leaving aside the deeper structure for a moment). Now consider how we generally tend to react to doxastic incompatibilities: Say that so far, I have believed that $p$ on good grounds, but as with most of my beliefs, I don't have any beliefs about the grounds of that belief or their degree of support. Now I am presented with excellent visual evidence for *non-p*: *I* immediately and automatically form or am moved to form the belief that *non-p* and notice that the two are incompatible. I might notice this either because it becomes directly transparent to me as a result of sitting down and reflecting on my beliefs or because I started feeling uneasy or uncomfortable, due to cognitive dissonance in the sense of Festinger's view (Festinger 1957).

At any rate, registering the incompatibility naturally prompts me to *re-evaluate* my belief that $p$. This means that I engage in a process of reasoning during which I identify the epistemic support for believing that $p$ or that *non-p* and compare the two. If I do well, I arrive at a result that is epistemically justified. Namely, if I adequately judge and weigh the support for each attitude and if I am rational and a good reasoner, I will most likely end up keeping the originally better supported belief and I will discard the less well supported one (though I might be less confident in the one I stick to than I was before, depending on the details of the case). The resulting attitude would then be doxastically justified on the basis of a competent piece of reasoning. If I do a bad job, on the other hand,

I will end up with an unjustified attitude on the basis of a flawed piece of reasoning. If I, for example, give the support for my belief that $p$ much more weight than it can be reasonably said to have because I really want $p$ to be true, if I am very distracted and thereby don't compare the weight of the relative support well, or if I simply lose interest and stop halfway through my reasoning, I might quite possibly end up with the originally less well propositionally supported belief and discard the one that was much better supported. My attitude would then be unjustified, even if I happened to pick the originally better supported one, because I would hold it as a result of bad reasoning.

I take this description of belief re-evaluation to be fairly uncontroversial, even though the details, as well as the degree of cognitive sophistication involved may vary. Sometimes the reasoning progresses in the form of conscious reflexion, for example when we deliberate whether to believe someone who tells us a dubious piece of gossip about a friend we know well. At other times, we can directly "see" which attitude is better supported and we make an immediate and mostly subconscious inferential step to discard the other one, for example when it is noticed that a newly formed belief stands in tension with a necessary truth. I want to point out two observations about this that will prove important: First, the re-evaluation of an attitude in response to registering its incompatibility with some other attitude is a paradigmatic example of reasoning. Second, dissolving incompatibilities between attitudes by re-evaluating them is something that we regularly do and that can be done in a way that produces a justified result. Accordingly, any theory of justification ought to (and does) allow for attitudes to be justified on the basis of good re-evaluative reasoning. I propose to employ the concept of belief re-evaluation for the analysis of undercutting defeat. Its usefulness for this purpose derives from two of its features. First, re-evaluation requires a "rebasing" of the belief. Second, at least in cases of defeat, re-evaluation features higher-order attitudes.

### 3.4.1 The Re-evaluation of Doxastic Attitudes and the Concept of Rebasing

I will turn first to the concept of rebasing. "Rebasing" describes a change in the surrounding doxastic structure of a doxastic attitude, namely, the replacement of one set of input with another as the total doxastic base of that attitude. Since we are fallible epistemic subjects, we sometimes hold beliefs on the basis of input that is not propositionally supportive of them to a sufficient degree. For example, $S$ might believe that $S^*$ charges too much rent on the basis of, among other things, the fact that $S^*$ looks shifty to $S$. $S$ might not consciously do so and if $S$ were to reflect on whether looking shifty is an indicator for charging too much rent, $S$ might notice that $S^*$'s looking shifty is not a good basis for the belief that she is charging too much rent and deny that it is, but as the case is, $S$ believes as she does in part because $S^*$ looks shifty. Let us assume both that $S^*$ looking shifty to $S$ is not propositionally supportive of $S$'s belief that $S^*$ is charging too much rent and that the basis of $S$'s belief contains further, highly supportive pieces of input, such that it does not crucially depend on the shiftiness-impression for its epistemic status. Now, I believe that the following is something that we can and, indeed, regularly do: In response to new information (or possibly even epistemically irrelevant influences) we stop holding the relevant doxastic attitude on the basis we are currently basing it on and start holding it on what we deem a better basis. Thus, if $S$ realizes that she believes that $S^*$ charges too much rent because, among other things, $S^*$ looks shifty to her and judges that this is not a good reason for the belief, she can and likely will, in response to this realization, ban the shiftiness-impression from the total doxastic base of her belief. This means that she stops using that impression as a base for her belief and continues to believe that $S^*$ charges too much rent solely on the basis of the other pieces of input in the original total doxastic base. Since the new, impoverished total doxastic base is not the same as before, she thus switches total doxastic bases for her belief. This description suggests the following principle:

RB:
A doxastic attitude $a$ of a subject $S$ is *rebased* in response to a stimulus $c$, iff at time $t_0$, $a$ has the total doxastic base $f_1$ and $c$ causes $a$ to be based on the total doxastic base $f_2$ at $t_2$ instead, where $f_1 \neq f_2$.

RB should not surprise anyone. Of course, we can discard what we take to be evidence from the bases of our attitudes when we learn that it is not supportive after all. We also add new input we acquire later or sometimes even discard a total doxastic base altogether and replace it with an entirely new one.[31] The entire history of science seems to be a testament to this, presumably because rebasing is such a common occurrence that almost every theory of justification has at least the resources to account for it, as I will show in the fifth chapter. For now, I want to lay out why RB is the key to understanding undercutting defeat, thereby motivating the Rebasing View that will be constructed on its basis.

To see how RB and undercutting defeat are related, consider the connection between rebasing and re-evaluation. When we re-evaluate a justified doxastic at-

---

[31] This happens, for example, when we believe only on the basis of one piece of input that turns out to be unsupportive or when a whole class of input is corrupted.

titude, we conduct a piece of reasoning that has as its result the sustenance or dropping of the attitude. When this happens, the doxastic support-relation between the original justifier and the re-evaluated attitude is severed, either to be reinstated alongside the additional confirmation from the (in this case reinforcing) re-evaluation, or to be committedly suspended. In either case, the re-evaluated attitude is rebased. What operations the re-evaluation contains depends on the newly acquired information that prompted it. In case that information appeals to the epistemic relationship between the re-evaluated attitude and its doxastic bases, it contains as components both an identification and an assessment of the doxastic bases of the re-evaluated attitude (what are the bases and are they positive?) and an identification and assessment of the epistemic relations between the bases and the re-evaluated attitude (do the bases support the relevant attitude, and if so, to what degree?). Naturally, this kind of re-evaluation is the one that is of most interest for the explanation of undercutting defeat. However, rebutting defeat can also be spelled out in terms of re-evaluation in a fruitful manner, as I will show later.

To illustrate the connection between re-evaluation and undercutting defeat, let us thus first assume that the relevant re-evaluation process investigates whether the original justifier supports the re-evaluated attitude to a sufficient degree. With this assumption in place, compare the following cases:

1) A subject $S$ justifiedly holds the doxastic attitude $a$ toward a proposition $p$ on the basis of $r$ and re-evaluates it. The reasoning process $S$ employs is good, the premises are justified and the operation is well conducted, such that its result is prima facie justified. The result of the re-evaluation is that $S$ gives up $a$.

2) A subject $S$ justifiedly holds the doxastic attitude $a$ toward a proposition $p$ on the basis of $r$ and re-evaluates it. The reasoning process $S$ employs is good, the premises are justified and the operation is well conducted, such that its result is prima facie justified. The result of the re-evaluation is that $S$ retains $a$.

3) A subject $S$ justifiedly holds the doxastic attitude $a$ toward a proposition $p$ on the basis of $r$ and re-evaluates it. The reasoning process $S$ employs is bad, the premises are unjustified and the operation is sloppily conducted, such that its result is not prima facie justified. The result of the re-evaluation is that $S$ gives up $a$.

4) A subject $S$ justifiedly holds the doxastic attitude $a$ toward a proposition $p$ on the basis of $r$ and re-evaluates it. The reasoning process $S$ employs is bad, the premises are unjustified and the operation is sloppily conducted, such that its result is not prima facie justified. The result of the re-evaluation is that $S$ retains $a$.

Intuitively, S is justified in retaining/giving up a in cases 1) and 2) and unjustified in doing so in cases 3) and 4). This suggests that whether we do a good job when re-evaluating an attitude makes a difference as to whether retaining or dropping the attitude will be justified.[32] However, if it were not rebased in the course of the re-evaluation, this could not be explained. The original justifier r would simply continue to make up a's total doxastic base and there would be no reason why a's epistemic status should change. Accordingly, it would be very hard to explain why S, in case 1) is *right* in giving up a. After all, if the re-evaluation made no difference to a's base, she would be giving up a well-founded attitude. Additionally, re-evaluation would become epistemically irrelevant. If r continued to be a's justifier, S would be justified in holding a in all four cases. This seems especially strange in case 4), where the attitude is retained after a bad piece of re-evaluative reasoning.

To see this, let us make case 4) a bit more vivid: Say S believes that domesticated sheep are kept under acceptable conditions (a) on the basis of reading a Wikipedia article (r). S then encounters her good friend Larry, a committed vegan, who presents some evidence that Wikipedia is not reliable with respect to animal welfare conditions. In response, S re-evaluates her belief. Thus, S considers Larry's points with respect to a's adequacy and endeavors to identify and likewise examine her original basis for a in light of this. Unfortunately, S does a really bad job. She really wants it to be true that sheep are kept in acceptable conditions to justify her consumption of wool and milk. She therefore partially misremembers the Wikipedia article, such that the one in her mind is different from the one she read. It seems much more persuasive to her in retrospect. In addition, she massively overestimates the article's relevance and weight. Furthermore, S (sloppily) tries to persuade herself that Larry's arguments are not well supported or irrelevant to the issue. In general, her bias leads her to making glaring mistakes in assessing r as the actual basis for her belief, as well as both the epistemic relations between it and Larry's arguments on the one hand and the belief on the other hand. She thereby comes to the conclusion that a is to be affirmed and thus holds on to it.

Clearly, the avoidable mistakes that S made during re-evaluation should make a difference to a's epistemic status. S's blatant failure to correctly identify

---

**32** One could argue that dropping an attitude is always *permitted* and thus never unjustified (see e.g. Nelson 2010). For the sake of simplicity, I will postpone accounting for this option to the next chapter and stick to the description given here. Note that this makes little difference, as one could also speak of dropping or retaining an attitude "fitting the input", instead of being justified or unjustified, where it may be permitted (and possibly neither justified nor unjustified) to drop a fitting attitude, but not to keep an attitude that is not fitting.

and evaluate the input relevant to *a* prevent her stubborn clinging to *a* from being epistemically OK (and, especially, from being justified). However, if *r* retained its status as *a*'s total doxastic base, this couldn't be true, since *r* on its own is good enough to provide justification and can act as justifier. The only thing that has changed is that there is now a bad re-evaluation process, but why would that make a difference to the epistemic status of *a*, if *a*'s surrounding doxastic structure has not changed at all? Given the conception of doxastic architecture at work here,[33] *S*'s mistakes can only make a difference to the justificatory status of the resulting attitude, if they are part of that attitude's base or were made during its basing.[34] Thus, since case 4) should not end up being a case of a justified attitude and since this must depend entirely on the quality of the re-evaluation process, *a*'s re-evaluation in 4) must make it the case that *a* is no longer (solely) based on *r*, but somehow depends on that process. Thus, in cases of re-evaluation, the relevant attitude is *rebased* from its original justifier to the re-evaluation process or to its input/premises, depending on what can generally play the role of a doxastic base. That is not to say that the original justifier doesn't continue to have influence, though it doesn't do so directly. Since re-evaluation consists in a new look at what counts in favor of or against the re-evaluated attitude, it will, if the re-evaluation is done well, be picked up by the process and its force will be taken into account.

We now have a picture in which, during a perfectly common cognitive operation, an attitude can lose its justification and be justifiedly given up. In cases where this happens in response to new information, that new information must thus amount to defeat. However, the goal is a full explanation of undercut-

---

[33] I am still assuming that the actual base of an attitude determines its epistemic status with respect to doxastic justification. Of course, epistemologists who hold that justification contains normative components need not accept this. It may, for example, be argued that the reason why *S*'s belief about the conditions of sheep is not justified is because its base *ought* to include the re-evaluation, even if it does not. I have no problem with this and will show later how such normative conceptions can make it easier to account for undercutting defeaters.

[34] You might think that this is not true, as the mistakes could be defeaters and defeaters don't need to be part of the defeated attitude's base in order to remove justification. First, this would have to work via normative/rational requirement and can thus only be true for theories of justification that somehow incorporate normative conditions and accordingly not, for example, for standard reliabilism. Second and more importantly, it is simply implausible that the mistakes *S* makes can be defeaters in the relevant sense in this case. They are not rebutting defeaters, as they have nothing to do with *a*'s subject matter and they can only be undercutting, if they concern *a*'s base. This in turn can only happen if *a* is based (or *S* is justified to believe that it is based) on the reasoning process that they are a part of. Thus, the mistakes can only make a difference if they are directly related to the attitude's base.

ting defeat that contains higher-order elements, as the previous sections suggested, and for that, more detail must be added to the description of re-evaluation.

As explained above, re-evaluation is a reasoning process that involves the assessment of the surrounding doxastic structure of an attitude. This includes first and foremost the identification and assessment of the total doxastic base and/or its epistemic relations to the re-evaluated attitude. The re-evaluation's result is the enactment of the conclusion of the reasoning process. For example, if it is discovered that the re-evaluated attitude is not sufficiently well supported after all, that result is enacted in the form of dropping the attitude. Clearly, a reasoning process that identifies and assesses a held doxastic attitude and its total doxastic base contains higher-order propositions as premises. Re-evaluation is essentially *about* other attitudes, after all. Let me simplify by depicting the process as an inference.

Assume that, for some reason, $S$ becomes suspicious of her attitude $a$ and re-evaluates it. She may reason as follows:

1) I should hold $a$, only if it is based on some piece of input $e$ and if $e$ is correct, $a$ is likely to be correct ($e$ is positive input with respect to $a$).

2) I hold $a$ on the basis of the piece of input $e^*$.

3) It is not true that if $e^*$ is correct, $a$ is likely to be correct.

---

4) I should not hold $a$.

It is important to note that premises like 2) are not supposed to represent higher-order *knowledge*. Specifically, $S$ could be wrong, but justified in believing that $e^*$ is a doxastic base for $a$.[35] However, as long as her higher-order belief here is justified, her reasoning process is epistemically fine. More will be said about the way in which higher-order assessment of the target-attitude proceeds in chapter 5.1. For now, the interesting observation is that this inference is riddled with higher-order propositions. 2) contains the identification of $a$'s actual total doxastic base, while 3) and 1) assess that base epistemically. Of course, an actual re-evaluation is likely to be less reflective in that the subject may just "see" that

---

[35] For reasons why introspection is not only fallible but may not even be a particularly good way of getting at the bases of our attitudes, see Grundmann (2009a). I do not want to commit to the thesis that introspection or self-knowledge is the only or even standard way of assessing the bases. I will assume, however, that we do have some way of doing so that can produce justified higher-order beliefs. Recall that this does not mean that we are always or even often right about what our attitudes are based on.

there is something wrong with one of her attitudes. The mechanisms of identifying and evaluating the base will nevertheless be engaged and it takes a step of reasoning to get from that to a conclusion about what to do with the attitude. We can thus say that re-evaluation is *broadly inferential*.

Re-evaluation often, but not exclusively,[36] happens *in light of the new information that prompted the re-evaluation*. Importantly, if it is prompted, re-evaluation does not only feature an assessment of the surrounding doxastic structure of the re-evaluated attitude but also an assessment of some of the information that prompted it and the relationship between the two. Defeaters are exactly the kind of new input that prompts re-evaluation. Thus, given that re-evaluation features higher-order attitudes and that undercutting defeaters characteristically rebut such higher-order attitudes, this is where they can do their work.

Importantly, the Demandingness Trilemma does not threaten here. The key feature of re-evaluation in this regard is that the higher-order premises *come into play as part of the target-attitude's re-evaluation* and are not an original part of the target-attitude's justificatory status. It is the identification and assessment of the original justifier and its relation to the target-attitude that prompts the subject form any kind of justification-relevant epistemic attitude or other form of awareness (see e.g. Klein 2014, p. 2722ff) toward propositions about the base or its quality. Furthermore, since re-evaluation involves rebasing, those attitudes, in virtue of being input to the re-evaluative reasoning process, are then crucial to the epistemic status of the re-evaluated attitude. Thus, in re-evaluation we already have a perfectly common phenomenon that involves reasoning with higher-order attitudes and those attitudes becoming highly relevant to the epistemic status of the affected lower-order attitude. This is exactly what is needed in order to get out of the Demandingness Trilemma. The idea behind the Rebasing Account of undercutting defeat is that undercutting defeaters are intimately connected to the re-evaluation of the target-attitude. Since defeater-prompted re-evaluation involves rebasing and reasoning with higher-order premises, the obtaining of undercutting defeaters *brings about* the higher-order attitudes that are then relevant to the epistemic status of the target-attitude and that can be rebutted by the defeater. At the same time, these higher-order

---

[36] Of course, one can also just sit down and re-evaluate an attitude one holds, for example, when it is really important for the attitude to be adequate (double-checking etc.). In those cases, no additional information over and above an assessment of the doxastic bases and their relation to the attitude is taken into account. However, for the purposes of investigating epistemic defeat, such cases are irrelevant. The defeater takes the guise of additional information that must be considered.

attitudes are not *generally* required for justification. In what follows, I will spell out the relation between undercutters and re-evaluation in more detail.

### 3.4.2 The Re-evaluation of Doxastic Attitudes and Higher-order Rebutting Defeat

There are two situations in which the re-evaluation of a doxastic attitude is, in some sense, required. The first one is an old acquaintance from the preceding sections: a situation where there is an incompatibility between at least two of the subject's doxastic attitudes. The second situation is one in which information about the quality of the doxastic bases of a specific lower-order attitude is received.

The first situation is familiar from previous discussion. Undercutting defeaters can produce such incompatibilities in the form of doxastic incompatibilities. Recall that this can happen when the defeater is a general piece of information about one's surroundings. For example, $S$ has the impression of a red wall in front of her and forms the corresponding belief. Then, $S$ learns that there is a red light, illuminating the room. This makes her take a more resisting stance toward color-impressions, which, prompted by the red-wall impression, leads her to (committedly) suspend judgment about the color of the wall. The adequate response to the incompatibility between suspension of judgment and the target-attitude is the re-evaluation of the incompatible attitudes and their bases.

In the second situation, the new information does not appeal to typical ways of attitude-formation but specifically targets individual bases.[37] For example: $S$ believes that there is a red wall in front of her, based on having an impression of such a wall. Now, instead of hearing that there is a red light in the room, a highly trustworthy observer tells $S$ that the total doxastic base of her red-wall belief doesn't support belief in the proposition that there is a red wall in front of $S$ (she just flat-out says that $S$'s impression does not support her belief). This information does not instill in $S$ the same sort of general resistance to red-wall-impressions as hearing about the red light does and supports suspension of judgment only insofar as it appeals to higher-order propositions about her actual base of the belief that the wall is red. However, there is little reason to assume that $S$ holds attitudes about these higher-order propositions or is aware of her commitment to them. It therefore does not allow the direct move to suspension

---

[37] This kind of defeater is also not covered by the Suspension Account and constitutes an additional counterexample against it.

of judgment that the first situation permits. Instead, it is more directly, even content-wise related to the target-attitude, given that it indicates that the target-attitude is not well founded. Since this implies a negative evaluation of that attitude, it prompts its re-evaluation without the detour via doxastic incompatibility. If one hears that one of one's doxastic attitudes is not sufficiently well supported, the adequate response should be to check whether this is true. Possible reasons are that we either generally presume that all of our attitudes are well founded, which is here contradicted for a specific attitude by the defeater, or that it is part of the concept of epistemic rationality that it is irrational (and thus norm-violating) to knowingly hold attitudes that are not well-founded. Note that the defeater's indication that the target-attitude is not well founded does not depend on the subject holding higher-order attitudes about the target-attitude beforehand. The defeater is indifferent with respect to what, specifically, supports the target-attitude or whether the subject has any beliefs about it. The subject is simply given the information that *whatever* her attitude is based on is not trustworthy and that is enough to require a re-evaluation. In the same way, learning that whatever is added to your favorite cereal in the last production step is poisonous is enough to make it reasonable for you to stop eating it, even if you don't know what, exactly, has been added.

Of course, there might be more situation-types that are occasions for re-evaluation but trying to find them all would miss the point of this exercise.[38] What is

---

**38** There is an interesting type of case that I have left out here. It seems that one can also obtain an undercutting defeater that supports suspension of judgment about the target-proposition and that doesn't unqualifiedly question the target-attitude's doxastic bases for the attitude of *suspension of judgment itself.* Call this kind of defeater a "same-state" defeater. For example, assume that two equally reliable testifiers make claims about the color of the widgets on the factory floor in a situation where no other information about this is available. One claims that they are red and the other claims that they are white. The subject responds to this input by justifiedly suspending judgment on the color of the widgets, based on both testimonies (they counterbalance each other). Now, the subject reads on an extremely reliable computer screen that the two testifiers are both under the influence of drugs that make them say nonsense. Intuitively, this new information supports suspension of judgment about the color of the widgets for the subject, while also functioning as an undercutting defeater. However, since the subject already suspends judgment, it seems that no conflict is produced. It seems to me that the reason why one has the intuition that there is defeat in this case is that we assume that the subject is aware of the fact that she bases her attitude on the testimony of the two testifiers and that doing so is only legitimate, if they are reliable. In variants of the case where it is made explicit that the subject is not aware of her relying on the testifiers at all, the intuition seems to vanish. This "awareness" can be cashed out in different ways (e.g. in terms of dispositional belief and the like) that presumably have in common that it can stand in doxastic conflicts with new information. The resulting conflict will be a higher-order conflict that affects the epistemic status of the lower-order target-

important here is that obtaining an undercutting defeater always creates such an occasion. The defeater propositionally supports either suspension of judgment about the target-proposition (where this is incompatible with the target-attitude) or it supports belief in the proposition that the target-attitude is not well founded. In either case, re-evaluating is the thing to do. The Rebasing Account that I am developing here essentially claims this: An undercutting defeater defeats in virtue of *requiring the re-evaluation* of the target-attitude and in virtue of *the shape that it gives a competent re-evaluation* of the target-attitude. In order to elucidate this position further, let me go through of the re-evaluation process that such a defeater demands.

Say that subject $S$ holds the justified belief that $p$ on the basis of the justifier $j$, where $j$ is a perceptual impression of $p$. $S$ learns from a trustworthy source that input like $j$ is not trustworthy under the circumstances ($d$) and immediately suspends judgement about $p$ in response. $S$ then registers that suspension of judgment about $p$ is incompatible with her belief that $p$ and consequently re-evaluates both attitudes. This means that $S$ investigates both $j$ as the total doxastic base of her belief that $p$, the support it offers to that belief and that she also takes into account $d$ and the support it enjoys. This can be depicted in the form of the following two inferences[39]:

For the target-attitude:

A1 $j$.

A2 If $j$, then probably $p$.

---

attitude of suspension top-down (a re-evaluation of the lower-order attitude will be part of the re-evaluation). If one finds this kind of awareness demanding, one can always resist the intuition that we can obtain same-state defeaters for many of our ordinary everyday-attitudes and claim that the two-testifiers scenario is not ordinary.

[39] I do not claim that re-evaluation always consists in full, conscious inferences. It is more likely that the reasoning employed in re-evaluation is much less cognitively demanding and proceeds via many silent premises and more or less direct moves from one step to the next. What I have in mind is something like Kent Bach's "default reasoning" (Bach 1985, p. 254), where the subject goes through each step with the underlying assumption that each follows from the previous one, without consciously reflecting on this. Alternatively, the cognitive demand of re-evaluation processes could be reduced by conceptualizing the premises not as attitudes, but as seemings or propositions one is merely aware of (cf. Cath 2011, pp. 132–134; Klein 2014, pp. 2722–2723. The exact form of the process, however, is for empirical science to discover. I am merely assuming that re-evaluative reasoning is broadly inferential and that it requires mental or cognitive states that have higher-order content in order to be performed properly in cases of undercutting defeat.

A3  If it is true that $j$ and that if $j$, then probably $p$, believe that $p$.

---

AK  Believe that $p$.

For the defeater:

B1  $d$.

B2  If $d$, then it is probably not true that: if $j$, then probably $p$.

B3  Believe that $p$ or disbelieve that $p$, only if there is some $x$, such that $x$ supports belief or disbelief in $p$.

B4  For every $x$, $x$ supports belief or disbelief in $p$, only if it is true that: if $x$, then probably $p$.

B5  If there is any $x$ available that supports belief or disbelief in $p$, it is $j$.

---

BK  Neither believe, nor disbelieve that $p$.

The important sentences in this structure are A1, A2, B1 and B2, as they describe the staging ground for the undercutter's ($d$) effect. The other premises contain conditions for justification, as well as, in the defeater-inference, the condition that $j$ is the total doxastic base of the target-attitude. These are merely needed to complete the inferences and nothing crucially depends on them (if they seem to lack detail or other formulations are preferred, they can be replaced with one's favorite alternatives).

During re-evaluation, the two inferences (or chains of reasoning) are conducted and their contents are checked against one another. Clearly, the conclusions, AK and BK, are incompatible with each other which explains the need to drop at least one of the related attitudes. In cases of competent re-evaluation in the face of *rebutting defeat*, re-evaluation would then straightforwardly consist of comparing the relative weights of the sets of input for the defeater and the target-attitude (represented by A1 and B1) and sticking with the better supported attitude, while dropping the less well supported one.

In cases of *undercutting defeat*, such as this one, it is not enough to weigh A1 and B1 against one another. This would be in accordance with the Suspension Account and overlook the higher-order rebuttal that is characteristic of undercutting defeat. Instead, the defeater's appeal to a higher-order premise is made explicit: A2 is logically incompatible with, jointly, B1 and B2. The defeater supports belief in the proposition that it is not true that $j$ is indicative of $p$ (B1 and B2). This incompatibility constitutes a rebutting defeater in B1 and B2 for the higher-order attitude in A2. But the justifiedness of that higher-order attitude is required for the move from $j$ to belief in $p$ (A1) which is part of the subject's assessment of her base for the belief that $p$ in the first chain. As a result, the first chain can no longer justifiedly establish the belief that $p$.

There are two things to be noted about this: First, A2 is not just something that $S$ is committed to in virtue of believing that $p$ on the basis of $j$, but, as a vital part of the re-evaluation initiated by the defeater, *a justified higher-order attitude*. Unlike an actual commitment to the supportiveness of $j$ that would arise from the original holding of the target-attitude on the basis of $j$, the higher-order belief that $j$ supports belief in $p$ need not be true but can enjoy misleading support. Furthermore (and importantly with regard to the Demandingness Dilemma), it was not necessary for the justification of the target-attitude beforehand but has become part of the new total doxastic base as a result of re-evaluation.

Second, in standard cases where the undercutter completely removes its target-attitude's justification, the relevant counterparts of B1 and B2 constitute *at least a successful* higher-order rebutter for A2. Recall that, in order to be successful, a rebutter has to support the negation of the target-proposition to a degree that neutralizes a sufficient portion of the original justifier to make the target-attitude unjustified. In general, due to the plausibility of the Exclusive Thesis, any rebutting defeater needs to have positive epistemic status. Since undercutting defeaters, on this picture, are a kind of rebutting defeater, the Exclusive Thesis holds for them, too. The degree to which an undercutting defeater thus undercuts the target-attitude's chain of reasoning depends on the relative weight of its support, as compared to the support that the higher-order premise leading to the target-attitude enjoys (if any). For cases of full undercutting defeat, the defeater counterbalances enough to fully remove justification for the higher-order premise. For cases of partial undercutting defeat, it merely weakens the justificatory status of the higher-order premise, which in turn weakens the status of the target-attitude that is supposed to be derived from it. Applied to the perceptual case I used as a template here, this means that the degree to which B1, the defeater, supports belief in the negation of the higher-order proposition that $j$ supports belief in $p$, A2, corresponds to the degree to which A2's support for the belief that $p$ is weakened.

Let us illustrate this with a more vivid case: Say, like many of us, A has some inductive support for the assumption that her color-perception in the room she is in is quite reliable (she has often formed beliefs about the color of objects in the room that turned out to be correct) and believes on the basis of color-perception that the wall is red. She is then told by a colleague that there are colored lamps in the room. The intuitive verdict on this case will covary with the trustworthiness we ascribe to the colleague's testimony in relation to the strength of A's inductive evidence. If we say that A's colleague is very trustworthy and that A has a moderate amount of inductive evidence, A's belief is intuitively fully undercut and must be given up. If we say that the colleague is only moderately trustworthy and that A has plenty of inductive evidence, A's belief about the color of the wall can intuitively be kept but is less well justified than before. This illustrates how the mechanics of rebutting defeat on the higher level influence the target-attitude's status on the lower level. Note that in typical cases of undercutting defeat, it does not take much independent support for the defeater to fully undercut otherwise strongly justified first-order attitudes. This is because their higher-order justification is often much less potent (examples will be discussed later). The question to what degree belief in propositions that claim reliability or trustworthiness with respect to basic methods of belief formation can be justified in general can be left open here, as any positive answer would amount to a refutation of skepticism, which would be unrealistic to attempt here. Sometimes we have additional support for the relevant higher-order beliefs (for example, when the lower-order attitude is based on a controlled experiment) and sometimes we must rely on whatever makes it legitimate to rely on certain basic ways of forming attitudes. The view proposed here merely requires that this "whatever" is such that it can be the content of a rebuttable higher-order belief.

Now it can be shown how this mechanic relates to some of the basic questions I aim to answer. What I set out to explain was, among other things, why holding on to a defeated attitude amounts to holding on to an *un*justified attitude. Fortunately, explaining undercutting defeat via re-evaluation has all the resources required to do so.

First of all, let us plausibly assume that, during re-evaluation, the re-evaluated attitude is replaced with an attitude of uncommitted suspension of judgment toward the target-proposition. That is, the target-attitude is temporarily given up while awaiting the results of the process. Presumably, it can then either be *reinstated* or it can be *replaced* with an alternative attitude, in case that is what the results of the re-evaluation demand.[40]

Second, recall that the epistemic status of the attitude that comes out of re-evaluation depends on the epistemic quality of that re-evaluation. Accordingly, $S$ might also have done a bad job in re-evaluating her attitudes, for example because she really wants $p$ to be true and therefore dogmatically disregards B1

---

[40] There may be the third option of simply dropping any attitude toward the target-proposition, depending on one's views on justification and epistemic normativity. This depends on the theory of justification in the background and will be discussed in chapter 5.

## 3.4 The Rebasing Account

and B2 (which together indicate that her justifier $j$ doesn't support her belief that $p$). In that case, $S$ is likely to end up sticking to the belief that $p$ in alignment with the conclusion of the argument supporting this, AK, and dismissing BK (the conclusion of the argument disputing it). Given that the re-evaluated belief is rebased from $j$ to the re-evaluation (or its input, depending on whether processes can serve as input), belief in $p$ would be unjustified, since AK rests on an inference from the defeated premise A2 (the supposition that the justifier $j$ supports the belief that $p$) as a result of faulty dogmatism. Thus, due to the informational state $S$ is in, there is no competent re-evaluation of her belief that $p$ open to her that has her continuing to hold that belief.

More generally, holding on to a defeated attitude is unjustified because the defeater brings about an epistemic state where the attitude can only be held on to on the basis of an incompetent re-evaluation or in the face of an unfulfilled requirement to run such a process (more details on this will follow in chapter 5). Note that it is also possible to explain why sticking to an undercut belief is unjustified, *even if the re-evaluation is done competently*. In the unusual case that one has correctly reasoned through the higher-order rebuttal, but simply reinstates the target-attitude anyway, holding the target-attitude is unjustified because it is then rebased to the re-evaluation, which is known to be an unsuitable base for it: One would be aware of the fact that, given one's available input, one cannot justifiedly reinstate the target-attitude but does so anyway. Why this is incompatible with the target-attitude being justified will later be spelled out in terms of different theories of justification.

Is there also a scenario where the subject re-evaluates, but *does* get to justifiedly reinstate her original attitude? There are at least two that can be seen immediately: First, re-evaluations in the *absence* of any defeaters will often permit this. For example, if I want to know why exactly I believe that polar bears live only at the north pole, I may re-evaluate my belief and reinstate it on the basis of my reasonably clear memory of being told so in school or googling it years ago. No weighing of conflicting input need be part of this process. Second, additional higher-order support for the target-attitude can enable its perseverance by strengthening the rebutted higher-order premise to a sufficient degree. This is what happens in THEORY, where Gerrit has independent support for the belief that his data supports his conclusion. During a re-evaluation of his belief, he gets to weigh it against the information about the drug intervention and reasonably come to the conclusion that the available support for the higher-order belief outweighs the conflicting information. As a result, he may reinstate his re-evaluated belief.

Summing up, in a paradigmatic case of undercutting defeat, a re-evaluation of defeater and target-attitude is required, due to the rational conflict the defeater creates. If done competently, this re-evaluation features the rebuttal of a higher-order belief. As a result, the subject can either justifiedly drop the target-attitude on the basis of the re-evaluation process (or its premises) and possibly replace it with an alternative or it can reinstate the target-attitude which is now, due to rebasing, based on an unsuited total doxastic base and thus unjustified. If the re-evaluation is done incompetently, on the other hand, its result will be based on an epistemically bad re-evaluation process that is incapable of conferring justification. Thus, if the subject reinstates the target-attitude in this situation, it will also be unjustified. These results fit the intuitions one has in the relevant cases of undercutting defeat. They also illustrate what it means for an undercutter to *shape the required re-evaluation in a certain way*. The undercutting defeater, via prompting re-evaluation, makes it the case that it is no longer an option to justifiedly stick to the target-attitude and thereby renders that attitude unjustified.

Undercutting defeaters thus turn out to have the following two characteristics:
1) Undercutting defeaters require a re-evaluation of their target-attitude that takes them into account.
2) Undercutting defeaters give a certain shape to a competent re-evaluation of their target-attitude which features the rebuttal of a higher-order belief about the doxastic bases of the target-attitude.

### 3.4.3 Formulating the Unpacked Version Rebasing Account of Undercutting Defeat

It is now time to modify the definitions for defeat and undercutting defeat in a way that incorporates the resources provided by the points made in the previous paragraphs. I will provide the proposed accounts first and then explain their components step by step.

Consider again the first characteristic of undercutting defeaters: Undercutting defeaters require a re-evaluation of their target-attitude that takes them into account. This feature allows a modification to the general analysis of defeat that forms the first component of the Rebasing View:

## 3.4 The Rebasing Account

Def-6:

$d$ is a defeater, iff

1. $d$ is a doxastic attitude or a piece of positive input for a doxastic attitude $A(q)$ about a proposition $q$ for a subject $S$ that is acquired by $S$ at time $t$

2. there is a doxastic attitude about $p$, $B(p)$, that is held by $S$ at $t$-1, such that

    2.1. $B(p)$ is doxastically supported to degree $x$ at $t$-1 and would, if reinstated, be so supported to degree $y$ at $t+2$, such that

        2.1.1. $x > y$ and

        2.1.2. the change from $x$ to $y$ is a result of $S$'s acquiring $d$ at $t$.

The definition of defeat changes in two ways.

First, it states in condition 2.1 that $B(p)$ *would be* supported to a lower degree as a result of acquiring the defeater, *only if it were reinstated*. This is because the definition needs room for my account of undercutting defeat: I assume that the target-attitude is non-committedly suspended during re-evaluation and can only be held unjustifiedly (or to be less well supported) if it is reinstated after re-evaluation. If it is dropped as the result of re-evaluation and thus not rebased, at no point is there an actual lower-order attitude that is unjustified. However, since dropping the target-attitude as a result of acquiring an undercutting defeater would still count as a case of defeat, the account must be able to accommodate it. This is achieved through the counterfactual formulation of 2.1. which is trivially fulfilled if the target-attitude is reinstated and substantially fulfilled if it is dropped.[41] Either way, 2. will be able to properly describe the effect of the defeater on the epistemic status of the target-attitude. Note that this accommodates an understanding of "rendering the target-attitude unjustified", at least for undercutting defeaters, that is somewhat unconventional. It does not work under the assumption that a defeater somehow *destroys* the justification of its target-attitude, but states that a defeater challenges (see Janvid 2017, p. 705) and thus "de-

---

[41] I am assuming here, following Lewis (1973, ch. 1.7), that counterfactuals can be fulfilled by the actual world. Should this assumption turn out to be unwarranted, I propose a reformulation in terms of dispositions, such that obtaining a defeater creates a disposition to reinstate the defeated attitude in an unjustified manner, with the reinstatement as a trigger-condition (for an overview over the mechanics of dispositions, see Choi and Fara 2018).

bases" an attitude and then *prevents* it from being justifiably reinstated.[42] This conception of a defeater's effect is a view that I want to defend, not only for undercutting defeaters but also, as I will motivate in the next chapter, for rebutting defeaters.

The second change concerns the point in time at which the target-attitude would be rendered unjustified by the defeater. It is now farther in the future (it was moved from $t$ to $t+2$ in condition 2.1). This is because, on the Rebasing View, undercutting defeaters defeat via an *intermediate step* of higher-order rebuttal during re-evaluation. Due to the fact that the higher-order belief that is rebutted must first be formed in the course of the reasoning process, this intermediate step must lie between acquiring the defeater and enacting the result of the re-evaluation (e.g. reinstating the target-attitude). To model this, a slightly larger time interval is needed.

With these modifications in place, the remainder of the Rebasing Account of Undercutting Defeat can now be formulated in terms of a conjunction of four conditions. I will first present the long, unpacked version of the analysis. To make it more accessible, I will go through it step by step and illustrate each step along the lines of the already familiar red-widgets case that involves a subject $S$ having an experience of red widgets on a production line. $S$ then hears from a reliable source that the widgets are illuminated by a red light. Keep in mind that all four conditions are meant to be connected by a conjunction and together give a full analysis of undercutting defeat:

Undercut-3:

$d$ is an undercutting defeater, iff

1. $d$ is a defeater:

    1.1. $d$ is a doxastic attitude or a piece of positive input for a doxastic attitude $A(q)$ about a proposition $q$ for a subject $S$ that is acquired by $S$ at time $t$

    1.2. there is a doxastic attitude about $p$, $B(p)$, that is held by $S$ at $t$-1, such that

    1.2.1. $B(p)$ is doxastically supported to degree $x$ at $t$-1 and would, if reinstated, be doxastically supported to degree $y$ at $t+3$, such that

---

[42] One can say that a defeater "preempts" its target-attitude being justified in the sense explicated by Constantin and Grundmann (2020).

1.2.1.1. $x > y$ and

1.2.1.2. the change from $x$ to $y$ is a result of $S$'s acquiring $d$ at $t$

*Condition 1.* is the by now familiar first condition that an undercutting defeater is also a defeater, because it constitutes a subclass. In the case of the red widgets, the information about the red lights acts in the role of $d$ and targets $S$'s belief that the widgets are red ($B(p)$). The remaining three conditions further explain why.

2. There is a set of input $j$ for $S$ at $t$-$1$ that $S$ would identify as the total doxastic base of $B(p)$, if $S$ were to competently re-evaluate $B(p)$

*Condition 2.* describes the content of the higher-order belief that the defeater rebuts. Since it specifies $j$ not as the target-attitude's actual justifier, but as the set of input $S$ would (justifiedly) identify as the justifier during a competent re-evaluation, it avoids the problems of the C-based Higher-Order account: $j$ need not be the actual justifier of the target-attitude (which would be part of a commitment's content that arises from actually basing $B(p)$ on $j$) but can be falsely taken to be that justifier on the basis of misleading input, such as in the modified MILK case. This amounts to the claim that undercutting defeaters target *higher-order propositions about the target-attitude's total doxastic base that the subject is propositionally justified to believe*. In the case of the red widgets, it is plausible that $S$ has reason to believe (and thus would believe, if she were to competently re-evaluate her belief about the red widgets) that her visual experience of red widgets is the justifier for her belief that the widgets are red. She would thus identify that experience as her justifier. This step connects the situation created by obtaining the defeater (described in condition 3.) with the higher-order rebuttal effect (described by condition 4.).

3. $A(q)$ is either

    3.1. Suspension of judgment about $q$, where $q$ is identical with $p$

    or

    3.2. Belief that $q$, where $q$ is the proposition that $B(p)$'s total doxastic base, whatever it may be, does not doxastically support $B(p)$ to a degree that is sufficient for justification

*Condition 3.* captures the two types of epistemic situation that obtaining an undercutting defeater produces, wherein re-evaluation becomes required.[43] 3.1 describes the situation where the defeater propositionally supports suspension of judgment about the target-proposition. 3.2 describes the situation in which the new information directly indicates that the target-attitude's doxastic base does not properly support the target-attitude. In combination with Condition 4., Condition 3. cashes out the idea that the higher-order belief targeted by the defeater is made relevant to the target-attitude's justification in virtue of the defeater creating an opportunity for re-evaluation.

In the case of the red widgets, the information about the red lights ($d$) propositionally supports, for $S$, suspension of judgment about the color of the widgets because color perception is the typical way to form color-beliefs for $S$ and the information about the red lights calls into question the epistemic quality of that way. Thus, $S$ is in a situation in which the newly acquired input propositionally supports suspension of judgment, which is captured by 3.1. This is one of the paradigmatic situations that were identified as requiring the subject to (competently) re-evaluate her attitude. Failing to re-evaluate will ideally immediately render the target-belief unjustified. However, this must be cashed out in very different ways by different theories of justification, the description of which must be postponed to chapter 5. Here, we can suppose that refusing or otherwise failing to (competently) re-evaluate when in a situation captured by condition 3. results in a loss of justification. For the red-widgets case, this would straightforwardly explain why the information about the red lights defeats $S$'s belief.

4.    $d$ is a rebutting defeater for $S$'s belief that $j$ doxastically supports $B(p)$ to a degree sufficient for justification, $B(j,s,p)$:

    If $S$ holds $B(j,s,p)$ and $d$ at $t+1$,

    4.1.    $d$ is a defeater for $B(j,s,p)$:

        4.1.1.    $d$ is a doxastic attitude or a piece of positive input for a doxastic attitude $A^*(q^*)$ with respect to a proposition $q^*$ for $S$ that is acquired by $S$ at time $t$

        4.1.2.    $S$ holds $B(j,s,p)$ at $t+1$, such that

            4.1.2.1.    $B(j,s,p)$ is supported to degree $x^*$ at $t+1$ and to degree $y^*$ at $t+2$, such that

---

[43] For conceptions of different ways in which a defeater might challenge the relevant higher-order belief, see Janvid (2017).

| | 4.1.2.1.1. | $x^* > y^*$ and |
|---|---|---|
| | 4.1.2.1.2. | the change from $x^*$ to $y^*$ is a result of $S$'s acquiring $d$ at $t$. |

4.2. Either

    4.2.1. $A^*(q^*)$ is belief that $q^*$ and $q^*$ is the negation of the proposition that $j$ sufficiently supports $B(p)$

or

    4.2.2. $A^*(q^*)$ is suspension of judgment about $q^*$ and $q^*$ is the proposition that $j$ sufficiently supports $B(p)$.

4.3. The input for $A(q)$ is independent of the input for $B(j,s,p)$.

*Condition 4.* specifies the sense in which an undercutting defeater is a potential higher-order rebutting defeater. The target for that rebuttal, $B(j,s,p)$, is the higher-order belief concerning what $S$ has justification to take to be $B(p)$'s total justifier, according to Condition 2.

The extended part of Condition 4. is formulated as a conditional with the antecedent "If $S$ holds $B(j,s,p)$ and $d$ at $t+1$" because $d$ only performs higher-order rebuttal, *if the targeted higher-order belief $B(j,s,p)$ is indeed formed*. If it is not, the relevant re-evaluation is either not performed at all or cannot be competent, which will also result in a loss of justification, as explained above.

The consequent of the extended part then explicates what is meant by an undercutter "prestructuring" re-evaluation. It simply applies the definition of rebutting defeat, Rebut-4, to the relationship between the undercutting defeater, $d$, and the higher-order attitude concerning the target-attitude's justifier, $B(j,s,p)$. All in all, Condition 4. tells us that an undercutting defeater will act as a higher-order rebutting defeater for the belief that $j$ supports the target-attitude, in case that higher-order belief is formed, which is required by the conditions for re-evaluation as given by Condition 3.

In the case of the red widgets, the information about the red light also acts as a potential higher-order rebutting defeater: Say $S$ re-evaluates her belief that the widgets are red in response to registering the incompatibility between her original lower-order belief that the widgets are red and suspension of judgment about the widgets, as propositionally supported by the new information about the red lights (in keeping with the requirement imposed on her in virtue of being in the situation described by 3.1). In the course of this, she forms the higher-order belief that her visual experience of red widgets, which she has identified as the justifier for her belief that the widgets are red, sufficiently supports her belief that the widgets are red ($B(j,s,p)$). Since, clearly, the information about the red lights propositionally supports the higher-order belief that it is *not the case* that her visual experience of red widgets sufficiently supports the belief that the widgets are red, it acts as a rebutting defeater for $S$'s other higher-order belief that her experience sufficiently supports her belief about the widgets' color. This is why it plausibly fulfills the consequent of condition 4. As a result, the only epistemically acceptable way for $S$ to finish her competent re-evaluation is to drop her belief that the widgets are red, as explained in the previous paragraphs. Thus, all things considered, $S$'s epistemic situation is such that all four conditions are fulfilled for the information that a red light illuminates the widgets. It is therefore correctly identified as an undercutting defeater by Undercut-3. In short, the red-light information provides input that supports suspension of judgment about the proposition believed by $S$, and $S$ is thereby in a situation in which she has to re-evaluate and form the higher-order belief that what she identifies as the justifier properly supports that lower-order belief and the input provided by the red-light information rebuts the higher-order belief, which makes it impossible for $S$ to justifiedly hold the lower-order belief.

These four conditions conjunctively make up the long and unpacked version of the Rebasing Account of Undercutting Defeat. Note that it describes the effect of a defeater as temporally extended along the following timeline: At $t\text{-}1$, $S$ justifiedly holds $B(p)$ on the basis of $j$. $S$ is in an epistemic position that would allow her to justifiedly form $B(j,s,p)$, if she were to assess the basis of $B(p)$. At $t$, $S$ obtains $d$. As a result, she is in one of the situations that require her to re-evaluate $B(p)$ at $t+1$, which would have her form or at least consider $B(j,s,p)$ on the basis of the positive input she has for it. $B(j,s,p)$ would then be rebutted by $d$, resulting in its loss of support at $t+2$. Due to the role $B(j,s,p)$ plays in the re-evaluation, that re-evaluation cannot support $B(p)$ to the same degree that $j$ originally did. Accordingly, $B(p)$ must at $t+2$ be much less well supported than at $t\text{-}1$. Of course, this is not to say that all of these events and doxastic changes always actually come to pass when an undercutting defeater is obtained, but, as argued before, due to rebasing, their failure to occur will likewise result in $B(p)$ losing doxastic support. So, Undercut-3 explicitly describes the characteristic effect that an undercutter has on the doxastic and logical structure surrounding its target-attitude, while securing its effect on a broader range.

### 3.4.4 Simplifying the Rebasing Account of Undercutting Defeat

From the outset, Undercut-3 looks complicated. One may recall Undercut-1, where the plausible defining characteristic of an undercutter was its indication that the target-attitude is not properly supported. However, this account provides a richer and more complete explanation of the phenomenon than any previously considered account. Thus, Undercut-3 is complicated because undercutting defeat is complicated (or at least more complicated than rebutting defeat). That said, its complexity does not imply that *suffering* undercutting defeat presupposes a particularly sophisticated cognitive apparatus in the subject. The theoretical reasons why an undercutter renders the target-attitude unjustified might refer to a complex web of relations within the surrounding doxastic structure, but the actual practices of registering incompatibilities and re-evaluating should be commonplace enough to not be overly taxing. However, as will be explained in the next section (3.5) dealing with possible objections, I do hold that, due to the potential cognitive demands of competent re-evaluation, suffering undercutting defeat requires a minimum of cognitive sophistication that might not be possessed by *every* epistemic subject. Those that lack the minimally required cognitive resources might thus be immune to undercutting defeat. However, this stance can be defended well enough.

In the meantime, Undercut-3 can be simplified to ease further discussion. The unpacked version of the Rebasing Account, as formulated in the previous paragraph, is clearly quite long and unwieldy, especially in light of the comparatively simple mechanics it ascribes to undercutters. The following version expresses comparatively simple mechanics ascribed to undercutting defeaters, while omitting extensive repetitions of included definitions and finer structure:

Undercut-3':

$d$ is an undercutting defeater, iff

1. $d$ is a defeater

and

2. There is a set of input $j$ of $S$ at $t\text{-}1$ that $S$ would identify as the total doxastic base of $B(p)$, if $S$ were to competently re-evaluate $B(p)$

and

3. $d$ is either

    3.1. positive input for suspension of judgment about $q$, where $q$ is identical with $p$

    or

3.2. the belief that $q$, where $q$ is the proposition that $B(p)$'s total doxastic base, whatever it may be, does not doxastically support $B(p)$ to a degree that is sufficient for justification

and

4. $d$ is a rebutting defeater for $S$'s belief that $j$ doxastically supports $B(p)$ to a degree sufficient for justification, $B(j,s,p)$.

As a quick reminder as to how these definitions feed into the rebasing/re-evaluation mechanism, we can add:

Rebasing/Re-evaluation and Undercutting:

1. $S$ is required to conduct a re-evaluation, $R(B(p))$, of her doxastic attitude $B(p)$ about proposition $p$, if $S$ obtains a doxastic attitude or a piece of positive input for a doxastic attitude $A(q)$ about a proposition $q$, such that

   1.1. $A(q)$ is suspension of judgment about $q$, where $q$ is identical with $p$ or

   1.2. $A(q)$ is belief that $q$, where $q$ is the proposition that $B(p)$'s total doxastic base, whatever it may be, does not doxastically support $B(p)$ to a degree that is sufficient for justification.

2. If $S$ conducts $R(B(p))$, $B(p)$ is rebased from its original total doxastic base, $j^*$, to $R(B(p))$ or its premises.

This summary states that obtaining an undercutting defeater in the form of a piece of input that questions the target-attitude's justifier is a sufficient condition for the requirement to re-evaluate the target-attitude. This, in turn, results in the rebasing of the target-attitude to the re-evaluation itself or its premises, as explained before. The re-evaluation contains the identification of $j$ as the target-attitude's justifier and the higher-order rebuttal of the associated belief.

Note that, while Undercut-3' is meant to ease reference to the account and to comprehensively express the key insights it is supposed to incorporate, it will be necessary to refer to the unpacked version, Undercut-3, in some of the discussion that follows. In the next paragraph, it will be tested whether the view can account for the central features of undercutting defeat, as unearthed in the discussion of other Higher-Order Accounts and the Suspension view. Since some of these features pertain to the details of the way in which undercutters pre-structure re-evaluation, the explanatory sufficiency of the account must be demonstrated along the lines of the unpacked version.

### 3.4.5 Accounting for the Key Features of Undercutting Defeat

Recall that three key features of undercutting defeat were illustrated during the discussion of the simple Suspension Account of Undercutting Defeat: source-sensitivity, the possibility of being counterbalanced by higher-order support, and a resistance to being weighed against the target-attitude's original justifier. How does Undercut-3 fare with respect to these features?

Let me begin with the phenomenon of *higher-order support*. Since the re-evaluation that forms an integral part of the unpacked explanation behind the account prominently contains higher-order rebuttal, the account can not only accommodate higher-order support, but even give a deep explanation for its protective effects. In the relevant example, THEORY, Gerrit has independent support for the proposition that he evaluated the evidence correctly, which protects his belief in his theory against a potential defeater in the guise of his colleague's testimony. Gerrit's highly competent supervisor has told him that he has done a good job and this is enough to keep him from having to worry about his colleague's assertion that his coffee has been laced with a reason-distorting drug during his work process.

Undercut-3 can explain this: The judgment of Gerrit's supervisor offers support for the higher-order belief that his evidence is sufficiently supportive with respect to his lower-order belief, such that the corresponding higher-order belief, $B(j,s,p)$, that is part of a competent re-evaluation of the target-attitude in light of the new information is not successfully rebutted by the colleague's assertion. The additional higher-order support far outweighs the grounds Gerrit's colleague gives him for doubting the relevant higher-order proposition. Thus, the higher-order support keeps the higher-order rebutter produced by the colleague's testimony from being successful, which would allow Gerrit to stick to his belief after competent re-evaluation.

However, the verdict that there is no defeat in such cases must be amended in light of what was already said about partial undercutting defeat. It is plausible that the colleague's testimony in THEORY, even if it is not sufficient to outweigh it completely, manages to at least partially neutralize the higher-order support offered by Gerrit's supervisor. It therefore counts as a partial higher-order rebutter and thus as a partial undercutting defeater. Even if the supervisor's judgment vastly outweighs the colleague's testimony, it is not implausible that Gerrit has to take it into account and at least become a little less certain. Compare the degree of support that Gerrit's belief in his theory would enjoy after a competent re-evaluation *without* the colleague's testimony to its degree of support *given* the colleague's testimony. It is highly plausible that the re-evaluation would have been more affirmative with respect to belief in the theory, if the colleague hadn't said anything troubling. In that case, Gerrit would have come out with a degree of support for his theory that is the result of an assessment of his reasons, strengthened by the higher-order support offered by his supervisor. In the absence of any contrary information, the resulting belief would have been strengthened to the degree that the higher-order support strengthened the relevant premise. Given the colleague's testimony, the total degree of support is lower, as it should make Gerrit *somewhat* more cautious (to make this effect more visible, we could also envision a case in which the colleague is more competent than Gerrit, but less competent than his supervisor). Undercut-3 captures this, since THEORY also fulfills condition 4. Accordingly, Undercut-3 rules that the colleague's testimony *is* an undercutting defeater, while the implemented theory of rebutting defeat explains why it is a partial one.

Next, let us look at *source-sensitivity*. Recall that undercutting defeaters are source-sensitive, on the subjective reading, in that one only obtains an undercutting defeater, if what one has propositional justification to take to be the bases of one's target-attitude include or otherwise involve the kind of input that the putative defeater calls into question. This was illustrated in a previous section by the MICRO example, where Ewald consciously bases his belief that a certain flower is red not on his red-impression, but on a microscopic analysis of the flower, such that the information that there is a red light shining on the flower in the wild does not undercut his belief.

Undercut-3 captures this feature: Condition 4. requires that an undercutting defeater be a rebutting defeater for belief in a higher-order proposition that is about the target-attitude's (presumed) total doxastic base, $j$. If Ewald were to competently re-evaluate his belief that the flower is red, he would not think that it was based on a red impression in the wild, since, having intentionally used a microscope, he is propositionally justified to believe that it is based on the microscopic examination, but not on a red-impression in the wild. A good assessment of the basis would therefore feature the former, rather than the latter.[44] Accordingly, the competent re-evaluation would not feature a higher-order premise in the belief-chain that the defeater can rebut, given that it does not concern microscopes, but color-impressions (and so, no propositional incompatibility can be detected). In fact, if Ewald, during re-evaluation, comes to believe that his belief is based on the microscopic examination, he will instead have *a rebut-*

---

[44] Of course, if Ewald had strong, misleading input indicating that his belief is, in fact, based on a visual impression of the flower in the wild, the defeater would indeed undercut his belief about the flower's colour. This is a corollary of the subjective reading of source-sensitivity and it gives the intuitively correct verdict, showing the subjective reading is superior to the objective reading.

*ter for the premise in the defeater-chain* which states that Ewald's belief is based on a red-impression in the wild, resulting in a collapse of the defeater-chain and a full reinstatement of the target-attitude on the basis of the re-evaluation, which is the intuitively correct result. Thus, MICRO fails Condition 4. and Undercut-3 therefore correctly rules that the new information is not an undercutting defeater, because it is not a rebutting defeater for belief in the corresponding higher-order proposition.

There is a second important observation that is connected with source-sensitivity. It allows undercutting defeaters to be partial defeaters in a special way that is different from the way in which rebutting defeaters can be partial. Undercutting defeaters are source-sensitive because the defeater can only successfully rebut higher-order beliefs that have the right content, namely, that are about the input that the subject competently assesses as bases of the target-attitude. Therefore, it can sever the support of some, but not all of a target-attitude's doxastic bases, merely lowering its degree of doxastic justification. Consider cases in which an attitude is based on more than one piece of input. Assume that subject $S$ believes that $p$ on the basis of two pieces of input, $j$ and $j^*$, where $j \neq j^*$ and where both $j$ and $j^*$ individually offer enough doxastic support for the belief that $p$ for that belief to be justified. $S$ then obtains a new piece of information, $d$, that fulfils Undercut-3 for $j$, i.e. it requires re-evaluation of the belief that $p$ and constitutes a (let us say successful) higher-order rebutter against the belief that $j$ sufficiently supports $S$'s belief that $p$. In that case, it counts as an undercutting defeater for the belief that $p$, *even though that belief remains justified* due to the untouched support provided by $j^*$. This is because in the relevant re-evaluation process, the defeater, due to its propositional content, could only ever successfully rebut premises that concern $j$, but not $j^*$. But because it does rebut premises concerning $j$, the defeater nevertheless shapes competent re-evaluation in a way that does not allow the rational reinstatement of the target-attitude with the same degree of confidence. It thus lowers the degree of total doxastic support that the belief enjoys to a degree that corresponds roughly to $j$'s degree of support.[45] At this point, Pollock's talk of defeaters defeating *reasons* (Pollock 1974, p. 42) can be integrated to some extent with the idea that defeaters

---

[45] Note that this effect would only occur if the re-evaluation occurred and were done in a competent way. Otherwise, the defeater would leave a reinstated target-attitude based on an incompetent process, rendering it wholly unjustified. This result is plausible, as it captures both the thought that the subject generally ought to lower her degree of confidence to the relevant degree in this situation, but also that, given that she bungles the whole re-evaluation, she should just withhold altogether. If she re-evaluated competently, she would have to lower her degree of confidence but given that she re-evaluates incompetently, she ought to suspend.

defeat *beliefs* (e.g. Bergmann 2005, p. 422) based on those reasons. An undercutting defeater defeats a reason, in Pollock's sense, in virtue of constituting a rebutter against the higher-order belief that the reason supports the belief based on it and it defeats a belief in virtue of shaping the re-evaluation in a way that makes sticking to the belief (with the same degree of confidence) on the basis of that reason unjustified. Both are true and interrelated.

It should be clear that Undercut-3 also gives the right verdict in the DEVICE-case, which turned out to be a case of rebutting defeat. The reason was that, while the defeater in that case could be *weighed against the original justifier*, undercutting defeaters generally cannot. Recall that Conrad has a device that analyzes available input and reliably tells him what doxastic attitude to take in a given situation. In this one instance, however, it gives a misleading recommendation that defeats a previously formed belief: Conrad believes that whales are mammals, based on a reading of a biology book, but the device recommends suspending judgment on whether whales are mammals. The recommendation renders Conrad's belief unjustified, but does not undercut it.

Like with MICRO, this is because the defeating recommendation of the device fails condition 4. Learning of the device's recommendation may support suspension of judgment and as such even create an opportunity for re-evaluation, but it does not indicate that there is anything wrong with basing attitudes on what Conrad has read in the book. Thus, it does not constitute a higher-order rebutter and therefore not an undercutting defeater. In this context, Undercut-3 helps to understand what is meant in Rebut-4 where it states that a rebutting defeater must be "independent of" the target-attitude's total doxastic base. We can say that two sets of input $j$ and $j^*$ are independent of one another, iff $j$ is neither positive input, nor a defeater for $j^*$ and vice versa. Clearly, then, rebutting defeaters are independent of the target-attitude's bases, while undercutting defeaters are not, given that they constitute higher-order rebutters. This further illustrates the crucial difference between the two types of defeaters.

Finally, there are some points to be made about the account's application to Sturgeon's MILK case. Recall that, roughly, the milk taster believes that the milk is OK on the basis of taste and smell, even though she does not believe that her belief is based on smell, but only on taste. She then learns that her nose is bunged up (see Sturgeon 2014, pp. 114–115). To make things a bit clearer, I will work with the modified variant of the case where the milk taster has obtained justification for believing that smell is irrelevant to judging whether the milk is OK (see Sturgeon 2014, p. 115).

Intuitively (and according to Sturgeon), the milk taster's belief is not undercut by the new information. Undercut-3 gives the same verdict. On the one hand, it can be argued that the information that her nose is bunged up, given all of her other attitudes, including her justified belief that smell is irrelevant to whether the milk is OK, does not require re-evaluation of the target-attitude. The would-be defeater indicates neither that she should generally suspend judgment on the status of the milk, nor that her particular belief is not well based. The case thus fails condition 3. On the other hand, even if re-evaluation were required, the milk taster would not be able to justifiedly identify smell as part of the total doxastic base for her belief, even if she re-evaluated competently. This is because she is justified to believe that smell is irrelevant to judging whether the milk is OK and thus, absent indication to the contrary, that it is not part of her milk-belief's total doxastic base.[46] If she were to competently assess the bases for her belief that the milk is OK, she would therefore also not form the corresponding higher-order belief that this lower-order belief is based on smell. Thus, the case fails condition 4. because it fails condition 2. for the right parts of the total doxastic base. Accordingly, Undercut-3 provides the right results for MILK.

Summing up, one can see that the Rebasing Account shares the explanatory power of the naïve higher-order account of undercutting defeat. It accommodates and explains central characteristics of undercutting defeat in the same way:

Table 2.

| Feature of UD/View | HOUD | Suspension Account | Rebasing Account | Case in point |
| --- | --- | --- | --- | --- |
| *Source-sensitive* | Yes | No | Yes | Micro |
| *Neutralized by higher-order support* | Yes | No | Yes | Theory |
| *Cannot rationally be weighed against justifier* | Yes | No | Yes | Device |

Furthermore, the Rebasing Account accounts for MILK, while being specifically designed to avoid the Demandingness Trilemma that plagues other Higher-Order Accounts. The use of the concept of rebasing in connection to the re-evaluation of doxastic attitudes allows an analysis that accommodates and fully explains the undercutting effect of undercutting defeaters as higher-order rebuttal, which not only reaches explanatory bedrock but also avoids higher-order conditions for justification in general. This is because it contains a mechanism for

---

[46] She can infer this from what she was taught in school, together with the assumption that she is a normal human being and reasonably good at using the right bases.

bringing higher-order attitudes into the picture and making them relevant to the target-attitude's epistemic status.

This concludes the introduction and formulation of the Rebasing Account of Undercutting Defeat. It was derived from general observations about the structure and normative features of the re-evaluation of doxastic attitudes and successfully tested for the right verdicts concerning key features of undercutting defeat. Before combining it with my account of rebutting defeat into a comprehensive picture, a number of objections must be addressed, in the next section. This will also highlight certain theoretical choices we have to make, if we want to give a complete account of the phenomenon. It is likely that my answers will not be satisfactory to representatives of every brand of epistemology. In this context, I will indicate what bullets I intend to bite and outline the cost of not biting them.

## 3.5 Some Objections

### 3.5.1 First Objection: The Rebasing Account Can't Deal with Counterexamples Any Better than its Rivals

Consider again Casullo's objections against the naïve Higher-Order Account. It should be clear that the Rebasing Account can deal with cases like the Unreflective Cognizer (a subject that contingently holds no higher-order attitudes whatsoever), since it does not require the antecedent presence of a higher-order belief in the subject, but rather prompts its formation by requiring re-evaluation. A more interesting question is whether it can also give the right verdict in the case of the Visualist. Here is Casullo's full formulation of that case:

> VISION: Subject $S$ is a normal person who begins with the belief that all her beliefs are based on sight. Let her start out with blocked ears, a desire to know whether there is a dog in her vicinity, and a firm presupposition that all her beliefs are based on sight. She unblocks her ears, it sounds as if there is a dog barking and she comes to believe, on that basis, that there is a dog in the vicinity. She is then told that hearing is unreliable in present circumstances. (Casullo 2016, p. 6)

VISION is a problematic case for the naïve Higher-Order Account because, intuitively, $S$ is unjustified in believing that there is a dog in the vicinity after being told that hearing is unreliable in the circumstances. The naïve Higher-Order Account cannot accommodate this because the subject believes that all her beliefs are based on sight and in that view, her beliefs can only be undercut by information that questions the reliability of sight. Thus, it gives the wrong verdict that $S$

continues to be justified in her dog-belief. Does the Rebasing Account do any better?

The answer depends on whether obtaining the information that hearing is unreliable under the circumstances creates a situation for $S$ that requires her to re-evaluate her belief that there is a dog in the vicinity. Recall that there are two typical kinds of new information, the acquisition of which creates such a situation: Either the information is general and stands in tension with the typical way to get the relevant truths under the circumstances and thereby suggests suspension of judgment, or it is specific and sheds doubt on the quality of the bases of a certain attitude directly and suggests suspension in this way. The information that hearing is currently unreliable is clearly general in character and can thus only belong to the first kind. However, the fact that $S$ believes that all beliefs are based on sight seems to prevent $S$ from operating under any typical assumptions about ways to get at the truth about dogs. If $S$ didn't have that belief, she would, based on her experience as an epistemic agent, likely tacitly assume that all beliefs about the presence of larger animals under her circumstances are based on sight or hearing. If so, the information that hearing is unreliable, together with the auditory impression of a dog, would support suspension of judgment about the presence of dogs and thus put that attitude on $S$'s mental table, so to speak. This would then lead to tension with any belief that there is a dog in the vicinity and thus require re-evaluation.

According to VISION's case description, however, $S$ cannot behave in this way because she is supposed to fully believe that all her beliefs are based on sight. In fact, $S$ will generally behave differently from most of us. Believing that all beliefs, actual and potential, are based on sight amounts to believing that sight is the only available source of input (for beliefs). Such a belief will, as full beliefs do, dispose $S$ to certain behavior. For example, if $S$ really believes that sight is the only source of input, she will be disposed to rub her eyes when she can't quite hear what is said, recommend eye doctors *whenever* someone systematically misses out on certain truths, wear blindfolds to shut out loud noises, be completely baffled by blind people's ability to ever obtain knowledge and touch hot plates with bare hands while looking away. Such a person is also certain to make different assumptions about typical ways to get at the truth and to form and dismiss certain doxastic attitudes in a way that is governed by operating principles that differ from those employed by most of us. Along the same lines, for $S$, the information that hearing is unreliable in VISION indeed does not require re-evaluation because her doxastic system does not contain the background assumptions and operating principles that would combine with it to support suspension of judgment in other epistemic subjects. For someone like $S$ in VISION, the Rebasing Account therefore agrees with the naïve Higher-Order Account and gives the verdict that her belief is not undercut by the new information.

The reason why I don't take this to be much of a problem is that a subject like $S$ that fully believes that all beliefs are based on sight is, contrary to Casullo's statement in the description of the VISION case, decidedly *not* a normal subject. Her higher-order belief disposes her to highly non-standard (from our perspective, even insane) behavior and it should be no surprise to anyone that what is rational for her to believe or do can differ wildly from what is rational for most people to believe or do. Accordingly, it should also come as no surprise that, in VISION, the fact that it is rational for us to re-evaluate and drop the belief about the dog says very little about whether this is also rational for her, given that she has a very strange background belief that massively affects *all* of her epistemic practices. So even if the defender of the Rebasing Account has to grant that there is no defeat in this case, she needn't be overly worried, as genuine intuitions about the epistemic status of someone like $S$ will be very hard to come by, given her overall extreme alienness. Certainly, they will not be clear enough to dismiss an otherwise promising view on undercutting defeat.

There is a weaker reading of some of the details of VISION, which is likely what Casullo has in mind: $S$ believes that all beliefs are based on sight in the sense that she consciously judges that they are so based and *when she thinks about the matter*, she acts and argues accordingly. However, there are also deeply ingrained, recalcitrant and causally active attitudes that stand in tension with this ostensive belief and that are responsible for much of $S$'s non-reflective behavior (and these are what we would consider "normal"). $S$ is then a normal subject in the sense that she, like everyone else, behaves in accordance with tacit assumptions about typical ways to get at certain truths that enable her to function as an epistemic agent. At the same time, she consciously believes that all of her beliefs are based on sight. She can thus be said to hold several, mutually exclusive attitudes about the sources of her beliefs, some consciously and some tacit. In this reading, $S$ can count as an irrational but normal subject, and VISION becomes a more serious case.

Fortunately, in this weaker reading, the Rebasing Account also gains the resources it needs to give the verdict that the information that hearing is unreliable under the circumstances is an undercutting defeater for $S$'s dog-belief: $S$'s tacit assumptions about the sources of her beliefs will be such that she regards hearing and seeing as typical ways to get at the truth about the presence of dogs. The defeater thus stands in tension with them and recommends suspension of judgment, creating a situation in which $S$ is required to re-evaluate the relevant attitudes. A competent re-evaluation will feature the realization that the belief that there is a dog in the vicinity is based on hearing and, consequently, the undercutting of the belief. Were *S* to dogmatically stick to her belief that all beliefs are based on sight, the re-evaluation would be a bad one and the result would be unjustified, which also fits the intuitions about VISION. Of course, *S*'s conflicting attitudes on typical sources of justification already introduce an element of epistemic shortcoming and require re-evaluation themselves. However, both possible outcomes can be accounted for: If *S* rationally ought to give up her tacit background assumptions, she becomes a radically non-normal epistemic subject (as in the strong reading). If she ought to give up her belief that all beliefs are based on vision, those assumptions are in place and allow the Rebasing Account to judge that she suffers undercutting defeat.

Let me sum up. Either: the statement that *S* believes that all beliefs are based on sight in VISION is given a strong reading. In that case, the Rebasing Account cannot accommodate the verdict that it is a case of undercutting defeat, but it doesn't have to because *S* becomes so atypical as an epistemic judgment that it becomes difficult to get clear intuitions from the case. Or: the statement is given a weaker reading, according to which *S* holds her belief that all beliefs are based on sight in addition to tacit, conflicting higher-order attitudes, in which case the intuition is secured, while the Rebasing Account can also give the right verdict. In any case, VISION and cases like it are no problem for the Rebasing Account. Note that the reason for this is the idea that beliefs about the sources of one's attitudes have a hard time replacing the deeply ingrained attitudes toward this matter that we typically have and need to have, in order to function as epistemic subjects. Of course, it is likely possible to construct a case where the re-evaluation-blocking attitude is more plausible and can be given a strong reading without undermining the intuition. In such cases, I am willing to bite the bullet and say that these are not cases of undercutting defeat. I don't take this to be a big bullet, as more plausible blocking attitudes also weaken the intuition that justification is lost.

### 3.5.2 Second Objection: The Rebasing Account Does Not Allow Undercutting Defeat for Unreflective Subjects

Points like Casullo's represent a certain general attitude toward defeaters that can be loosely associated with externalist positions in epistemology. The idea is that whether a new piece of information defeats depends on the *facts*, that is, on the actual doxastic structure surrounding the target-attitude (specifically, its actual doxastic bases), and not on what the subject is justified to believe about this. Sturgeon's position with respect to undercutters, on the other hand, represents a more internalist-flavored approach to the matter, where an undercutter only gets to undercut if the subject registers or has access to its connection to the target-attitude in some way. The MILK-case supports this latter picture by illustrating that the bare facts are not enough to explain undercutting defeat. Further support comes from my argument that accounts that do not feature some form of incompatibility between the defeater and some other attitude do not reach explanatory bedrock.

In spite of seeming friendly to Internalism, the Rebasing Account is supposed to accommodate those results without committing to either internalist or externalist positions in epistemology. It could now be argued, however, that the Rebasing Account is too favorable toward a broadly internalist viewpoint in that it avoids only the most demanding internalist conditions, like higher-order conditions on justification, but nevertheless takes an internalist stance on more moderate but still controversial issues. The foundations of the account appear lopsided in that they are sensitive to relatively sophisticated objections against broadly externalist views but only acknowledge the most fundamental objections against their internalist counterparts. An objection against the Rebasing Account of undercutting defeat may thus run as follows: Since the view posits a number of cognitively demanding background conditions for at least some forms of defeasibility, like assumptions about standard ways to form beliefs in given situations, the capacity to assess and compare the bases of one's doxastic attitudes and the disposition to suspend judgment in cases of incompatibilities, it makes such defeasibility still too cognitively demanding. This worry is especially pressing for undercutting defeat, as it is supposed to feature higher-order beliefs and reasoning. Thus, one may argue that the *mere lack* of sophisticated attitudes on the part of unreflective subjects already poses a problem.

By way of responding to this point, let us look at the following case:

> UNASSUMER: Imagine that a person, call her the "Unassumer", has no beliefs whatsoever about the sources of her beliefs about dogs. This includes background assumptions about typical ways to form dog-beliefs for all common situations. One day, the Unassumer is outside, hears a dog bark and forms the belief that there is a dog in the vicinity on that basis. She then learns from a reliable source that hearing is unreliable in her current circumstances. She is so unassuming about the sources of her beliefs that she makes no connection at all between the new information and her dog-belief.

If it is granted that the Unassumer's dog-belief is initially justified, one can now ask whether the case is plausibly a case of undercutting defeat. If it is, the Rebasing Account cannot accommodate that verdict, since the new information does not stand in tension with any background assumptions about standard ways and thus does not support suspension of judgment for the Unassumer. Accordingly, it also does not create a situation for her that requires re-evaluation.

Several issues with the case and the verdict it is supposed to evoke can be pointed out in response.

First, in standard case descriptions of undercutting defeat, no information about any higher-order attitudes is given. The reason is not necessarily that people usually don't have any, but that it is assumed that the protagonists only have those that any adult epistemic subject is expected to hold. In section 3.3 and in the previous paragraph, I suggested that background assumptions about the ways we typically form certain beliefs are very common and explain a lot about typical epistemic behavior. If this is correct, intuitions about the Unassumer should be reevaluated in light of the degree to which her epistemic life must depart from that of a normal human subject. Having no higher-order attitudes at all may well make her so different from the rest of us that invulnerability to undercutting defeat will not seem as strange as it first appears.

This points to a second issue: Notably, any defeat-intuition about UNASSUMER is much weaker than the intuition in standard cases like LEAVE or Pollock's red widgets case. A plausible explanation is that in standard cases, we feel that the subject *should* make the connection between the new information and the target-attitude, *because we expect them to operate under certain higher-order background assumptions* that the defeater stands in tension with. Once it is made explicit, like in UNASSUMER, that no such background assumptions are in place, this principle cannot systematize the intuition. If there is no tension between cognitive items like doxastic attitudes or assumptions, the only thing that the subject could be obliged to be aware of is a tension between the defeater and some external proposition, e.g. in the form of a commitment, about her actual total doxastic base. But, as I argued, it is very difficult to motivate the thesis that one generally ought to track such commitments and thus, it is hard to see why exactly the Unassumer should make any new connections between defeater and belief. Cases like UNASSUMER are supposed to reopen an explanatory gap by screening off background assumptions and re-evaluation, which are the resources that the Rebasing Account uses to close that gap. However, given the relative weakness of the intuition and the Unassumer's deviation from epistemic normality, the presence of the gap in the case works less against the Rebasing Account than it does against the thesis that undercutting defeat should be possible for subjects who operate under no higher-order assumptions, no matter how basic or broad. The thesis that complete higher-order ignorance protects from undercutting defeat is not so implausible, neither intuitively nor theoretically, that we should refuse to accept it on pains of sacrificing the explanatory power of higher-order conflicts and bite the bullet on cases like MILK, where it is especially natural to assume.

A final point with respect to the Unassumer can be seen to make the case a bit less isolated. There seem to be real-life cases of subjects that make no higher-order assumptions with respect to typical ways of attitude-formation, namely (among others), young children. The issue of young children and other cognitively less sophisticated epistemic subjects will be dealt with in more details in the next paragraph. Still, it will be useful to already unveil the stance I take on the matter: I hold that young children, if they really do not make any silent higher-order assumptions at all, are not cognitively sophisticated enough to be subject to at least some forms of undercutting defeat. Part of the reason for this (though not the whole truth) could be that they haven't been around long enough to develop such assumptions, which would have them miss out on opportunities for epistemic improvement. Since the Unassumer seems to be like a young child in that respect, I also hold that the Unassumer does not suffer undercutting defeat either.

One might think that this stance seems problematic because it "punishes" cognitive sophistication. It appears to imply that less sophisticated agents' doxastic attitudes are less likely to be undercut and thus more often justified and less vulnerable than the attitudes of more sophisticated agents. While a lowered likelihood of undercutting defeat for less sophisticated subjects is indeed a consequence of my view, it does, against appearances, not follow that they also have better justified attitudes in general. A lack of higher-order background assumptions about typical ways to form doxastic attitudes immunizes against undercutting, but, as Grundmann (2009a) shows, it is plausible that it also leaves such subjects without an important tool for calibrating their attitudes to the truth. An advantage of being able to take into account general undercutting information is that it provides additional opportunities for checking the quality of the bases for one's doxastic attitudes and thus increase their adequacy-likelihood. While unsophisticated agents may less often be in situations where new information renders their attitudes unjustified, those attitudes are also less well connected to the truth, precisely because they cannot take such new information into account. A thermometer that shows the temperature and also has a detection mechanism for malfunctions is a better thermometer than one that lacks this detection mechanism, even though the latter provides support for a larger total number of justified attitudes throughout its lifespan than the former (because it allows for more justified but false attitudes to be based on its data). Likewise, the Unassumer may end up with a larger total number of justified attitudes than a normal adult subject, but she will also likely have more misleadingly justified and inadequate or false attitudes than a normal adult subject. Furthermore, we may think that the Unassumer can be criticized for just that reason: She *ought* to make higher-order assumptions about typical ways of attitude-formation because she blinds herself to important sources of information that help correct mistakes. Thus, while she cannot be criticized for unjustifiedly believing that there is a dog nearby on the Rebasing Account (since that belief comes out justified), she can still be criticized for epistemic shortcomings, which helps explain the intuition that there is *something* that the Unassumer does wrong.

To sum up: The Rebasing Account cannot account for a verdict about UNASSUMER, according to which the Unassumer's belief that there is a dog nearby is defeated. However, this is not a problem because i) the Unassumer is far from being a normal epistemic subject, which corrupts the intuition; ii) the intuition about the case is far weaker than about paradigmatic cases of undercutting defeat to begin with; and iii) the intuition can be explained by pointing to other epistemic shortcomings of the Unassumer that arise on the Rebasing Account, namely, her lack of access to an important corrective mechanism.

### 3.5.3 Third Objection: The Rebasing Account Does Not Allow Undercutting Defeat for Cognitively Unsophisticated Subjects

As Casullo's objections suggest, an even more pressing worry concerning the demandingness of the Rebasing Account is that its background requirements render cognitively less sophisticated subjects *systematically immune* against undercutting defeaters, which is implausible. One consequence of this is that whether one can be subject to undercutting defeat might depend on purely contingent facts about one's cognitive capacities and behavior and is thus to some extent arbitrary.

The idea behind criticisms of this kind is that even theoretically more complicated kinds of defeat, like undercutting defeat, should be easy to come by and that susceptibility to them is a hallmark of any epistemic subject. The Rebasing Account, however, conceives of undercutting defeat in a way that 1) makes higher-order background assumptions a condition for the possibility of undercutting defeat from general information, and 2) also requires a subject to have at least the capacity to reflect and re-evaluate doxastic attitudes in order for that subject to be vulnerable to undercutting defeat. Points like Casullo's suggest that the Rebasing Account therefore cannot be an adequate account, since it is obviously not the case that all epistemic agents meet its requirements for undercutter-vulnerability.

A particularly clear example are young children (this is thoroughly discussed with respect to defeat and testimony in Lackey 2008, pp. 195–220). It is plausible to assume that young children often do not operate under background assumptions about typical ways to get at the truth with respect to certain propositions in certain situations. This is because such assumptions presumably form gradually as a result of the exercise of different ways of attitude-formation. Young children have had much less opportunity than adults to exercise their attitude-formation methods. It may also be true that some higher-order propositions are too abstract for children to properly grasp, even implicitly (cf. Lackey 2008, p. 204) and slowly become available as their cognitive system matures. Note that the absence of *assumptions about typical ways of forming attitudes* should not mean that children cannot have higher-order attitudes at all. After all, it should at least be treated as a possibility that young children may have access to higher-order attitudes through simple introspection. If they do, they will turn out to be possible victims of undercutting defeat on the Rebasing Account with regards to their introspectively examined attitudes (at least if their access is sophisticated enough to allow for higher-order rebuttal). Whatever the exact nature and extent of available higher-order access, young children will *generally* turn out to be less vulnerable to undercutting defeat than adults in proportion to the degree to which they form fewer and less sophisticated higher-order attitudes. The mechanics behind this should be clear enough by now. Young children tend to fail condition 1) to the same degree to which they lack higher-order attitudes expected from adults. As for condition 2), it is plausible that young children are often unable to draw proper inferences from and to relatively abstract propositions. Specifically, it seems as though they are not well equipped to perform competent re-evaluations of their doxastic attitudes, especially when those re-evaluations contain higher-order premises (in simpler cases of rebutting defeat, for example, young children may well be able to re-evaluate competently). Accordingly, one could make the argument that a defeater cannot require young children to re-evaluate in cases where they can't fulfill this requirement, i.e., cases of undercutting defeat. They thus seem to fail condition 2). For these reasons, it seems that young children are invulnerable to undercutting defeat on the Rebasing Account.

Furthermore, the view presents a lopsided picture of epistemic support relations in the following way: It is extremely plausible that children can have knowledge and thus epistemic justification from various sources (e.g. Alston 1989a, p. 164; Moser 1991, p. 158; Burge 2003, pp. 503–504). On the Rebasing Account, this can be accepted, but it must be denied that young children, while able to *obtain* justification just like adults, cannot *lose* justification just like adults. This seems like an arbitrary asymmetry.

If it is really plausible that young children can suffer undercutting defeat, this is a bullet I intend to bite. I hold that only subjects that have reached a certain level of cognitive sophistication, which allows for higher-order attitudes and re-evaluation and which contains background assumptions about typical ways to form doxastic attitudes, are vulnerable to undercutting defeat. First, just because some epistemic phenomena, like justification or even knowledge, can be found in less sophisticated subjects, it doesn't follow that all of them can.[47] It is quite plausible that an epistemic subject's opportunities, responsibilities and sources of doubt expand as she matures. It should really not be that surprising that increasing cognitive capabilities go hand in hand with the development of more complex epistemic connections and behavior. So, the bullet I want to bite should not be a hard pill to swallow at all.

Second, the thesis that all epistemic subjects should be vulnerable to undercutting defeat is not well motivated. It presumably either rests on certain intuitions or on the thought that it would be strange to think of cognitively less sophisticated subjects as possessing a significant epistemic advantage in being immune to undercutters. If it is an intuition that does the work here, it should be far from clear what intuition this is supposed to be, exactly, and whether it is strong enough to establish undercutting defeat for young children. In the case of undercutting defeat, I find it plausible that we should only take the doxastic attitudes of young children to be undercuttable insofar as we hold them responsible for the bases they hold them on, and that we should only hold them responsible in this way if we expect them to be at least in principle able to form attitudes toward basing relations and re-evaluate them. Maybe rudimentary abilities to this effect are possessed at a younger age than those worried about cognitive demandingness suspect. If so, this fact can explain the intuitions behind the worry. But even if this is not so, the strength of such intuitions is dubious. Take, for instance, a three-year-old who is barely able to understand moderately complex sentences. The child sees a red surface and forms the justified belief that there is a red surface in front of her. Now, her mother *falsely* tells her that there is a red light behind her. Stipulate that the three-year-old is utterly incapable of making the connection between this new piece of information and her red-belief. Is it really plausible to say that the child is now no longer justified in believing that the surface is red (cf. Lackey 2008, pp. 204–207)? Note that all the explanations that come to mind in cases of adults don't work here: We don't expect the child to make the connection, there is no substantive sense in which the child is behaving irresponsibly and it is at least odd to say that the child *ought* to see that there is something wrong with her belief. One reason for this is that it is not just a certain higher-order attitude that is *absent* in the picture, like in UN-ASSUMER, but in this example, the subject is completely *incapable of forming one*

---

[47] In this I agree with Thomas Raleigh who argued that cognitive sophistication is required in order to form an attitude of suspension of judgment at the European Epistemology Network Meeting 2016 in Paris.

in the first place. So, intuitions about young children in cases of putative undercutting defeat should not move us overly much.

What about the epistemic advantage that immunity to undercutting defeat seems to give young children? As I already explained in the discussion of UNASSUMER, there are numerous things to say about the child's epistemic setup that tell us why not being vulnerable to undercutting defeaters is not an overall epistemic advantage. So, there is little theoretical reason to insist on undercutting defeaters for young children. It seems, then, that the thesis that every epistemic subject, including cognitively less sophisticated ones, must potentially be subject to undercutting defeat is undermotivated.

The price to pay for accepting the Rebasing Account, if one considers it a price, is the vulnerability of cognitively less sophisticated subjects to at least undercutting defeat. If one is unwilling to pay it, however, I hope that what I have said in this section shifts the burden of proof, so that it now rests on the proponent of the vulnerability-thesis. It should have become clear that satisfactorily explaining defeat is not as easy as it seems and, given the number of examples and theoretical considerations discussed in this book so far, pretty much everything, including the defeasibility of child-beliefs, is fair game. There is no reason to think that subjects that lack any higher-order attitudes and cannot re-evaluate must behave in the exact same way in the face of defeat as other subjects do. This section also concludes the development of the Rebasing Account of Undercutting Defeat. It has come a long way and a large number of issues have been discussed in connection with it. This has brought up a number of interesting questions with respect to defeat that reveal its complexity. Due to the order of discussion, some of these questions have been asked of accounts of undercutting defeat, but not of rebutting defeat. In the next chapter, this will be rectified and the final versions of my accounts of defeat in general, rebutting defeat, and undercutting defeat will be formulated.

# 4 Putting Things Together

In this section, I want to make the picture presented so far more comprehensive. A question that arises from the discussion of undercutting defeat is how it relates to rebutting defeat. For example, a pivotal point in the analysis of undercutting defeat was that obtaining an undercutting defeater constitutes a situation in which re-evaluation is required because it introduces tension within the subject's noetic system. Shouldn't obtaining rebutting defeaters do the exact same thing? But if it does, why is re-evaluation so important to undercutting defeat, while rebutting defeat seems to be perfectly explicable without it?

In this section, I will argue that this impression is misleading. The account of rebutting defeat presented in chapter 2 can and should be adapted to the re-evaluation framework, producing a Rebasing Account of Rebutting Defeat. Such an account will be much more flexible and will open up a whole new range of interesting phenomena that can be explained. The second goal for this chapter is to take a second step back and position the Rebasing Account among general pictures of defeat: the Causal View, the Reason-Neutralizing View and the Reasons-Against-Belief View. So far, I have been defending a version of the Causal View, which commits me to respond to general objections against the more general framework. Furthermore, it will be helpful to explore the extent to which the Rebasing Account agrees with other programs, like Loughrist's (2015) Reason-Against-Belief View.[1] This will also touch upon issues concerning theories of justification, which will provide an ideal staging ground for the next chapter.

## 4.1 The Extended Account of Rebutting Defeat

Recall that, in the view of rebutting defeat espoused in chapter 2, a rebutting defeater re-configures the pool of available input in a way that leaves the target-attitude less well propositionally supported. Call this the "Basic Account". Since propositional support does not involve basing, it seems that re-evaluation has nothing worthwhile to add to the Basic Account. Furthermore, one may think that it turns out that rebutting defeat is fundamentally different from undercutting defeat, given that the latter, but not the former, is explained through cognitive processes like re-evaluation. This is not necessarily a problem, as undercutting defeat seems to *characteristically* go beyond propositional support. So, it

---

[1] There are rough proposals for modifications to Pollock's original account that also emphasize the reason-for relation (Chandler 2013; Wheeler 2014).

may not be that surprising that its mechanism is unique. However, there are theoretical reasons that put pressure on this divergence. For instance, the situation one finds oneself in when obtaining a rebutting defeater appears to be sufficiently analogous to the state of tension that obtaining an undercutting defeater generates to motivate the question why re-evaluation would only be required in cases of undercutting defeat.

My response to this will be to understand rebutting defeaters, too, as requiring and pre-structuring re-evaluation processes and thereby targeting doxastic justification, instead of merely affecting the composition of the available input. Call this account the "Extended Account". Keeping in mind that the Extended Account assumes that a situation in which one obtains input for belief in the negation of, or suspension of judgment about, a proposition one believes is a situation in which one suffers epistemic defeat, it can be formulated as follows:

Rebut-5:

$d$ is a rebutting defeater, iff

1. $d$ is a defeater.
2. There is a set of input $j$ of $S$ at $t\text{-}1$ that $S$ would identify as the total doxastic base of (the target-attitude) $B(p)$, if $S$ were to competently re-evaluate $B(p)$.
3. $A(q)$ (the doxastic attitude supported by $d$) is either

    3.1.    the belief that $q$ and $q$ is the negation of $p$

    or

    3.2.    suspension of judgement about $q$ and $q$ is identical with $p$.

4. $S$ is propositionally justified to believe that $d$ is independent of $j$.

Condition 3. describes the situation of doxastic incompatibility created by the defeater in which re-evaluation is required. Condition 4. acknowledges the fact that the Extended Account relocates the rebutting effect to the reasoning-process of re-evaluation, where what is justified for the subject to believe about the total doxastic base of the target-attitude, $j$, and the support offered by $d$ are more important than the actual state of affairs concerning the relationship between $d$ and $j$. After all, it is supposed to play by the rules of (internal) rationality. The rules and characteristics of re-evaluation are then left to capture the weighing and comparing of $d$ with $j$ that a rebutter engenders. This comparison is built into the analysis of rebutting defeat on the Extended Account.

## 4.1 The Extended Account of Rebutting Defeat — 149

Furthermore, since obtaining a rebutting defeater is supposed to require re-evaluation in this picture as well, the Extended Account of rebutting defeat also adds to the conditions of the re-evaluation/rebasing principle:

Rebasing/Re-evaluation and Defeat:

1. $S$ is required (or prompted) to conduct a re-evaluation, $R(B(p))$, of her doxastic attitude $B(p)$ about proposition $p$, if $S$ obtains a doxastic attitude or a piece of positive input for a doxastic attitude $A(q)$ about a proposition $q$, such that

    1.1. $A(q)$ is belief that $q$, where $q$ is the negation of $p$ or

    1.2. $A(q)$ is suspension of judgment about $q$, where $q$ is identical with $p$ or

    1.3. $A(q)$ is belief that $q$, where $q$ is the proposition that $B(p)$'s total doxastic base, whatever it may be, does not doxastically support $B(p)$ to a degree that is sufficient for justification.

2. If $S$ conducts $R(B(p))$, $B(p)$ is rebased from its original total doxastic base, $j^*$, to $R(B(p))$ or its premises.

The sufficient conditions for the requirement to re-evaluate have been added to in the form of 1.1, which describes the characteristic support for the negation of the target-proposition that a rebutting defeater offers. 1.2 already covers the special case of a rebutting defeater supporting suspension of judgment.

Now, how does it relate to the Basic Account? It can be shown that the two have different extensions. Consider the following case:

> IDLE DEFEATER: Joe reviews video games for a living. In a month, the yearly new first-person shooter title will come out and Joe has now obtained justification to believe that it will contain a predatory element that is intended to dupe the customer out of money (e.g. because a developer leaks this information). This is a very strong reason for him to believe that the game will be bad. A few weeks later, however, Joe has not thought about the predatory game element so long that only targeted reflection will make it available for basing beliefs about the game on for him. He is then invited to a test-play session, during which he notices two things in order: First, he sees that the game has brilliant graphics, which makes him tentatively believe that it will be a good game. Second, he notes that the game is horribly balanced, which indicates to Joe that the game will be bad. Joe estimates the influences of graphics and balancing to be roughly equally relevant to the overall quality of the game.

On the face of it, noticing the bad balancing during his test game is a successful rebutting defeater for Joe's belief that the game will be good and this is certainly the verdict Rebut-3 gives. However, it seems to be inappropriate, once we assume that Joe re-evaluates his belief in response to obtaining that defeater. He will, among other things, assess the input that is available to him. Now, the case is set up in a way that reflecting on information regarding the game's quality will make him remember that there will be a predatory element in the game upon release. As a result, *during and after re-evaluation, Joe has a significant piece of input available that he lacks before re-evaluation.* We can therefore say that, in such a case, re-evaluation is *generative* with respect to input.

When re-evaluation is generative, the case verdicts of the Basic Account and the Extended Account must diverge: Assume that combining the information about the predatory element with the information about the unbalanced gameplay results in so much input against the belief that the game will be good (in relation to the input provided by noting the good graphics) that IDLE DEFEATER becomes a case of perfect rebuttal. In that case, a competent re-evaluation for Joe would be one during which all three available pieces of input are combined, such that Joe can justifiably believe that the game will be bad on their collective basis. Since all three pieces of input are only available during re-evaluation and since the information about graphics and balancing alone are fairly well balanced with respect to their support or challenge of the target-attitude, the Basic Account and the Extended Account give different verdicts on this case: On the Basic Account, it is a case of successful rebutting defeat, while, on the Extended Account, it is a case of perfect rebuttal.

I do not wish to argue that either verdict is the intuitive one. But there are good theoretical reasons for preferring the Extended Account. Specifically, the different results transfer nicely to structural differences between propositional and doxastic justification. As already acknowledged, the Basic Account describes a change in the epistemic status of the target-attitude for the subject with respect to propositional justification, depicting a rebutter as changing the configuration of the available input such that it no longer propositionally supports the target-attitude to the same degree as before. Whether or not that input forms the basis of the target-attitude is left open, so that the account is silent on whether and how rebutting defeaters can remove doxastic justification. On the Extended Account, a rebutting defeater, just like an undercutting defeater, requires re-evaluation. Since re-evaluation includes rebasing, this explains how a rebutting defeater can affect doxastic justification: It normally requires the subject to weigh and compare its support with the support of the original justifier and to include it in the premises for re-evaluation, which are part of the new total doxastic base. If that base is less supportive than the original base, defeat has occurred.² Accordingly, any argument that favors doxastic justification over propositional justification with respect to epistemic relevance is an argument that favors the Extended Account over the Basic Account.

It is easy to find cases that suggest that doxastic justification is what "we really care about" when we do Epistemology, like Lehrer's racist-case: Raco is a racist who believes on the basis of his prejudices that people of a certain ethnicity are especially susceptible to a disease. He then becomes a doctor and acquires a lot of excellent medical evidence that this is indeed true. However, he does not employ is new knowledge as the basis for his belief, but continues to hold it on the basis of his prejudices (cf. Lehrer 2000, pp. 196–197). It is intuitively clear that Raco's racist belief is unjustified, which shows that it is natural to think of justification in terms of doxastic justification. It is equally natural to think of rebutting defeat as targeting doxastic justification. Imagine, for example, that subject $S$ justifiably believes that $p$ on the basis of $r$ but $r$ is only a fraction of $S$'s total available input for $p$ and that the rest of that input also propositionally supports belief in $p$. Accordingly, $S$ has more potential justifiers available than she is using. If $S$ then obtains a rebutting defeater for her belief that suffices to counterbalance $r$, but not the large amount of additional positive input $S$ has available, it still seems that giving up the belief in response is at the very least permitted for $S$. This is difficult to explain, if the basing relation is ignored and the focus lies squarely on propositional justification.

Of course, it is not uncontroversial to put such a strong focus on doxastic justification. After all, Evidentialism is a respectable view on epistemic justification that focuses much more on propositional support (cf. e.g. Conee and Feldman 1985; Conee and Feldman 2004b; Conee and Feldman 2008).³ Regardless, there is another reason for preferring the Extended Account: It provides theoretical unity. As shown in the previous chapter, undercutting defeat targets the support relations between a belief and its justifier. Since the notion of *justifier* includes the basing relation, undercutting defeat characteristically does not

---

**2** Depending on one's notion of "availability", it is possible that the Extended Account shows more coextension with the Basic Account than I give it credit for here. If everything that is available is such that the subject can be expected to use it in competent re-evaluation, for example, any attitude that is doxastically justified based on re-evaluation will also be propositionally justified. Cases like IDLE DEFEATER would then also turn out to be incoherent but can be replaced with similar cases that do not involve the kind of shallow forgetting that is at work here. However, I don't want to commit myself to the relevant notions of availability and requirement, especially since doing so leads into epistemically deep waters.
**3** However, such views will have to accept steep commitments if they are to make sense of undercutting defeat, as I will discuss in more detail in the next chapter.

concern propositional, but doxastic justification. In addition, there is little reason to think that *rebutting* defeat, on the other hand, really does characteristically concern propositional justification. At the root of this idea lies the realization that a straightforward aggregation of the defeater with the reasons one has in favor of the target-attitude gives us the results we expect. This aggregation-principle, however, is not exclusive to the Basic Account of Rebutting Defeat. After all, the defeater can be aggregated only with the input that the subject can reasonably identify as the target-attitude's doxastic basis just as well, as the Extended Account suggests. Thus, the fact that rebutting defeaters can be straightforwardly aggregated with and weighed against already possessed input does not favor the Basic Account. Therefore, given that undercutting and rebutting defeaters are supposed to be subclasses of the same kind (defeat), why would one insist that rebutting defeaters target propositional justification? Following the Extended Account in taking them to target doxastic justification puts them into the same box as undercutting defeaters while preserving all the relevant intuitions.

Importantly, this is not to say that rebutting defeaters do not *also* affect propositional justification. It is still true that they reconfigure the pool of available input. The Extended Account does not deny this, but adds a framework that describes the defeater's effect on a relevant portion of that input and that can contain generative components. It is thus extended in the sense that it provides a more versatile theoretical instrument that allows it to cover generative cases and to explain how and why rebutting defeaters manage to affect doxastic justification, which they intuitively clearly do.

## 4.2 A Defense of Causal Accounts of Defeat

It is now time to address a pressing question that was postponed in the first chapter: So far, I have been pursuing the project of formulating an account of defeat, according to which the acquisition of defeaters characteristically results in a loss of justification. This has been dubbed a "causal" account of defeat. I have done little, until now, to establish the sensibility of such a project. Yet, there are alternatives. The most prominent opponent of a causal account of defeat is what can be called a reasons-based, or front-door approach to defeat. In such a view, defeaters are not characterized by their effect, but by what they are reasons for or against.

In what follows, I will first show how and where these two types of account come apart. Relevant cases will be discussed as potential counterexamples to the Rebasing Account I have formulated. Next, I will take a closer look at a reasons-based account of defeat and attempt to show that there is a central kind of case that the Rebasing Account is much better equipped to deal with. Questions of theoretical unity will also be addressed.

These discussions will also highlight why the project of formulating a causal account of defeat has not been defended until this point: First, a viable version of a causal account was needed. It is only with the introduction of the re-evaluation-framework that a causal view like the Rebasing Account gains the resources it needs to address the complications of generative cases. In addition, it is particularly well equipped to handle matters of theoretical unity. Only with a sophisticated causal view in place can the project of causal accounts of defeat be shown to be viable. So, it is only now that this can be undertaken.

### 4.2.1 Attempting to Account for Double-Agent Cases, While Preserving Theoretical Unity

Interestingly, it is precisely the possibility of generative doxastic processes that poses a problem not just to the Rebasing Account, but to causal accounts of defeat in general. Causal accounts characterize defeat through its characteristic effect on the justificatory status of the target-attitude (they lower or remove justification). The problem is that it may not be true that defeaters always lower the degree of justification of their target-attitudes. Timothy Loughrist presents a kind of case that is supposed to establish this and that he calls "double-agent case" (Loughrist 2015, p. 76). Here is an example of such a case:

> DOUBLE-AGENT: Mounira believes that the Chinese invented fireworks because she saw it on the history channel. When she tells her friend Paul, whom she knows to be trustworthy, he remarks: "Don't believe anything you hear on the history channel. They make crazy suggestions about aliens in history. So, they are really unreliable, but the Chinese fireworks thing is true.[4]

In order to bring out the idea behind this case, let us assume that the support that seeing something on the history channel lends to Mounira's belief that the Chinese invented fireworks is *as good as* the support that Paul's claim that the Chinese invented fireworks lends to that belief.[5] The question is then: Is

---

[4] Chandler's (2013) lightswitch-case can be seen as similar, if it is provided that the subject learns of the power-out that cuts the connection between her flipping a lightswitch and the light turning on in the hallway and of the backup generator that powers the light in the event of a power-out at the same time.
[5] If one thinks that, if it is true that the history channel is unreliable, seeing something on it does not provide any support to believing what one sees (i.e., if one thinks that a source

Paul's claim *that the history channel is unreliable, but that the Chinese invented fireworks* a defeater for Mounira's belief *that the Chinese invented fireworks*, given that Mounira retains the same amount of propositional support that her belief had before hearing from Paul?

Loughrist thinks that it is. His reason is essentially that the mechanics behind the effect that Paul's testimony arguably has on the surrounding doxastic structure of Mounira's belief are the same as the one behind paradigmatic cases of defeat (cf. Loughrist 2015, pp. 62–66). There certainly seems to be some truth to that. While Mounira can hold her fireworks-belief after receiving the new information with the same level of justification as before receiving that information, it is not like she can just ignore Paul's testimony. After all, it tells her that the basis for her belief is not sufficiently supportive, while it also offers an alternative basis. So, it prompts Mounira to rebase her belief on the basis that she now has reason to think is better. This is very close to what an undercutting defeater does, except that such a defeater, in paradigmatic cases, does not also offer a new basis for belief, but a new basis for suspension of judgment.

Accordingly, DOUBLE-AGENT is a case in which a subject is presented with new input that requires the rebasing of a previously held attitude by indicating that attitude to be based on an unsuitable set of input, *but* it is also a case in which the subject can reinstate her attitude with the same degree of justification. If the structural analogy to undercutting defeat is sufficient to establish DOUBLE-AGENT as a case of defeat, it is a very troublesome counterexample to causal accounts of defeat. Such accounts define a defeater through its justification-lowering effect, after all, and, in a double-agent case no such lowering takes place.

However, one may argue that the putative defeater in such a case, like Paul's statement "The history channel is unreliable, but the Chinese fireworks thing is true", is actually not to be considered a single epistemic item (i.e., a defeater). In DOUBLE-AGENT, it is plausible that Paul's conjunctive statement contains two items: the conjunct concerning the reliability of the history channel is an undercutting defeater, while the conjunct concerning Chinese fireworks is an additional piece of positive input for Mounira's belief. A defender of a causal account could then evade the counterexample by changing the definition of a defeater so that additional epistemic items are screened off, for example by defining a de-

---

must be objectively OK in some sense in order to provide epistemic support), the case can be configured in a way that still makes it possible to accept this hypothesis. One can assume that a) the history channel is reliable, b) Paul is a reliable testifier and c) in this particular instance, Paul is wrong about the history channel, but right about the Chinese inventing fireworks. This would result in a configuration of the case as a case of misleading undercutting defeat, which is compatible with the externalist requirement.

feater as a new piece of information that, *if it were the only piece of information acquired* at a specific point in time, would lower the degree of justification of the target-attitude. One could then obtain defeaters in addition to further positive input without losing justification, since it is still true that, were the defeater acquired alone, justification *would* be lost. This suggests the following modification to my causal account of defeat:

Def-7:

d is a defeater, iff

1.  d is a doxastic attitude or a piece of positive input for a doxastic attitude $A(q)$ about a proposition $q$ for a subject $S$,

2.  there is a doxastic attitude about $p$, $B(p)$, that is held by $S$ at $t$-$1$, such that, if d and only d were to be acquired by $S$ at time $t$:

    2.1.  $B(p)$ would be doxastically supported to degree $x$ at $t$-$1$ and would, if reinstated, be so supported to degree $y$ at $t+2$, such that

        2.1.1.  $x > y$ and

        2.1.2.  the change from $x$ to $y$ would be a result of $S$'s acquiring d at $t$.

The new counterfactual formulations can be found in condition 2.[6]

Loughrist acknowledges that the question of how to carve up new information into epistemic items arises with respect to double-agent cases but argues, against the dialectical move proposed here. He proposes both that one can have a belief that has a a logical conjunction as its content and that beliefs can be defeaters. Thus, why would the conjunction that is the content of Paul's statement not be able to serve as one item that acts as a defeater? Accordingly, he thinks that restricting the ways of carving up new information in the way done here would be ad hoc (cf. Loughrist 2015, pp. 53–54).

---

[6] Note that a counterfactual twist of course invites the usual troubles with counterexamples from disruptive factors that counterfactual accounts are often beset by (see Shope 1978). I have no solution for these to offer here. My stance is rather that there has to be *some* way of isolating the defeater, such that only it is obtained and nothing else changes, as far as possible. Maybe this can be done by way of ceteris paribus conditions or by relying on the modality of dispositions. Whatever the correct modal modifier turns out to be can be put into the definition instead of the counterfactual I will be using here for simplicity's sake.

The problem with this response is that there are structural differences between the two conjuncts that the defender of the causal account justifiedly wants to pry apart. The two conjuncts in Paul's statement quite clearly play different roles when it comes to the impact that their acceptance has on Mounira's epistemic situation, which can be seen once one considers them in isolation: As already indicated, the defeating conjunct would lower the target-attitude's degree of support. The confirming conjunct, on the other hand, would raise the degree of support. Furthermore, the two conjuncts cannot easily be further dismantled into even smaller epistemic items, since they are expressible in atomic sentences. What this indicates is not, as Loughrist suggests, that defeaters *themselves* can double as pieces of positive input but that defeaters need not be entire beliefs. They can be parts of beliefs in the sense that they can be believed content, where that content does not exhaust the entire content of a full belief.[7] When defeaters occur as smaller parts of a larger package of new information, they may not end up lowering the target-attitude's degree of justification. This, however, does not mean that they are not still best characterized by their typical effect on the justificatory status of that attitude, which is captured by their effect in isolation. After all, only when we observe the behavior of an item in isolation are we able to determine its functional profile, and that profile is what makes something a defeater. Loughrist seems to generally agree with this, as he also relies on functional features to motivate the idea that Paul's statement in DOUBLE-AGENT is a defeater in the first place. So, it is somewhat surprising that he lumps epistemic items that function as positive input and items that function as defeaters together.

Of course, this only establishes that new information that comes in the form of complex propositions and that acts as a double agent can be dealt with by causal accounts. There are other cases of double agency that are more problematic and that arise from the previously discussed potential generativity of re-evaluative reasoning. Consider the following variant of IDLE DEFEATER (the important changes are highlighted):

IDLE EVIDENCE: Joe reviews video games for a living. In a month, the yearly new first-person shooter title will come out and Joe has now obtained justification to believe that *it will have a highly motivating progression system* ($r^I$). This is a good reason for him to believe that *the game will be good* ($p$) and it *is the only input he has to go on* for now. A few weeks later,

---

[7] It seems to me that Loughrist suggests that a belief in a conjunction is not the same thing as two beliefs that are each in a conjunct. Under the assumption that this is true (and I am inclined to accept this), defeaters can be partial beliefs. Otherwise, double-agent cases turn out to be far less convincing than assumed.

however, Joe has not thought about the progression system for so long that only targeted reflection will make it available for him to base doxastic attitudes about the game on it. He is then invited to a test-play session, during which he notices two things in order: First, he sees that the game has brilliant graphics ($r^2$), which makes him tentatively believe that it will be good. Second, he notes that the game is horribly balanced ($r^3$), which indicates to Joe that the game will be bad (*not-p*). Joe estimates the influences of graphics and balancing to be roughly equally relevant to the overall quality of the game.[8]

The candidate for defeater-status in this case is $r^2$. It is the new information that puts the target-attitude (belief that *p*) into question.

First, assume, analogously to the structure in IDLE DEFEATER, that the new information suggesting that the target-belief is false is as weighty as the dormant input suggesting that it is true. That is, $r^1$ supports Joe's belief that *p* to a degree that is equal to the degree to which $r^3$ supports belief in *not-p*. Now, consider what would happen during the re-evaluation that is required by the conflict in Joe's noetic system arising from the combination of his tentative belief that *p* (as a response to acquiring $r^2$) and the belief that *not-p*, which is supported by $r^3$: As stipulated in the example, during a competent re-evaluation Joe would recall that the game will have a motivating progression system ($r^1$), which supports belief that *p*. Since $r^1$ and $r^3$ are equally weighty, their support for and against the belief that *p* is cancelled out. As a result, the only piece of input that remains, all things considered, supportive of the belief that *p* is $r^2$. Since $r^2$ is sufficient to doxastically justify the belief that *p* and since the degree to which it does so remains unchanged from before obtaining $r^3$, Joe can reinstate his belief that *p* after re-evaluation with the same degree of confidence as before. It will turn out to be justified to the same degree that it was before obtaining the putative defeater, $r^2$.

Putting a gloss on this kind of case, we can say that certain generative cases are such that obtaining new information that prompts re-evaluation also

---

8 The case is reminiscent of a case presented by Kvanvig against Plantinga's (1994) view. There, the justifier of the target-attitude contains a piece of input that fully defeats a newly obtained piece of information that would otherwise have defeated the target-attitude (Kvanvig 2007). Kvanvig argues that the new information ought to be identified as a defeater and the relevant part of the justifier as a defeater-defeater. Backdoor-approaches like Plantinga's and – to an extent – mine have difficulties explaining this. Note that the specific problem this case raises for Plantinga's view does not apply to the Rebasing Account: The noetic system to which the defeater requires the subject to move does not contain the target-attitude, which can thus not be unjustified. On the Rebasing Account, defeaters are not defined in terms of entire noetic systems and the relevant effect the defeater and defeater-defeater plausibly have can be located within re-evaluation processes. A defender of the Rebasing Account can then proceed to give the answer I propose in the next paragraph.

prompts the "activation" of additional positive input which then becomes doxastically relevant and counterbalances or undercuts the new information. As a result, the target-attitude does not lose justification. For that reason, Def-7 rules that such a case is not a case of defeat. IDLE EVIDENCE works in a similar fashion as DOUBLE-AGENT is supposed to work, but it is not ruled out by the counterfactual formulation due to the fact that $r^2$, the best candidate for defeater status, is not complex. The potential problem here is that, since the case has many of the hallmarks of a defeat case, such as the inducing of a doxastic incompatibility and a requirement to re-evaluate, one may be tempted to say that it is a case of defeat.[9]

In response, we can first note that the dispute here seems to be a merely verbal one. After all, it is not like a defender of a causal account cannot give an informative description of cases like IDLE EVIDENCE that links them to defeat and that can account for the case's structural features. For example, one could say that the new information in IDLE EVIDENCE is a *potential* rebutting defeater. This labelling would parallel the one used in my earlier discussion concerning the epistemic status of defeaters, where I proposed to call a defeater that is itself defeated a "potential defeater" in an attempt to reserve the term "defeater" for justification-destroying input. A potential defeater could be said to offer propositional support for the negation of the target-proposition; it thus fulfills one of the Rebasing Account's (really any causal account's) most important conditions for identifying rebutting defeaters. It thereby has the potential to be a defeater in that, if no other input is present (or some other antecedent condition), it is disposed to lower the target-attitude's degree of justification. Bergmann's "power defeaters" (Bergmann 2006, p. 155) work in just this fashion: Power defeaters can be present before their target-attitude is present. What makes them related to "newly acquired state" (Bergmann 2006, p. 156) defeaters is that they are disposed to defeat certain attitudes as soon as they are formed.[10] Admittedly, such

---

**9** Loughrist (2015, p. 76) also seems to find this *intuitively* plausible. Since defeat is not a concept that is easily accessible from an everyday-perspective, however, and since I, for one, don't share that intuition, I remain somewhat skeptical of this line of argument.
**10** The kind of defeater that I have been investigating is a somewhat broader version of, in Bergmann's terminology, a "newly acquired state defeater" (Bergmann 2006, p. 156), which is characterized as a newly acquired mental state, like a belief or an experience, that "makes" the target-attitude unjustified (Bergmann 2006, p. 156) or "as a result of which" (Bergmann 2005, p. 422) the target-attitude becomes unjustified. Accordingly, Bergmann also subscribes to a causal view on at least one type of defeater. He also postulates other kinds of defeater, namely "continuing defeaters" and the already mentioned "power defeaters" (Bergmann 2006, p. 155). As seen in the previous section, power defeaters can be seen as equivalent to what I have called "potential defeaters". Continuing defeaters are supposed to be newly acquired defeaters (the

conditionals are tricky constructions (Kvanvig 2007) but note that they do not exhaust the causal defeatist's tools for dealing with the relevant cases. The parallels between the structure of the competent re-evaluations prompted by $r^2$ in IDLE EVIDENCE and by paradigmatic cases of rebutting defeaters, such as overhearing the lawyer in LEAVE, can be diagnosed in any case. If the notion of a potential defeater can be put to use in this fashion, the proponent of a causal account and those that would want to classify IDLE EVIDENCE as a case of defeat merely disagree over what label is appropriate for new pieces of information that act as double agents in generative cases.

Now, somebody like Loughrist would argue that labelling them differently is both a commitment of a causal account and unmotivated because it neglects considerations of *theoretical unity*. Two points can be raised against this contention.

First, theoretical unity is not overlooked in the defeater/potential defeater nomenclature, given that, trivially, every defeater also is a potential defeater. If one were to drop the general definition of a defeater and the first condition of the definitions of rebutting and undercutting defeaters, one would be left with an account that describes only the direction of the epistemic support that the different kinds of defeater provide. A causal defeatist would label this an account of potential defeat. Why not stop there and switch the label to actual defeat? Because the resulting, impoverished account tells us only that rebutting defeaters support suspension of judgment or belief in the negation of the target-proposi-

---

kind of defeater I have been discussing thus far) that continue to render the target-attitude unjustified, in case it is not dropped in response to acquiring the defeater (cf. Bergmann 2006, pp. 157–159). For example, overhearing the lawyer in LEAVE is a newly acquired defeater, but if Mara holds on to her belief that no more leave is due, the memory of overhearing the lawyer continues to make that belief unjustified and is thus a continuing defeater in Bergmann's view. The Rebasing Account's focus on doxastic justification and the mechanics of re-evaluation make the distinction between a newly acquired and a continuing defeater superfluous. Newly acquired defeaters are all that is needed. Once a defeater has lowered the degree of justification of its target-attitude, it stays lowered until further cognitive operations change the composition of the justifier again. After all, the effect of a defeater is taken to be the initiation of a process that rebases the target-attitude and that is incapable of producing a new total doxastic base for the target-attitude that offers the same or a higher degree of epistemic support for that attitude as before acquiring the defeater. Even if the defeater is forgotten afterwards, this effect is not so easily reverted, just as forgetting a piece of positive input that functions as a justifier for one of one's attitudes does not automatically result in that attitude losing justification. Thus, continuing defeaters add nothing to the picture. This may change, however, if one takes the target of defeat to be propositional justification, as Bergmann seems to do. Still, even if a defeater needs to continue to be part of the surrounding doxastic structure on that assumption, it is not so clear why *newly acquired defeaters* should then work in a significantly different manner.

tion (where these conflict with the target-attitude), and that undercutting defeaters support suspension of judgment or belief in the proposition that the target-attitude is not well based. If this were to exhaust what can be said about defeaters, these two types would turn out to have very little in common from a structural standpoint. What unifies them is that they engender a requirement to re-evaluate and the content of the definition of defeat. Thus, according to the Rebasing Account and similar views, when we are interested in structural similarities between defeater-types, we can ask what it would take to turn a potential defeater into an actual one. This does not just provide theoretical unity but is also illuminating when it comes to non-standard cases. For example, in double-agent cases we can recognize the new information as a potential defeater because we can see that subtracting the inactive input or additional content in propositionally complex new information characteristic of such cases will turn a double-agent case into a typical case of defeat. Furthermore, if one is interested in the question under what circumstances one's attitudes may lose justification, causal accounts of defeat will have more to say than other views because the former have to take theories of justification into account to a much greater degree. This may be worthwhile because it seems that loss of justification is very often the relevant area of interest, not just in philosophy, but in everyday life.

Second, behind the appeal to theoretical unity stands the thought that the smaller-scale effects of a putative defeater matter more to its identity than the larger-scale effects it has on the subject's noetic system. This is a tempting thought, but it runs the danger of leaving out crucial features that are hidden in the larger structure. This point ties into a larger argument that can be made in favor of causal accounts like the Rebasing Account. Specifically, I will now give an argument to *prefer* this view over a seemingly more straightforward alternative: Loughrist's Reasons-Against-Belief View.

### 4.2.2 Against the Reasons-Against-Belief Theory of Defeat

So far, I have tried to show that a causal account like the Rebasing Account has the resources to deal even with particularly troublesome double-agent cases that arise from the potential generativity of re-evaluation. Next, I will argue that the production of theoretical unity through an effect-describing condition on defeat, as on a causal account, allows deeper and much more plausible distinctions between defeater-types than a reasons-based view such as Loughrist's is capable of.

To begin with, let us look at the core motivation for preferring a reasons-based view: Stepping temporarily outside of the terminology used thus far, one gets the impression that a defeater, at its core, is merely *a* reason not to hold a certain doxastic attitude on a certain basis, and whether or not this leads to a loss of justification depends on all kinds of other factors, including dormant reasons as in IDLE EVIDENCE. Loughrist takes this idea very seriously, which leads him to formulate his own favored account of defeat as follows:

> The Revised Epistemic Reasons-Against-Belief Theory:
> $S$'s belief that $r$ would be a defeater with respect to $S$'s belief that $q$ if and only if $S$'s belief that $r$ would be an epistemic reason for $S$ to not believe that $q$ on some basis. (Loughrist 2015, p. 88–89)

For ease of access, I will refer to this view with the shorthand "RABT" ("reasons-against-belief theory").

Notably, Loughrist doesn't think it necessary to make a strong distinction between rebutting and undercutting defeaters. In RABT, a new piece of information is an undercutting defeater, in case it is a *source-sensitive* defeater and one holds the target-attitude on the basis of the relevant source. If one holds it on the basis of any other source, the new information does not constitute a reason against the attitude and no defeat occurs. The new information is a rebutting defeater, in case it is *source-neutral* and one holds the target-attitude on the basis of any source whatsoever (cf. Loughrist 2015, p. 86, 87). Thus, the only distinction between rebutting and undercutting defeat turns out to be source-sensitivity/source-neutrality.

The problem is that this completely overlooks the higher-order interactions characteristic of undercutting defeat. For instance, there is nothing in RABT's characterization of an undercutting defeater that prevents the weighing and comparing of the defeater with the original justifier from being legitimate, even though this is prohibited by the nature of *undercutting*. Loughrist is aware of this apparent corollary of his view and points out that some higher-order interaction can still be accounted for. Sticking to his terminology, a reason is "self-promoting", that is, a reason $r$ for belief in $p$ does not just recommend believing that $p$, but believing that *p on the basis of r* (cf. Loughrist 2015, pp. 95–99). A reason is thus taken to contain a higher-order element. A suitable undercutting defeater, $d$, understood as a reason to not believe that $p$ on the basis of $r$ is thus not just a reason against the belief that $p$ but also a reason against the higher-order commitment that $p$ is to be believed on the basis of $r$. It "negatively promotes".

This looks like it captures the higher-order features of undercutting defeat but it can be shown that it ultimately doesn't. It still follows from RABT that, if $r$ is much weightier than $d$, justification for the belief that $p$ is left intact (and only partially lowered). After all, in a case of undercutting defeat one would have one reason to believe that $p$ on the basis of $r$ ($r$ itself) and one reason not to that same thing ($d$). What one is then to believe seems to be a matter of which reason is better. Justification will then still merely be a function of reasons for and against believing (cf. Loughrist 2015, p. 93). But then, the higher-order features of undercutting defeat do not make any difference. Loughrist might have succeeded in enriching his account by stipulating that an undercutting defeater is also a higher-order rebutter, but the thesis that reasons are self-promoting and that undercutters are also first-order reasons keeps the addition from accounting for the functional differences between the two defeater-types. The following case both illustrates this and shows how implausible the implications are:

> FEEBLE: Schliemann is looking for the location of ancient Troy. After a long search with many dead ends, he is now fairly certain that it stood at location $L$ because he has amassed a large body of evidence for this hypothesis: Local legends and ancient accounts were cross-referenced with scientific data, ruins were found and unearthed, modern machinery was used to determine dates etc. The evidence is so overwhelming that Schliemann has started working on an article that boldly claims his success. One night he notices that all of the data he has amassed has been handled by his faithful assistant Larry before Schliemann got to see it himself. Schliemann knows that Larry has been feeling extremely sorry for him after encountering so many dead ends in their search and he has recently learned that Larry is, in fact, in love with him. Schliemann's immediate suspicion that Larry has tempered with the evidence and will continue to do so if left unchecked in order to make him feel better is somewhat confirmed when he finds a historical document among his assistant's possessions that he hasn't seen before.

In this case, it is plausible that Schliemann's belief that Troy stood at location $L$ is undercut and thus rendered unjustified by the realization that Larry appears to have tempered with the evidence.[11] This is the case, even though the justifier for that belief is extremely weighty (a host of archeological evidence), whereas the defeater is only comparatively weakly supported (Larry's love and pity and the single unknown document). Due to the extreme imbalance between the weights of the two pieces of input, any account that holds that undercutting defeaters

---

[11] If one does not find this plausible for this case, it should not be hard to find alternatives. Imagine, for example, that you clearly see a masked robber running from the store, which gives you extremely good reason to believe that the store was robbed. However, this very weighty justifier can be undercut by a comparatively weakly supported defeater, like reading a faded, snow-covered billboard that informs you that dressing up like robbers and faking robberies is a town tradition.

can be weighed against the target-attitude's justifier cannot account for this verdict.

The point can be reinforced: Assume that the evidence of Larry's tempering is misleading and that Larry does his job as he should. Imagine then what would happen if Schliemann did not act on his suspicion but continued to collect further evidence about Troy at location $L$, such that his pool of positive input for his belief that Troy lies at $L$ grows ever larger. Given that he still has some justification to believe that Larry tempers with all of the incoming evidence, it intuitively continues to be illegitimate for Schliemann to rely on that growing body of positive input for his belief that Troy stood at $L$, no matter how large it gets. It would clearly be irrational of Schliemann to one day claim: "Look at all this evidence. I have no idea whether it actually supports my belief but there is so much of it that my belief must be justified." From his perspective, this would be like believing that Troy stood at $L$ on the basis of a great amount of more or less random information that may or may not support the belief or even be on topic. If that were legitimate, we could justify any belief, no matter how crazy, just by gathering heaps of arbitrarily selected input. This is clearly wrong.

This result is hard to avoid if one holds that undercutting defeaters, the very kind of information used to figure out whether a piece of input is supportive or not, can be outweighed by the very input we are having doubts about. In a view like RABT, there must come a point where Schliemann gets to justifiedly believe that Troy stood at $L$ based on his ever-growing pool of evidence, even though he has reason to believe that all of that evidence has been tampered with. If justification is supposed to be a function of reasons for and against belief, the function that would correctly describe what is happening in FEEBLE cannot be structurally too similar to the one that describes what is happening in cases like LEAVE. That is, even if one could produce a weighing-principle that lets the evidence of Larry's tempering counterbalance the collected evidence in FEEBLE, that principle will get all standard cases of rebutting defeat wrong, where the weighing and comparing of input is straightforward. An account of undercutting defeat featuring higher-order rebutting defeat, on the other hand, can easily explain what is happening in FEEBLE, since it would not allow the weighing of the new input against the weighty first-order justifier, but only against the associated higher-order belief, which is typically much less well supported.

Importantly, belief in the higher-order proposition that the justifier supports the target-attitude is *not* supported by the original justifier itself (it is not self-promoting in the relevant sense). In this example, Schliemann's oversight over the archeological procedures, for instance, may give him some reason to believe the higher-order proposition that his evidence supports his belief that Troy lies at $L$. But the evidence itself does not support that higher-order belief and so his belief that Troy lies at $L$ (absent the defeater) can be much better justified than the higher-order belief. Accordingly, obtaining a successful lower-order rebutting defeater is much harder for Schliemann than obtaining a successful higher-order rebutting defeater (an undercutter). This divide between lower- and higher-order epistemic status is both independently plausible and fits the intuitions about FEEBLE. It explains why the further gathering of lower-order evidence has no bearing on the force of the defeater. Opening up this divide is not an option in Loughrist's framework, however. For him, the *only* difference between undercutting and rebutting defeaters is source-sensitivity, that is, the fact that rebutting defeaters tell us not to hold the target-attitude on *any* basis, while undercutting defeaters tell us not to hold it on a *specific* basis. Both defeater-types merely *promote* in the same way that other reasons do, one source-specifically, the other generally. They thus have no special, isolated bearing on the higher level. This is why RABT can capture both kinds of defeater. The problem is that, clearly, promotion must be compatible with the normal way of weighing and comparing reasons in cases of rebutting defeat. Therefore, it must be compatible with doing so in cases of undercutting defeat.

Again, in a case of undercutting defeat one would have one reason to believe that $p$ on the basis of $r$ ($r$ itself), and one reason not to do that same thing ($d$). It is an integral part of Loughrist's account that this should be so, given that all reasons have higher-order components via promotion: A justifier self-promotes and a defeater promotes negatively against it. Their higher-order components interact in the same way as their first-order components do. But FEEBLE shows not only that undercutting defeaters cannot be weighed against other reasons in the normal way, but also that they cannot be weighed against them *at all*. Otherwise, Schliemann will eventually end up justified and that is clearly the wrong verdict. Even if undercutters have weight on the lower level as direct reasons, their higher-order component must go beyond mere source-sensitivity.

What this shows is that the standard of theoretical unity that Loughrist is after is not achievable for rebutting and undercutting defeaters. Source-neutrality or sensitivity is not the only difference between them. As far as I can tell, what they have in common are two broad features: First, they both support the negation of a proposition one believes or has justification to believe (first-level for rebutting defeaters, higher-level for undercutting defeaters). Second, they both at least tend to have an adverse effect on the justificatory status of the target-attitude, be it partial, successful or perfect. Given that a specification of the first feature would be required for a satisfactory account, while also establishing crucial differences between the defeater-types, the second feature is still the best bet for a unifying condition. Furthermore, a reason-based account like RABT cannot easily buy into the framework of higher-order rebuttal for undercutting defeat.

Still, it must be noted that double-agent cases like IDLE EVIDENCE admittedly put pressure on causal accounts and the somewhat gerrymandered concept of a potential defeater is needed to achieve full extensional adequacy. So, there may well be room for improvement and if a Reasons-based Account can implement a deeper distinction between the defeater-types, it will turn out to be a serious contender.

Nevertheless, the result of this section should be a successful defense of the broader project of a causal account with regards to potential counterexamples in the form of double-agent cases. At the same time, it has become clear that such cases are quite relevant to the project and, depending on one's view on my responses, might not have been fully accounted for. As a second result, it was seen that the causal account's rival, a reasons-based account of defeat, has its own set of, potentially more difficult, problems to contend with. Specifically, it encounters difficulties when confronted with the screening-off effect engendered by the higher-order component of undercutting defeat. This is illustrated by cases where additional first-order support from the same undercut source is gathered.

In the last paragraph of this section, I will now state the final version of the Rebasing Account of Undercutting Defeat, before moving on to applying it to broader topics in epistemology.

## 4.3 The Rebasing Account of Undercutting Defeat in its Final Form

It is time to fully state the Rebasing Account of Defeat. For the final version, numerical markers can be removed:

Def:

$d$ is a defeater, iff

1. $d$ is a doxastic attitude or a piece of positive input for a doxastic attitude $A(q)$ about a proposition $q$ for a subject $S$,
2. there is a doxastic attitude about $p$, $B(p)$, that is held by $S$ at $t$-1, such that, if $d$ and only $d$ were to be acquired by $S$ at time $t$:

    2.1. $B(p)$ would be doxastically supported to degree $x$ at $t$-1 and would, if reinstated, be so supported to degree $y$ at $t+2$, such that

    2.1.1. $x > y$ and

    2.1.2.  the change from *x* to *y* would be a result of *S*'s acquiring *d* at *t*.

Rebut:

*d* is a rebutting defeater, iff

1. *d* is a defeater.
2. There is a set of input *j* of *S* at *t-1* that *S* would identify as the total doxastic base of $B(p)$[12], if *S* were to competently re-evaluate $B(p)$.
3. $A(q)$ is either

  3.1.  the belief that *q* and *q* is the negation of *p*

 or

  3.2.  suspension of judgement about *q* and *q* is identical with *p*.

4. *S* is propositionally justified to believe that *d* is independent of *j*.

Undercut':

*d* is an undercutting defeater, iff

1. *d* is a defeater.
2. There is a set of input *j* of *S* at *t-1* that *S* would identify as the total doxastic base of $B(p)$, if *S* were to competently re-evaluate $B(p)$.
3. *d* is either

  3.1.  positive input for suspension of judgment about *q*, where *q* is identical with *p*

 or

  3.2.  the belief that *q*, where *q* is the proposition that $B(p)$'s total doxastic base, whatever it may be, does not doxastically support $B(p)$ to a degree that is sufficient for justification.

---

[12] The target-belief.

4. If there is a belief $B(j,s,p)$ that $j$ doxastically supports $B(p)$ to a degree sufficient for justification which is held by $S$ at $t$, $d$ is a rebutting defeater for $B(j,s,p)$.

Rebasing/Re-evaluation and Defeat:

1. $S$ is required (or prompted) to conduct a re-evaluation, $R(B(p))$, of her doxastic attitude $B(p)$ about proposition $p$, if $S$ obtains a doxastic attitude or a piece of positive input for a doxastic attitude $A(q)$ about a proposition $q$, such that

    1.1. $A(q)$ is belief that $q$, where $p$ is the negation of $p$ or

    1.2. $A(q)$ is suspension of judgment about $q$, where $q$ is identical with $p$ or

    1.3. $A(q)$ is belief that $q$, where $q$ is the proposition that $B(p)$'s total doxastic base, whatever it may be, does not doxastically support $B(p)$ to a degree that is sufficient for justification.

2. If $S$ conducts $R(B(p))$, $B(p)$ is rebased from its original total doxastic base, $j^*$, to $R(B(p))$ or its premises.

The more unified treatment of undercutting and rebutting defeat enabled by the Extended Account of Rebutting Defeat also allows me to elaborate on the "as a result of" locution from Def. Seeing as the account defended here is a causal account, it must be understood in a causal sense: The typical *effect* of the defeater-acquisition is a situation in which re-evaluation of the target-attitude is required and in which a competent re-evaluation will result in either a reinstatement of the target-attitude with a lower degree of justification (and thus possibly a lower degree of belief/disbelief/suspension, depending on whether doxastic attitudes are thought of as graded) or in dropping the target-attitude. This is because the defeater constitutes either a higher-order rebutter or a lower-order rebutter. I will look at the relationship between the defeater and the presumed requirement to re-evaluate in the next chapter.

It is time to sum up the chapter's findings. The Rebasing Account of Defeat has been completed and fully stated. First, it was seen that there is some reason to adapt the re-evaluation framework used in the analysis of undercutting defeat to the phenomenon of rebutting defeat. I therefore adopted the Extensive Account of rebutting defeat. This step resulted in a more comprehensive and interconnected picture of defeat in which a rebutting defeater's modification of available input turned out to be the fundamental mechanism behind both defeater-types. At the same time, the potential generativity of reasoning-processes also opened the door to particularly troublesome double-agent cases, which cast doubt on the more general features of the Rebasing Account, namely, its causal character. This created the need to lend some additional relevance to potential, as opposed to actual defeaters. While this seems to be a bullet to bite, it could also be shown that a causal account's contender, a reasons-based account of defeat, while able to provide somewhat greater theoretical unity, conflates relatively deep distinction between the defeater-types. Specifically, RABT entails that both defeater-types can be weighed against the target-attitude's justifier, which is highly implausible in cases of undercutting defeat. A causal account featuring higher-order rebuttal, on the other hand, crucially avoids the possibility of weighing in cases of undercutting, but not rebutting, defeat. Thus, since causal accounts, unlike their reason-based competitors, can feature higher-order rebuttal as a characteristic of undercutting defeaters without running into the Demandingness Dilemma, they can take structural differences between defeaters more seriously. In the next chapter, I will fill in the details of the Rebasing Account, applying it to different theories of justification. Specifically, I will look at the normative character of defeat and how it may relate to epistemic justification in a range of different views.

# 5 Defeat and Epistemic Justification

According to the view defended thus far, a defeater of either type is a piece of input, the acquisition of which creates an incompatibility in one's noetic system, which puts one in a situation where the target-attitude is to be re-evaluated. Re-evaluation consists of an assessment of the justifier, that is, the total doxastic base, of the target-attitude and a piece of reasoning involving the resulting higher-order beliefs. What shape a competent re-evaluation can take depends on the type of defeater obtained.

In order to fix and simplify language, from this point onward the Rebasing Account will be assessed in terms of the following template case: Subject $S$ holds target-attitude $B(p)$ about proposition $p$ on the basis of justifier $j$ and obtains a (potential) defeater $d$ for $B(p)$. In order to cover partial defeat, $B(p)$ can here be understood as a maximally specific attitude: either as an attitude with a specific degree of justification or as a graded attitude with a specific degree of confidence. A partial defeater then recommends giving up $B(p)$ and replacing it with a similar attitude on a lower level of the relevant scale. Call the re-evaluation of $B(p)$ "$R(B(p))$" and the set of higher-order beliefs involved in it "$HO(B(p))$". The claim so far has been that $d$ defeats $B(p)$ by creating a situation in which $R(B(p))$ is required for $S$ and where $R(B(p))$ must result in dropping $B(p)$, if it is to count as competent.

Until this point, nothing has been said on how the normative terms of *requirement* or *competent* are to be understood. Since defeaters affect justification, this is because it depends on the normative resources a given theory of justification can bring to bear on filling them in. For example, an evidentialist will only be able to accommodate the Rebasing account if she can reasonably say that the evidential norm alone accounts for both the requirement to re-evaluate and the relevant restrictions on its competence.

My first goal in this chapter is to examine and evaluate claims like this and thereby suggest how different theories of justification can fill in the details of the Rebasing Account. As far as they succeed, they can be said to have the conceptual resources to accommodate the phenomenon of defeat.

My second goal concerns unearthing the potential contribution that a given theory of justification, in turn, can make to the explanation of defeat. On a causal account of defeat, it makes very little sense for a theory of justification to straightforwardly make it a condition on justification that the subject have no defeater. This would amount to the claim that a given attitude is not justified because of an epistemic item that causes it not to be justified, which borders on being trivial. It is not the nature of defeat – removing justification – that is of most interest when looking at specific theories of justification, but the theoretical scaffolding that supports the explanation for this nature. This means that by filling in the details of Rebut and Undercut, assuming that these two basic types are exhaustive, as I have argued, we get a full explanation why Def holds. Ideally, a theory of justification completes these accounts of rebutting and undercutting defeat and thereby automatically accounts for the phenomenon of defeat in general. Therefore, the focus of discussion in this context should not lie on Def and, in order to avoid confusing near-trivial consequences, must even screen off the first conditions in Rebut and Undercut, since they reiterate Def. Instead, I want to examine how a theory of justification can connect with what determines the characteristic functional roles of rebutting and undercutting defeat, which is described in the conditions of Rebut and Undercut, excluding the first one.[1]

To make this easier to handle, I will use the following *impoverished* versions of Rebut and Undercut in this chapter:

Rebut$^i$:

$d$ is a rebutting$^i$ defeater, iff

1. There is a set of input $j$ of $S$ at $t$-$1$ that $S$ would identify as the total doxastic base of the target-attitude $B(p)$, if $S$ were to competently re-evaluate $B(p)$.

2. $d$ is either the doxastic attitude $A(q)$, or input that propositionally supports $A(q)$.

3. $A(q)$ is either

    3.1. the belief that $q$ and $q$ is the negation of $p$

    or

    3.2. suspension of judgement about $q$ and $q$ is identical with $p$.

4. $S$ is propositionally justified to believe that $d$ is independent of $j$.

Undercut$^i$:

$d$ is an undercutting$^i$ defeater, iff

---

[1] The defeater-conditions in these accounts are required for the reasons I discussed when looking at double-agent cases, so I cannot just scrap them.

1. There is a set of input $j$ of $S$ at $t\text{-}1$ that $S$ would identify as the total doxastic base of target-attitude $B(p)$, if $S$ were to competently re-evaluate $B(p)$.
2. $d$ is either

    2.1. positive input for suspension of judgment about $q$, where $q$ is identical with $p$

    or

    2.2. the belief that $q$, where $q$ is the proposition that $B(p)$'s total doxastic base, whatever it may be, does not doxastically support $B(p)$ to a degree that is sufficient for justification.

3. If there is a belief $B(j,s,p)$ that $j$ doxastically supports $B(p)$ to a degree sufficient for justification which is held by $S$ at $t$, $d$ is a rebutting$^i$ defeater for $B(j,s,p)$.

Keep in mind that these versions are only intended to make the discussion simpler, even though they get pretty close to the real thing.

Of course, the two goals formulated for this chapter are not separate, but blend with each other. It is still helpful to keep in mind that adapting the Rebasing Account to theories of justification is never just intended to show that the relevant theory can accommodate the view, but also to indicate how it contributes to a full-fledged explanation of defeat. Defeat is not just an addendum or caveat to justification, but its flipside.

The chapter will be structured as follows: First, I will look at a deontologist conception of justification. This will shed light on the normative characteristics of defeat on the account proposed here. Second, I will proceed similarly for an access-internalist take on evidentialism and a basic version of process reliabilism, where these theories are taken to represent (reasonable) opposite endpoints on a range of theories of justification ordered with respect to the degree to which awareness-restrictions are placed on what counts as input. From these restrictions arise different sets of theoretical resources for accommodating defeat and I will investigate why and to what extent these resources suffice with respect to Rebut$^i$ and Undercut$^i$. In the fourth and last part, I will build on these results and discuss the concept of *normative defeat*. I will argue that the putative phenomenon of defeat from *input one should have had*, which is usually associated with this term, is only plausible under specific, highly controversial assumptions. However, the resources of strongly historical theories of justification, like basic process reliabilism, do not seem to be extensive enough to cover the related and much more plausible phenomenon of *input one should have been aware of.* If this is the case, such theories have to treat this phenomenon as an instance of normative defeat and add suitable conditions. In general, since I have used normatively loaded terms like "required" or "accessible" rather freely in the previous chapters, this chapter will lead to some further clarification and expansion of the Rebasing Account of defeat and may even turn out somewhat revisionary, due to the specifics of certain views on justification. These revisions should leave the basic structure of defeaters intact and make sense within the frameworks of the relevant theories.

## 5.1 Defeat and Epistemic Norms

It may seem that the most straightforward approach to defeat starts from the perspective of a deontological conception of justification. In such a picture, whether or not an attitude is justified depends on whether the subject, in holding it, does not fail any of her epistemic *obligations, responsibilities or duties*. I will speak of "obligations" by treating the term as equivalent to "responsibilities" and "duties", as not much hangs on possible differences between these. For my purposes, a generic version of the view will be sufficient:

> Deontological Justification (DJ):
> $S$ is justified in holding $B(p)$, if and only if $S$ holds $B(p)$ while it is not the case that $S$ is obliged to refrain from holding $B(p)$. (cf. Steup 2017)

Keep in mind that, in order to gloss over issues concerning degrees of justification and defeat, I stipulated in the chapter's introduction that $B(p)$ is to be understood as a maximally specific attitude, that is, as an attitude that comes with some marker of degree attached (like a degree of confidence). Let us therefore set these matters aside for the purposes of this section. There is a large number of controversial questions surrounding a view like DJ and the idea of epistemic obligations in general. For the purposes of this book, I will ignore most of them, because they touch upon the general viability of a deontological conception of justification, which is not my subject. I will not attempt to defend or criticize the view on that level, since I am solely interested in the ways it may deal with defeat. Specifically, for this section, I will presuppose that we have sufficient voluntary control over the right parts of our epistemic lives to allow for substantial epistemic obligations.[2] I will further presuppose that it is plausible that

---

[2] This claim is famously debated by Alston (1988) and also e. g. in Feldman (2001). I will remain silent on what the "right parts of our epistemic lives" are. This is because many assume that epis-

fulfilling one's epistemic obligations is necessary and sufficient for epistemic justification.[3] I do not want to fully endorse these claims, but I merely wish to point out that a deontological view of justification can accommodate the Rebasing Account of defeat. Debating the general pros and cons of that view would add nothing to this goal.

Recall that one of the crucial thoughts behind defeat is that holding on to a target-attitude (with the same degree of confidence) in the face of either a rebutting or an undercutting defeater amounts to holding that attitude unjustifiedly. In order to make this work in DJ, there must be an epistemic obligation that is violated when one fails to revise the target-attitude in the presence of such a defeater. This will be an obligation to refrain from holding the target-attitude in circumstances of rebuttal or undercutting. Call this the no-defeater obligation:

No-Defeater Obligation:
$S$ is obliged to refrain from holding $B(p)$, if $S$ has obtained a rebutting$^i$ or an undercutting$^i$ defeater for $B(p)$.

Rebut$^i$ and Undercut$^i$ are then supposed to be plugged in. The No-Defeater Obligation itself is fine in principle. However, it is a very unsatisfactory adaptation of the Rebasing Account in a number of respects: It does nothing to further elaborate Rebut$^i$ and Undercut$^i$ and it glosses over substantial contributions that deontologism could make to the analysis of defeat. To see this, we can look at the foundations of the No-Defeater Obligation: Plausibly, there are obligations that govern the initialization and the process of re-evaluation and which are simpler and more basic than the No-Defeater Obligation. These simpler obligations ground the No-Defeater Obligation. Since the goal then becomes to determine which obligations are suitable to ground Rebut$^i$ and Undercut$^i$ (assuming that accommodating the Rebasing Account is necessary in order to accommodate defeat), the method of choice will be to find basic obligations that regulate those components of the Rebasing Account that must be filled in.

Two types of such basic obligations can be straightforwardly identified: Type 1 obliges to re-evaluate in situations in which $B(p)$ is held together with $d$. It will fix if and in what sense $R(B(p))$ is "required". Type 2 governs the re-evaluation itself and determines whether it contains the violation of general epistemic obligations. It thus explains what it means for a re-evaluation to count as "compe-

---

temic obligations concern doxastic attitudes (e.g. Feldman 2002a), but it has also been claimed that they may be *practices* or *states of affairs* (cf. Alston 1988; Robitzsch, Andrea (née Andrea Kruse) Manuscript).
**3** For an overview over some problems with this assumption, see for example Pappas (2017).

tent". Of course, Type 1 and Type 2 obligations can overlap, possibly coming down to one very general obligation.

### 5.1.1 Type-1 Obligations: Obligations to Re-evaluate

To begin with, Type 1 obligations might be said to oblige to re-evaluate doxastic attitudes in case they conflict with other doxastic attitudes or with attitudes one doesn't hold but is aware of being supported by the available input. These were the types of situation that I identified as getting defeat off the ground. However, it can be seen that an obligation that only demands this will not be much more fundamental than the No-Defeater Obligation itself. A better candidate would be an obligation that obliges one to refrain from holding *conflicting* attitudes. After all, it is doxastic conflict that is supposed to prompt re-evaluation.

Thus, let us consider the following Type 1 obligation:

No-Conflict Obligation:
$S$ is obliged to refrain from holding $B(p)$ together with $A(q)$, where $B(p)$ and $A(q)$ conflict with each other.

What does it take for two attitudes to conflict with each other? This was already answered, at least for the type of conflict that is relevant for defeat: Two attitudes conflict with each other , just in case they have *content that is logically incompatible* or they are *doxastically incompatible*. This comes down to the idea that attitudes are incompatible in case they cannot be rationally held simultaneously, either because doing so would render a noetic system incoherent or because they are by their nature non-cotenable (McFarlane 2007).

The idea behind the No-Conflict Obligation lies close to the heart of defeat, but it is not strong enough to fulfill the role of a Type 1 obligation. It could, for example, be satisfied simply by $S$ refraining from forming the attitude $A(q)$, even though it is supported by a newly acquired piece of input $d$ that acts as a defeater.[4] Thus, if the No-Conflict Obligation were to exhaust the resources that a defender of DJ could bring to bear on the matter of defeat, $S$ could have obtained $d$, but still fail to be obliged to refrain from holding $B(p)$, simply because $S$ dismisses $d$ without ever forming $A(q)$. This would mean that $B(p)$ turns out justified in a case of defeat – an unacceptable result.

Since the issue is that there are cases where one can have obtained a defeater without that defeater being a doxastic attitude, the solution is a Type 1 obli-

---

[4] Recall that, according to Def, input,can itself play the defeater-role.

gation that focuses on input, rather than on the attitudes themselves. The conflict then continues to be relevant because it arises between the attitude held and the attitude best supported by the newly acquired input:

> Negative Updating Obligation:
> S is obliged to refrain from holding $B(p)$ at time $t$, if S acquires a new set of input, $d$ (and only $d$), at $t$, such that $d$ propositionally supports $A(q)$, where $B(p)$ and $A(q)$ conflict with each other.

Clearly, the Negative Updating Obligation describes a special case of a more general obligation that has to do with the general fit between one's attitude and the total input available. Also, it is assumed here that there is an obligation requiring a subject to only hold attitudes that are doxastically supported to a sufficient degree and that must be satisfied for $B(p)$ before $t$ in cases of defeat. However, since the precise way of spelling out these more fundamental parts of a deontological view is not my goal here and can be left to the defender of DJ, the Negative Updating Obligation is a satisfactory candidate for the role of Type 1 obligation. It is sufficiently basic to explain why the No-Defeater Obligation holds and it marks the minimum in terms of conceptual resources that the defender of a deontological view on justification needs in order to account for the first joint in the Rebasing Account of Defeat: Whatever general epistemic obligations are postulated, they should entail the Negative Updating Obligation. Otherwise, it becomes difficult to make sense of defeat in a very fundamental way, given that all the theories of defeat discussed so far agree that defeaters work at least in part by changing the balance of the available input in a negative direction with respect to the target-attitude.

With the Negative Updating Obligation in place as our Type 1 obligation, we can describe in what sense re-evaluation is required in cases of defeat. When one holds $B(p)$ and acquires $d$, one has at least two options, each of which would satisfy the obligation: 1. Competently re-evaluate $B(p)$ in light of $d$, 2. directly drop $B(p)$ (and possibly ignore $d$). Note that these two options have the same result because a competent re-evaluation in a case of defeat will not result in the reinstatement of $B(p)$. The difference is that re-evaluation can result in justified, committed suspension of judgment or some other new attitude that is best supported by the available input, whereas directly giving up $B(p)$ amounts to "opting out" of the epistemic game regarding $p$ altogether.[5] Doing so will result in having

---

5 Further, even more substantive differences arise if we do not interpret $B(p)$ here as a maximally specific attitude. In that case, competent re-evaluation may also result in keeping $B(p)$ with a different degree of justification – a result that is completely precluded by directly dropping $B(p)$.

no attitude at all about *p*, which one may think to be an option that is always open to an epistemic agent. More precisely, the idea behind option 2. is that epistemic obligations can be thought to be *negative*, in the sense that only ever prohibit holding certain doxastic attitudes but never require the subject to do so.⁶

While I certainly do not want to commit myself to the view that epistemic obligations are always negative, I will assume it for the rest of this section, in order to demonstrate that the Rebasing Account can be accommodated by this more demanding framework. If it can, the same should be unproblematic for a framework that includes positive epistemic obligations, because such a view has more normative substance and can straightforwardly contain an obligation to re-evaluate in cases of defeat. Thus, the sense in which re-evaluation is required in response to obtaining a defeater will for now be understood as conditional: If the subject decides to hold any doxastic attitude about the target-proposition, the Negative Updating Obligation obliges her to competently re-evaluate the target-attitude in case she obtains input that propositionally supports an attitude that is incompatible with the target-attitude.

### 5.1.2 Type-2 Obligations: Obligations to Re-evaluate in a Certain Way

It is now time to explain in detail how further epistemic obligations connect different parts of a re-evaluation and how a competent re-evaluation is to be distinguished from an incompetent one. This is where Type 2 obligations come into play. Roughly, a full re-evaluation process consists of three steps, each of which is the subject is obliged to perform (at least conditionally) by a Type 2 obligation. The epistemic quality of the steps (whether they are competently executed) is then a matter of more general criteria for justification and rationality that I will leave to the proponent of DJ to spell out, since she would need to do so in any case. In addition, there is a Type 2 obligation concerning the extent to which re-evaluation is conducted as a process.⁷

To begin with, let us look at this latter, larger-scale Type 2 obligation. If any of the three parts of the full re-evaluation is left out, e.g. due to dogmatism, lack of time or laziness, it cannot provide doxastic justification for committed belief, disbelief or suspension of judgment after rebasing. Imagine that Marla starts to re-evaluate her belief that Frank is due no more leave. She assesses the original

---

6 For a position that claims that all epistemic obligations are negative, see Nelson 2010.
7 Naturally, these Type 2 obligations are not meant to be basic obligations. They, too, must be derivable from more fundamental epistemic norms.

justifier she holds this belief on and is about to evaluate it in light of the defeater. However, at that moment a police officer enters her office and hurries her outside because of a bomb threat, leaving the third step untouched. In that situation, re-instating the belief that Frank is due no more leave or forming any other kind of attitude on this matter would clearly not be justified for Marla, because the re-evaluation process this would be based on is unfinished and thus either it itself is not a supportive basis or it wouldn't allow for proper basing on its premises. Marla is thus stuck with the uncommitted suspension of judgment adopted during re-evaluation. She is not in a position to hold *any* committed doxastic attitude on the matter of Frank's leave and would have to pick the re-evaluation back up or opt out of the issue.

Accordingly, running the *full* re-evaluation is the only way to come to a justified doxastic attitude on the matter in a case of defeat. This gives us the first Type 2 obligation:

> Type 2, the First: S is obliged to refrain from holding a committed doxastic attitude about $p$ based on $R(B(p))$, in case S does not fully run $R(B(p))$.

Keep in mind that holding an attitude about $p$ *on the basis of $R(B(p))$* is the only way of doing so in cases of defeat. This is because, in such cases, the Negative Updating Obligation kicks in and requires either re-evaluation or opting out of the matter completely, which would amount to simply refraining from holding any attitude on the target-proposition at all. Importantly, this includes committed suspension of judgment. Opting out requires one to uncommittedly suspend.

Next, we can turn to the Type 2 obligations that stitch together re-evaluation itself. As already mentioned, the re-evaluation of a doxastic attitude can be seen as, roughly, proceeding in three steps. I will first characterize these steps and formulate informal "guiding questions" for them that make their objectives apparent. These are only for illustration purposes, however. I will use the term "target-attitude" here because I am mostly interested in defeat but, of course, Type 2 obligations govern re-evaluations with other prompts, too.

First, the re-evaluated attitude is uncommittedly suspended and its original justifier is assessed. The guiding question here is: Why did I hold this doxastic attitude on this matter to begin with? The objective of this step is an *assessment* of the target-attitude's original justifier. It is important to remember that the results of this step may or may not be correct and thus may or may not contain the actual justifier. A competent assessment, just like a justified attitude, is not infallible and may lead one astray due to misleading input or performance error.

Second, the connection between the justifier and the target-attitude is confirmed. The guiding question here is: Is my basis for holding my doxastic attitude supportive with respect to that attitude and if so, to what degree? This may be answered by running an inference from the higher-order beliefs about the justifier resulting from the first step to the target-attitude. Alternatively, the connection can be somehow "seen" directly. For a competent re-evaluation, either way must be followed in accordance with general epistemic quality standards.

Third, it is determined, on the basis of the previous steps' results, what type of attitude with what degree of confidence (or some other grading marker) it is suitable to hold on the matter. This step takes into account additional information obtained or so far unused after forming the re-evaluated attitude, most prominently: the defeater. Thus, the third step contains any weighing and comparing of higher- or first-order support that may take place. Again, the comparison of support must be undertaken in accordance with general epistemic standards. As a result, the original attitude may be reinstated or committedly suspended.[8] The guiding question here is: What attitude should I hold on this matter, all things considered?

Next, I will go through each step and try to formulate an obligation to perform this specific step. Since the epistemic operations that make up a given step consist of relatively commonplace formations of attitudes and evaluations of input, competently performing a step amounts to performing it in accordance with general epistemic quality standards.

Recall that the guiding question for the first step of re-evaluation, the assessment of the target-attitude's original justifier, is: Why did I hold this attitude on this matter? The most straightforward way of completing this step is to form higher-order attitudes about the bases of the target-attitude. Let me illustrate this via LEAVE: As a first step in a re-evaluation process, Marla may attempt to recall on what basis she started believing that Frank is due no more leave, remember reading the regulations and, as a result, form the higher-order belief that she holds her belief because she read the regulations. This would constitute an assessment of the target-attitudes original justifier and, assuming that her memory is epistemically fine and no other information is available, also a competent one. A *competent* assessment of the justifier is thus one that aims at identifying the target-attitude's justifier and results in justified higher-order attitudes concerning the identity and possibly quality of the justifier. An *incompetent* assessment is simply a poorly executed process of this kind that results in unjustified higher-order attitudes or none at all. If Marla, for example, is subject to extreme bias when it comes to her own past competence in forming doxastic attitudes, she may let this color her memories and overestimate the force of the original justifier or imagine herself relying on more input than she had in

---

**8** Or possibly the result could be no attitude at all, depending on the details of the case.

## 5.1 Defeat and Epistemic Norms — 179

the past. Thus, whatever an account like DJ deems to be the right conditions on justification determines whether the first step is competently executed.

Of course, the highly explicit and intellectualized description I have used to describe the step here is unlikely to be correct in everyday-cases of re-evaluation. Realistically, Marla's memory will supply her with an impression of the basis of her belief in a direct and hard-wired manner. This impression may well not coalesce into a full belief but remain at the level of cognitive representation and as such find its way into the re-evaluation process, most of which will run subconsciously. In that case, justification for the relevant higher-order attitudes may not be the right concept to determine the quality of the first step. Alternatively, one could then speak of the higher-order representations resulting from a subconscious assessment of the available input in a good or bad manner. Badness and goodness evaluations can be understood as analogous to some of the standards for justification. Spelling out the details here would lead too far afield but I am confident that any theory of justification has the resources to provide them for the weaker concepts of good or bad representation-formations. I will say more on the more realistic description at a later point.

Keeping in mind that assessing the original justifier of the target-attitude involves forming higher-order attitudes (or at least higher-order representations) concerning the target-attitude's doxastic bases, the next Type 2 obligation can be formulated as follows:

Type 2, the Second:
If $S$ is obliged to fully run $R(B(p))$, $S$ is obliged to competently assess $j$.

Notice that Type 2, the Second is also a conditional obligation. Together with the Negative Updating Obligation and Type 2, the First, it entails that a subject is obliged to competently assess the justifier of the target-belief in cases of defeat, if it intends to hold a committed attitude about the target-proposition. This is because the only other option, according to the Negative Updating Obligation, is opting out, and because the assessment of the justifier is part of a full re-evaluation of the target-attitude, which is in turn required by Type 2, the First under these circumstances. Type 2, the Second is also still a negative obligation in a sense, because it permits the subject to refrain from holding any attitude at all on the matter (to opt out). It merely places conditions on what is permitted, if a committed attitude about the target-proposition is the subject's goal.

The question guiding the second step of re-evaluation was: Is my basis for holding this doxastic attitude on this matter supportive with respect to the attitude and if so, to what degree? Let us assume that this question is answered by way of running an inference from the higher-order attitudes that resulted from an assessment of the target-attitude's justifier to the target-attitude. To then answer the question, further higher-order attitudes (or representations) concerning the connection between what one has assessed as the justifier in the first step and the target-attitude must be formed as a further result. For example, having determined her reading the regulations as the target-attitude's justifier, Marla can run an inference from that perceived justifier, together with known a priori and a posteriori epistemic background principles, to the belief that Frank is due no more leave. Success could then prompt the conclusion that her justifier supports her belief (to some degree).

Alternatively, and more realistically in any moderately simple case, she can directly "see" (through the employment of hard-wired cognitive faculties) that her reading the regulations supports her belief and come to the relevant conclusion in this more direct way. Either process can be seen as a *further assessment* that concerns the relation of epistemic support between the result of the previous assessment of the justifier and the target-attitude. Whether the second step has then been conducted competently will, again, depend on whether the inference was valid or the direct uncolored observation and on whether the resulting higher-order attitude concerning lower-order support-relations turns out justified. The Type-2 obligation that requires the execution of the second step looks similar to the previous one:

Type 2, the Third:
If $S$ is obliged to fully run $R(B(p))$ and has assessed $j$, $S$ is obliged to competently assess the epistemic support-relation between the result of her assessment of $j$ and $B(p)$.

The final Type 2 obligation can be found through considering the guiding question of the third step of re-evaluation: What attitude should I hold on this matter, all things considered? Being the natural conclusion to any complete re-evaluation process, the answer to this question is enacted by forming a doxastic attitude on the target-proposition. In a competent execution of the third step, this attitude is typically belief, disbelief or committed suspension of judgment and it is formed as an epistemically adequate (given general standards of justification) response to acquiring the results of the two assessments performed in the previous two steps. One of these would amount to a reinstatement of the target-attitude, which is precluded for a competent re-evaluation in a case of defeat. In the case of Marla, for example, the third step of a competent re-evaluation would presumably be the formation of the belief that Frank *is* due more leave on the basis of her previous realizations that 1) she holds her original belief that he is not due more leave on the basis of having read the regulations (from the first step) and 2) that the lawyer's testimony offers much better support against her belief than her having read the regulations offers in favor of it (from the second step). Reinstating her belief that Frank is due no more leave would amount to performing this final step incompetently in this case because it does not fit the results from the previously performed assessments, due to the nature of the defeater and, again, general epistemic standards. Naturally, a subject that is obliged to run a re-evaluation in full is also obliged to complete it by making up their mind about its results. The relevant final Type 2 obligation can therefore be stated as follows:

> Type 2, the Fourth:
> If $S$ is obliged to fully run $R(B(p))$ and has assessed $j$ and the epistemic support-relation between the result of her assessment of $j$ and $B(p)$, $S$ is obliged to form a doxastic attitude toward $p$ on the basis of her assessment of $j$ and her assessment of the epistemic support-relation between the result of her assessment of $j$ and $B(p)$.

Type 2, the Fourth takes the other Type 2 obligations as its components, which captures the idea of re-evaluation as an interlocking process, instead of a series of independent steps. Taken together, Type 2, the First, Second, Third and Fourth complete my proposal for the epistemic norms that ensure that obtaining defeaters requires full re-evaluations with specific steps. Furthermore, general norms of justification that determine when the formation of the attitudes required by these obligations are epistemically adequate, distinguish the steps of a competent re-evaluation from those of an incompetent one. Taking these normative standards together, we get the following characterization:

> $R(B(p))$ is competent, in case
>
> 1. $S$ conducts $R(B(p))$ in full,
> 2. $S$ comes to hold justified attitudes or otherwise warranted representations concerning $j$,
> 3. $S$ comes to hold justified attitudes or otherwise warranted representations concerning the epistemic support-relation between the result of her assessment of $j$ and $B(p)$ and
> 4. $S$ forms a first-order attitude $B^*(p)$ on the basis of her assessment of $j$ and her assessment of the epistemic support-relation between the result of her assessment of $j$ and $B(p)$, such that $B^*(p)$ is doxastically justified.

This can be put together with the Negative Updating Obligation and Type 2, the First, such that it gives us the result we want: In case $S$ holds $B(p)$ and acquires $d$, $S$ only avoids violating an epistemic obligation either by directly dropping $B(p)$

(satisfying the Negative Updating Obligation) or by running $R(B(p))$ competently (satisfying the Negative Updating Obligation and all Type 2 obligations, conditional on S's decision to re-evaluate instead of opting out). Due to the Exclusive Thesis and the Type 2 obligations governing competent re-evaluation, the latter response will result in $S$ replacing $B(p)$ with some other attitude toward $p$, the exact nature of which depends on the defeater.

The Negative Updating Obligation (or some other, similar obligation related to the No-Conflict Obligation) acts as Type 1 obligation and provides the link between defeat and re-evaluation that Def, Rebut and Undercut need to get off the ground. It fills in the details of what it means that a defeater (as it turns out, *conditionally*) "requires" the subject to re-evaluate in terms of a deontological conception of justification. Furthermore, the Type 2 obligations identified explicate what it means for the defeater to pre-structure re-evaluation and, assuming the plugged-in general standards for justification allow this, account for the structural differences between defeater-types by regulating lower- or higher-order rebuttal. Together, they contribute to a full (deontological) explanation of the phenomenon of epistemic defeat and, since they are in principle derivable from more general obligations, they show how Def, Rebut and Undercut can be accommodated under a deontological framework. Furthermore, since the obligations identified in this section leave open what standards actually hold for epistemic justification, they give one a good idea of the *normative profile* of defeaters. Any theory of justification that can derive these Type 1 and Type 2 obligations from its normative resources can rely on the explanation given here.

## 5.2 Defeat and Internalism

Evidentialism and Reliabilism are two of the more popular theories of epistemic justification currently discussed in philosophy. Where a deontological conception focuses on the normative profile of the term "justified", these two theories attempt to give an account of what justification is in a more language-independent sense. The goal is to characterize a property of true beliefs that at least somewhat qualifies them for knowledge and that accounts for their superior epistemic status (Goldman and Beddor 2016; Kelly 2016).

I will focus here on a relatively pure and decidedly access-internalist version of Evidentialism that contains clear normative elements and contrast it with a staunchly externalist and purely descriptive version of Reliabilism, while keeping both model views as generic as possible. I hope to show that these clear-cut accounts can accommodate Def, Rebut and Undercut straightforwardly, which I take to provide a convincing reason to think that the account of defeat presented in this book will be acceptable to epistemologists of almost any persuasion within the spectrum between the two positions. However, this reason must ultimately come down to circumstantial evidence, which is all I can provide here. Still, it should at least motivate epistemologists to fully spell out accommodations of the Rebasing Account for their favorite views on the spectrum.

### 5.2.1 Introducing a Simple Internalist Picture

The idea behind Evidentialism is quite simple and can be expressed in the following generic account:

> Generic Evidentialism:
> $S$'s doxastic attitude $B(p)$ is justified, just in case $S$'s total evidence, $E$, sufficiently supports $B(p)$. (see Conee 2004, p. 261; Mittag IEP)

On the surface, Generic Evidentialism roughly corresponds to the version of that view championed by Conee and Feldman (2008). However, Generic Evidentialism must be kept easy to swallow for internalists of many stripes. It must be quickly restricted or adapted if required. In order to ensure this, it deviates from Conee and Feldman's view in some substantial features that are revealed in the answers to the following questions: 1. What is evidence and what does having it mean?; 2. What comprises $S$'s total evidence?; 3. What does it mean for one's total evidence to sufficiently support an attitude?

Within the boundaries of an access-internalist picture of Evidentialism, the first question can be answered through the following minimalist account:

> Generic Evidence:
>
> $e$ is a piece of evidence concerning $p$ for $S$, just in case
>
> 1) $e$ is accessible for $S$ by reflection and
>
> 2) $e$ epistemically supports some doxastic attitude about $p$ for $S$.

Thus, for example, one has evidence supporting the belief that the government is trustworthy, if one can recall politicians keeping their pre-election promises in the past. "Accessible by reflection" is taken here to roughly mean that it lies within scope of the subject's abilities to form predominantly true beliefs about $e$ through (normal and effortless) reflection, where this may or may not include conscious observation or memories of experiences. This may serve as a substitute for the idea that evidence has, in some sense, to be mentally "possessed" (Mittag IEP). Note that not much hangs on the exact way of spelling out the internal-accessibility criterion here. Determining what counts as evidence constitutes the first step of an Evidentialist accommodation of Rebut$^j$ and Undercut$^j$. The inclusive term "input" that has been used so far in this book is thereby replaced with the term "evidence". Recall that input was supposed to be whatever the subject has available for basing her doxastic attitudes on. Evidentialism automatically gives a more specific account of input by claiming that only evidence, here characterized as whatever is accessible by reflection, can serve as input. Let me make a number of remarks as to the restrictiveness of Generic Evidence.

The view sketched here allows for external facts to serve as evidence (cf. Gibbons 2006), as long as they are somehow accessible by reflection. An example would be the fact that grass is green, which is accessible through the ability to recall an experience of green grass. In that case, one could say that the *experienced fact* that grass is green counts as evidence for one to believe that it is green. At the same time, a similarly accessible, but non-veridical *mere experience* of pink grass (for example, the result of a trickster's machinations) can also serve as evidence. By design, this conception of evidence is thus quite permissive. Of course, the Evidentialist is free to add further restrictions, such that only accessible internal states, such as beliefs or experiences, can be evidence (Conee and Feldman 2004a) or even that only currently occurrent internal states are evidence (Feldman 2004). However, such further restrictions make no difference to the general way in which Evidentialism can accommodate the view of defeat under consideration, because that view turns on re-evaluation, which in turn depends first and foremost on access. Therefore, the weaker Generic Evidence is preferable for my purposes.[9]

Generic Evidence can be further enriched by constraints derived from the structure of justification. One may, for example, admit as evidence only those accessible states that are "foundational" in the sense of not being in need of support through further evidence themselves, such as external states or experiences (Mittag IEP). In order to preserve a generic or standard form of internalist evidentialism, I will follow Conee and Feldman (2008, pp. 87–88) in assuming that beliefs can be "intermediate" evidence in that they derive their evidential force

---

[9] Of course, one could also hold that evidence is internally located, but need not be accessible. The reason why this purely mentalist kind of view will be omitted here is that it is in many relevant respects more akin to an externalist view of justification than access-internalist variants are. Specifically, the fact that it unqualifiedly locates input on the "inside" makes very little difference to the mechanics of re-evaluation, which turns on the subject assessing the relevant justifier. The reliabilist account of defeat I give in the next section can just as well be applied to such a view.

from foundational evidence. It follows that evidence needs to have some positive epistemic status in order to support, just like defeaters need to have some positive epistemic status in order to defeat. This is a point that will be important in this discussion.

The second question is about what comprises a subject's total evidence. It can be answered fairly quickly, as it corresponds to the ideas on balancing of total available input for incompatible attitudes discussed in the chapter on rebutting defeat. One's total evidence $E$ concerning $p$ is composed of all evidence one has that supports (or defeats) any of the three possible doxastic attitudes one can take toward $p$ (cf. Conee and Feldman 2008, p. 83, 84). Which doxastic attitude $E$ itself supports then depends on the relative balance of all the evidence concerning $p$ contained in it (cf. Conee 2004, p. 269). If the evidence supporting belief is weightier than the evidence supporting disbelief or suspension, $E$ itself supports belief in $p$ to a degree that corresponds to the size and weight of the portion of the evidence supporting belief that is not fully counterbalanced by the evidence supporting an incompatible attitude. Of course, intermediary evidence in the form of beliefs should not be taken to add to the weight and balance of the total evidence over and above the foundational evidence they derive their force from.[10]

The third question must be broken down: One can ask what it means for a subject's total evidence to *sufficiently* support an attitude, or one can ask what it means for it to *support* an attitude in general. So far, I have been assuming that there is some threshold that total epistemic support must cross in order for the supported attitude to count as justified, without further specifying where exactly this threshold lies. Since doing so is a task for any theory of justification, but, given the possibility of partial defeat, not necessarily for a satisfactory account of defeat, I will set this issue aside and continue to assume that some acceptable characterization of the threshold and the notion of sufficient support can be given.

Of more interest for an evidentialist accommodation of defeat is the question what it means for evidence to support an attitude in general. A variety of responses are possible. For example, one can say that the total evidence must objectively make the correctness of the relevant attitude *probable*,[11] that the atti-

---

[10] However, it seems that a rebutter for intermediary evidence can also act as a rebutter for its evidential foundation.
[11] This idea lies at the root of Bayesian confirmation theory. See e.g. Jeffrey 1992, 2004; Horwich 2016.

tude must *seem correct*[12] to the subject, or that the correctness of the attitude must be part of the *best available explanation*[13] for the evidence. This issue, too, need not be settled here, but whatever solution is accepted, its broader features are relevant to the accommodation of defeat.

Let's use the word "Connector" to describe whatever state of affairs connects evidence and target-attitude and makes it so that subject $S$'s total evidence $E$ supports $S$'s attitude $B(p)$.. The Connector can be a seeming, an available explanation, a fact about probabilities or whatever the Evidentialist of the relevant persuasion thinks it is. Depending on the degree to which a given Evidentialist is inclined toward internalism, the Connector will either turn out to be part of the total evidence $E$ or it will be external to $E$. This leads us to the following broad ways of spelling out the concept of evidential support:

*Generic Support 1:* $E$ supports $B(p)$ for $S$, just in case the Connector is included in $E$.

*Generic Support 2:* $E$ supports $B(p)$ for $S$, just in case the Connector exists.

The stoutly internalist Evidentialist I am considering here will opt for Generic Support 1 and hold that the Connector is itself part of the evidence. However, Generic Support 2 will be touched upon when more moderately internalist versions are considered later.

There is one last feature of Generic Evidentialism that must be addressed. In general, Evidentialism is a theory of propositional justification (e.g. McCain 2014, pp. 84–85). Still, it is supposed to have the resources to underpin doxastic justification as well. The idea is that, in addition to being (propositionally) justified, an attitude can also be "well-founded" (e.g. Conee and Feldman 1985, p. 24, 2008, fn. 1; McCain 2014, p. 85, 118). Relying on the broadly causal understanding of basing I have been using so far, this can be understood as follows:

Generic Well-Foundedness:
$S$'s doxastic attitude $B(p)$ is well-founded, just in case
1. $S$'s total evidence, $E$, sufficiently supports $B(p)$ and
2. $B(p)$ is based on $E$.

---

**12** The view that something like an evidential seeming is what justifies doxastic attitudes is called *Phenomenal Conservatism* (e.g. Huemer 2001, 2007).
**13** See Conee and Feldman 2008, 2011.

With these generic Evidentialist notions in place, we can now have a look at the Evidentialist's options for accommodating the Rebasing Account of Epistemic Defeat.

### 5.2.2 An Internalist Accommodation of Epistemic Defeat

It is tempting to think that Generic Evidentialism can accommodate defeat without reference to re-evaluation or rebasing, since the notion of total evidence has a weighing and balancing mechanism already built-in. Pollock's original account is intended to make use of this.

Starting with rebutting defeat, the idea is that the original total evidence $E^*$, that is, the total evidence possessed by the subject before obtaining the defeater, together with the defeater $d$, no longer sufficiently supports the target-attitude $B(p)$. Given Generic Support, this must come down to the thesis that the presence of a rebutting defeater neutralizes the Connector (to some extent) because the new set of total evidence $E$, which includes $d$, no longer supports $B(p)$ with the same strength as before obtaining $d$. This can be made plausible, given the way a rebutting defeater reconfigures the pool of total evidence, as explained in chapter 2.

Things are not as straightforward when it comes to undercutting defeaters. The built-in weighing mechanism does not account for them directly, since undercutting defeaters cannot be weighed against lower-order evidence but only against higher-order evidence, as the FEEBLE-case from the previous chapter illustrates. How can Generic Evidentialism make sense of this, given that the primary mechanism by which what is supported by one's evidence is fixed consists in expanding or reducing the set of total evidence? An undercutting defeater can be taken to affect the Connector, most straightforwardly by removing or neutralizing it. This is in line with the intuition that undercutting defeaters show that the (lower-order) evidence one has relied on so far does not really support the target-attitude.[14] Applying the idea to SCHOOL, one could say that, as a result of acquiring the defeater, James' evidence for the belief that his daughter is skipping school in SCHOOL *vanishes* (as evidence for that belief, in any case) because he loses the Connector that makes it support his belief. Whether this can be made plausible clearly depends on how one characterizes the Connector.

---

[14] This is also in line with Feldman's best-explanation view, given that an undercutting defeater presumably makes it the case that the truth of the target-belief is no longer the best available explanation for the evidence.

To make the Generic Evidentialist's life in this regard as easy as possible, I will assume both Generic Support 1, according to which the Connector is part of the subject's evidence, and the idea that the Connector *contains appropriate higher-order information* linking the lower-order evidence to the target-proposition. It may thus be, for example, a higher-order attitude or an experience containing a higher-order proposition. Such a view may be demanding but it seems to capture undercutting defeat: Because the Connector is evidence itself, it must be either foundational or intermediate evidence and thus have positive epistemic status. This also means that it can be rebutted, and since undercutting defeaters are higher-order rebutting defeaters which characteristically target higher-order attitudes that affirm a proper connection between the first-order evidence and the target-attitude, it can thus be claimed that undercutting defeaters characteristically *rebut the Connector*. The Connector then ceases being evidence, which in turn means that the lower-order evidence that it connected to the target-attitude does so as well.

If $c$ is the Connector that is responsible for $E^*$-$c$ (the subset of $E^*$ containing all evidence with the exception of $c$) supporting $B(p)$, it is also responsible for $E^*$ supporting $B(p)$. Obtaining an undercutting defeater $d$ then neutralizes $c$ in $E^*$, which results in $c$ ceasing to be part of $E^*$ and $E^*$-$c$ ceasing to be evidence for $B(p)$. The new set of total evidence $E$ can then be said to be either empty or to contain only $d$. In general, this can also be utilized to cover cases of partial undercutting, since the degree of justification that the target-attitude enjoys is decreased in correspondence with the weight of the disconnected evidence. $E$ may then contain evidence that supports $B(p)$ due to another Connector that is not neutralized by $d$. This seems to be the right result.

One may have some qualms accepting this explanation. It is not, or at least not always, plausible that an undercutting defeater makes the first-order evidence *vanish*, which would be a result of the rebuttal of the Connector on this picture. One may, for example, think that James in SCHOOL does not lose evidence for the belief that his daughter is skipping school. Instead, he acquires new information that *bars him from relying* on this evidence under his specific circumstances.[15] *Generally,* seeing someone dressed like one's daughter leaving a coffee shop during school hours is evidence for her skipping school. Given Thomas' testimony, though, James can simply not rely on it. This type of description is certainly potentially controversial for SCHOOL, but it is quite plausible in cases

---

**15** This characterisation of undercutting fits especially well with any position in which the Connector is not necessarily accessible, e.g. where it consists in objective evidential probabilities. Such a view is incompatible with the idea that defeaters can remove the Connector, given that defeaters can be misleading.

where the original evidence is conclusive, i.e. where the target-proposition logically follows from it. Imagine a logician arriving at the conclusion of a deductively valid argument as a result of a hugely complex derivation. The original evidence for that conclusion (the premises) necessitates the truth of the conclusion, which makes it overwhelmingly plausible that it is evidence, no matter what anyone thinks. Still, if all his colleagues disagree with the logician's conviction that the conclusion follows from the premises, it seems that he may lose justification for belief in it. Such cases will be analyzed in greater detail in the next chapter. Note that the re-evaluation and replacement-mechanic can potentially solve this issue for Generic Evidentialism. They make it possible that the logician's belief, after re-evaluation, is not based on the conclusive evidence it started out with, but on a new set of evidence that accommodates the defeater's effect. So, prima facie, a detour through re-evaluation is at least potentially useful and possibly even conceptually required for Generic Evidentialism, in order to properly accommodate intuitions here. Still, since it seems to get the central verdicts for cases of undercutting defeat right, and since intuitions about the presence or absence of evidence may not touch more technical notions of the term *evidence*, the Generic Evidentialist may well insist that the Connector-rebuttal option is a perfectly serviceable account of undercutting defeat.

So far, these accounts only tell us how a defeater may remove propositional justification. While cases like DOUBLE-AGENT will likely spell trouble for it, it can be granted, I think, that they do a reasonably good job. However, the Evidentialist still needs to explain how defeaters can remove doxastic justification, which is where a proper accommodation of the Rebasing Account becomes useful, if not necessary. At first glance, explaining why defeaters remove doxastic justification on Generic Evidentialism is easy, since Generic Well-Foundedness ensures that a defeated attitude is not doxastically justified either: The defeater is part of $E$ and thus, since condition 2. demands that $B(p)$ be based on $E$, ignoring the defeater and retaining the maximally specific target-attitude $B(p)$ will amount to $B(p)$ not being well-founded. Thus, a defeater, just through the weight and direction of its propositional support, ensures that the defeated attitude is neither propositionally nor doxastically justified (to the same degree as before). This impression of ease is deceptive, however, which can be seen as soon as one looks more closely.

As neat as this picture seems, it implicitly relies on something like the Rebasing Account's mechanism for feeding the front-door properties of rebutting defeaters into the complex re-evaluation-machinery that governs changes in the target-attitude's status with respect to doxastic justification. For while the Evidentialist may be content with Generic Well-Foundedness as an account of what doxastic justification consists in and with the derivable view on why having obtained a rebutting defeater is inconsistent with it, this already presupposes that the defeater is required to become part of the target-attitude's total doxastic base. Generic Well-Foundedness demands that the subject base her attitude on all the evidence she possesses. Since the defeater becomes part of that evidence when it is obtained, this amounts to the demand that the target-attitude be *re-based* from the original set of total evidence $E^*$, to the new set $E$. The Rebasing Account explains how the process that amounts to rebasing – re-evaluation – is, in turn, required by the points of conflict between $E^*$ and $E$.

Now, if Evidentialism indeed presupposes that rebasing is to take place in cases of defeat, it had better also provide the conceptual resources to account for it. Specifically, if it is found plausible that the Rebasing Account gives us the best picture of the relationship between defeat and rebasing (as I have argued at length) and that the obligations established in the previous section really describe a defeater's normative profile, Evidentialism must be capable of deriving the Type 1 and Type 2 obligations I stated from the norms it takes to underlie epistemic practice.[16] Thus, the accommodation of the phenomenon of defeat requires the Evidentialist to show that the obligations governing re-evaluation and rebasing are derivable from a norm connecting the holding of attitudes and the possession of evidence. An example that can be assumed for the purposes of this work is the following generic version of what we can call the "Evidence Norm": $S$ is permitted to hold doxastic attitude $B(p)$ about $p$, only if $B(p)$ fits (and is based on) $S$'s total evidence $E$. Given that the Type 1 and Type 2 obligations from the previous section all received a broadly negative formulation and that Evidentialism provides general standards for justification, we can make a substantial attempt at fully accommodating the Rebasing Account.

Covering Type 1 obligations can be straightforwardly accomplished in Evidentialist terms: Both rebutting and undercutting defeaters change the composition and directional weight of the subject's total evidence $E$ by introducing support for an attitude incompatible with the target-attitude. Since the target-attitude $B(p)$ will then no longer fit $E$, the Evidence Norm kicks in and prohibits holding on to $B(p)$. If a well-founded attitude about $p$ is the subject's goal, she must base it on the new total set of evidence $E$, rather than its original justifier, $E^*$. As I have argued, this happens by way of fully re-evaluating $B(p)$. As a result, the Evidence Norm requires the subject to either opt out and drop $B(p)$ or to re-evaluate $B(p)$, thus serving as a Type 1 obligation.

---

[16] Of course, this presupposes that justification is taken to be essentially normative by the Evidentialist. The Reliabilist must take a different tack, as I will explain shortly.

## 5.2 Defeat and Internalism — 191

Similarly, since the total available evidence at this point does not permit holding on to the target-attitude (in the same way as before) and since the only way to properly respond to this is to opt out or to rebase and possibly modify the relevant attitude, it only permits holding on to an attitude that is the resulut of *full* re-evaluation. Thus, the Evidence Norm also underpins the Type 2 obligations discussed before.

Now, one might think that claiming that the total evidence available permits full re-evaluation is a stretch. The idea behind the concept of evidence, it might be argued, is that it only permits the *holding* of attitudes and not the forming of attitudes in particular ways. It can be answered, however, that this, again, leaves open how Evidentialism can account for well-foundedness or doxastic justification. Given the limited options to react to new information that normal human subjects have, it seems that changes in the total available evidence must indirectly engender "practical" requirements to perform broadly cognitive operations like re-evaluation. This is because as soon as the basing relation enters the picture, changes in evidence must normatively (through the Evidence Norm) govern changes in basing. This is what Type 1 and Type 2 obligations describe. Importantly, however, the claim is not that the new evidence that results from obtaining a defeater itself requires re-evaluation. The claim is that that new evidence only allows holding the attitude that results from competent re-evaluation, such that, given that the only way to hold this attitude in a well-founded manner is re-evaluation, obtaining a new set of total evidence requires re-evaluation. Stated more abstractly: The epistemic obligations triggered by obtaining a defeater coincide with respect to their trigger conditions with practical obligations to run full re-evaluations.

To make the option to re-evaluate explicable in Evidentialist terms, the three steps of re-evaluation must now be shown to be governed by the Evidence Norm, producing an Evidentialist account of a competent re-evaluation.

During $R(B(p))$, (i) the set of evidence that served as $B(p)$'s original justifier, $E^*$, is assessed in light of the subject's total evidence concerning $E^*$. The result of that assessment is the formation of higher-order attitudes concerning identifying $E^*$ and the obtaining of corresponding higher-order evidence $E'$.

(ii) Taking into account the defeater $d$ and $E'$, $E^*$'s support-relation to $B(p)$ is assessed, resulting in corresponding higher-order attitudes and higher-order evidence $E''$. At least some of the resulting higher-order attitudes will amount to an assessment of the Connector, insofar as they are about the support relation between the remaining evidence in the original justifier and the target-attitude. Depending on the relevant background theory, they might even become the Connector.

(iii) A new attitude $B^*(p)$ is formed on the basis of the subject's new set of total relevant evidence $E$, which includes $d$, $E'$ and $E''$. In the case of a rebutting defeater, $E$ can include $E^*$ (depending on available evidence in step i) because $E'$ and $E''$ ideally allow the justified belief that $E^*$ supports $B(p)$ (no higher-order rebuttal through $d$). In the case of an undercutting defeater, $E$ ideally does not include $E^*$ because deriving $E'$ and $E''$ involves higher-order rebuttal, resulting in $E^*$ ceasing to be evidence for $B(p)$ according to Generic Evidentialism.

The specific characteristics of Evidentialism come into play with regards to the conditions that need to be fulfilled in order to run a re-evaluation competently: A competent re-evaluation can be distinguished from an incompetent one in terms of whether $E'$, $E''$ and $B(p)^*$ include (or support) *justified* attitudes, in the sense that they are based on sufficiently supportive sets of total evidence. Thus, Evidentialism adds conditions under which re-evaluation produces justified results.

To make this whole characterization more accessible, consider a case of misleading undercutting defeat:

> RED-FALSE: Mariko observes an assembly line putting together widgets through a factory window. The widgets appear red and so Mariko forms the belief that the widgets are red. She is right, the widgets are indeed red. Along comes Farid, a coworker she knows to be very trustworthy. Farid wants to prank Mariko today, however, and tells her that there is a red light beneath the factory window that illuminates all the widgets. Mariko simply ignores Farid's testimony and holds on to her belief that the widgets are red.

This is a classic case of undercutting defeat and it should be reasonably uncontroversial that Mariko loses justification for her belief that the widgets are red. Furthermore, we saw earlier that the best way to explain why defeat is happening here is by way of higher-order rebutting defeat, which is illustrated, among others, by cases of defeater-defeat through higher-order support. The effect for this case is that the defeater (Farid's testimony) neutralizes Mariko's original justifier (her red-widgets-experience). This comes down to Mariko's degree of justification for the belief that the widgets are red after receiving Farid's testimony being just as high (or low) as it would be if he did not have an experience of red widgets. This is an expression of the observation that Farid's testimony makes it illegitimate to further rely on that experience.

The scheme I developed can easily be applied to RED-FALSE: After receiving Farid's testimony, Mariko's total evidence no longer supports her belief that the widgets are red. The Evidence Norm (indirectly) requires her to either drop any belief about their color or to form a different attitude. If she opts to do the latter, she must re-evaluate her previous belief in light of the new total evidence. During re-evaluation, her original evidence $E^*$ for her belief (the red-widgets experience) and its support-relations with respect to the color of the widgets must be (re-)assessed in light of Farid's testimony $d$ and her other higher-order evidence. The results of this assessment are then also evidence ($E'$ and $E''$). In the case at hand, Mariko's higher-order evidence, together with Farid's testimony are such that the Evidence Norm will not allow Mariko to justifiedly believe that her experience properly supports her belief. In Generic Evidentialism, the results of re-evaluation amount to rebuttal of the Connector, which results in $E^*$ ceasing to be evidence for $B(p)$. Accordingly, the Evidence Norm prohibits reinstating $B(p)$ because Mariko has no more evidence for it. This is the right result for RED-FALSE.

### 5.2.3 A Problem for Moderately Internalist Versions of Evidentialism

Before moving on, I want to make a few brief remarks on less demandingly internalist versions of Evidentialism and their relation to defeat. Specifically, it is worthwhile to point out a structural issue with Evidentialist views that are unwilling to take up the relatively demanding nature of the Connector that I assumed here. Such views may be unable to properly model the undercutting of other evidence that, in Generic Evidentialism, turned out to amount to deleting other evidence.

According to the Evidence Norm, holding an attitude that fits the total evidence available is justified. Assume now that the Connector is not itself part of that evidence, but some fact about the truth- or correctness-related connection between the total evidence and the target-attitude, while everything else is defined as in Generic Evidentialism. Call this view "Moderate Evidentialism". The Connector may, for example, be a fact about the evidence raising the truth-probability of the target-attitude. Moderate Evidentialism has a similar problem as the Suspension Account when it comes to explaining undercutting defeat: It fails to explain the fact that undercutting defeaters not only somehow clash with the target-attitude but also neutralize other evidence through undercutting effects.[17]

To see this, consider RED-FALSE again. The question that arises with respect to Moderate Evidentialism is how the intuitive verdict that the defeater neutral-

---

[17] As Christensen (2010a, pp. 204–205) points out, on views like Moderate Evidentialism, undercutting defeat looks similar to another variant of source-sensitive defeat that will be discussed later under the heading of "higher-order defeat". The important point is that this other variant is much more controversial than undercutting defeat, further underscoring the point I am making here.

izes the support from Mariko's visual impression of red widgets is supposed to be accommodated. Since the defeater is misleading, Mariko's experience objectively still makes it more likely that the widgets are red, so why would it not raise her belief's degree of justification?

The standard Evidentialist answer is that her experience, together with Farid's testimony, does not make it more likely that the widgets are red, but this just seems like a restatement of the verdict on the case rather than an explanation. To be sure, it is plausible that this should be so, but what is needed is an Evidentialist account of *why* this is so, preferably in terms of higher-order rebutting defeat. Generic Evidentialism can give us just such an explanation: Part of Mariko's evidence is the Connector, which is a contentful, accessible state with positive epistemic status that claims, roughly, that her red-widgets experience supports the belief that the widgets are red. This state is logically incompatible with the proposition that the experience does not support the relevant belief, which is supported by the false information that there is a red light shining on the widgets. As a result, the Connector is rebutted and ceases to be part of Mariko's evidence for the belief that the widgets are red. In turn, her red-widgets experience also ceases to be evidence for that belief, yielding the result that it is neutralized.

It is not at all clear whether Moderate Evidentialism can tell the same story because, in this view, the Connector is not an independent part of Mariko's evidence in this demanding sense and thus cannot be straightforwardly rebutted. It is an external fact about the relationship between Mariko's experience and her belief and, given that the defeater in this case is misleading, it remains true that relying on her experience makes it quite likely that her belief is true. This would even be the case were she to rely on both her experience *and* the defeating evidence. This is because there are no rebutting defeaters for facts, only for doxastic attitudes. So, the Moderate Evidentialist owes us an explanation as to why Farid's testimony makes it the case that Mariko's red-experience is no longer evidence for her belief.

The underlying point is that, as soon as the Connector is conceived of as, in some sense, external to the subject, it becomes difficult to account for misleading undercutting defeaters because it becomes difficult to account for higher-order rebuttal. Let us say that $B(p)$ is Mariko's belief that the widgets are red and that $E^*$ is her original visual impression of red widgets. The challenge is to accommodate the strong intuition that $B(p)$'s degree of justification is no longer affected by $E^*$ because $E^*$ is undercut by Farid's testimony. How can this "undercutting" be spelled out, if not through $E^*$'s vanishing? One might say that Mariko still has the evidence $E^*$ for holding $B(p)$, but that she also has compelling evidence that requires her to "doxastically ignore" $E^*$ as a potential doxastic base for $B(p)$ in the form of Farid's testimony. Thus, she has supportive evidence, but she cannot rely on it in a way that would produce doxastic justification. Since she also has no other evidence that may serve as the new basis for $B(p)$, she therefore cannot hold $B(p)$ in a well-founded manner. As a result, she is barred from having doxastic justification for $B(p)$, though she may still have propositional justification.

This description seems pre-theoretically adequate, although it would require the Evidentialist to expand her set of epistemic norms so as to allow for this systematic difference between propositional and doxastic justification. The Evidence Norm, together with Generic Well-Foundedness does not provide the conceptual resources needed to explain why Mariko's belief that the widgets are red would turn out unjustified, assuming that she reinstates it after re-evaluation on the basis of a set of total evidence that does de facto support that belief (because it contains her red-widgets impression).[18] Thus, as long as Moderate Evidentialism does not come with an expanded normative inventory or an enriched account of doxastic justification, I present cases like RED-FALSE as a counterargument against Moderate Evidentialism. It is not enough to claim that the original evidence, together with the defeater, is not evidence for the target-belief – that claim must be cashed out in a way that explains how an undercutting defeater can interact with the Connector such that the right result is produced.

This concludes the accommodation of the Rebasing Account to a staunchly internalist theory of justification – Generic Evidentialism. It was seen both that such a view can provide the resources needed to account for Type 1 and Type 2 obligations and that the Rebasing Account, by filling in an important blank when it comes to defeat of doxastic justification, can make an important contribution to the view's explanatory power. However, it was also seen that these results do rely on a demanding conception of the Connector that is in line with staunch internalism but that may well be rejected by more moderate Evidentialists. If the notion is given a more externalist characterization, however, Evidentialism's conceptual resources do not easily allow for an explanation of undercutting defeat.

---

**18** If some sort of rebutting effect were postulated, RED-FALSE would still serve as a counterexample because the loss in justification would not be describable in a way that has it correspond to the weight of the original justifier in every plausible case. Furthermore, cases like FEEBLE would also not be covered.

## 5.3 Defeat and Externalism

### 5.3.1 Simple Reliabilism

Let me now turn to externalist theories of justification. To represent this end of the spectrum, a staunchly externalist and descriptive version of the most prominent externalist theory can be formulated: Generic Reliabilism.

> Generic Reliabilism:
> $S$'s doxastic attitude $B(p)$ is justified, just in case $B(p)$ is the result of a process that is (sufficiently) reliable (adapted from Goldman 2012).

First, it must be noted that Generic Reliabilism is much more concerned with doxastic justification than Generic Evidentialism was. This is because being a result of a given process can be taken to imply that the resulting attitude is based on that process in the sense that it now depends for its justificatory status on its credentials.[19] Thus, rather than content-related states like having evidence, it is *the quality of the process itself* that is relevant to justification. That quality is judged in terms of its reliability, that is, in terms of its capability of ensuring a correct or true attitude. The two key components of this account are then clearly *process* and *reliability*. Since matters surrounding these components are complex and somewhat controversial,[20] they will have to be characterized in the broadest strokes.

Starting with the process, the kind that comes to mind when considering justification is the attitude-formation process that results in the original formation of the relevant attitude. One may ask whether this process needs to be (wholly) cognitive or whether it can also involve other physical processes, such as the reflection of light off of objects or the mechanisms of the receptors within the human eye. For the purposes of this discussion, the answer does not matter overly much and so the following broad characterization will be assumed:

---

[19] It could also be thought that, in virtue of resulting from the process, the attitude is based on the process' input. However, since talk about the input to the relevant processes gets one into epistemically deep waters, I will assume here that it is the process itself that does the basing. Still, it should be clear that what I will be saying here can be said just as well about a conception of Reliabilism that deals with process-inputs.

[20] This is especially the case where matters like the "generality problem" or reference classes are concerned (see e.g. Conee and Feldman 1998; Alston 1995; Goldman and Beddor 2016; Pollock and Cruz 1999), but also when it comes to the details of what constitutes reliability (e.g. Alston 1995; Goldman 2009; Goldman 2012; Frise 2018).

Generic Attitude-Formation Process:
$P(B(p))$ is an attitude-formation process, just in case $P(B(p))$ is a process of type $T$, where the running of a $T$-process at time $t$ typically results in the formation of a new doxastic attitude on some proposition $p$, such that no doxastic attitude on $p$ was held immediately before $t$.

Before discussing this, it must further be noted that there are a number of general issues with Generic Attitude-Formation Process characterization that are controversial and cannot be addressed here. For instance, I do not intend to attempt to solve the generality problem (see Conee and Feldman 1998) and so it must remain an open question how it is to be individuated or what it means, exactly, that running T-processes *typically* results in doxastic attitudes (although I do think that we have a solid intuitive grasp on these matters, at least when ignoring some detail). Similarly, it is difficult to get more concrete than "suitable input" without getting into deep waters. Importantly, I still wish to stay neutral on what can count as input in this context. Whatever can engage an attitude-formation process can be input, including states of affairs outside of the subject's cognitive system and other beliefs. A Reliabilist may want to restrict this somewhat (e.g. Comesaña 2010), but for a generic version it seems preferable to be inclusive. This also means that it will be left open whether attitude-formation processes must be fully cognitive, as mentioned above.

Still, even given all these caveats, it should be reasonably intelligible what an attitude-formation process may consist in. Now, notice that an attitude-formation process, according to this conception, characteristically results in a *new* attitude, that is, a result of the process is a doxastic attitude on some proposition that the subject has so far not entertained a doxastic attitude on at the time the process is run. Specifically, this means that an attitude-formation process does not reinstate or change an existing attitude, as re-evaluation may. One of the reasons reliabilism traditionally struggles with the accommodation of defeaters is that considering only attitude-formation processes is too restrictive, as this leaves out the idea of re-evaluation completely. We will see, too, that loosening this often implicit restriction gives Generic Reliabilism much more extensive resources for dealing with defeat than one may suspect.

But before discussing this, we need some conception of an attitude-formation process being *reliable*:

Generic Reliability:
A process $P(B(p))$ is reliable, just in case i) $P(B(p))$ is of a type $T$ that typically results in a subject $S$ holding some doxastic attitude, ii) $T$ is such that the attitudes resulting from running processes that belong to it are correct in a sufficiently high percentage of (possible) instances. (adapted from Goldman 2012, 2009; see also Goldman and Beddor 2016; Goldman 2009; Frise 2018)

Leaving general issues aside, there are two points about this account that require clarification. First, I will assume that the exact frequency with which a reliable process needs to produce correct attitudes in order to serve as an epistemic justifier should coincide with a more general threshold of epistemic support that an attitude must enjoy in order to count as justified (which will continue to be presupposed in this context). Second, having reliability judgments quantify over *possible* instances of running the relevant process makes it possible to run a reliable process for the first or even the only time in a given possible world and get a justified (but possibly false) attitude out of it.

Generic Reliabilism comes fairly close to Goldman's original account of process reliabilism (Goldman 2012) and is thus not too much of an idealization. It also illustrates nicely the general problem reliabilism has when it comes to accommodating defeat. The thought behind a Reliabilist theory is that an attitude's justificatory status depends on the genesis of the attitude, not on synchronic features like having evidence or being subject to obligations. This makes justified attitudes comparatively easy to come by and avoids the over-intellectualization that a classical Cartesian internalism struggles with (Alston 1989b, ch. 8; Greco 1990; Bergmann 2006, ch. 1; Kornblith 2012, ch. 1).

### 5.3.2 Reliabilism's Trouble with Defeat

The problem is that Generic Reliabilism's focus on the qualities of attitude-formation processes also makes it hard to *lose* justification later. To understand this better, recall RED-FALSE: Intuitively, Mariko's belief that the widgets are red is no longer justified after receiving Farid's testimony. This is because it calls the basis of her belief into question and so it becomes irrational for her to continue to rely on it. However, from a Reliabilist perspective, everything seems to be fine with Mariko's belief, even if she ignores Farid's testimony. It has been formed via perception, which is a (generally) reliable attitude-formation process under Mariko's circumstances, so it should turn out justified in a view like Generic Reliabilism. The problem is that most versions of reliabilism amount to a *genetic* or historical theory of justification. They are concerned with the quality of the way in which the subject came to hold an attitude and not necessarily with synchronous considerations of epistemic rationality (cf. Constantin 2020). By the time the defeater shows up, everything capable of determining the target-attitude's justificatory status is already set and done. Applied to RED-FALSE, the issue is that, when Mariko obtains Farid's testimony, the attitude-formation process that led her to hold the belief that the widgets are red and the quality of which is supposed to determine the belief's justificatory status is already finished and cannot be retroactively changed by the testimony. In fact, retroactively changing a finished process turns out to be the only way to remove justification in such a view, and this idea is hard to reconcile with any account of causation. Intuitions about defeat, on the other hand, are primarily driven by intuitions about rationality. Here, no such problem seems to crop up because facts about what attitude is currently rational to hold, unlike facts about the causal origin of the target-attitude, can easily change with the gathering of more input.[21] Thus, it seems that the plausibility of defeat supports a framework for justification that includes restrictions from principles of (a certain form of) rationality, which are incompatible with the core idea behind genetic theories of justification.

Of course, the problem has been recognized before. In response, Goldman proposes to add a synchronic condition to reliabilism: A subject *S*'s doxastic attitude *B(p)* is justified only if there is no process *p2* available to *S*, such that i) *p1* and *p2* are not identical, ii) *p2* is reliable and iii) had *S* employed *p2* in addition to *p1* in forming a doxastic attitude about *p*, *S* would not have formed *B(p)* (cf. Goldman 2012). This account seems to take care of RED-FALSE: Having obtained Farid's testimony, Mariko now can be said to have a process for coming to attitudes about the color of the widgets available that, if she ran it in addition to her vision-process (and if she did so competently), would prevent her from believing that the widgets are red. One may even be tempted to combine this view with the Rebasing Account and claim that running the two processes *combined* amounts to running a single process that looks like a re-evaluation of Mariko's belief that the widgets are red.

However, there are a number of severe problems with this alternative-processes approach. First, counterexamples can be levelled against it: Beddor (2015) shows that having an alternative reliable process available is not necessary for defeat because cases can be constructed where one suffers defeat, even though certain psychological states make the relevant alternative processes un-

---

21 See Constantin 2020. Baker-Hytch and Benton (2015) press a similar point.

available. An example would be defeating testimony by someone whom one hates so much that one is psychologically incapable of taking it into account. Beddor further argues that having alternative processes available is not sufficient either, because there could be legitimate doubts in one's doxastic system that are so far removed from one's consciousness that they don't intuitively defeat, even though they make the relevant alternative processes available (cf. Beddor 2015, pp. 150–155).

Second, cases like RED-FALSE can be modified so that the defeater cannot be acquired by a reliable process, while still intuitively defeating (Baker-Hytch and Benton 2015, pp. 50–53): Imagine that Farid is excellent at appearing trustworthy while being a pathological liar. It still seems as though Mariko's belief is defeated, even though she has no alternative reliable process available. Farid's testimony is highly unreliable in this case, after all. Note that this intuition changes drastically once it is assumed that Mariko has internally accessible reason to think that Farid is a liar, which further illustrates that intuitions about defeat are driven by intuitions about internalist-flavored rationality.

Finally, Goldman's solution does not seem to fit well with what can be called the "spirit" of reliabilism (cf. Grundmann 2009b; Constantin 2020). It is not concerned with the genesis of a belief, but rather sneaks in synchronic conditions to specifically deal with defeat, which seems ad hoc.

In light of these problems, let us put the alternative-processes approach aside. Instead, it can be proposed that a better reliabilist way to deal with defeat is to focus on process types other than *formation*-processes that can serve as bases for doxastic attitudes. Specifically, we need processes that take place in the present and that can therefore be affected by the presence defeaters (at least whenever a defeater is obtained). Of course, the idea here is that a re-evaluation process is just the searched-after alternative (cf. Constantin 2020).

Now, one might think that the move from abandoning focus on formation-processes to re-evaluation processes is too quick. There is another kind of process that (partly) takes place in the present and that is already well established, after all: sustaining processes. As the name suggests, a sustaining process is responsible for continuing to hold or for reaffirming an attitude. Couldn't one say that a defeater somehow renders an attitude's sustaining process unreliable, showing that no complicated re-evaluation mechanic is needed? Philosophers have thought for some time that the formation-process isn't the only process relevant for the justificatory status of the target-attitude. In cases where a belief, for example, is intuitively held for reasons that differ from those it was formed in response to, a reliabilist explanation may be that the process that *sustains* the belief, and is thus responsible for is justificatory status, is not its formation-process (Goldman 2012, pp. 36–37; Swain 1985, pp. 71–76; Conee and Feldman 1998, pp. 1–4; Frances 2008, p. 242; Grundmann 2009b, p. 67).

First it must be noted that this already sounds a lot like a gloss over the rebasing mechanic I proposed in chapter 3. The cases where it seems most like there must be a second kind of process at work are cases where the subject starts out with one justifier for her attitude and ends up with another. Whether the supposed second process is indeed a re-evaluation process or whether it may be something else depends on the details of one's account of sustaining processes. If one understands sustaining processes to be structurally much like formation processes, in that they are *temporally limited* series of changes that have *as their final result* some doxastic attitude, there must be a close relationship between the rebasing/re-evaluation framework and the idea of sustaining processes, as there are many plausible claims one can make connecting the two. For example, it seems that a re-evaluation process is a *kind of* sustaining process and that a process is a sustaining, rather than a formation process, just in case the relevant attitude *was rebased* to it. If sustaining processes are understood in this way as *reaffirming* or *reinstating* processes, one can directly see how well the Rebasing Account of Defeat fits with the resulting reliabilist picture of justification: Defeaters initiate new sustaining processes that must obey certain principles (those of a competent re-evaluation, for instance) in order to be reliable, and that are structured in ways that allow only for certain justified outcomes (dropping or weakening the defeated attitude).

However, one may also understand sustaining processes in a substantially different way that tries for a more straightforward accommodation of defeat. In this view, a sustaining process is a temporally extensive, *ongoing* process that *continuously brings it about* that the subject holds the relevant doxastic attitude. One can then try to accommodate defeat by claiming that such a process is only reliable, if it is sensitive to defeaters. In this picture, every justified doxastic attitude must either be freshly formed or rely on an ongoing sustaining process. This amounts to abandoning the genetic character of Generic Reliabilism in favor of a synchronic view that still seems to avoid over-intellectualization, as sustaining processes need not be consciously run. One may think that this provides further advantages, as the view seems to straightforwardly accommodate cases like RED-FALSE: If Mariko ignores the defeater provided by her coworker, it follows that the ongoing process sustaining her belief that the widgets are red is not sensitive to undercutting information. It follows further that the process is not sufficiently reliable to justify the belief because processes that are not sensitive to defeating information are very unlikely to produce a sufficiently good ratio of correct to incorrect attitudes. Thus, holding on to the target-attitude in the presence of the defeater is incompatible with the target-attitude's justification. It then seems that ongoing sustaining processes provide all that is needed to accommodate defeat.

However, there are significant problems with this seemingly simple solution. First, while it may not over-*intellectualize*, in a specific sense of that term, it still makes extreme demands of a normal human subject's cognitive capacity. It is cognitively extremely demanding to postulate an ongoing process for every single justified attitude that a given subject happens to have. I may well hold hundreds or thousands of justified doxastic attitudes, but it seems unlikely that enough cognitive capacity to account for that many sustaining processes is permanently engaged with these attitudes (cf. Constantin 2020). In fact, it is unlikely that I even *have* the required capacities.

Second, in the resulting picture of defeat, a defeater does not *remove* justification at all. If the process that Mariko's belief is based on is insensitive to defeaters at the time of receiving the defeater, it must have been so before that time (if we assume that attitudes start being based on sustaining processes almost right after their formation). But then it follows from the idea that such lack of sensitivity is incompatible with justification that her belief that the widgets are red *wasn't justified to begin with* when the defeater is obtained (cf. Constantin 2020). Thus, the defeater does not remove justification from the target-attitude but rather unmasks the attitude as unjustified. But that is not the intuition one has in standard cases of defeat. Thus, the seemingly simpler view does not target the right phenomenon.

Finally (and most damningly), the presence of a defeater is not related to unreliability in the right way. The intuition behind defeat is that the presence of a defeater is not compatible with justification. If this is supposed to be explained in terms of the relationship between the presence of a defeater with the reliability of the sustaining process, it must be assumed that a sustaining process that misses even one defeater must automatically be unreliable (in the sense of not being sufficiently reliable for justification). This amounts to the claim that a process's sensitivity to defeaters must be perfect (cf. Constantin 2020). But why would anyone accept such high standards? A process need not be perfectly reliable in order to confer justification, so why should it have to be perfectly reliable when it comes to detecting defeaters? This argument may seem familiar in light of my discussion of the Inclusive Thesis on the epistemic status of defeaters. That is because it also points to a disanalogy between defeat and justification that must be assumed for purely ad hoc reasons. It should be clear that trying to justify this assumption more deeply is not worth it, given the alternative offered by the Rebasing Account.

### 5.3.3 Reliabilism and the Rebasing Account of Undercutting Defeat

In light of the problems raised in the previous paragraph, let us proceed with the idea that the process that is affected by a defeater is neither an attitude-formation process, nor an ongoing sustaining process, but instead a re-evaluation process. This is the first step in a Reliabilist accommodation of the Rebasing Account. In what follows, I will sketch a straightforward accommodation of the Rebasing Account of defeat and thus of defeaters in general in reliabilist terms.

To see how the accommodation may proceed, consider a variant of RED-FALSE that ends after Mariko is offered her co-worker's testimony (leaving her stubborn refusal to revise her belief for later). That is, consider RED-FALSE up until the point when the defeater is obtained by Mariko. When Mariko is offered the undercutting testimony, she will normally register the incompatibility between the suspension of judgment supported by the defeater and her belief. How exactly this is modelled is not so easy to say, but some pointers have already been given in the chapter on undercutting defeat. The idea is that suspension of judgment on the target-attitude comes to be "set on the mental table", that is, it shows up and is processed in the subject's cognitive system as a live option. This is supposedly the result of the detection of tension between the defeater's content and what is represented or archived as a typical way to get at certain information (in this case, the color of objects) or of direct questioning of the used process, depending on what higher-order attitudes can be found in the subject's noetic system.[22]

The details of this have already been discussed in previous chapters, but it must be stressed that they may represent an additional commitment for the reliabilist, since the resources needed to create tension between an undercutting defeater and the target-belief must be provided. If it is agreed that undercutters appeal to higher-order propositions, this will mean the assumption of higher-order material in standard noetic systems. As explained earlier, I do not consider this too problematic, but it is something to keep in mind. A reliabilist not willing to take such commitments on board may have to reject undercutting defeat as well (cf. Constantin 2020). So, as before, the first step is to explain how a defeater introduces an incompatibility. This incompatibility must, in a *descriptive* theo-

---

[22] As a consequence, a subject with no higher-order attitudes at all about typical ways etc. will not be able to suffer undercutting defeat. One may or may not consider this a problematic consequence (I do not, for reasons discussed in the chapter on undercutting defeat). In any case, it is a consequence the (generic) reliabilist must accept if she wishes to preserve the spirit of her view.

ry like Generic Reliabilism, be taken to cause or prompt, rather than require, re-evaluation.

Returning to the analysis of RED-FALSE, the doxastic incompatibility between the suspension of judgment on whether the widgets are red, raised as an option by the defeater, and Mariko's belief that the widgets are red will cause cognitive dissonance.[23] This, in turn prompts a re-evaluation process comparing two chains of reasoning, an idealization of which has been described before:

For the target-attitude:

    A1  The widgets appear red.

    A2  If the widgets appear red, they probably are red.

    A3  If it is true that the widgets appear red and that if they appear red, then they probably are red, believe that the widgets are red.

---

    AK  Believe that the widgets are red.

For the defeater:

    B1  There is a red light shining on the widgets.

    B2  If there is a red light shining on the widgets, then it is probably not true that: if the widgets appear red, then they probably are red.

    B3  Believe that the widgets are red or disbelieve that the widgets are red, only if there is some x, such that x supports belief or disbelief in the proposition that the widgets are red.

    B4  For every x, x only supports belief or disbelief in the proposition that the widgets are red, if it is true that: if x, then the widgets are probably red.

    B5  If there is any x that supports belief or disbelief in the proposition that the widgets are red, it is that the widgets appear red.

---

    BK  Neither believe, nor disbelieve that the widgets are red.

---

23 A sensation of discomfort that can be caused by detecting inconsistencies between beliefs and other doxastic states.

For cases of rebutting defeat, the chains for the target-attitude and the defeater will look more similar and lack the premise-incompatibility that is characteristic of undercutting defeat. I will restrict the discussion here to cases of misleading undercutting defeat like RED-FALSE, since the adaptation of the results for other kinds of defeaters should be obvious in light of the previous chapters.

Next, let us look at the Generic Reliabilist's resources when it comes to accounting for re-evaluative reasoning. Note that, since re-evaluation involves reasoning, the conditions under which re-evaluation processes like the one depicted here are reliable under normal circumstances broadly correspond to the conditions under which reasoning processes in general are reliable. Given the way re-evaluation has been set up, it should be understood as essentially inferential. Standardly, an inferential process is considered to be reliable, just in case 1) its premises are the results of reliable (here in accordance with Generic Reliability) processes and 2) the process of drawing the inference is conditionally reliable, that is, is such that, if the premises fed into it are the results of reliable processes, the conclusion will be the result of a reliable process (cf. Goldman 2012; Boghossian 2003). What does it take for an inferential process to be conditionally reliable? The rules to which it complies must be such that it is truth-conducive (or correctness-conducive) (cf. Boghossian 2003; Priest 2008). This means that it must produce a high ratio of correct attitudes, if it is fed a high ratio of correct attitudes as premises. In worlds relevantly like ours, this will be achieved in case the rules conform to the rules of *rational* inference in the pre-theoretical sense. That is, what is commonly considered a good or logical or valid inference is considered a truth-conducive and thus reliable inference.

The idea here is that, when it comes to reasoning, the Reliabilist requirements for justification are sufficient for the standards of rationality, which is not obviously true of other attitude-basing processes (think of relying on the testimony of an outwardly trustworthy, but de facto unreliable testifier). Given that obtaining defeaters prompts re-evaluation and that re-evaluation processes replace the original basis of the target-attitude, as argued in the previous chapter, this would allow Reliabilism to accommodate the rationality-driven intuitions in cases of defeat because, in cases of defeat, the process that determines the epistemic status of the target-attitude after registering the defeater is the re-evaluating reasoning-process (Constantin 2020). In the case at hand, the two chains of reasoning involved in the re-evaluation of Mariko's widget-belief depicted above model rational inferences and replace the process by which Mariko arrived at the belief that the widgets are red as the basis of that belief, should it be reinstated after re-evaluation.

In addition, the cognitive operations implementing the chains, producing their input (assessments of the target-attitude's bases) and relating them to one another (assessments of incompatibilities between premises or conclusions) are expressed in the three-step structure discussed in previous sections. The pre-theoretical reliability-standards for reasoning-processes can be said to include the Type 2 obligations that connect the steps in that a re-evaluation process is plausibly only reliable if it is run in full and the steps properly interlock.

Finally, competent re-evaluations can be distinguished from incompetent ones by observing whether the assessment- and inference processes run during the steps are (conditionally) reliable. If a target-attitude is reinstated as the result of re-evaluation, its justificatory status depends on whether the re-evaluation process was competent. A defeater changes the subject's epistemic situation, such that no competent re-evaluation reinstating the target-attitude is possible: After hearing from Farid that there is a red light shining on the widgets, there is no conditionally reliable way for Mariko to reason from an assessment of her belief's doxastic bases in light of the defeater to the original way she held her belief. Reinstating it is sure to violate reliabilist conditions for justification at some point.

### 5.3.4 Testing the Reliabilist Accommodation of the Rebasing Account: Rebasing and Chaining

The framework described so far can now be tested by checking whether it gives the correct result for cases where a target-attitude is kept in spite of the presence of a defeater. We want to say that such an attitude must be unjustified because it effectively amounts to rejecting the defeater without a proper epistemic basis for doing so. To understand this better, recall the original case-variant of RED-FALSE, in which Mariko simply sticks to her belief that the widgets are red, despite Farid's testimony. How can the account developed here accommodate the intuition of unjustifiedness in that case?

It depends on the details of the processes that are run. Consider what would be the case if Mariko ran the inferences depicted in the previous paragraph and, despite registering the tension between the premises concerning the reliability of her belief's basis, A2 and B1/B2, reinstated her belief that the widgets are red at the end of re-evaluation. In that case, the attitude held on the basis of the re-evaluation process would not fit the process and thus not be reliably produced. It would then not turn out justified either.

A similar result is obtained if the re-evaluation is done incompetently (in the sense established in the section on the normative profile of defeaters), such that the higher-order rebuttal is overlooked or ignored. In that case, the process itself would be unreliable because it would not conform to pre-theoretical standards of rationality. Again, Mariko's kept belief would turn out unjustified. The only move open to Mariko after re-evaluation that would leave her with no unjustified attitudes is to permanently give up the target-attitude and possibly suspend judgment on the basis of the re-evaluation process (enacting the conclusion of the B-chain which is not undercut).

This conforms with the intuitions about RED-FALSE and, more generally, with intuitions concerning rationality in cases of defeat, while staying fully true to Generic Reliabilism: the justificatory status of the relevant attitude is fully determined by the reliability of the process it is a result of and thus based on, which is re-evaluation in cases of defeat. This is due to the rebasing-effect of re-evaluation. Furthermore, because re-evaluations are pieces of reasoning conforming to pre-theoretical standards of rationality and because they feature higher-order premises, higher-order rebuttal will occur in (at least partially competent) re-evaluations in cases of undercutting defeat (as shown in the discussion above), while a simple comparison of the weight of the premises will occur in cases of rebutting defeat, where no premise-incompatibilities crop up. This lets the reliability of the relevant re-evaluation process depend on just those factors that drive intuitions in the varied cases of defeat.

Put slightly differently, the Generic Reliabilist can tell the following story in order to account for defeat: When a defeater is obtained, it creates a doxastic incompatibility by causing the consideration of a doxastic attitude as a live option that is in conflict with the target-attitude. This, in turn, creates cognitive dissonance, prompting a re-evaluation process to which the target-attitude, if reinstated, is rebased. If the target-attitude is reinstated, whether it is justified depends on the quality of the re-evaluation process, which in turn depends on whether it is run in full and whether the attitudes formed during its steps are reliably formed. In plausible cases of defeat, the defeater precludes the possibility of a competent re-evaluation that results in a reinstatement of the target-attitude. Importantly, as soon as a re-evaluation process is considered as an alternative to a formation-process with regards to basing, the re-evaluative mechanics described so far slot into place and a coherent picture of defeat develops that relies only on the very basic resources Generic Reliabilism can bring to the table.

While it seems that the Rebasing Account is tailor-made for a theory like Generic Reliabilism, there are a number of issues that must be addressed. First, more must be said about the way the re-evaluation is initiated by the acquisition of defeaters and its role as a doxastic base. In the first chapter, "being based on" for doxastic attitudes was spelled out as a causal notion. Since, in Generic Reliabilism, being the result of a formation or sustaining process amounts to being based on that process or its input, it follows that the way in which re-evaluation is initiated and replaces the original process as the base must also be spelled out in causal terms. Specifically, in order to accommodate the rebasing effect, the Generic Reliabilist must postulate that obtaining a defeater not only causes the initiation of re-evaluation, but also that, from then on, the re-evaluation process and not the formation process is the cause of the subject holding the target-attitude, in case it is reinstated. Whether this is plausible is a matter of debate, given that, in case the target-attitude is reinstated after re-evaluation, one may think that the original formation-process is just as good a candidate for the role of cause as the re-evaluation process is. After all, there is a clear sense in which Mariko, having dismissed Farid's testimony, still believes that the widgets are red as a causal result of having seen them. The Generic Reliabilist must explain away this intuition or show it to rest on a confusion. To make her stance somewhat more plausible, she might propose the following case: S has her car painted red. That night, a group of colorblind hooligans comes by and spray-paints the car red. What is the cause of the car being red the next morning? Since what makes the car red is the micro-configuration of its surface and since that configuration is wholly a result of the hooligans' actions, one can say that the car is now red because of the hooligans and no longer because S had it painted red (Constantin 2020).[24]

The second issue to be addressed concerns the fallibility of reliable processes. Sine Generic Reliability merely requires a reliable process to be such that a high percentage, but not *all*, of the attitudes resulting from a given process are correct, the following scenario is possible: Mariko receives the defeater, re-evaluates and reinstates the target-attitude, even though she has only used reliable processes. One of them simply misfired. In other words, it is possible for a competent re-evaluation to nevertheless produce the wrong conclusion because it need not be an infallible re-evaluation. In such cases, the Generic Reliabilist will have to conclude that the reinstated target-attitude is justified.

A first response is that this result is not nearly as bad as the problems that the alternative ways of conceiving of defeaters discussed so far run into. After all, the defeater has not been ignored. Instead, it has led to a re-evaluation of the target-attitude and that should already go a long way toward accounting for the intuition that a defeater cannot just be ignored. So, one may just bite the bullet at this point. Still more can be said if we pursue a strategy first presented in

---

[24] This can be made more plausible by highlighting the relations of causal influence (in the sense of Lewis 2000) between the color of the car and the two candidate causes: While variances in the way the car was originally painted red make absolutely no difference to the current color of the car, such variances in the way the hooligans spray-painted it do. For example, had S painted it in a slightly darker shade, it would still have the exact coloring the hooligans gave it, whereas, had the hooligans used a darker red, the car would have been a darker red in the end.

Constantin 2020: Let us assume that in the original version of RED-FALSE, Mariko reinstates her belief that the widgets are red despite the co-worker's testimony, but that she does not do so because she unwarrantedly dismisses that testimony, but simply because she re-evaluated and the corresponding reasoning-process misfired in this particular case (she made a *performance error*). While it must be admitted that, at that particular point in time, her reinstated belief is justified, this still leaves Mariko with an incompatibility in her noetic system between suspension of judgment (as supported by Farid's testimony) and her belief, which will trigger yet another re-evaluation. That second re-evaluation will then ideally result in giving up the target-belief, but, of course, it is possible that it, too, misfires. In that case, a third re-evaluation will be triggered by the remaining incompatibility and so on. Since every re-evaluation is reliable in this scenario (otherwise the resulting attitudes end up unjustified and the chain ends), the likelihood of the higher-order rebuttal being detected and the target-attitude being given up will approach 100%, given enough chained re-evaluations. Thus, even though reliable re-evaluation processes are not infallible, the mechanism as a whole is.

One may reasonably object that this is an artificial solution in that it is psychologically unrealistic. No normal epistemic subject will go through enough re-evaluations to secure this result. Rather, we normally stop after one or two. Fortunately, this can, for the most part, easily be accommodated and helps the framework deliver the right results, depending on the reasons for stopping.

First, I do not think it at all unrealistic that a noetic system is built in a way that increases the reliability of its processes, where practical, by chaining together repetitions of them. Thus, when there is enough time and cognitive resources, it makes sense for a noetic system, whose goal is to form a good ratio of correct attitudes, to repeat attitude-formation, sustaining and reinstating-processes in order to lower the likelihood of performance errors occurring and increase reliability. Admittedly, however, this must be left to speculation to an extent. Still, it is at least not at all obvious that chaining processes is in general psychologically unrealistic.

Next, consider the following, psychologically more realistic, though somewhat improbable description: Mariko reliably re-evaluates her belief that the widgets are red, makes a performance error and, prompted by the retained incompatible attitudes, re-evaluates again, unfortunately repeating the performance error. However, after the second re-evaluation, her noetic system marks the resulting conflicting attitudes as "checked and unproblematic" and moves on. This somewhat metaphorical description can be understood as Mariko tacitly forming a higher-order attitude concerning the epistemic status of the attitudes coming out of re-evaluation that blocks further re-evaluations (like the belief that the apparent incompatibility is not an actual incompatibility). If this is what stops further re-evaluations, there is no problem. The new higher-order attitude may actually make it rational to hold two doxastically incompatible attitudes at the same time.

Finally, it may be that Mariko, at some point, fails to pick up on the fact that her noetic system contains doxastically incompatible attitudes, such that no further re-evaluation is triggered. This last option leads to a more general question: Assume that a subject simply fails to register the incompatibility generated by obtaining a defeater and thus no re-evaluation is triggered. Will the Rebasing Account allow Generic Reliabilism to hold that defeat still occurs in such cases? If the answer is *no* and if the reason for stopping to re-evaluate is that the incompatibility is no longer registered, the result will be that, after several misfired but reliable re-evaluations, Mariko's belief that the widgets are red will end up being justified, in spite of having obtained an undercutting defeater for it. Since this would not amount to fully ignoring the defeater, this result may not be inacceptable, but it does generalize to cases where it seems to be.

### 5.3.5 Testing the Reliabilist Accommodation of the Rebasing Account: Active and Passive Ignorance

The last point made in the previous paragraph concerning the possibility of simply failing to register an incompatibility points to a deeper potential problem. Since Generic Reliabilism is a purely descriptive theory of justification, it cannot tie the justificatory status of the defeated attitude to whether or not re-evaluation is *required* in such cases. Therefore, the Generic Reliabilist must postulate that, necessarily, in every case of defeat, re-evaluation must de facto be caused to occur. In this, genetic theories of justification diverge perhaps most strikingly from the views discussed so far when it comes to defeat. They lack the normative resources to have incompatibilities in a subject's attitude-system straightforwardly disqualify at least one of the incompatible attitudes from being justified. But what can be said about intuitive cases of defeat that are grounded in nothing but such an incompatibility?

To get a better grip on the issue, let us distinguish between two ways of ignoring a defeater: active ignoring and passive ignoring (cf. Constantin 2020).[25] When actively ignoring a piece of information with respect to some matter or proposition, one displays behavior that is perhaps most akin to a refusal to ac-

---

25 These correspond to a similar distinction made in Grundmann (2009b).

knowledge its epistemic relevance for that matter/proposition (cf. e.g. Reed 2006, p. 190). In contrast, a new piece of information is passively ignored with respect to a matter or proposition, just in case it is not processed by the noetic system in such a way that the relevant processes that can take it as input are engaged. Passively ignoring a defeater amounts to contingently failing to register the incompatibility between the attitude supported by the defeater and the target-attitude, such that no relevant process, like re-evaluation, is triggered. The two thus established ways of ignoring new information must be dealt with in different ways from a Reliabilist perspective.

Clearly, in a case in which Mariko dismisses Farid's testimony because she hates him personally, her belief's justification is intuitively still defeated by that testimony. Her active choice to ignore that testimony makes this intuition even stronger because it underlines Mariko's perceived irrationality. Generic Reliabilism, coupled with the Rebasing Account, can deal with such cases. Active ignoring by itself already requires registering the connection between the incompatible attitudes and at least rudimentary re-evaluation. Let us say that Mariko undervalues Farid's testimony because she hates him. Therefore, in order to select a given piece of input for undervaluing, she has to register that the piece is available for belief-basing processes to operate on and to be a piece of testimony by Farid. These propositions are higher-order and not standardly assessed whenever Mariko receives a new piece of input. They are thus the ideal candidates for cropping up during re-evaluation, just like the higher-order attitudes defeaters appeal to. Therefore, receiving the hated Farid's testimony may trigger re-evaluation, during which Mariko's hatred leads to irrational steps or premature abortion of the process (Mariko may, for example, simply stop considering something when it turns out that it comes from a source she actively ignores), rendering it unreliable.

What this suggests is that the Rebasing Account delivers an additional analytic tool that helps accounting for active ignoring. In this view, one actively ignores a new piece of information in virtue of dismissing it or giving it too little weight during a re-evaluative reasoning process triggered by receiving it. This can lead to that process either becoming unreliable or being aborted prematurely. Generic Reliabilism can thus say that irrational active ignoring not only results in unjustified attitudes, but necessarily triggers, and is even best explained in terms of, re-evaluation (cf. Constantin 2020). Thus, actively ignoring a defeater leaves the target-attitude unjustified.

The same explanation is not so well suited for accounting for passive ignoring. In order to passively ignore a piece of information, it need not be marked or recognized as of a certain type or from a certain source. It simply happens that the processes that would normally be triggered by receiving it and that tend to connect it to other held attitudes fail to engage. This corresponds to the subject not "seeing" the connection (in the case of defeat: incompatibility) between the new information and a previously held attitude. A suitable variant of RED-FALSE that illustrates this would be one where Mariko receives Farid's testimony, but, due to an extremely rare cognitive malfunction or because she is slightly distracted, does not "put two and two together" and holds on to her belief that the widgets are red, while also believing that they are illuminated by a red light. Intuitively, it seems that her belief about the color of the widgets is now defeated. But because she doesn't register the connection between defeater and target-attitude, no re-evaluation occurs. If she sustains her belief, this kind of case is a clear counterexample to a Generic Reliabilist adaptation of the Rebasing Account, since it would judge that Mariko's belief remains justified.

There are two ways to respond to this. The first is to bite the bullet on cases such as this one and accept that they are, despite appearances, not cases of defeat, but cases of mere potential defeat. This stance can be supported by an argument from analogy. Consider my philosophical belief system. I have been doing philosophy for years now and started out being really interested in metaphysics, later switching to epistemology. When I was doing metaphysics, let us assume that I formed a number of sophisticated theoretical beliefs in that area that were very well supported by my available input. It is very likely that some of these beliefs, through extremely long and complicated inferential relations, can be shown to be incompatible with some of the (let us assume equally well supported) epistemological beliefs I hold today. This is very hard, maybe even impossible, for me to detect, and becomes even harder given the temporal distance between me forming my metaphysical beliefs and me forming my epistemological beliefs. Now, it seems odd to say that my epistemological beliefs are not justified because of extremely subtle incompatibilities with "far away" metaphysical beliefs (cf. Constantin 2020). More generally, our noetic systems are bound to contain logical incompatibilities between far apart attitudes. These can be extremely complicated and are generally almost impossible to avoid. It seems to me that this should not mean that the involved attitudes are automatically ruled out as justified.[26] But of course unregistered, far apart incompatibil-

---

[26] This idea is likely to be highly controversial, given that the view that consistency is a minimal requirement for rational belief can be described as a consensus view (Huttegger 2017, p. 14). That is why I cannot commit to it at this point. Still, the idea that incompatible attitudes can nevertheless be justified may be feasible, especially for views on justification that don't care too much about rationality, like Generic Reliabilism. Also, there are some independent reasons for thinking that consistency may not be a requirement for rationality after all (see e.g. Christensen 2004; Pryor 2018).

ities can be seen as cases of passively ignored potential defeaters. Thus, it is open to the Generic Reliabilist to generally reject the idea that mere incompatibility is sufficient for defeat, motivated by cases of far apart incompatibilities that amount only to cases of mere potential defeat. This would then motivate biting the bullet on cases of passively ignored potential defeaters like the variant of RED-FALSE discussed earlier. This is the response I prefer, but it is an admittedly controversial one.

The second response would be to admit that Generic Reliabilism (or any pure version of Standard Process Reliabilism) is unable to deal with cases of passively ignored potential defeaters and must add some synchronic, possibly normative condition to account for them. In this view, passively ignored potential defeaters are not doxastic defeaters at all but "normative defeaters", that is, potentially defeating, true propositions one ought to be aware of. Still, this second response is compatible with a specific picture of defeat that does not need to admit such normative defeaters across the board. This will be picked up in the next section.

With these issues (for the most part) resolved, the picture developed in this section can be seen to show a reasonably smooth Generic Reliabilist account of defeat that makes good use of the Rebasing Account, supplementing it with the required minimum of conceptual resources to fill in the blanks. The Rebasing Account appears, in many ways, tailor-made for a "purist" version of reliabilism, such as Generic Reliabilism. With the resources such a view has for accounting for conditionally reliable reasoning, the rebasing-effect of re-evaluation processes ensures that the intuitive verdicts for especially tricky cases of misleading undercutting defeat, such as RED-FALSE, can be given without the need to add synchronic conditions to an otherwise fully genetic theory of justification. Some additional explanatory work must be done to address a number of issues arising from the purely descriptive nature of Generic Reliabilism, however. While most of these worries, such as the view's ability to provide a coherent causal picture of the succession of basing relations involved and the accommodation of cases of active ignoring, can be resolved, the intuition that justification is removed in cases of passively ignored potential defeaters is difficult to account for. This is because, at its core, the intuition is driven by normative impressions: One *ought to* register the fact that the new information is incompatible with one's attitudes. The Generic Reliabilist may bite the bullet on the relevant cases on the basis of their analogy to cases of far apart incompatibilities. If she is not willing to do so, an additional, synchronic and normative condition on justification must be added to the account that deals with such normative defeaters.

## 5.4 Normative Defeaters

So far, I have been dealing exclusively with doxastic defeaters. That is, I have been dealing with defeaters that are already part of the noetic system and, for the most part, whose incompatibility with the target-attitude has been registered by that system. The notion of doxastic defeater that has been relied on is notably broader than some that have been considered in the literature. Specifically, since defeaters can be input, under the broad, neutral definition of the term I have given in chapter 1, they can be anything from external facts to beliefs, as long as they are available for basing attitudes on.[27] I left the meaning of "available" open to be filled in by a given theory of justification. As we saw in the last section, however, normative intuitions in certain cases of defeat seem to stretch the class of things that can act as defeaters beyond the class that a given theory of justification considers as input, or at least as the kind of input that can act as a defeater.

This is why it is now common to distinguish doxastic from *normative defeat* (cf. e.g. Lackey 1999, p. 487; Lackey 2000, ch. 1–3; Lackey 2005, p. 640ff; Reed 2006, p. 190, 191; Lackey 2008, pp. 253–257; Grundmann 2011; Lackey 2014; Cloos 2015, p. 3012ff; Goldberg 2017b; Pritchard 2018, p. 3071ff).[28] Normative defeaters are not input, but *potential* input in the sense of not being possessed, but being in easy reach of the subject. The idea is then that potential input also has defeating power. Two important notes must be taken here.

First, I take normative defeaters to target justification, rather than knowledge.[29] This must be mentioned because the two may come apart. That is, it may be possible to find potentially available input that is incompatible with

---

[27] In contrast, philosophers have placed more thorough restrictions on the notion. We already saw that Pollock thinks of them as reasons which can be beliefs or experiences. Some think that they can be beliefs or doubts (Reed 2006) or, more broadly, mental states (Bergmann 2006, pp. 154–160). As explained before, I prefer a functional individuation of defeaters. Whatever does what a defeater does is a defeater. Accordingly, the only point at which the inclusion or exclusion of the defeater in the subject's mental life becomes relevant is when it comes to the accommodation of the functional account by a given theory of justification that puts certain constraints on where justification-relevant factors are to be found.

[28] Meeker 2004) and Gibbons (2006) also deal with normative defeat, though they use different labels.

[29] Some, like Meeker (2004), Gibbons (2006), Reed (2006) or Goldberg (2016, 2017a, 2017b, 2018) also consider evidence one should have to defeat justification. So does Lackey (2008), though she discusses normative defeaters with respect to knowledge in earlier work (e.g. 1999a, 2005).

knowledge, but not with justification.³⁰ Such pure "knowledge-defeaters" appeal to components of knowledge other than justification and will thus work systematically differently from the defeater-types I have been discussing and will thus also need their own theory.

Second, what I discuss as "normative defeaters" are not the kind of defeaters that the proponents of Defeasibility Theories of Knowledge have in mind (see e.g. Lehrer and Paxson 1969; Harman 1980, 1973, and for an overview Grundmann 2011). That is, normative defeaters are not just true propositions that preclude knowledge in virtue of being potential justification-defeaters, but they also need some further connection to the subject, like being ignored only at pains of epistemic negligence.

In keeping with the idea that defeat is a legitimate epistemic phenomenon in its own right, the postulation of normative defeaters must be underpinned by plausible cases and general considerations concerning justification, rather than the need to accommodate Gettier-style examples within a theory of knowledge. For ease of expression, I will follow Lackey (e.g. Lackey 2005, fn. 12) in using the expression "factual defeater" to refer to a true proposition such that, if it were available as input, it would act as a doxastic defeater, but also such that it is *not true that one should have it*. This is the kind of defeater that specifically targets knowledge and was introduced by way of the defeasibility theory of knowledge to deal with Gettier-style cases (for an overview, see Grundmann 2013). Since this is an approach to defeat that specifically refrains from treating it as an independent phenomenon, I will not deal with it here. Importantly then, I am concerned here with normative, rather than factual defeaters, which target first and foremost justification and only target knowledge insofar as justification is required for knowledge.

### 5.4.1 Assessing the Case for the Possibility of Normative Defeat

To begin with, I will look at commonly advanced cases of putative normative defeat and attempt to show that the existence of normative defeaters cannot be established relying on them without some substantive background assumptions. Specifically, it can be shown that, in many cases, the perceived epistemic failure can be explained in a way that does not involve normative defeaters.

---

30 For an attempt at finding such cases, see Gibbons (2013, p. 210 ff).

Commonly (and ignoring technical terminology for a moment), normative defeaters are taken to be counterevidence one does not have but *should possess*.[31] Here is an illustrating example by John Gibbons:

> FRIDGE: John has good reason to believe that there are eggs in the fridge. When he tries to make an omelet that morning, however, he notices that they have gone off and throws them away. Because he has to leave for work now, he writes on a post-it that there are no more eggs and puts it on the fridge, which is where he and his wife Julia always put such information. Later that day, Julia comes home, planning to bake a cake. The fridge is within her field of vision, but she doesn't pay attention to the possible presence of post-its. Because she remembers the carton of eggs she saw in the fridge yesterday, she assumes that there are still eggs in the fridge and leaves to shop only for the other ingredients. While she normally checks the fridge for post-its because she knows that that is where relevant household-information is shared, she doesn't do that on this particular day. (adapted from Gibbons 2006, p. 22)

Is Julia's belief that there are still eggs in the fridge justified? Those partial to the distinction between doxastic and normative defeaters have the intuition that it is not. This is explained in the following way: There is evidence that Julia should have had (the post-it) and that would have shown her clearly that her belief about the eggs is false. She should have had this evidence because the post-it was available to her, given that the fridge was in her visual range, that checking it is her common practice and that she knows that there may well have an important post-it on it. Thus, the evidence from the post-it defeats the justification of Julia's belief that there are eggs in the fridge (cf. Gibbons 2006, pp. 22–24). Returning to my terminology, there is a fact (the post-it) that, in a given theory of justification, is not part of Julia's input, i.e., that is not available to her for basing doxastic attitudes on. That fact should have been noticed by her, however, and thus should have been input available for basing (in the relevant sense). Furthermore, if it were input, it would be a doxastic defeater for Julia's belief about the eggs. The case then seems to suggest that this potential for doxastic defeat is sufficient for actual defeat.

First, it must be noted that this does not prove much from a theoretical standpoint. This is because an important factor that influences the classification

---

[31] Sometimes it is also claimed that a normative defeater is a belief one should have held because of evidence one should be aware of (cf. Lackey 2005, p. 639). This leads back to the question of what, exactly, can play the defeater-role. Since, in such cases, there must be evidence one should have had in any case (otherwise one could not explain why one should have had a certain belief), I will continue to treat the evidence, rather than the belief, as the putative defeater. This is also in line with the idea that states other than beliefs can be defeaters, which was argued for earlier.

of such cases is what counts as input in a given theory of justification. Imagine a hypothetical theory that is extremely liberal when it comes to what the subject has available for basing and that treats the post-it in FRIDGE, say, and a clear visual impression of a lack of eggs in the fridge as on a par in this regard. From the perspective of such a theory, FRIDGE is a straightforward case of doxastic defeat and the post-it works exactly like the defeaters in LEAVE, SCHOOL, etc. The idea behind normative defeat, however, is that there might be defeaters that are not part of the surrounding doxastic structure and that are not *actual*, but merely *potential* input. Our hypothetical inclusive theory would thus not need to accept normative defeaters at all, while still being able to provide defeat-verdicts for the relevant cases.

In general, the notion becomes increasingly more interesting the more restrictive the constraint a given theory of justification puts on what counts as input. Imagine for the sake of contrast a theory that would count only *beliefs* as input. Such a super-restrictive theory would not be able to count reading and understanding the post-it as a doxastic defeater, as long as no belief is formed. It would thus have to absolutely accept that there are cases of normative defeat, since it is clearly plausible that reading and understanding the post-it removes justification for the belief that there are eggs in the fridge and since it has to count such a case as a case of normative defeat (cf. Goldberg 2017a, p. 2864). What this shows is that pointing to apparent cases of normative defeat can just as well be understood as an argument to loosen restrictions on what is available to doxastically support beliefs, as it can be understood as suggesting that we need a whole new category of defeaters. It could be the basis for an argument for the hypothesis that even unregistered facts can be in a relevant sense *available* for basing attitudes on sometimes. After all, input is supposed to be what is available for basing and there is no in-principle reason why this should only cover cognitively registered items.

Correspondingly, a given theory's chances of successfully resisting the need to accept normative defeaters for theoretical reasons depends on the notion of input it employs and why, since the degree of its restrictiveness determines the plausibility of apparent cases of normative defeat it may be confronted with. This seldom appreciated point is clearly important to Generic Reliabilism's chances of dealing with passively ignored defeaters, but it also highlights the following point: A theory of justification that rules out seemingly plausible candidates for input-status for good reason will be able to bring the same good reason to bear on ruling out seemingly plausible factors as defeaters. Thus, any theory that provides arguments for ruling out unread post-its as input has the very same arguments at its disposal for ruling out unread post-its as defeaters. Since it may still have intuitions to account for, this means that whether there are normative defeaters is a complicated, highly theory-dependent issue, and it also means that it almost necessarily fails to be obvious whether there are normative defeaters, even if convincing cases can be found. The same is not true for doxastic defeaters, since, whatever a given theory counts as input, it counts as a potential doxastic defeater because doxastic defeaters simply are input for certain negations, as I argued at length. So, any theory of justification must accept doxastic defeaters, whereas whether it has reason to accept normative defeaters depends on the relevant details. The need to do so is not nearly as obvious as their proponents often seem to think.

Of course, it would also be too quick to reduce the apparent cases of normative defeat discussed in the literature to mere producers of case-intuitions. The cases do suggest some theoretical underpinning, at which we will look next. The most straightforward explanation for cases of normative defeat appeals to epistemic duties and responsibilities: In failing to look at the fridge before going shopping, Julia failed to check what she has good reason to believe to be an important source of input. Thereby, she irresponsibly avoided crucial information she would have obtained, had she done what an epistemically responsible subject would have done. If an epistemic duty to check readily available sources can be made plausible, one can also say that Julia shirked such a duty. The result is an irresponsibly formed or retained belief (that there are eggs in the fridge), which is then seen to be unjustified.

This responsibility-driven explanation gets further support from the fact that the strength of the defeater-intuition co-varies with the perceived egregiousness of the irresponsible behavior in a range of cases.[32] To understand this better, compare the following two cases:

> NEWSPAPER: Arthur believes that the mayor of his hometown has been accepting bribes on the basis of a report in a trusted television program. This is indeed true. He further knows that the program leans toward the liberal political spectrum and, although it is generally quite reliable, may make a mistake every now and then (it is reliable enough for justification, however). The belief suits him quite well because, as a staunch liberal, he dislikes the conservative mayor and wants to see her disgraced. One day later, Arthur considers buying a (trusted and reliable) newspaper. However, he can see that the front cover promises news on the mayor's conduct and, while the report may well affirm what Arthur already believes about the bribes, he refrains from buying the newspaper because he does not wish to ex-

---

[32] Gibbons (2006, pp. 23–24) also shows that the intuition co-varies with egregiousness of irresponsibility by inviting us to imagine a sequence of versions of the FRIDGE-case, such that the post-it gets progressively bigger until it is billboard-sized. He claims that the intuition also becomes progressively stronger. Meeker (2004, pp. 162–163) shows co-variance between the strength of the normative component of cases with defeat-intuitions as well.

pose his belief to possible refutation. The newspaper report, in fact, claims to expose the television program as mistaken, due to a misinformation campaign by the liberals, and (mistakenly) states that the mayor has not taken bribes.

STAKES: Xi wants to take the 09:15 train to work as she does every day and thus plans to be at the station at 09:12. She relies on her excellent memory of the schedule in determining when to be at the station, and the train will indeed depart at 09:15. Unbeknownst to her, however, the online schedule for the train mistakenly shows that there is construction in progress and that the train leaves at 09:10 today. A quick check of the online schedule on her phone would have informed Xi of this. Missing the train would result in Xi arriving 15 minutes late at work. While this would normally not be a problem, also unbeknownst to Xi, her boss stormed into the office this morning and screamed that anyone who was going to be late today would lose their job.

In NEWSPAPER, Arthur's perceived epistemic irresponsibility in refraining from buying the newspaper is quite egregious because he insulates himself willingly from new input. This, in turn, also strengthens the impression that there is something wrong with Arthur's belief that the mayor has been taking bribes on the second day – we get a defeat-intuition. In STAKES, on the other hand, Xi seems to behave quite responsibly from an epistemic point of view: She has taken the 09:15 train countless times in the past and knows its normal schedule extremely well. Also, it is very unlikely from her perspective that she will get into any kind of trouble at work for an unforeseen delay. Still, there is a clear sense in which it would have been easy for Xi to possess the information about the schedule change and in which it would be very good for her to possess that information. However, it would be something of a stretch, I think, to claim that Xi was irresponsible in not double-checking the train times (if one has a different intuition here, the case can be modified to strengthen her misleading reasons). Even if not, the degree of irresponsibility one could plausibly ascribe to her will be much lower than the degree ascribable to Arthur in NEWSPAPER.

Furthermore, the intuition that Xi's belief in STAKES is not justified is correspondingly weaker than the intuition that Arthur's belief that the mayor has been taking bribes is not justified.[33] A rather more natural characterization of the former case would be that Xi's epistemic behavior is fine in the sense that it suffices to make errors sufficiently unlikely. She simply has bad luck and ends up in a case where such an error occurs. That is why calling her epistemic

---

33 Cases like STAKES look like candidates that demarcate the line of distinction between a doxastic or normative defeater and a factual defeater: The information Xi misses may well prevent *knowledge* and thus count as a factual defeater, while it does not seem incompatible with *justification* and thus not count as a doxastic or normative defeater (of course, assuming that these intuitions are shared for the case).

behavior "unfortunate" is more fitting than calling it "irresponsible". In contrast, Arthur's epistemic behavior with respect to the newspaper in NEWSPAPER is quite reckless to begin with, such that epistemic fault can be found with it from the start. "Unfortunate" seems too friendly a term in this case. Therefore, it appears that the plausibility of normative defeat depends on the intuitive plausibility of an incompatibility between epistemic irresponsibility and justification.

If normative defeat is indeed grounded in the notion of epistemic responsibility or duty in the sense examined here, however, there are at least two good reasons to be doubtful of the existence of normative defeaters. The first reason is an application of the previous observation that the dialectical situation for normative defeat is remarkably complicated. Current theories of justification acknowledge that the common-language notion of justification heavily involves duty and responsibility, but, for good reason, prefer more technical notions when it comes to epistemic justification (Steup 2017). Such theories will say of some cases that, while it looks as though an attitude is justified because it is, in a pre-theoretical sense, responsibly held, that attitude is still not justified, e.g. because it was not reliably formed, does not fit the total evidence or is not virtuous.[34] We would expect such a theory to treat defeat similarly (cf. Lackey 2005, p. 643), so why should its proponent not resist at least some cases of putative normative defeat, given that they are driven by just those intuitions surrounding pre-theoretically understood responsibility and duty?

The second issue has to do with the nature and scope of the epistemic responsibilities at play. For many putative cases of normative defeat, the relevant intuition has an alternative explanation that does not require the putative normative defeater: The subject lacks justification because she was *generally irresponsible* in not checking a known source of potential counter-information. If we think that behaving epistemically irresponsibly is incompatible with justification, it is the fact that the subjects in paradigmatic cases of putative normative defeat behave irresponsibly that explains why they are not justified and not the fact that there is a piece of potential input available that they should have, but did not, take into account.

To see this, compare two versions of FRIDGE. One version is the original setup for the case in which Julia does not properly examine the fridge and misses the post-it in her field of vision. In the other version, she also fails to properly examine the fridge, but John has also forgotten to put a post-it there. Thus, in this second version, there is no piece of input she should have had, but she

---

[34] Lackey (2005, p. 643, 644) also makes this point to show that irresponsibility and justification (and thus defeat) can come apart.

still behaves irresponsibly by not properly examining the fridge. As a result, we get a case-pair where the two cases differ only in one relevant factor, that is, the presence of the putative normative defeater in the form of the post-it on the fridge. First, the intuition one has in this second version of the case where the post-it is missing seems to be exactly the same as in the original version (at least for me): Julia's belief that there are eggs in the fridge is not justified. Second, this can be explained in the exact same way considered above: She behaves epistemically recklessly in neglecting to properly check a known and easily available source of potential defeating input (the fridge). These results are not that surprising, considering the observation that the strength of the intuition concerning lack of justification becomes weaker when the egregiousness of the irresponsible behavior is lowered, as demonstrated by the contrast between NEWSPAPER and STAKES.[35]

So, what we find is that a case-pair where the cases seem to differ only in the existence or presence of the putative normative defeater and nothing else, as far as the epistemic perspective of the subject in the bad epistemic position is concerned, evokes the same intuition concerning justification. It would follow that such cases do not establish the phenomenon of normative defeat. Furthermore, the reason for this is systematic, if it is assumed that what drives intuitions in putative cases of normative defeat is the notion of epistemic irresponsibility in a general sense. What such cases emphasize is that intuitions about epistemic responsibility influence intuitions about justification, and that is hardly news. What would be needed, then, to establish normative defeat?

One way would be to find a case-type where i) there exists a true proposition that is not input, but that should be input for the subject and that, if it were input, would defeat the target-attitude, ii) that evokes clear intuitions of defeat, such that the bullet is not easily bitten and iii) is such that a variation of the case that lacks the true proposition or where the proposition has a relevantly different content but is otherwise the same does not evoke the defeat-intuition (this is the lesson from the case-pair analysis with regards to FRIDGE). Since NEWSPAPER, and not STAKES, evokes a defeat-intuition, such a case will be much more difficult to find than it may seem. Note that, at this point, two case-types have been ruled out as clearly establishing normative defeat: cases where the defeater is part of the noetic system, such as the variant of Fridge in which Julia reads and understands the post-it, but doesn't otherwise react to it (most theories of

---

[35] This also suggests another case-pair that is equally relevant and where the putative normative defeater is present in both cases, but in one case the subject behaves irresponsibly and in the other it does not. If we find, as I suspect, that the intuitions concerning justification co-vary with the presence of epistemically irresponsible behavior, the same argument can be made.

justification would count those as doxastic defeaters) and cases where the subject behaves irresponsibly in a general manner, such as NEWSPAPER (the putative normative defeater is not shown to do the explanatory work). What is left?

Defenders of normative defeaters like, for example, Gibbons (2006, pp. 23–24), Lackey (cf. Lackey 2005, pp. 642–644, 2008, pp. 255–257) and Goldberg (e.g. Goldberg 2016) disagree with me on what has been said so far. They would argue that I gave a misleading underpinning explanation for the phenomenon. The subjects in cases of normative defeat, according to them, do not irresponsibly *refrain from checking a known source of potential defeating information*, but rather irresponsibly *refrain from reacting to a true proposition that would defeat their justification and that they ought to be aware of*. They neglect their responsibility for *that particular* true proposition (cf. Gibbons 2006, pp. 22–26).

Jennifer Lackey presents a case-pair similar to the one discussed in the previous paragraph, in which one is supposed to have different intuitions. This would support the idea that the existence of the putative normative defeater itself is what makes the difference with respect to the epistemic quality of the target-attitude. This would fit the bill regarding the kind of case it would take to establish normative defeat. Here is her case:

> NEWSPAPER-2: Arthur correctly believes that the mayor has been taking bribes, based on the reliable testimony of his aunt Lola (who does not disclose her sources). Unbeknownst to him, at time *t1*, every newspaper and radio program plausibly claim that the mayor has not been taking bribes, however, but is the victim of a liberal misinformation-campaign. These news-outlets are easily available to Arthur, he simply doesn't think to check them. In fact, there is no such campaign. Instead, the mayor's party has successfully managed to dupe the news-outlets into thinking that there is and that the mayor is innocent. Since Arthur is unaware of this, he continues to believe that the mayor has been taking bribes. At *t2*, the news-outlets unmask the ruse of the mayor's party and start broadcasting and writing that the mayor has been taking bribes. Arthur still doesn't check and continues to believe as he did before. (adapted from a case in Lackey 2005, p. 640, 2008, pp. 253–254)

Lackey claims that Arthur's belief that the mayor has been taking bribes is defeated by the radio and newspaper reports that he misses out on. She then explicitly rules out the negligence-based explanation I have motivated and holds that, at *t2*, Arthur's belief becomes justified again because the reports go away. Accordingly, it must be the reports themselves that make the difference because Arthur does not retroactively become more responsible at *t2*. Thus, she presents a case that contains a relevant case-pair and claims that the defeating effect is present, just in case the input Arthur should have but misses out on is present. It is supposed that the missed true proposition or fact itself is what prevents Arthur from getting the epistemic goods, not the fact that he should have checked for it (cf. Lackey 2005, p. 642, 643). Lackey derives part of her motivation for stressing the importance of normative defeat from the observation that restricting the class of things that can be defeaters to *beliefs* seems to implausibly discount intuitively clear cases of defeat (cf. Lackey 1999, p. 475; Reed 2006, p. 189, 190).

In response, it must first be noted that this observation is already borne out by the wide definition of input and the flexible view on what can play the defeater-role I have been employing. Thus, in the present view, defeaters are far from being restricted to beliefs. They are most often input, which can include anything at all that may serve as a doxastic base. Still, clearly, this does not cover the putative normative defeater in NEWSPAPER-2, at least for any theory in which the reports don't count as input, such as Generic Evidentialism and Generic Reliabilism.

However, it is not at all clear to me that Lackey's verdict on the case is correct. I tend to have the intuition that Arthur is justified at $t1$, as well as at $t2$. So far, this may just be a conflict of intuitions (although I do think that the intuition is far from strong in either case), but two points can be made to back up doubts about the case's impact. First, it seems that there is no big difference between Arthur at $t1$ in NEWSPAPER-2 and Xi in STAKES. In the immediate epistemic vicinity of both subjects, there is a true proposition or fact that, if they were aware of it, would make them highly irrational in believing as they do. In fact, being aware of it would be even more important for Xi, given the high stakes involved for her. However, intuitively, Xi is justified in believing that the train will leave at 09:15. Still, if Arthur is responsible for the reports he misses, why wouldn't Xi also be responsible for information displayed on the easily available online schedule, given that it is at least as close to her perspective as the newspaper reports are for Arthur? In addition, consider how easy it would be to lose justification if subjects in situations like Xi's should also be said to be unjustified. As soon as any, in principle detectable, deviation from the regular states of affairs occurs in our everyday lives, like unexpected construction work, changes in the schedules of others etc., we would lose justification for otherwise extremely well supported attitudes, which could even have skeptical results.

Similarly, misleading others implausibly becomes much less deplorable in certain cases. Imagine a political committee deciding on a decisive new traffic rule and only after that rule has been decided, informing the public through the radio. This is done with this kind of timing with the intention of fining as many drivers as possible. A driver who just happens to not have the radio on at that moment and who breaks this brand-new rule can then be fully blamed for this because he can be said to be responsible for the radio report and was not justified in believing that it was OK to drive as he did. As a result, releasing relevant information at the last possible moment, as the committee does, is, in fact, a good way of putting epistemic blame on the victims of such practices. This seems implausible: The reason why such practices seem deplorable is because it is illegitimate to put the epistemic blame on the victim. A better description of such a situation would be that such practices are epistemically unfair because situations are created in which the victims have good justification for believing as they do. This makes according behavior more likely and enables cashing in on that behavior. The general point would be that anyone who judges that Arthur is unjustified at *t1* must say the same of Xi and that this judgment will overgeneralize significantly.

The second point to be made is a repetition of the observation that in virtually any view of doxastic defeat, defeaters are input, in some sense or other, that is not systematically different from any other kind. On the account of defeat proposed in this book, rebutting defeaters are most often positive input for belief in the negation of the target-proposition (or suspension of judgment about that proposition), while undercutting defeaters are standardly positive input for belief in the proposition that it is false that the target-attitude's original justifier supports that attitude. So, defeaters are input that *supports* some attitude. If one thinks of a normative defeater as input, in the sense of being available for basing, the question arises why there should only be normative defeat and not also normative support. Doxastic defeaters defeat *in virtue of* supporting something, after all, and it is not at all implausible to think that apparent normative defeaters defeat because they are potential input one should have had that supports some attitude that is incompatible with the one one already holds.

But if potential input can defeat by supporting, why, then, can it not also *just* support? Applied to NEWSPAPER-2, one may thus ask why Arthur's belief is defeated by the news-reports at *t1*, but does not enjoy additional justification by the changed reports at *t2* (Goldberg 2016, p. 456, fn. 12; cf. Goldberg 2017b, p. 339 ff). If the answer is that this would not be intuitively plausible, this, together with the parallels with STAKES, sheds all the more doubt on the significance of the intuition that Arthur suffers defeat in the first place. At the very least, the proponent of normative defeat owes an explanation as to why there is such an asymmetry between defeaters and supporting input in the normative case. The discussion of a similar proposed asymmetry between defeaters and supporting reasons with respect to the question whether defeaters need to be supported in order to defeat suggests that this is a tall order, since the very same considerations could be brought to bear here.

One final point can be made regarding the examples given in this section. I have taken care to describe the cases in such a way that the putative normative defeater has no connection to the subject's noetic system. One may think that this leaves them short of making the best case for normative defeat. For example,

## 5.4 Normative Defeaters — 225

one may want to make a distinction between NEWSPAPER-2 and STAKES: While Arthur has some independent justification to suspect that there is significant evidence pertaining to his belief in the newspaper (he is justified in taking the newspaper to be likely to contain such information), Xi has no such special justification for thinking that there is such evidence. Thus, in one case, the subject is justified to believe that *there is significant and relevant potential input* but *doesn't know what that potential input says or what it supports*, while in the other case the subject is not justified to believe that there is such input. The difference could be thought to come down to a difference in there being *expectable* further input.

The problem with this description of the situation can be summed up by the question that immediately presents itself: Why is Arthur's input supporting the proposition that there is significant, relevant input he hasn't obtained and that might easily count against his belief not itself a *doxastic* defeater? If it is, this will explain the relevant intuition in a much smoother way than the postulation of a normative defeater would. Furthermore, it is quite plausible that input propositionally supporting the belief that there is information that may easily show one's attitude to be false acts as a doxastic (rebutting) defeater. After all, if I have reason to believe that there is evidence that may easily show that my belief is false, I also have reason to believe that my belief may easily be false – a clear case of doxastic, rebutting defeat. This point makes the need for case-pairs that feature no difference in background input apparent. An explanation-relevant difference in the possessed input of the protagonists will explain a difference in intuition without having to recur to putative normative defeat at all.

Summing up, there are then three reasons why the case for normative defeat is overstated: First, given that normative defeaters are supposed to be potential input, that is, propositions that would be input were the subject aware of them, what counts as a normative defeater depends on what a given theory of justification counts as input. The more inclusive the notion, the more far-fetched and less convincing the relevant cases turn out. The need to accommodate them thus fluctuates with the details of the given theory. Also, for input-wise more restrictive theories, this tends to render apparent cases of normative defeat cases that the relevant theory is already committed to bite the bullet on, in which case they will be resisted. Second, for many seemingly convincing cases of apparent normative defeat, there is a second explanation for the intuition aside from the presence of the putative defeater in the form of a lack of more general epistemic responsibility. This is illustrated by the case-pair discussed for FRIDGE. If such a case-pair is possible, the alternative explanation must first be ruled out in order to take the relevant case to establish the phenomenon of normative defeat. Finally, even if unproblematic cases can be found, one may still worry that the postulation of the epistemic significance of input one should have had overgeneralizes. Parallel cases such as STAKES yield counterintuitive results and one would have to find an explanation as to why such evidence can't also offer additional support, rather than only defeat.

### 5.4.2 Remaining Motivations to Accept the Possibility of Normative Defeat: The Example of Goldberg's View

Given all this, I am nevertheless not generally opposed to postulating the existence of normative defeaters. One may well be concerned about cases such as the ones discussed here, while still preferring conceptions of input that don't allow them to count as cases of doxastic defeat. Philosophers who have such concerns sometimes also hold theories of justification that do include such conceptions and also favor irresponsible unawareness of specific propositions over general irresponsibility as an explanation for the relevant cases. Such a theory-driven motivation can be a good reason to accept NEWSPAPER-2 and possibly cases like STAKES as cases of defeat.

A recent example of such a view is the account of, in part, socially determined justification by Sanford Goldberg (developed in Goldberg 2016, 2017a, 2017b, 2018). Goldberg can motivate the idea that it is the neglected piece of information itself and not the behavior that leads to its neglect that prevents the target-belief from being justified. He thinks that, in virtue of belonging to a society with certain epistemic practices and standards, one can be properly expected to possess the relevant information and be held responsible for evidence one misses out on but should have had (Goldberg 2018, ch. 6). Thus, if one's doctor does not know some new revelation that would show her beliefs about one's condition to be false because she did not read the latest research, one can justifiedly criticize her for not knowing about it and her beliefs about one's condition would not be justified. If there was no such revelation, on the other hand, one would be perfectly happy with the doctor's performance and her beliefs about one's condition would be justified (cf. Goldberg 2017b, p. 345, 2018, p. 162). Thus, the idea is that the social practices and expectations are sensitive to actually missed, relevant information, rather than, more broadly, epistemically irresponsible behavior. As a result, it is the presence of the putative normative defeater itself that makes the difference, such that properly adapted case-pairs like the one's previously discussed will be given different verdicts with respect to justification.

The idea that defeat can be grounded in social expectations goes back to attempts to deal with cases originally proposed by Harman (cf. Harman 1968, pp. 172–173, 1980, p. 164). In response to Harman's observations, Pollock proposes a new class of defeaters: socially sensitive defeaters (cf. Pollock and Cruz 1999, pp. 192–193).[36] While this notion was originally centered on knowledge, it has been applied to justification since Meeker 2004. These positions may not be quite developed enough to give us normative defeat, however, given the complicated theoretical issues pointed out in this section. That is not to say that better developed positions don't exist.

The already mentioned view by Goldberg (presented in its full form in Goldberg 2018) is a rich theory describing evidence one should have had, normative defeat and justification in general. He also rightly addresses the question that previous accounts leave out and that I have raised in response to the examples above: What is the epistemic significance of supporting true propositions one should be aware of, if any, and what is the difference to putative normative defeaters? Goldberg's position is that potentially defeating propositions one should be aware of present an "epistemic ceiling" (Goldberg 2016, p. 449) in that it can lower justification, but not increase it (cf. Goldberg 2016, pp. 459–460, 2017b). He holds this not only for cases where the subject has no direct epistemic relationship with that putative defeater (no higher-order input indicating that there is the putative defeater), but even for cases where the subject has excellent reason to believe that the propositions it should be aware of support the target-attitude (Goldberg 2016, pp. 457–461). I disagree with him on this point and will elaborate my position in the next chapter when discussing higher-order/lower-order interactions between input.

In general, it must be noted that much of Goldberg's framework is controversial since the heavy emphasis on social practices may be felt to go too far (consider epistemic subjects on lonely islands and the extremely high overriding force of social expectations). Similarly, his account rests on the assumption that social expectations and practices do select for neglected information, rather than epistemic irresponsibility. This, too, is not obvious, although Goldberg does a lot to motivate the point. Another significant worry would be that the norms derived from social environments are not actually epistemic norms, but practical or even narrowly social norms. Those could secure the relevant case-verdicts but they could also skew the results with respect to *epistemic* justification. In general, I do not want to take up a position on Goldberg's view here, however. If one

---

**36** Another earlier version of the view can already be found in Harman (1973) and also Kornblith (1983).

finds the idea of normative defeaters plausible, a theory like his is a good way to properly explain and integrate them. Conversely, the theory also presents a good example of normative defeaters resulting naturally from a general picture of justification and defeat.

### 5.4.3 The Rebasing Account and Normative Defeat: Passively Ignored Defeaters as Normative Defeaters?

To round out this chapter, I will now suggest how the Rebasing Account can help analyze cases like the ones discussed in this section as cases of defeat for those theories that would favor such an analysis.

Since, as their label suggests, normative defeaters function in a distinctly normative manner, the most straightforward way to account for them would be to treat them as *potential* doxastic defeaters, which have already been introduced in the previous chapter. The central idea would be that, instead of *doxastically* pre-structuring re-evaluation, they could be said to *normatively* pre-structure re-evaluation. The way to construct such an account, roughly, would proceed in three steps. First, one identifies informative cases of normative defeat and extrapolates the content of the defeating items. Second, one determines the Type-1 and Type-2 obligations one wishes to take on board. An evidentialist will pick only the Evidential Norm, while other Philosophers may go for some or all of the positive or negative obligations discussed in the section on the normative structure of defeaters. Finally, the selected norms must be utilized to explain i) why the subject ought to possess the normative defeater and what their potential shortcoming is if they do not and ii) how the content of the normative defeater, if obtained, would impact a competent re-evaluation of the target-attitude and thereby pre-structure it in the ways laid out in previous chapters. Concerning ii), it must be ensured that the results of re-evaluation conform with the defeat-intuitions in the relevant cases.

Obviously, achieving these three goals puts some serious constraints on the epistemic obligations one chooses to accept. The social norms Goldberg has in mind may fit the bill and so might a large chunk of the Type-2 obligations governing re-evaluation that were listed and explained in the first section of this chapter. In general, at least the Type-2 obligations required to get the Rebasing Account off the ground for normative defeaters will be relatively broad and not too demanding, given that, for the most part, they are general norms for reasoning processes that should be uncontroversial to most normatively inclined epistemologists. Note that, as I argued in the previous section, the rules connecting the steps of re-evaluation can be accommodated by epistemologists of most, or possibly all, stripes.

The relevant Type-1 obligations are more tricky to set up properly, but they are difficult to find independently of the Rebasing Account, as the criticisms that can be levelled against normative defeat show. To illustrate a Rebasing Account of normative defeat, consider FRIDGE again and let us assume with Goldberg that the social practice of checking the fridge before shopping for groceries grounds an epistemic requirement for Julia to possess the information on the post-it. What makes that information a normative defeater? First, due to the social practices at play, the normative defeater is properly connected to the subject, opening the door for suitable Type-1 obligations. Second, given that Julia is obliged to be aware of the content of the message on the post-it, she is also obliged to process it in accordance with the norms governing the registering of noetic incompatibilities and re-evaluative reasoning processes, plausibly assuming that one is generally obliged to treat new information in an epistemically acceptable way. That way, Type-2 obligations enter the picture. This should result in an obligation to give up her belief that there are eggs in the fridge because the information on the post-it makes a re-evaluation process that does not result in giving up the target-belief incompetent. After all, that information successfully neutralizes the original justifier for that belief by counterbalancing it. This amounts to the information on the post-it normatively pre-structuring the relevant re-evaluation process, which in turn allows a Rebasing Account of normative defeat to get off the ground. A Rebasing Account of normative defeat is then preferable to its competitors for the same reasons that prefer the Rebasing Account of doxastic defeat and that have been extensively discussed in the previous chapters.

Finally, let me return to the Generic Reliabilist accommodation of the Rebasing Account of defeat. The result of the previous section on Generic Reliabilism was that there are plausible cases of defeat that cannot be easily accounted for: cases of passively ignored defeaters. We can now see that a Generic Reliabilist concerned about these cases could postulate that passively ignored defeaters are, in fact, normative defeaters.[37] Pursuing this idea, one may ask how cases of passively ignored defeat relate to the cases of apparent normative defeat discussed in this section. An obvious difference is that passively ignored defeaters are part of the subject's noetic system. It is their connection to the target-attitude

---

**37** Gibbons (2006) could be read as suggesting this. If in his case the post-it within the field of vision can be counted as input, as it may in Generic Reliabilism, his version of FRIDGE may be a case of passively ignored defeat. His proposal of how to deal with the case is then very close to what I have to say here. Goldberg (2017a), too, seems to group passively ignored defeaters and normative defeaters together.

that is missed, rather than the defeating information itself. Accordingly, in Generic Reliabilism, one gets cases of normative defeat of the most intuitively convincing type: cases where one fails to do proper housekeeping with respect to one's own noetic system.

Specifically, the case of passively ignored defeat discussed in the previous section where the subject does not register the connection between a co-worker telling her about a red light with her belief that the widgets in front of her are red is structurally analogous to the most plausible variant of FRIDGE where John reads and understands but doesn't otherwise react to the post-it. What the Generic Reliabilist may thus want to account for are cases in which the information is part of the input, but not properly put into relation with the target-attitude. She need *not* also account for cases where there is some external information that is not part of the input, but that would shed light on the target-attitude if it were. This makes it easier to find plausible normative conditions to add to Generic Reliabilism that help account for them. Following the line of thought in Constantin 2020, they can be selected such that cases of passively ignored defeaters are taken care of, while the more controversial cases like NEWSPAPER, STAKES, NEWSPAPER-2 and the original version of FRIDGE do not turn out to be cases of defeat.

Specifically, turning first to Type-1 obligations, while it is not at all obvious that one has an obligation to actively look for additional input while holding already justified doxastic attitudes, even if there is no special reason to think that defeaters are likely, it is quite plausible that one is obliged to look out for incompatibilities between pieces of input within one's own noetic system.[38] In contrast, the scope for potential Type-1 obligations that get violated in cases like the original version of FRIDGE etc. is somewhat difficult to figure out, at least if one is not willing to subscribe to factual defeaters as well. In such cases, the input one fails to but should have does not merely exist somewhere but is also easily available to the subject in some substantial sense. In FRIDGE, for example, the post-it is not supposed to be a normative defeater just in virtue of existing as a potential piece of input, but rather in virtue of doing so *and being relatively easily available* to Julia (one of the reasons why her behavior may be seen as irresponsible). Spelling out the exact sense of "available" that feeds into the relevant obligations in this picture is tricky – certainly more difficult than spelling it out for cases of passively ignored defeaters in which the defeating item is already part of the subject's epistemic perspective.

---

[38] Goldberg holds an account – coherence-infused reliabilism – that emphasizes this feature and that seems to be the kind of Reliabilist account I consider here (see Goldberg 2018, ch. 4).

What this shows is that not all purported cases of normative defeat must be treated alike. It is certainly an option to have one's theory of justification account for some, but not others. Accordingly, Generic Reliabilism, and indeed any theory of justification that cannot treat passively ignored defeaters as doxastic defeaters, has the option to i) accept passively ignored defeaters as normative defeaters, while ii) rejecting unpossessed, potential input one should have had as normative defeaters.

This may well be an attractive position. The defeating power of potential input one should have is tied to controversial theoretical assumptions and does not seem to be consistently backed by plausible cases, whereas passively ignored defeaters consistently evoke the intuition that justification is lost and require much less debatable Type-1 obligations to explain them (no noetic incompatibilities, rather than no incompatibilities with available, potential input). Furthermore, while the Generic Reliabilist willing to account for passively ignored defeaters would need to add some synchronic, normative condition to her otherwise descriptive theory, such a condition is limited in scope and plausible enough. It would merely need to ensure that re-evaluation is required, in case there is input in one's noetic system that supports an attitude that is incompatible with the simultaneously held target-attitude.[39] If she wanted to account for input that is not, but should be, part of the noetic system as normative defeat as well, the required new condition would need to bring with it a whole host of controversial further positions on a range of issues.

Finally, limiting the accepted cases to those of passively ignored defeat also severely limits the degree to which the resulting new view diverges from "pure" reliabilism and that might be worthwhile for some. In general, if the proponent of a genetic theory of justification wishes to account for passively ignored defeaters instead of biting the bullet on them, it is open to them to modify their position in a way that analyzes passively ignored defeaters in the way normative defeaters are commonly analyzed, while rejecting cases of input one should have had as cases of normative defeat. One could also say that it is open to them to accept only those cases of putative normative defeat as cases of actual normative defeat that are also cases of passively ignored defeat.

This concludes the accommodation of the Rebasing Account of Defeat to different theories of justification. Starting with normative or obligation-centered theories, I examined what can be called the normative structure of defeaters. Two kinds of obligations were identified that could serve to underpin the Rebas-

---

**39** This could, of course, be spelled out in terms of processes alone and thus come down to Goldman's previously discussed alternative-processes solution to the problem of defeat.

ing Account: Type-1 obligations that connect the incompatibility produced by the defeater with re-evaluation, and Type-2 obligations that tie together re-evaluation. It was shown that these obligations can be spelled out as negative obligations and reduced to few, not particularly controversial general obligations. Furthermore, within the structure created by these obligations, competent re-evaluations can be distinguished from incompetent ones in terms of the results of the re-evaluation conforming to general standards on justification that depend on the given theory. Second, I introduced two generic versions of purist internalist and externalist theories of justification and I discussed what resources they have for accommodating the Rebasing Account and where they are lacking in this regard. Finally, I addressed the possibility of normative defeaters in response to the Generic Reliabilist problem with passively ignored defeaters. I argued that it is far from obvious that there are normative defeaters and that accepting passively ignored defeaters as normative defeaters can be divorced from accepting normative defeaters across the board, opening up theoretical space for Generic Reliabilism. In the final chapter, I will now try to apply the account of defeat presented so far to an interesting and epistemically relevant phenomenon: disagreement. This will also allow me to take a stance with respect to the general function of higher-order input.

# 6 Defeat and Disagreement

In the final chapter of this work, I want to give my take on currently debated issues relating to higher-order information and disagreement. So far, the discussion has been, in many ways, highly theoretical. This is fine, given that the goal has been to develop a framework for a widely accepted and virtually ubiquitous phenomenon that is neutral with respect to theories of justification – a task that naturally moves from relatively uncontroversial every-day cases to their theoretical capture. Having accomplished that task, I now want to highlight that the project is more than a theoretical game and that it can give illuminating insights with respect to actual epistemic practice. It can help determine what to do, epistemically speaking, in unclear everyday-situations like disagreement. Thereby, the discussion is led from explanation to application. In doing so, I also hope to show that the Rebasing Account of Defeat can shed further light on the question how higher-order input relates to first-order input – a question that has gathered some interest recently. I will start with discussing what one is rationally obliged to do with one's view when confronted with a disagreeing peer, and I'll try to frame possible answers in terms of defeaters and kinds of defeaters. I will then distinguish a range of cases where different kinds of new input are obtained and relate them to kinds of defeaters. I will then use the results as a starting base to formulate an argument for a specific position concerning the epistemology of disagreement, namely, Strong Conciliationism.

Higher-order propositions have played a rather prominent role in the discussion so far. Some arguments have been given as to why they may play a role in undercutting defeat, and the phenomena of higher-order rebutting defeat and additional higher-order support have also been addressed. In this chapter, higher-order input will be discussed more generally still. There are two popular approaches philosophers take to this issue that differ more in background than in essence.

One approach starts with the search for the rules of epistemic rationality and the phenomenon of enkrasia (it seems that, if one rationally believes that one ought to Φ, then one is rationally required to intend to Φ).[1] This then raises the question what one rationally ought to do in cases where the enkratic requirement is in tension with other rational rules, namely cases where one has good reason to Φ, while also having good reason to think that one doesn't have good reason to Φ. The other path starts with the question what one rationally

---

[1] Examples for approaches to the topic from this direction are Egan and Elga 2005; Schechter 2013; Schoenfield 2015; Sliwa and Horowitz 2015; Titelbaum 2015; Christensen 2016.

ought to do with one's attitude, given that someone whom one has good reason to take to be just as likely to be right disagrees. In cases where both parties draw on the same first-order input, it may then turn out that one has, in fact, formed one's attitude as a correct response to the input, but that one also has good reason to doubt that very fact.

In this chapter, I will approach the topic from the perspective of an epistemologist interested in the phenomenon of disagreement. Two reasons motivate this: First, I take it that what the relevant rational rules say is informed, to some extent, by what a given theory designates as the rationality-determining factors. In the case of the literature surrounding the enkratic requirement and first-order/higher-order conflicts, the debate is heavily influenced by the idea that (first-order) evidence determines what is rational/justified to believe, as the Evidence Norm would have it. This leads to tension with the enkratic requirement in cases of misleading higher-order evidence (cf. e.g. Sliwa and Horowitz 2015; Silva 2017). A thorough commentary on this would require an exhaustive evaluation of both the enkratic requirement and the Evidence Norm. This would not only go beyond the scope of this chapter but also seem inappropriate, given that, in the service of theory-neutrality, a commitment to Evidentialism and the Evidence Norm must be avoided. [2]

Second, I am interested in applying the theory developed so far to epistemic practice. The question about what we rationally ought to do with our opinions when confronted with other people who disagree is highly relevant in our social, political, ethical and everyday lives, in which we are regularly confronted with disagreement. As I will try to show, the account of defeat developed thus far provides a powerful argument to decide what to do in such cases that derives its weight from a general framework of higher-order input. This can be developed from the accounts of defeat established so far and from case-analysis. Furthermore, I will make an attempt to show that perceived differences between undercutting and *higher-order defeaters*, which target the subject's competence rather than the epistemic connections between justifier and target-attitude, vanish to an extent when observed through the lens of the Rebasing Account. The goal will be to distinguish these two types of defeater as subsets of the set of source-sensitive defeaters that are not deeply distinguishable, thus unifying them under the general framework of the Rebasing Account.

---

[2] For the record, I have certain sympathies with the point made in Silva (2017) on this issue. The distinction between propositional and doxastic justification should have a more prominent place in this debate. This would also expose the unduly strict limits that the idea that first-order evidence determines rational/justificatory status imposes on the epistemic evaluations of these cases.

## 6.1 Disagreement

### 6.1.1 Examples and Basic Terminology

To get a grip on the issue at hand, consider the following, well-known case of disagreement:

> RESTAURANT: Dominik and Miriam have known each other for years and are well aware that they get things right when they are doing simple mental math roughly equally often. Today, they are going to a restaurant with a couple of friends. After the meal, everybody decides to split the bill evenly. The waiter brings them the bill showing the total and Miriam and Dominik both do mental math in trying to figure out how much each participant has to pay. Miriam comes up with 31 Euros, while Dominik's result is 33 Euros. They share their results.[3]

Assuming Miriam's perspective for a moment, it seems intuitive that she would be epistemically wrong to continue to believe that each participant has to pay 31 Euros after she learns that Dominik has come up with 33 Euros. In fact, suspension of judgment on her part seems to be the correct reaction. Part of the explanation for this must be the fact that both Miriam and Dominik have reason to believe that their opponent in the disagreement over the restaurant bill is as likely to get things right as they are themselves (cf. Elga 2007, p. 488 ff; Enoch 2010, p. 956). This bit is not too controversial, so let us first introduce a number of concepts that help describe what is going on so far and that can also be accepted by both sides in the debate I will sketch in this section.

First, I take it that RESTAURANT is a case of peer-*disagreement* because Miriam and Dominik hold attitudes for which the following principle is fulfilled:

Disagreement:
Person $A$ and person $B$ are in a disagreement at time $t$, iff $A$ and $B$ believe propositions $p$ and $q$, respectively, such that $p$ and $q$ cannot both be true.

It must be mentioned that *Disagreement* is not uncontroversial. It may overgeneralize and predict disagreements where, intuitively, there are none (e.g. Marques 2014). Also, it does not capture a disagreement between a belief-holder and someone who suspends judgment (see e.g. Palmira 2013) or between subjects having different credences encoding the same flat-out attitude about the same proposition (cf. MacFarlane 2014, ch. 6). Since I will not address these important issues in detail because I have another point to make, I will simply flag them

---

[3] The case is adapted from Christensen's (2007, p. 193) original version.

here and assume *Disagreement* for the purposes of this discussion. It should be a plausible enough account for a large swath of disagreement-cases.

Second, RESTAURANT is a case of *peer*-disagreement because Miriam and Dominik have reason to take each other to be *epistemic peers*. The gloss that epistemic peerness is given in the case description implies that peers are roughly equally good at the relevant epistemic evaluation. This is supposed to underpin the "rational pressure" that Miriam and Dominik's realization that they disagree with each other exerts on them, respectively, to give up their beliefs about the bill splitting.

This description is still too metaphorical, although already quite intelligible. In an attempt to clear it up, let us ask why Miriam may feel compelled to become less confident in her belief that she and Dominik each have to pay 31 Euros by her realization that Dominik disagrees with her. A straightforward answer is that, from her perspective, Dominik stands a good chance of being right about the issue. In fact, since he is usually right on matters of mental math as often as Miriam is, he is also as likely to be right about the bill shares as Miriam is. What this suggests is that what generates rational pressure here is the fact that both Dominik and Miriam, in knowing each other's track record on mental math, can make the reasonable judgment that their relative likelihood to be right or wrong about the bill shares is roughly equally high. This suggests the following conception of epistemic peerhood:

Peerhood:
Person $A$ and person $B$ are epistemic peers with respect to a proposition $p$ at time $t$, iff, $A$ and $B$ are equally likely to hold a true belief about $p$ at $t$ (adapted from Enoch 2010, p. 956).[4]

This account of peerhood will be assumed for the rest of this chapter.[5]

A couple of notes are in order. First, the time-relativity of peerhood implicit in this conception disassociates *general* characteristics of the disagreeing parties from the epistemic situation they are in in a given case of peer-disagreement. The idea is that knowledge about another person's track record or epistemic character may *justify* one in taking that person as a peer in a given situation, but it is not *constitutive* of peerness. To see this, consider that in cases like RESTAURANT, actual peerhood between the parties of the disagreement is not what drives the

---

[4] See also White 2009; Sosa 2010.
[5] An assumption is appropriate here because there is some disagreement over how peerhood is to be understood (for an overview, see Gelfert 2011). Nevertheless, I believe that this assumption gets at the heart of the matter because it can be accepted, at least for the purpose of the present argument, by defenders of both the Equal Weight View and the Total Evidence View.

relevant intuition. It is rather the fact that Dominik and Miriam, respectively, have sufficiently good reasons to justifiedly take each other to be peers. That is, if it were the case that Miriam was, in fact, slightly better than Dominik in mental math, but Dominik had excellent reason to believe that they are equally good, the intuitive verdict would be the same. Thus, what generates the relevant rational pressure is that the parties are justified to believe that *Peerhood* is fulfilled between them. Second, as before, I purposefully refer to beliefs in this definition, rather than attitudes. This is because, for now, I want to avoid the previously mentioned question of how to model disagreement with an agnostic. Finally, if one is unhappy with the use of the concept of probability in *Peerhood*, one may plug in other concepts in its stead.[6]

Finally, there is at least some agreement between broadly conciliatory positions on disagreement about the idea that peer-disagreement presents a *defeater* for the disagreement-grounding beliefs of the disagreeing parties (see e.g. Grundmann 2013; Matheson 2015a). That is to say that having justification for believing that a peer disagrees with one *at least somewhat lowers the degree of support* that the contentious belief enjoys. Given that disagreement is guaranteed to offer no *further* support for the contentious belief, denying this claim would amount to holding that learning that someone whom one justifiedly judges to be as likely to be right as oneself about the matter disagrees with oneself is no input for one's belief at all. In other words: Denying that recognized disagreement defeats amounts to claiming that disagreement has no epistemic relevance to the contentious belief at all. This or a slightly weaker version of this Steadfast view has been defended by some philosophers (cf. van Inwagen 1996; Kelly 2005; Bergmann 2009) but the view that peer-disagreement has at least some defeating force has proven more plausible.[7]

What is controversial between the more widely accepted broadly conciliatory positions is what kind of defeater such disagreement amounts to. If it is a defeater that affects the relation between the input and the target-belief, such as an undercutting defeater, its effects will differ significantly from the effects of disagreement as a (partial) rebutting defeater. As will be seen next, the most prominent positions on the impact of peer-disagreement can be distinguished nicely by the nature of the defeater they postulate peer-disagreement to provide.

---

**6** Elga (2007), for example, seems to rely on conditional credences, rather than something like truth-probabilities.

**7** Indicators for this are that generally plausible motivations for Steadfast responses are rarely supposed to establish the adequacy of Steadfast responses for all or even most cases of disagreement (e.g. Enoch 2010; Lackey 2010) and that fully Steadfast positions have been revised (see the move from Kelly 2005 to Kelly 2010).

## 6.1.2 Disagreement as a Defeater: Strong and Weak Versions of Conciliationism

In this paragraph, two versions of a broadly Conciliationist view on peer-disagreement will be distinguished: Strong and Weak Conciliationism. It will be shown how the difference between the two can be cashed out as a difference in the defeater-type that each view takes disagreement to constitute. This distinction will be the basis for a theory-driven argument for Strong Conciliationism in the next paragraph that draws on what has been learned about defeaters so far.

According to *Strong Conciliationism*, being confronted with a disagreeing peer amounts to being in a situation in which one rationally ought to modify the contentious belief as though one had lost the first-order input it was originally based on. Assuming that this also pertains to justification, this amounts to the claim that, *in cases of peer-disagreement, the degree of justification that the contentious belief enjoys is equal to the degree of justification it would enjoy if one didn't have the input it was originally based on.*[8] This is supposed to be a corollary of the idea that, in cases such as RESTAURANT, one ought to "bracket" the input one originally relied on (Elga 2007, p. 489; Christensen 2010a, p. 195).

One of Strong Conciliationism's most prominent proponents, David Christensen, motivates this position (roughly) as follows: Each out of two parties to a peer-disagreement has good reason to believe that at least one of the involved parties has made a mistake because they cannot both be right. Furthermore, they have good reason to believe that the likelihood that they themselves have made the mistake is just as high as the likelihood that their opponent has made the mistake because they have good reason to take each other to be epistemic peers with respect to the contentious proposition at the time of the disagreement. As a result, both parties have good reason to believe that the likelihood that they have made a mistake is, at least, 0.5, which is far too high to reasonably stick to their original belief (Christensen 2007, p. 197 ff).[9] This motivates the view that peer-disagreement provides full defeaters. What kind of de-

---

[8] This may or may not result in a recommendation to suspend judgment or to "split the difference" (Christensen 2007, p. 203) etc. It seems to me that these blanket-recommendations are too coarse grained. It is simply unlikely that, from the idea that peer-disagreement somehow neutralizes the input at play at the beginning, we can predict the rational attitude for every possible case, especially in light of generative-defeat phenomena or the possibility that defeaters can double as reasons (cf. Constantin and Grundmann 2020).

[9] Conversely, the chance of being right is no higher than, at best, 0.5 and that is equivalent to tossing a coin on the truth of the belief.

feater is at play will then depend on the kind of mistake that is made likely by the disagreement.

A Strong Conciliationist thinks that this mistake renders the original input rationally unusable. In a standard case of peer-disagreement like RESTAURANT the input is shared between the two parties. Both Miriam and Dominik rely on the total shown by the bill and general mathematical principles they both know in coming up with their beliefs about the shares. The mistake that must have been made by at least one party must then be a mistake with respect to the *correct evaluation* of the input. That is, at least one party must have misjudged the support- or defeat- relationship between the shared input and the positions of the parties. Another way of putting this would be to say that at least one side has based their attitude *improperly* on the input. This leads Christensen to the "Independence Principle" (Christensen 2009, p. 758), according to which being confronted with a disagreeing peer requires one to rely only on input independent of the disagreement, that is, one is to rely only on input that does not serve as the doxastic bases for the beliefs of the parties.

Accordingly, in Strong Conciliationism, the kind of defeater provided by learning of a disagreeing peer is or is akin to an undercutting defeater. It is the kind of defeater that targets the relationship between the input and the target-attitude, broadly conceived, rather than the correctness of the target-attitude or the veracity of the input. As was seen earlier, this entails that the kind of defeat at play is *source-sensitive*.[10] I will leave open for now whether there may be kinds of source-sensitive defeaters that are not undercutting defeaters and characterize the broader class as follows:

S-Def:

$d$ is a source-sensitive defeater iff

1. $d$ is a defeater for subject $S$ with respect to $S$'s doxastic attitude $B(p)$ (in the sense established earlier)

2. Whether $d$ is a defeater for $S$ with respect to $B(p)$ depends on $S$ relying on input $j$ as her total doxastic base for $B(p)$.

Condition 2. is supposed to express the thought that a source-sensitive defeater defeats by questioning a specific source of input or epistemic relations concerning a specific set or kind of input. As a result, whether such defeat occurs de-

---

[10] We will see later that not all source-sensitive defeaters need be undercutting defeaters. That is why I will go with the broader label here.

pends on whether the subject actually relies on the input targeted by the defeater. This has been discussed in the chapter on undercutting defeat.

We have seen that Strong Conciliationism postulates that standard cases of peer-disagreement provide a *source-sensitive defeater*. Strong Conciliationism's dialectical opponent in this context is *Weak Conciliationism*. A proponent of Weak Conciliationism holds that being confronted with a disagreeing, recognized peer never (or only in extremely rare fringe cases) rationally requires one to modify the contentious belief as though one had lost the first-order input it was originally based on. Instead, it must be modified so that it reflects the degree of support offered by a set of *total input* that results from *adding* the input gained from learning about the disagreement to the contentious belief's original doxastic basis, that is, to the input that the contentious belief was originally based on (Kelly 2010, pp. 198–208). In terms of justification, the idea is that the degree of justification that the contentious belief enjoys depends on the degree of support that the set of total input possessed at the time of the disagreement offers to it, where that set results from adding the input gained from learning about the disagreement to the belief's original doxastic basis.

In this picture, the original doxastic basis does not *lose* epistemic significance for the contentious belief but is merely counterbalanced to a degree by the information from disagreement. Accordingly, what reaction to peer disagreement is required depends on its weight, relative to the weight of the disagreement which is taken to propositionally support disbelief or suspension of judgment (Kelly 2010, p. 203). In some cases, the input gained from learning about the disagreement will completely "swamp" (Kelly 2010, p. 144) the original doxastic basis and generate results that are intuitive for cases often championed by Strong Conciliationists. In other cases, the original doxastic basis makes up enough of the total input to justifiedly stick to the contentious belief. To understand this better, consider the application of the view to RESTAURANT. How to go about this depends on what, exactly, is characterized as the relevant input. Essentially, the proponent of Weak Conciliationism has two options here. According to the first option, Miriam and Dominik have some input for their beliefs, aside from the disagreement itself. In that case, given that this input will continue to offer support for their beliefs in a Steadfast view, it cannot be guaranteed that they will be required to give up their beliefs. This will depend on whether their original input has sufficient weight relative to the disagreement. According to the second option, Miriam and Dominik have no other input, independently of the disagreement.

In any case, Weak Conciliationism cannot (and probably will not) give the same verdict as Strong Conciliationism, which states that Miriam and Dominik's degree of confidence must be such that it does not take their original doxastic bases into account. Alternatively, it can somehow be made plausible that Miriam and Dominik have no other input available for their beliefs (implausible as that may seem), aside from their disagreement, in which case Strong Conciliationism's verdict becomes available to proponents of Weak Conciliationism.[11]

Now, how is Weak Conciliationism to be spelled out in terms of defeat? Roughly, in Weak Conciliationism, learning that a peer disagrees provides one with a (full or partial) *rebutting* defeater. However, there is an interesting twist to this that relates back to the special characteristics of peer-disagreement. Consider the following line of thought by Kelly (cf. Kelly 2010, pp. 135–150): Let us assume, plausibly enough, that realizing that we are in a disagreement with a peer gives us some higher-order input that relates to the question whether the shared lower-order input supports our contentious belief. That is, learning that Dominik in RESTAURANT believes that each share is 33 Euros, based on the shared information from the bill, supports the proposition that the shared information between him and Miriam supports that each share is 33 Euros. At the same time, learning that Miriam believes that each share is 31 Euros, based on the shared information from the bill, supports the contrary proposition that the shared information supports that each share is 31 Euros. As a result, both Miriam and Dominik have the following four pieces of input:

1. The information on the bill about the total
2. The information that Miriam believes that each share is 31 Euros on the basis of the bill
3. The information that Dominik believes that each share is 33 Euros on the basis of the bill
4. The information that Miriam and Dominik are peers about mental math

Because of 4., 2. and 3. offer equally strong support for the respective higher-order beliefs: The information that Miriam believes that each share is 31 Euros on the basis of the bill supports the higher-order belief that the bill supports that each share is 31 Euros to the same degree as the information that Dominik believes that each share is 33 Euros on the basis of the bill supports the higher-order belief that the bill supports that each share is 33 Euros. Accordingly, 2. and 3. should cancel each other out. If so, this leaves both Miriam and Dominik only with their original doxastic bases: 1. This seems to support the result that both

---

**11** Even though much depends on these tricky details, this is not to suggest that Weak Conciliationism is less plausible in general. Thomas Kelly (2010, 2013) describes a range of cases that show that it has significant explanatory resources and may even treat some cases better than certain versions of Conciliationism can.

Miriam and Dominik may justifiedly continue to believe as they do on the basis of 1. in spite of the disagreement.

However, it remains true that 2. and 3. *together* support *suspension of judgment* about the amount of each share for both Dominik and Miriam, which is incompatible with them continuing to hold their beliefs as before the disagreement. Thus, because their total input now contains a set of input that supports suspension of judgment, due to the disagreement, Miriam's and Dominik's beliefs are rendered less well justified than they were before the disagreement. The case is thus supposed to be a case of rebutting defeat where the rebutting defeater supports suspension of judgment (analogous to DEVICE).

It seems to me that this is the best Steadfast attempt to accommodate the higher-order relevance of disagreement. To emphasize how this kind of defeat by disagreement is supposed to stand in contrast with the kind that Strong Conciliationism proposes, we can say that disagreement, in Weak Conciliationism, provides a *source-neutral* defeater:

N-Def:

$d$ is a source-neutral defeater iff

1.  $d$ is a defeater for subject $S$ with respect to $S$'s doxastic attitude $B(p)$.
2.  Whether $d$ is a defeater for $S$ with respect to $B(p)$ is independent of $S$ relying on input $j$ as her total doxastic base for $B(p)$.

Condition 2. captures the idea that a source-neutral defeater lowers justification, no matter what the original justifier for the target-attitude happened to be – a characteristic of rebutting defeat that was remarked upon in previous chapters. Most notably, while a source-sensitive defeater's strength depends on the strength of the original justifier it pertains to, a source-neutral defeater's strength depends on the degree of support it enjoys, relative to the degree of support the original justifier provided. A source-sensitive defeater's significance increases with the significance of the originally relied-upon input it suggests to be untrustworthy. In contrast, a source-neutral defeater's significance increases with the degree of support it enjoys. In order to decide between Strong Conciliationism and the Steadfast view, it will be instructive to see how this works in detail.

## 6.2 A Theory-driven Argument for Strong Conciliationism

Given the way I have traced the debate so far, the central difference between Strong Conciliationism and Weak Conciliationism is the kind of defeater they take disagreement to present. The next step is to test their claims in this regard. Instead of directly evaluating their verdicts on given cases of disagreement, this will be done in two steps: First, I will present clear cases of source-neutral and source-sensitive support and defeat and highlight their structural characteristics, which should be familiar by now. This will give us a general framework that describes the epistemic impact that source-neutral and source-sensitive support and defeat have in general (in more detail than just in regard to increasing and lowering degrees of justification). Then, I will show that there is an easy recipe to construct cases of disagreement that are structurally analogous to the various defeater-cases. As a result, it can be seen that the kind of defeater at play depends on whether the input that the two parties to a peer-disagreement rely on in holding their contentious beliefs is shared between them.

For those cases where this is given (which are often at the center of the disagreement-debate), it can be shown that Strong Conciliationism gives the right verdict, that is, the verdict that best fits the previously developed general framework. The type of defeater at work here is a source-sensitive defeater. For cases where the input is not shared, proponents of both positions should be able to agree that Weak Conciliationism's treatment is adequate. This would vindicate the verdict to that effect given in Grundmann (2013). Since the Strong Conciliationist idea that input is rendered rationally unusable is only made plausible for cases of shared input, this should not be a point of disagreement in any case. Thus, I will be presenting a new argument from disagreement-independent observations about the structure of defeat for the assessment of the requirements of peer-disagreement that offers support for Strong Conciliationism with respect to the treatment of cases of shared input and, more generally, Grundmann's observation that the kind of defeater produced by peer-disagreement depends on whether the input is shared between parties to the disagreement.

### 6.2.1 Source-neutral and Source-sensitive Support and Defeat

Recall that S-def and N-def entail that what makes a piece of input a source-sensitive or a source-neutral defeater is whether it defeats *independently* of what serves as the target-attitude's original justifier. This concept has been explored in great detail already. Now, a natural idea is to wonder whether there is also source-sensitive and source-neutral doxastic *support*. There is some reason to think that there is, as the cases I will discuss here suggest. The idea is that, parallel to the distinction between S-def and N-def, a source-neutrally supporting doxastic base supports an attitude independently of whether there is another, original doxastic base that supports the target-attitude. A source-sensitively supporting doxastic base raises the degree of justification of an attitude, only if there is another, original doxastic base of a certain type that also supports the target-attitude. The former kind of support is so familiar that we take it for granted, while the other kind is less obvious.

To make these distinctions clearer and more plausible, let us begin with a case-pair highlighting source-neutral support and defeat.

> SNS: At $t1$, Freya believes that the gate her flight leaves from, gate 51, is around the corner on the basis of the man at the service desk having told her so. At $t2$, she then sees a sign on the wall with an arrow that points around the corner and says "gate 51". She then re-evaluates and starts relying on both the man at the service desk's testimony and on seeing the sign as a total doxastic base for her belief that gate 51 is around the corner.

Let us call Freya's original doxastic basis, the man at the desk's testimony, $r1$ and the newly acquired piece of input that she adds to that base, seeing the sign, $r2$. It should be intuitively highly plausible that Freya's belief that the gate is around the corner at $t2$ is justified to a higher degree than it was at $t1$. This is because her total doxastic base at $t2$ consists of $r2$ in addition to $r1$. The relevant observation is that $r2$ offers *source-neutral* doxastic support to Freya's belief. This is the standard kind of support that we are dealing with in our everyday epistemic practice. It can be seen that $r2$ offers source-neutral doxastic support by considering the following thought: If Freya had not had $r1$ at $t1$ and if she had then come across $r2$ and formed her belief based on $r2$, that belief would still have been doxastically justified. Therefore, $r2$ must be able to offer doxastic support on its own, independently of other doxastic bases.

Things are different in the next case.

> SSS: At $t1$, Freya believes that the gate her flight leaves from, gate 51, is around the corner on the basis of the man at the service desk having told her so. At $t2$, she comes across a customer double-checking a piece of information with another airport employee that she was given by a man fitting the description of the man at the service desk who told her about the gate. Freya overhears the airport employee credibly ensuring the customer that the man at the service desk is the company's most trusted and reliable customer service operative. She then re-evaluates and starts relying on both the man at the service desk's testimony and on the second employee's assurance as a total doxastic base for her belief that gate 51 is around the corner.

As before, let's call Freya's original base $r1$ and the new information, here the second employee's testimony, $r2$. The following verdict on SSS is intuitively plausible: The degree of justification of Freya's belief that gate 51 is around the corner at $t2$ is higher than it was at $t1$. Since the only relevant difference in Freya's epistemic state between $t1$ and $t2$ is the addition of $r2$ as a doxastic base for the be-

## 6.2 A Theory-driven Argument for Strong Conciliationism — 245

lief, this suggests that *r2* supports her belief. The important observation is that it must do so source-sensitively, that is, the support depends on Freya *also* relying on *r1* at *t2*. This can be seen by conducting the dependence-test from the previous paragraph: If Freya is assumed not to have *r1* at *t1*, the intuition that the degree of justification of her belief rises at *t2* vanishes. If the man at the service desk had not told Freya that gate 51 is around the corner, learning that the man is extremely trustworthy intuitively would do nothing to improve the status of her belief that gate 51 is around the corner. However, *given that the man at the service desk told her that the gate is around the corner*, learning about his trustworthiness *does* improve the belief's epistemic status. Thus, *r2*'s support for Freya's belief is dependent on her holding the belief on the basis of *r1* in SSS.

Before moving on to the analogous kinds of defeat, a caveat must be addressed. It is not obvious that the degree of justification of Freya's belief in SSS increases because *r2* offers doxastic support to the belief. Instead it is possible that it somehow enhances the support offered by *r1*. Which of these options is realized in cases like SSS depends on what it means for a piece of input to support an attitude, which is determined by the analytic tools a given theory of justification brings to the table. If this is understood in terms of probability-raising, for example, *r2* will turn out to support Freya's, whereas a different explanation for the verdict on SSS must be found in views that postulate a more direct, propositional connection between input and target-attitude. In keeping with the goals of the book so far, I will leave the details open here in order to stay neutral. Let us therefore say that a piece of input *r* source-sensitively supports a doxastic attitude *B(p)*, just in case the degree of justification of *B(p)* rises as a result of *B(p)* being (also) based on *r*. This conception is a bit looser than the support-relation that was used so far and should allow for a multitude of ways to accommodate the verdict on SSS.

With these observations and simple modifications in place, we can now turn to a similar case-pair for defeat.

> SND: At *t1*, Freya believes that the gate her flight leaves from, gate 51, is around the corner on the basis of the man at the service desk having told her so. At *t2*, she then sees a sign on the wall with an arrow that points straight ahead and says "gate 51". She then re-evaluates and starts relying on both the man at the service desk's testimony and on seeing the sign as a total doxastic base for her belief that gate 51 is around the corner.

SND is a typical case of rebutting defeat: At *t1*, Freya justifiedly believes that gate 51 is around the corner on the basis of *r1* (the service desk information). At *t2*, she starts relying on both *r1* and a new piece of input that supports the negation of the proposition that gate 51 is around the corner – the sign pointing straight ahead. The resulting total doxastic base consisting of *r1* and *r2* is less supportive of her belief that gate 51 is around the corner than *r1* alone has been. Thus, that belief is less well justified at *t2* than it was at *t1*. The input provided by the sign is a source-neutral defeater because it fits N-def: Since it lowers the target-belief's degree of justification, it is clearly a defeater and it is source-neutral because it is true in SND that, if Freya had not had *r1*, *r2* would still have lowered the degree of support that the target-belief enjoyed or justified a belief in the negation of the target-proposition to a degree that is equal to the degree to which it lowers the justification of Freya's belief in SND. *r2*'s defeating is therefore independent of whether Freya has *r1*. This should be familiar by now.

So will be the case for source-sensitive defeat:

> SSD: At *t1*, Freya believes that the gate her flight leaves from, gate 51, is around the corner on the basis of the man at the service desk having told her so. At *t2*, she comes across a customer double-checking a piece of information with another airport employee that she was given by a man fitting the description of the man at the service desk who told her about the gate. Freya overhears the airport employee credibly ensuring the customer that the man at the service desk is close to being fired because he often shows up drunk and gives highly unreliable information to customers. She then re-evaluates and starts relying on the results of that process and on the second employee's assurance as a total doxastic base for her belief that gate 51 is around the corner.

SSD is a standard case of undercutting defeat, so that Freya's belief loses all its original justification. The input gained from overhearing the second employee (*r2*) supports belief in the higher-order proposition that the original justifier for Freya's belief that the gate is around the corner, the service desk man's testimony (*r1*), does not properly support the latter belief (the target-attitude). The re-evaluation process that has her add *r2* to the target-attitude's total doxastic base is then competent only if Freya stops giving weight to *r1* as a result, as explained in previous chapters. This results in her belief that the gate is around the corner having a lower degree of justification at *t2* than it did at *t1*, where the degree to which it is lower conforms to the degree of support that *r1* offered to the belief at *t1*. Thus, at *t2*, the degree of justification of Freya's belief that the gate is around the corner is equal to the degree of justification it would have if she had no reason at all for holding it. The source-sensitivity test shows furthermore that (unsurprisingly) the defeater at play is source-sensitive: It is a defeater because it lowers the target-attitude's degree of justification and it is source-sensitive because the defeating-effect would not have been observed if Freya had not relied on *r1* at *t1* as a doxastic base for the target-attitude. Had she, for example, believed that the gate is around the corner on the basis of seeing a sign that shows "gate 51" and an arrow pointing around the corner, overhearing the second employee's description of the service desk man's epistemic credentials would intuitively (and according to the Rebasing Account) have done nothing to lower original degree of justification for Freya's belief that the gate is around the corner. This shows that the defeating-effect of the new information depends on what serves as the target-attitude's original justifier, so that the defeater in SSD fulfills S-def.

An important observation is that source-sensitive support and defeat both work by way of supporting or rebutting the relevant higher-order proposition: $r2$ in SSS supports Freya's belief that the gate is around the corner in virtue supporting belief in the higher-order proposition that the service desk man's testimony offers good support for that belief. In SSD, $r2$ defeats Freya's belief in virtue of rebutting the same higher-order belief. This explains why obtaining *both* new pieces of source-sensitive input – the supporting one and the defeating one – would influence the justificatory status of Freya's belief about the gate such that it is worse than in SSS, but better than in SSD. In fact, $r2$ in SSS would help *protect* Freya's belief against the defeating effects of $r2$ in SSD. This is a side-effect of the nature of undercutting defeat as higher-order rebutting defeat discussed in an earlier chapter: The two pieces of input for the relevant higher-order belief counterbalance each other, weakening the undermining effect of the defeating component. Note that all this is not to say that all source-sensitive defeaters must be undercutting defeaters. I will address the question whether there are other kinds of source-sensitive defeaters in the next section.

### 6.2.2 The Argument for Strong Conciliationism

Now we can turn to the question what kind of defeater is obtained in cases of peer-disagreement. A point that has received some attention in the debate (e.g. Grundmann 2013; Matheson 2015b, ch. 1.2, 1.3), but that is still often under-appreciated, is that what kind of defeater an instance of recognized peer-disagreement offers to its participants depends on whether the two parties share the input that makes up their respective original justifiers.

To see this, compare the following two variants of a typical case of peer-disagreement:

> VIRUS-DIFFERENT: Peter and Petra are both students of Biology who are in the same year of their courses and justifiedly regard each other as epistemic peers when it comes to their fields and consider each other to be equally thorough, careful and adherent to similarly high epistemic standards. Peter reads the influential monograph "The Wonderful World of the Virus" (WWV), while Petra reads the similarly important book "Fascination Virus" (FV). Both books thoroughly discuss the question whether viruses are lifeforms ($p$). Neither Peter nor Petra have previously considered that question and neither of them has any rel-

evant information on the matter, aside from what they read in the respective books. Solely based on the data and arguments in the respective books, they form conflicting, initially justified, beliefs on the question. Peter believes that viruses are lifeforms, while Petra believes that they are not.

VIRUS-SAME: Peter and Petra are both students of Biology who are in the same year of their courses and justifiedly regard each other as epistemic peers when it comes to their fields and consider each other to be equally thorough, careful and adherent to similarly high epistemic standards. They both read the influential monograph "The Wonderful World of the Virus" (WWV) which thoroughly discusses the question whether viruses are lifeforms ($p$). Neither Peter nor Petra have previously considered that question and neither of them has any relevant information on the matter, aside from what they read in the respective books. Solely based on the data and arguments in the book, they form conflicting, initially justified, beliefs on the question. Peter believes that viruses are lifeforms, while Petra believes that they are not.

Obviously, the only difference between VIRUS-DIFFERENT and VIRUS-SAME is that, in the former case, Peter and Petra rely on *different* sets of input that they obtained from reading WWV and FV, respectively, as justifiers for their respective beliefs about the lifeform-status of viruses, while, in the latter case, they rely on the very same set of input obtained from reading WWV. Next, consider the *total set of input available* to, for instance, Peter *after* learning about their disagreement:

In VIRUS-DIFFERENT:

1) The data and arguments in WWV

2) The fact that Peter concluded that $p$ from the data and arguments in WWV

3) The fact that Petra concluded that $not$-$p$ from the data and arguments in FV

In VIRUS-SAME:

a) The data and arguments in WWV

b) The fact that Peter concluded that $p$ from the data and arguments in WWV

c) The fact that Petra concluded that $not$-$p$ from the data and arguments in WWV

First, let us assume that part of what goes into the epistemic relevance of the pieces of input 2) and b) in the respective cases is a self-assessment on Peter's part that takes into account his expertise and track-record, such that it offers independent support. This may not seem too plausible for the everyday-kind of case, but it seems plausible enough for a self-reflecting subject that we will assume Peter to be in these cases.[12] The question at hand is how Peter's awareness of Petra's peerness with respect to him on the matter at hand influences the way in which 2) and 3) and a) and b), respectively, influence the epistemic relevance/weight of 1) and a) regarding Peter's belief that $p$. Since both Strong Conciliationism and Weak Conciliationism agree that 3) and c) present Peter with a defeater for his belief, but disagree over what kind of defeater, the answer to this question will decide which side gets it right.

Starting with VIRUS-DIFFERENT, what kind of defeater does 3), the fact that Petra comes to disbelieve that $p$ on the basis of data from a different book, present to Peter's belief that $p$? Since Petra relies on a different set of input from Peter (she uses FV, while he uses WWV) in coming to her conclusion, the information that her conclusion differs from Peter's (the defeater) cannot rebut a belief in the higher-order proposition that the data and arguments in WWV supports the belief that viruses are lifeforms. To illustrate: After learning about their disagreement, Peter's justification for the higher-order belief that what he learned from WWV supports the lower-order belief that viruses are lifeforms (the target-attitude) is no worse than it was before learning of the disagreement. However, his justification for the belief that viruses are lifeforms is. As a consequence, the defeating effect of the disagreement is independent of the fact that Peter relies on WWV in forming his belief. Had he instead read a different book, say "Going Viral", finding out that Petra has read FV and disagrees with him would still intuitively have generated pressure on him to modify his belief. Thus, the defeater that the disagreement in VIRUS-DIFFERENT presents fulfills N-Def and is *source-neutral and not source-sensitive*.

This can be made sense of if one considers the role that Petra's reading of FV plays in all of this. Since Peter justifiedly believes that Petra is just as good at gathering and evaluating input as he is himself, he also has justification for the belief that her belief that viruses are not lifeforms is just as well supported as his belief that they are. While he has not read FV, he justifiedly believes that his peer Petra has and that she believes that $p$ is false on the basis of its contents, which in turn gives him justification to believe that the input Petra obtained from FV supports the belief that $p$ is false to a degree that is comparable

---

12 In fact, I do find it plausible that a subconscious self-assessment goes into most everyday-attitude formations, but this is not the place to discuss this point.

with the support provided by the input he gathered from WWV.[13] This amounts to Peter having justification to believe *that there is input that supports the negation of what he believes*. Furthermore, since Peter has justification to take Petra to be his peer, which amounts to roughly equal likelihood to get things right, he also has justification to believe that the not-$p$-supporting input (FV) that he has justification to take to be there is roughly as supportive of belief in $p$ being false as the input he relies on (WWV) is supportive of believing that $p$.[14]

Put in terms of Peter's total evidence, 3) [The fact that Petra concluded that *not-p* from the data and arguments in FV] gives Peter reason to believe that there is something like 1) [The data and arguments in WWV], roughly inheriting 1)'s weight as input that supports belief in the negation of $p$. 2) [The fact that Peter concluded that $p$ from the data and arguments in WWV] cannot also fulfill this particular role with respect to 1) supporting belief that $p$ since this would amount to illegitimately counting 1), on which Peter already relies directly, twice. This is not to say that Peter's awareness of him being a competent biologist does not give 2) *some* positive impact on the justificatory status of his belief. After all, his competence does make it less likely that he has made a mistake. But, since lowering the likelihood of a mistake is not the same as direct propositional support, that impact is not derived from the direct supporting relationship between WWV and $p$ and thus doesn't give WWV more weight than it has anyway. Finally, because Peter and Petra reasonably take each other to be peers, 3) can fully counterbalance 1). This leaves Peter with no counterbalanced support for his belief that $p$ and thus a total set of input that does not support belief in $p$. Since this is the result of obtaining 3), learning about the disagreement gives Peter a rebutting defeater.

What can do the explanatory work getting us from the observation that Peter now has a disagreeing peer (who relies on different input than he does himself) to the defeating effect that the disagreement with Petra has on Peter's belief is a principle that has been put on the table by Feldman (2007, 2014): Evidence of evidence is evidence. The idea behind this principle is that whenever one has input $r$ that supports believing that there exists some other directly supporting potential input for believing that $p$, without possessing that potential input itself,

---

**13** This is especially plausible if we assume that Peter and Petra are equally confident regarding their beliefs about viruses being lifeforms.

**14** Of course, equal likelihood to be right need not come down to equal input and equal competence. The two components may be differently prominent on the sides of the parties to a disagreement. However, to keep things simple, I will assume that they are equally prominent and assume that it is obvious that the argument, in a slightly more complicated version, can be worked out for alternative distributions without loss.

*r* itself supports belief in *p*. This can, for example, explain why reading in a newspaper that there is scientific evidence for the existence of quarks can justify one in believing that there are quarks, even though one does not possess that evidence oneself.

While the evidence-of-evidence-is-evidence principle is controversial (e.g. Fitelson 2012; Roche 2014; Comesaña and Tal 2015a, 2015b), something in its neighborhood must be plausible enough to suggest itself for the explanation of this defeating effect. To establish this at least minimally, consider another example: Holmes arrives at the scene of a robbery and asks what evidence has been secured so far. He is told by Watson that not much was found but that they have one key piece of evidence that clearly establishes that Moriarty is the culprit. Unfortunately, while the extremely reliable Watson has seen that key piece of evidence, in his elation at having found the culprit so quickly, he forgot what the evidence consisted of (say it was a videotape) after it was sent to the station. In this situation, it seems that Holmes may justifiedly believe that Moriarty is the culprit, even though he has no access to input that would establish this directly. What he has to go on is input (Watson's testimony) that supports that there is such directly establishing input (the videotape). Other cases can be constructed after a simple fashion: The subject in question can use observations about the behavior of other subjects as input that supports belief in some proposition where the best explanation for the others' behavior is their access to evidence for the truth of that proposition. This kind of structure is surely familiar enough from everyday life so that it offers good reason to assume that there must be a legitimate epistemic principle connecting such indirect support with justification. The underlying principle can then be shown to apply in cases of peer disagreement where the two sides rely on different sets of input, such as VIRUS-DIFFERENT.

Thus, the disagreement gives Peter input that supports belief in the proposition that there is input that supports the negation of his belief that *p* to an extent (due to Petra's peerness) that is roughly equal to the support offered by his reading of WWV. According to the relevant evidence-of-evidence principle, this amounts to him having input that supports the belief that *p* is false, which fully counterbalances the input he originally relied on in coming to believe that *p*. As we have seen, in 3) Peter has thereby obtained a source-neutral rebutting defeater that fully counterbalances his original input.[15]

---

**15** Of course, the weight of the evidence that there is evidence against the belief will not, in fact, be *exactly* as weighty as the evidence Peter possesses himself. After all, the removed status (for him) of Petra's evidence introduces an additional error possibility. However, if the peerness assumption is well justified, the removed evidence will still suffice to rebut Peter's belief to an

While this looks like it might get the Strong Conciliationist into trouble, seeing as she claims that peer-disagreement provides one with a *source-sensitive* defeater, actual Strong Conciliationists are unlikely to be worried by this result. This is because, first, even though both parties to the disagreement in cases structurally similar to VIRUS-DIFFERENT may justifiedly continue to rely on their original justifiers, the peerness-assumption still results in epistemic symmetry: Both get a *full* rebutting defeater from learning of the other's opinion. Next, let us see what kind of defeater the disagreement in that case gives Peter.

Unlike in VIRUS-DIFFERENT, the input Peter receives from learning about his peer Petra's disagreement in VIRUS-SAME does rebut belief in the higher-order proposition that the input he obtained from reading WWV epistemically supports the belief that $p$. This is because what the fact that Petra believes that $p$ is false on the basis of WWV, that is, on the same source that Peter himself relies on in believing that $p$ is true, indicates to Peter that it is false that he has judged the direction of the propositional support offered by WWV correctly. At least one of the two peers must have made a mistake and the kind of mistake at issue must concern the way they came to their conclusions from the data and arguments in WWV, since that is the only input that could have justified their beliefs before the disagreement and it is stipulated that they were justified at that point. Furthermore, since they are peers and take each other to be equally likely to get things right, the likelihood that Peter made the mistake cannot be justifiedly believed by him to be lower than Petra's chance. Since the defeater thus targets the relation between WWV and Peter's belief that $p$, it amounts to a *source-sensitive* defeater because its epistemic relevance depends on Peter relying on WWV as his justifier.[16]

---

extent sufficient to make belief unjustified. At the very least, Peter has good reason to believe that there is evidence that is as weighty as his own that counts against his belief. Also, it is of course always possible to fiddle with the weights of the involved evidences to produce the results suggested here.

16 Note that, given that the defeater in VIRUS-SAME is supposed to be source-sensitive, one must be able to explain how the set of input consisting of b) and c) appeals to the higher-order proposition that WWV supports belief that $p$ in the right way. In SSD, things are clear: The information that the service desk man is an unreliable testifier directly indicates that that proposition is false. In VIRUS-SAME, Peter justifiedly believes that he and Petra and are peers and that they disagree, which justifies the belief that there is a roughly 50% chance that he has made a mistake in judging the direction and weight of WWV. Accordingly, b) and c) together propositionally justify Peter to suspend judgment on whether he may justifiedly believe that $p$, based on WWV. Why think that having to suspend judgment on the relevant higher-order proposition defeats the connected lower-order belief? The reason is that the case is analogous in relevant points to a similar version of the classic red-wall case of undercutting defeat: Say a subject

So far, this is the Strong Conciliationist's analysis of the case. To show that it is the right one, we can examine structural similarities between Virus-Same and SSD: First, we can follow Kelly (2005, 2010) in treating b) [The fact that Peter concluded that $p$ from the data and arguments in WWV] and c) [The fact that Petra concluded that *not-p* from the data and arguments in WWV] as a unified set of input. Specifically, we can assume that it is legitimate for Peter to take into account the observation that he, as a competent epistemic subject, has formed a specific belief on a specific basis. No one would claim that, in a case of disagreement, the parties cannot rationally rely on the observation *that they hold the position they do*. Thus, in standard cases of disagreement, input like b) and c) can be straightforwardly aggregated as pieces of input "pulling in opposite directions".[17] Given the peerness-assumption, b) and c) furthermore have the same epistemic weight and thus counterbalance each other fully. As a result, the set of input consisting of b) and c) propositionally supports suspension of judgment. Now, Kelly claims that the set *independently* supports suspension of judgment about $p$ and proposes simply adding it to a) [The data and arguments in WWV] and treating it as the kind of rebutting defeater obtained by Conrad in Device (Kelly 2010, pp. 202–208). If this is correct, the set (and thus the new input consisting in learning about the disagreement) acts as a source-neutral, rebutting defeater.

To establish the Strong Conciliationist's analysis against this claim, it can be shown that the defeater at play here fails condition 2. of N-Def: independence from the original doxastic base of the target-attitude. To see how one may go about this, let us briefly return to SSD. In order to test whether the defeater in SSD fulfills condition 2., we considered a version of the case where Freya relies not on the service desk man's testimony, but on a different piece of input as her original doxastic base. In that test-version, it turned out to be implausible to claim that her belief is defeated by the new information she receives. We can run a similar test for Virus-Same by constructing a test-version of the case:

---

looks at a wall that seems red to her. Now she is told by a trusted testifier that there is a trickster running around that comes by the place roughly 50% of the time. When he does come by, he places a red light behind the observer of the wall (based on an example in Sosa 2002). Even though the support for the defeating proposition about the red lamp is weaker than in the original case, such that the subject has to suspend judgment now on whether there is a red lamp behind her, intuitively, the subject's belief that the wall is red is still undercut.

**17** What this assumes is that there is no undermining relationship between beliefs about who says what. This is, of course, not necessarily true, since parties to a disagreement could, in principle, also disagree about *that*. We will leave such cases aside for the current discussion, as they may provide self-undermining defeaters.

VIRUS-SAME*: The Biology-student Peter believes that viruses are lifeforms ($p$). However, he does not rely on the data and arguments in WWV in coming to his conclusion that this is so, but on the testimony of his trustworthy Biology professor. Still, he has read WWV and he does think that the input it provides supports the belief that viruses are lifeforms (let us accept for the purposes of the argument that this can amount to him "concluding" that they are from WWV). Still, Peter does not make WWV part of his total doxastic base for his belief. Peter's epistemic peer with regards to viruses, Petra, however, believes that viruses are not lifeforms, based on having read WWV.

In VIRUS-SAME*, unlike in the test-version of SSD, one gets the impression that Peter may, in fact, obtain a defeater.

Still, a case can be made for the view that it is *not a defeater for his contentious belief* that viruses are lifeforms, but only for his *independent higher-order belief that WWV supports belief that p*, which, importantly, is not doxastically related to his contentious belief. In VIRUS-SAME*, Peter and Petra hold conflicting *beliefs* about $p$. They also, additionally, come to conflicting *conclusions* about $p$ on the basis of WWV (this could be depicted in terms of conflicting higher-order beliefs about the relationship between WWV and $p$). Their conclusions are mutually defeated by the fact that the other person disagrees, be this by way of source-neutral or source-sensitive defeater[18]. This is a point of agreement between Strong and Weak Conciliationism, after all.

However, WWV is not part of the doxastic base of Peter's belief that $p$, so that the degree of doxastic justification that his belief that $p$ enjoys is not negatively affected by this disagreement between conclusions: To be sure, the set of input consisting of b) and c) supports suspension of judgment on whether $p$, *given WWV*. But why would that fact affect the epistemic status of Peter's *testimony-based* belief? Yet, the Weak Conciliationist's conditions for defeat of that testimony-based belief through disagreement are met in VIRUS-SAME*: Peter's total available input contains a) [The data and arguments in WWV], b) [The fact that Peter concluded that $p$ from the data and arguments in WWV] and c) [The fact that Petra concluded that *not-p* from the data and arguments in WWV]. He is aware of disagreement on whether $p$ with his peer Petra, and they come to different conclusions on the basis of WWV. This supports suspension of judgment. Still, his belief that $p$ is not defeated, both intuitively and because there is little theoretical motivation for claiming otherwise.

The latter point can be emphasized by illustrating the structure of this somewhat abstract case: The secondary, conclusion-related disagreement screens off the direct rebutting effect that comes from a disagreeing peer. Otherwise, the hy-

---

[18] The argument I am about to present shows it to be a source-sensitive defeater.

pothesis would be untestable because a testifier's claim that what one believes is false (and thus any kind of disagreement) always automatically reverts to being a rebutting defeater if the input is not shared (as the analysis of VIRUS-DIFFERENT shows). The question to be investigated is what kind of defeater *the set of input supporting suspension of judgment* amounts to, and that set is left intact and not screened off by anything. The observation that it has no bearing on Peter's testimony-based belief and does not defeat it is then telling. If this analysis is correct, the test-case for VIRUS-SAME is not a case of defeat in the relevant sense. This proves that the defeater obtained from disagreement in cases of shared input like VIRUS-SAME is source-sensitive. It fails condition 2. of N-Def and it fulfills S-Def: There are relevant cases where, if Peter relied on a different set of input as the original doxastic base, his belief would turn out justified.

Before moving on, let me briefly discuss a possible objection against this argument. One could claim that the analysis given for VIRUS-SAME* also rules out cases of different input like VIRUS-DIFFERENT as source-neutral. Consider a similar test-version of VIRUS-DIFFERENT: Peter and Petra disagree on whether $p$. They come to different conclusions about $p$ on the basis of two different sets of input, $r1$ for Peter and $r2$ for Petra, while Peter actually bases his belief on a *third* set, $r3$ and not on $r1$. It seems that, in that case, Peter's belief is also not defeated by the disagreement, which seems to suggest that the defeater at play in the original Virus-different case must be source-sensitive because it fulfills S-Def. At the same time, given what was said before, it should be uncontroversial that the disagreement in VIRUS-DIFFERENT does *not* provide Peter with a source-sensitive, but with a source-neutral defeater! The case has the subject possess a non-undermined set of supporting input, $r1$, that is not used, but that potentially counterbalances the input from disagreement, here driven by $r2$. In the case sketched, a competent re-evaluation is likely to result in Peter holding on to the contentious belief. It would see Peter rely on his original doxastic base, $r3$, as well as $r1$ and the input from disagreement containing $r2$, which would result in Peter holding the belief that $p$ on the basis of a set of input that supports the belief to a degree that corresponds to degree to which $r3$, alone, supports it because $r1$ and $r2$ counterbalance each other.

As a first step toward a response, it is important to note that things are significantly different in VIRUS-SAME*: In that case, there is no third set of unused input that kicks into relevance during re-evaluation. The only unused set of input is the one shared with Petra and that set will not offer Peter further support for his belief, due to the disagreement over what conclusion to draw from it. For this reason, a competent re-evaluation on Peter's part in VIRUS-SAME* need not expand the total doxastic base of his belief that $p$. In the test-version of VIRUS-DIFFERENT at consideration here, however, it is just the addition of the unused set of supporting input counterbalancing Petra's doxastic base that saves his belief's justificatory status from being negatively affected by the disagreement. So, in the test-version of VIRUS-DIFFERENT, the doxastic base needs to be extended to account for the no-defeat intuition by a set of input *that is directly involved in the disagreement.*

This difference between the cases underlies the difficulties of analyzing cases of peer-disagreement. A disagreeing peer always comes with a doxastic base. Thus, if one moves away from a case like VIRUS-SAME with regards to what plays that role, one moves from a case where there is only one set of input serving as two original doxastic bases to a case like VIRUS-SAME*, where the same set only serves as the opponent's original doxastic base. Thus, one also moves to a situation where both parties suddenly have input that (indirectly) counts against their position. This is why finding a good test-case for VIRUS-SAME is so difficult. As explained, the additional changes made to the case in VIRUS-SAME* (Peter's doxastically inert judgment on WWV) are supposed to screen off this effect.

The observation that similar changes to VIRUS-DIFFERENT only produce similar end-results because they tend to generate pressure to add disagreement-involved input to the target-attitude's doxastic bases shows that, in cases where the input is not shared, these effects *cannot* be screened off. This is significant because it shows that the relevant modification to VIRUS-DIFFERENT is not really a test case for source-sensitivity: It implicitly assumes that the Peter's original doxastic base in VIRUS-DIFFERENT, $r1$, comes back into use in response to encountering the defeater in the modified case. Note that, if it were stipulated that Peter does not take $r1$ into account during re-evaluation, the re-evaluation would be incompetent and his belief would be defeated. Going even further, even if it could be made plausible that this kind of re-evaluation is competent after all, the fact that $r3$, the supporting input Peter would then rely on, is counterbalanced by Petra's $r2$ would still defeat Peter's belief that $p$. Thus, apparent source-sensitivity test-cases for cases of disagreement with different sets of input either do not amount to real or suitable test-cases for source-sensitivity, or the test-cases show that the defeater from disagreement is indeed source-neutral. Cases like VIRUS-SAME*, on the other hand, are true test-cases showing that the defeater from disagreement in shared-input cases is source-sensitive.

All of this should establish the following two points: First, cases like VIRUS-DIFFERENT are relevantly similar to SND and fulfill N-Def. They present the parties to the disagreement with a source-neutral defeater. This is in keeping with Weak Conciliationism but should also be unproblematic from the perspective of Strong Conciliationism. Second, cases like VIRUS-SAME, on the other hand, are relevantly similar to SSD and fulfil S-Def. They present the parties to the disagreement with a source-sensitive defeater. This in turn requires the parties to bracket their original justifier, which vindicates Strong Conciliationism and shows that Weak Conciliationism mischaracterizes the effect of learning about peer-disagreement in cases of shared input. At the same time, the present discussion highlights that one must pay careful attention to the distribution of input in a given case of disagreement. Peer-disagreement is not some special, sui generis epistemic situation but simply a complex situation that requires a complex theoretical analysis with the general tools of epistemology.

This is also part of the reason why the issue of *uniqueness* has not come up in this discussion. Uniqueness is a principle, according to which a given set of input only ever justifies *one* specific doxastic attitude (Feldman 2007; White 2005). If it fails, it seems that Strong Conciliationism is in trouble because the attitudes of both parties to a disagreement might be justified, based on the same, shared input. Given the strength of the principle, it should be unsurprising that it has been subjected to substantial criticism (e.g. Rosen 2001; Kelly 2010; Ballantyne and Coffman 2011). As soon as we think about Strong Conciliationism as postulating that peer-disagreement provides the parties with a certain kind of defeater, however, this issue becomes irrelevant: Say party A and party B recognize each other as peers and disagree about whether *p* (belief and disbelief). Their shared input, *e*, is such that both belief and disbelief can be justifedly held on its basis (uniqueness fails for it). Whether A's and B's beliefs regarding *p* are undercut, however, depends on whether they have reason to believe that *e* permits both. After all, even if uniqueness fails generally, in the vast majority of cases where we disagree on the basis of the same input, one of the attitudes at play is bound to fail to be justified on the basis of that input. If A and B have no reason to believe that their case is different, it doesn't matter that *e* technically permits both their beliefs; they will still obtain a defeater for the reasons given above. If they do have such reason, it will act as a defeater-defeater for the defeater from disagreement, neatly explaining why in this case both attitudes can be maintained. If we understand Strong Conciliationism as a thesis about the kind of defeater that disagreement (potentially) provides in such cases, all of this is part of the package because it is part of the nature and structure of defeat that defeater-defeat is possible.

Therefore, if the focus of the debate should lie on the kind of defeater provided by peer-disagreement, as argued by me and Grundmann (2013), the truth or falsity of uniqueness has no impact on it, as no relevant position presupposes it in the first place. Any position that does will severely underestimate the complexity of disagreement-situations. It is not possible to establish that a given subject must always behave in a specific way in such situations because the precise impact of the defeater depends on many variables that may receive different values in different cases. This should have become clear from all the previous discussions.

## 6.3 The Rebasing Account of Higher-Order Defeat

In the last part of this chapter, I want to address the idea that the source-sensitive defeater in a case of peer-disagreement with shared input is not a classic undercutting defeater but belongs to some new class. So far in this book, it was observed that undercutting defeaters are source-sensitive and that peer-disagreement in cases of shared input provides one with a source-sensitive defeater. This seems to suggest that such disagreement simply produces an undercutting defeater for the disagreeing parties. Everything said about disagreement so far seems to be compatible with this hypothesis. However, it has been rejected in the literature with authors pointing out a number of differences between what I proposed to be source-sensitive defeat in cases of peer-disagreement and undercutting defeaters (Feldman 2005; e.g. Christensen 2010a; Lasonen-Aarnio 2014; DiPaolo forthcoming).[19] Let us call the former *higher-order defeat*.

### 6.3.1 Higher-order Defeaters and Undercutting Defeaters

To get a better idea of where the supposed difference between undercutting and higher-order defeat lies, it makes sense to take a closer look at the aforementioned "bracketing" of lower-order input that a higher-order defeater is supposed to be doing. The idea behind the concept is this: To say that a set of input is to be bracketed is not to say that it now fails to support the target-proposition. Instead, it has become somehow *improper to rely on it* as a doxastic base for a belief in that proposition, whether or not it is actually supportive (cf. Christensen 2010a). In contrast, undercutting defeaters are classically taken to "destroy" support-relations between input and the target-attitude, as we saw in previous chapters. Thus, an undercutting defeater supposedly makes it the case that the affected input no longer supports (is no longer positive input with respect to) the target-attitude.

---

[19] Lasonen-Aarnio, in fact, argues that the proposed source-sensitive defeater here is not a defeater at all. Her arguments are supposed to show that appropriate rules of rationality cannot be found to ground the relevant requirements. I hope to avoid these issues in virtue of having shown that the mechanics of re-evaluation do not require sui generis norms and by demonstrating that all source-sensitive defeaters can be explained through this framework.

## 6.3 The Rebasing Account of Higher-Order Defeat — 259

As a first comment on this, it must be noted that matters are not as simple as this and depend on the details of a given theory of justification.[20] More generally, one can immediately see why this support-destructive conception of defeat, much more than the idea of an input-bracketing higher-order defeater, is easier to reconcile with frameworks that place emphasis on propositional justification. After all, a support-destroying defeater necessarily affects the composition of the total available input, while a bracketing defeater places certain restrictions on which input can be used as a doxastic base, leaving its composition completely intact. I will leave these issues aside for the purposes of this discussion, having already put a firm focus on doxastic justification.[21]

What is more important is that undercutting defeaters differ from supposed higher-order defeaters with regards to what they themselves support. An undercutting defeater supports belief in the proposition that the relevant lower-order input does not support the target-attitude. A higher-order defeater somehow indicates that relying on the relevant lower-order input is improper. Accordingly, undercutting and higher-order defeaters seem to target *different higher-order beliefs* for the higher-order rebuttal that is characteristic of source-sensitive defeat. This difference results in different applicability conditions for the two defeater types. Consider the following case:

FLIGHT: At time *t*, Andy is piloting an airplane to Hawaii. She is confident that she has enough fuel to get there because five minutes ago (at *t-1*) she came to this conclusion by

---

**20** Within this debate, such matters are often stated in terms of evidence. The idea here is then that a higher-order defeater does not change the fact that some set of evidence evidentially supports the target-attitude, while an undercutting defeater is supposed to do just that. This points back to Pollock's previously discussed idea that a more classical kind of defeater defeats precisely because a given set of evidence, together with the defeater, is not evidence for the target-attitude. I have already problematized this idea in the third chapter and in the previous chapter. Ultimately, whether it is true that an undercutting defeater destroys evidential support will depend on where one finds the Connector within one's evidentialist framework. As shown before, on strongly internalist forms, like Generic Evidentialism, it may well turn out to be true (and the distinction thus to be valid) because undercutting defeaters rebut the Connector. In less internalist views, like Moderate Evidentialism (and all fully externalist theories, of course), the Connector stays in place and so the evidence stays supportive. In such a view, undercutting defeaters can be expected to have the same kind of bracketing effect that higher-orders are supposed to have. So, the distinction based on the defeater's effect on support-relations will be highly dependent on the theory of justification in the background.

**21** There is some reason to think that many of the issues that arise with higher-order defeaters with respect to propositional justification disappear, once the relevant claims are taken to appeal to doxastic justification. As stated earlier, I have sympathies with the view expressed by Silva (2017) on this matter.

way of a calculation based on the following set of input $I^t$:
- A full tank contains 20,000 miles worth of fuel.
- The tank is ¾ full.
- Hawaii lies 16,000 miles from Andy's point of departure.
- Andy has flown 5,000 miles toward Hawaii.

In a case like this, one may think that it is not possible for Andy to obtain an undercutting defeater for her belief that she has enough fuel. To see this, let us assume that her capacity for mental math is well developed, so that, looking at $I^t$, it is perfectly obvious to her that she has enough fuel. Further assume that this comes down to her gaining a priori insight into the fact that $I^t$ deductively entails that she has enough fuel. Thus, in FLIGHT, she is aware of the fact that her justifier *conclusively* supports her belief. In such a situation, it may seem impossible that Andy could obtain an undercutting for her belief. Put slightly differently, there is no further trustworthy information she could obtain that shows that her justifier does not sufficiently support her belief.[22] First, she always has a defeater-defeater because she can simply *see* that it does. Second, since the proposition she believes follows deductively from her input and since deductive inferences are monotonous (adding premises does not affect their validity), obtaining more information cannot negatively affect the relevant support-relation.

While I am somewhat skeptical of the overall plausibility of this line of thought, it is sufficiently tempting to at least conclude that it is not obvious that one can have undercutting defeaters for cases of relying on conclusively supporting input. In contrast, it is overwhelmingly plausible that one can have higher-order defeaters in such situations. Consider the following case:

> HYPOXIA: At time $t$, Andy is piloting an airplane to Hawaii. She is confident that she has enough fuel to get there because five minutes ago (at $t$-1) she came to this conclusion by way of a calculation based on the following input $I^t$:
> - A full tank contains 20,000 miles worth of fuel.
> - The tank is ¾ full.
> - Hawaii was 16,000 miles from Andy's point of departure.
> - Andy has flown 5,000 miles toward Hawaii.
>
> At $t$, air traffic control provides her with a credible warning that, as a result of a drop in her oxygen supply that has now been compensated for, any reasoning she's done in the last five minutes has probably been wildly unreliable without her noticing. This is a common effect of hypoxia, a loss of oxygen in the brain (case adapted from Elga 2013; DiPaolo forthcoming).

---

22 Based on thoughts in Christensen 2010a, p. 196 ff.

It seems intuitively clear that learning that she was likely subject to hypoxia when she did her calculation does not rationally allow Andy to simply keep to her belief that she has enough fuel (for the same verdict on this and similar cases, see Christensen 2010b; Elga 2013; Schechter 2013; DiPaolo forthcoming).

Assuming that the set of four points of data Andy takes as input to her calculation serve as her justifier, note that this defeater does not support belief in the proposition that Andy's justifier does not really support her belief about the fuel. Instead, it indicates that Andy has made a *performance error* when coming to her conclusion. That is, the information that she has suffered from hypoxia tells Andy nothing about the mathematical relations between the input she relied on and her conclusion, but it tells her that she has misjudged these relations. Because we are not perfect input-processing machines, this kind of error is always a possibility for us, no matter how watertight the actual support-relations between our justifiers and our doxastic attitudes are. Therefore, it is always possible to receive information that tells us that we are *now* in a situation where we have made such an error. If this kind of information amounts to a defeater, as HYPOXIA indicates, the defeater at play cannot be an undercutting defeater but must be a higher-order defeater.

Furthermore, the case highlights an additional, informal difference between the two defeater-types that is sometimes pointed to in the literature: In the cases of undercutting defeat discussed so far, the defeater resulted in the subject having support for thinking that it *would amount to holding an unjustified attitude if the subject continued to hold* her attitude on the basis of the affected input. In contrast, in cases like HYPOXIA, the defeater gives Andy support for thinking that her belief about the fuel *was never justified to begin with*. An undercutting defeater gives one new information in light of which one must make a change. A higher-order defeater gives one new information in light of which a change should have been made already (cf. Lasonen-Aarnio 2014, p. 317).

So, all things considered, we can conclude that there is significant evidence for making a distinction between undercutting and higher-order defeaters as subclasses of the broader class of source-sensitive defeaters. At the same time, they share the more general features of source-sensitive defeaters, specifically, their appeal to higher-order propositions. In the remainder of this section, I will model higher-order defeaters within the Rebasing Account. This process will simply adapt the framework developed for undercutting defeaters to higher-order defeaters, since, as the discussion so far already suggests, the main difference between the two types of source-sensitive defeaters lies in the content of the higher-order attitude they rebut. As we will see, this way of distinguishing source-sensitive defeaters will also allow me to make even finer-grained distinctions within the class of higher-order defeaters.

### 6.3.2 Complex and Simple Cases of Higher-Order Defeat

The strategy I will employ in examining higher-order defeat will be to analyze a number of cases of putative higher-order defeat. I will then show that certain structural features of the cases correspond to features of the relevant competent re-evaluation, which in turn allow us to distinguish three classes of higher-order defeaters. To get started, let me introduce a structural distinction between case-types:

> Call a case of putative higher-order defeat *complex*, iff a competent re-evaluation on the part of the subject *does not feature a re-use* of the original justifier.

> Call a case of putative higher-order defeat *simple*, iff a competent re-evaluation on the part of the subject *does feature a re-use* of the original justifier.

To see how this distinction contributes to the effects of a defeater in the relevant cases, we can employ versions of the hypoxia-case, beginning with the already familiar, complex one:

> HYPOXIA-C: At time $t$, Andy is piloting an airplane to Hawaii. She is confident that she has enough fuel to get there because five minutes ago (at $t\text{-}1$) she activated the autopilot and, because she is bad at mentally, but not otherwise, evaluating mathematical evidence, used pen and paper to slowly and carefully figure this out on the basis of the following input, $I_1$:
> - A full tank contains 20,000 miles worth of fuel.
> - The tank is ¾ full.
> - Hawaii is 16,000 miles from Andy's point of departure.
> - Andy has flown 5,000 miles toward Hawaii.
>
> Unfortunately, the autopilot broke right after she did her calculations, so that she cannot repeat them now. At $t$, air traffic control provides her with a credible warning that, as a result of a drop in her oxygen supply that has now been compensated for, any reasoning she's done in the last five minutes has probably been distorted without her knowing it but now everything is fine again.

Intuitively, Andy is required to give up her belief that she has enough fuel and should suspend judgment because she has no properly usable grounds for belief or disbelief. What makes this case complex is the fact that Andy at $t$ cannot activate the autopilot, so that she cannot come to any conclusions from $I^t$. Thus, any re-evaluation at $t$ cannot feature $I^t$ itself.

It is at this point that we can get an idea of the higher-order proposition targeted by the relevant higher-order defeater: Normally, when we are in situations where we cannot re-use our original input during re-evaluation, we rely *on our own past competence:* For example, imagine you do a calculation with pen and paper as to how much your friend owes you. When you meet that friend a few days later and she offers a tentative challenge to your results (she may say something like "Just looking at the figures, it looks like I may owe a little less"), you may incorporate her judgment into the basis of your belief about the amount owed by quickly re-evaluating. At the same time, you can plausibly respond that you did the calculations and that the amount you came up with is very likely to be the one owed. The explanation for this is that, during re-evaluation, you can weigh the fact that you, a reasonably reliable everyday-mathematician, arrived at the relevant result on the basis of the available data against the rebutting defeater obtained from your friend's cursory assessment and that your past calculation sufficiently outweighs that defeater. Since you do not repeat your calculation, you are thereby effectively replacing as your belief's total doxastic base the original data you used during that calculation (the recorded figures of amounts lent on a given occasion, for example) with something like your memory of having done the calculation as a competent calculator.

The schema suggested here can do a lot of explanatory work when it comes to HYPOXIA-C. Intuitively, Andy's belief that she has enough fuel is defeated by the information that she was suffering from hypoxia when she did the calculation. This can be explained in the following way: Since she cannot repeat the calculation, she must rely on her own past competence instead of the data by adopting a higher-order belief about her having performed a competent calculation in the past during re-evaluation. That belief is then rebutted by the hypoxia-information indicating that her past calculation was not competent after all, resulting in an undermining effect. The chains of inference she could run during such a re-evaluation may look like this:

1) I am a reasonably competent mathematician in flight-related matters.
2) I came to the conclusion that I have enough fuel on the basis of the available data at *t-1*.
3) If I am a reasonably competent mathematician in flight-related matters and if I came to the conclusion that I have enough fuel at *t-1*, then it is probably true that I have enough fuel.
4) Therefore, I may reasonably believe that I have enough fuel.

a) My belief that I have enough fuel is justified, only if it is true that [if I am a reasonably competent mathematician in flight-related matters and if I came to the conclusion that I have enough fuel at *t-1*, then it is probably true that I have enough fuel].
b) I have likely been subject to hypoxia at *t-1*.

c) If I have been subjected to hypoxia at *t-1*, it is probably not true that [if I am a reasonably competent mathematician in flight-related matters and if I came to the conclusion that I have enough fuel at *t-1*, then it is probably true that I have enough fuel].
d) Therefore, a belief that I have enough fuel is unlikely to be justified.
e) Therefore, I may not reasonably believe that I have enough fuel.

As in the case of undercutting defeat, premises in the second, defeater-related chain, b) and c), rebut a crucial premise in the belief-related chain, 3). Thus, the higher-order defeater in HYPOXIA-C seems to have a higher-order rebutting effect that is structurally analogous to a standard undercutting defeater, except that it rebuts a higher-order belief about one's own past competence, rather than a belief about the support-relation between the original justifier and the target-attitude. As in the case of undercutting defeat, this leaves Andy with the only option to suspend judgment. This explanation neatly captures the intuitions about the case. Furthermore, we can explain why higher-order defeaters, but not undercutting defeaters are possible for certain cases of conclusive input, like HYPOXIA-C: In complex cases, the originally relied-upon input ceases to be part of the target- attitude's total doxastic base during re-evaluation. The reliance on one's own past competence replacing it can in turn be undermined by higher-order defeaters, which characteristically target that competence.

Now, the picture developed here is not obviously correct. In fact, we commonly take ourselves to believe on the basis of actual truth-supporting reasons or evidence, rather than on memories of our own supposed competence. It is by no means proposed here that this should not be correct for the vast majority of our doxastic attitudes. To see this, consider how the analysis from relying on one's past competence exploits the idea that re-evaluation brings a doxastic change: The idea that Andy, in the present, cannot re-use her calculation *becomes* epistemically relevant as a result of obtaining the defeater because the defeater exerts pressure on her to rebase her belief. Because her circumstances have changed, what is available for basing has also changed and this is how the defeater gains purchase, illustrating how context-dependent higher-order defeaters are. It is not claimed that it is always or even often true that the input one originally relied on cannot be relied on again at the point of re-evaluation (although it may; I want to stay silent on this empirical question). The claim made here is merely that, in cases where re-evaluation is required and where the original justifier cannot be re-used during re-evaluation, that is, in complex cases, we rely on our own past competence and this is what explains why new information that sheds doubt in that competence sometimes defeats.

## 6.3 The Rebasing Account of Higher-Order Defeat — 265

Such situations can be contrasted with *simple* cases, in which we get a different result:

HYPOXIA-S: At time $t$, Andy is piloting an airplane to Hawaii. She is confident that she has enough fuel to get there because five minutes ago (at $t$-$1$) she used her considerable skill in mental calculations to quickly figure out that this is so on the basis of mentally laying out and evaluating the easily accessed mathematical evidence, $I_1$:
- A full tank contains 20,000 miles worth of fuel.
- The tank is ¾ full.
- Hawaii is 16,000 miles from Andy's point of departure.
- Andy has flown 5,000 miles toward Hawaii.

Andy's skill is such that she could repeat this calculation in her head at any time. At $t$, air traffic control provides her with a credible warning that, as a result of a drop in her oxygen supply, any reasoning she's done in the last five minutes has probably been distorted without her knowing it but now everything is fine again.

The difference between this case and HYPOXIA-C is that it is far less clear that Andy has to suspend judgment on whether she has enough fuel.

To bring this out, we can enrich the case a little by supposing that the math is so easy and that Andy is so good at it that she can just "see" that she has enough fuel. Given my framework, this can be explained straightforwardly. HYPOXIA-S is a simple case in that Andy can, at $t$, assess the data *again* with her considerable competence. Therefore, she can rely on the data itself as a premise, rather than on her own past competence, during re-evaluation. A competent re-evaluation on her part would thus not contain 1) and 2) in the target-attitude's chain but the original mathematical data about the tank's fuel level, distances etc. The hypoxia-related chain (not a defeater-chain in this example) is the same as in the complex case. Because the information about past hypoxia does not pertain to the epistemic connection between this data and the belief that Andy has enough fuel, the premises in the target-attitude's chain are not rebutted by the premises in the hypoxia-related chain and thus no undermining and no defeat occurs. Indeed, because the target-attitude's chain contains mathematical data perfectly fit for basing the belief on, premise a) in the hypoxia-related chain is shown to be false instead. As a result, it is the hypoxia-related chain, rather than the target-attitude's chain that collapses, so that a competent re-evaluation on Andy's part in HYPOXIA-S will result in her reinstating the belief that she has enough fuel. Thus, the fact that she contingently is in the position of being able to reuse her original justifier during re-evaluation makes a crucial difference with respect to the question whether the new higher-order information concerning her past competence amounts to a higher-order defeater. More generally put: Higher-order information shedding doubt on one's own past competence amounts to a defeater in complex, but not in simple cases.

### 6.3.3 Persistent, Fleeting and Infectious Higher-Order Defeaters

There is a small wrinkle in the distinctions made in the previous paragraph. In the present picture, the information provided by air traffic control in the simple case, HYPOXIA-S, does not render it *persistently* unjustified for Andy to believe that she has enough fuel, but that is not to say that it has no epistemic consequences at all. For if one accepts the Rebasing framework for such cases, the new information does bring some requirements to the table and cannot simply be ignored, in spite of the fact that they do not result in Andy's belief becoming unjustified. If Andy in HYPOXIA-S were to simply disregard air traffic control's information, she would not re-evaluate at all and therefore also not base her belief on [mental math at $t$], but on [mental math at $t$-$1$] and, given the hypoxia-information, there is clearly something wrong with that. After all, she has reason to believe that the process that originally led to her holding her belief is flawed and this seems to be incompatible with justification in the case, given that the new information targets just her original way of getting her belief. Thus, while Andy may quickly and easily reinstate her belief that she has enough fuel in response to learning about the hypoxia warning, she may not simply disregard that warning.

This principle is already somewhat familiar from previous chapters: Even a defeater that does not prevent the reinstatement of the target-attitude still requires uncommitted suspension of judgment during re-evaluation. Since air traffic control's warning therefore does have the potential to defeat and prompts/requires a change in the target-belief's doxastic status, albeit a temporarily limited one, we may call the kind of pseudo-defeater provided in simple cases like HYPOXIA-S a *fleeting* higher-order defeater.[23] It may be contrasted with the kind of defeater provided in complex cases like HYPOXIA-C, which engenders more permanent doxastic changes and which can be called a *persistent* higher-order defeater.

There is a third kind of case that has a unique structure. In the complex and simple cases discussed so far, the defeater is only aimed at the *original* use of the

---

23 It may be thought that what I have said concerning causal accounts of defeat is incompatible with classifying the higher-order information in simple cases as a defeater here. That may be correct, and if so, I have no problem withdrawing defeater-status from it. Nevertheless, I prefer the label here because there is a (in this case) significant difference between the well-supported information about the hypoxia and, for example, a completely unsupported piece of information that suggests that something is wrong with one's belief. As I argued in chapter 2, we definitely do not want the latter to turn out to be a defeater, while this is somewhat more plausible for the former.

input that forms the target-attitude's original justifier. There are cases of defeat, however, where the defeater "infects" *any* potential use of the input. Here is an example:

> HYPOXIA-I: At time *t*, Andy is piloting an airplane to Hawaii. She is confident that she has enough fuel to get there because five minutes ago (at *t-1*) she used her considerable skill in mental calculations to quickly figure out that this is so on the basis of mentally laying out and evaluating the easily accessed evidence, $I_1$:
> - A full tank contains 20,000 miles worth of fuel.
> - The tank is ¾ full.
> - Hawaii was 16,000 miles from Andy's point of departure.
> - Andy has flown 5,000 miles toward Hawaii.
>
> At *t*, air traffic control provides her with a credible warning that, prior to taking off, she has secretly been given a drug by a competitor that completely distorts her general reasoning without her noticing. Since her entire water supply was laced with it, the drug is very likely to still be in effect.

This variant of the case is inspired by Christensen's (2010a, p. 187) drug-case. Intuitively, Andy is no longer justified in holding the belief that she has enough fuel. Furthermore, because air-traffic control's warning indicates not only that her original way of coming to believe that she has enough fuel on the basis of *I1* was unsuited, but also that any present or (near) future way of exploiting *I1* will be unsuited, due to the influence of the drug. Thus, there is no competent re-evaluation open to Andy that would have her reinstate her belief that she has enough fuel.

Let us assume that the defeater in the case is misleading, that is, Andy is not, in fact, under the influence of the drug. Still, the information that she has been given the drug supports suspension of judgment, prompting re-evaluation. During that re-evaluation, Andy is capable of re-using *I1* because she is a competent mental mathematician. Since the information about the drug does not indicate that *I1* fails to support the belief that she has enough fuel but targets Andy's attitude-formation processes. Therefore, no higher-order rebuttal and no undercutting effect occurs. Normally, this would result in Andy being able to reinstate her belief. However, the epistemic quality of coming to the conclusion that she has enough fuel on the basis of *I1* during the re-evaluation is *itself* indicated to be subpar by the information about the drug. At the end of the re-evaluation, Andy is left with a belief that she has enough fuel to be reinstated, while the information about the drug, given that it also concerns her reasoning *during the process that would lead to that reinstatement*, continues to support suspension of judgment with respect to whether she has enough fuel. This means that the doxastic incompatibility introduced by the defeater is not dissolved by the re-evaluation, which would require *another* re-evaluation. But one can already see that further iterations of the process will not yield any different results, given that the drug-information affects them all. A justified reinstatement of the belief that Andy has enough fuel is not possible, which explains the defeating effect of the information about the drug.

Structurally, the defeater does not affect the reasoning chain concerning the target-attitude during re-evaluation but undermines the presumption that the re-evaluation process as a whole is epistemically legitimate, which requires further investigation and makes that process unsuitable as a doxastic base. Since it does this to every potential re-evaluation process, the defeater can be called an *infectious* higher-order defeater because it "infects" all following iterations. In a case of infectious higher-order defeat like HYPOXIA-I, it does not matter whether one is in a complex or a simple case. Even if the original data is reusable, the process cannot be used as a justifier, due to the general nature of the defeater. Cases of infectious higher-order defeat are cases where one has independent reason to think that some universally applicable epistemic capacity is disrupted, leaving no way out of the problematic situation. It is difficult to say what one is to do in that situation, given that justified suspension of judgment is also not an option. It would have to be based on the disrupted faculty.[24]

### 6.3.4 Peer-Disagreement and Higher-Order Defeat

Summing up, we find that, in higher-order defeaters, a second type of source-sensitive defeaters can be found. Such defeaters can be distinguished from undercutting defeaters by looking at the content of the higher-order belief they rebut during re-evaluation: While undercutting defeaters target beliefs concerning the support-relations between original doxastic base and target-attitude, higher-order defeaters target beliefs expressing reliance on one's own past competence. This further enables the subdivision of the class of higher-order defeater into the two types of higher-order defeater – fleeting and persistent – which differ with respect to whether they allow a reinstatement of the target-attitude after re-evaluation, depending on whether the subject is in a simple or in a complex case. A special variant of higher-order defeat is infectious higher-order defeat,

---

**24** One option would be to postulate a requirement for a *complete absence of any doxastic attitude* toward the target-proposition, if feasible. This is not implausible, given that the epistemic situation in cases of infectious higher-order defeat seems to be quite similar to the phenomenon of *higher-order doubt* (Alexander 2013), which amounts to support for the belief that *no* first-order attitude will be adequate.

which has a persistent defeating effect, regardless of whether it applies to a simple or a complex case.

Now, let us apply the resulting taxonomy to the phenomenon of peer-disagreement. The type of higher-order defeater one often finds in cases of peer-disagreement is the persistent higher-order defeater. This is especially plausible, if one looks at time-slices of disagreement that do not feature a renewed evaluation of the shared input. Similarly, if the shared input is painstakingly evaluated again by both sides but the disagreement persists, the persisting disagreement may provide one with a recurred persistent higher-order defeater. This kind of persistent disagreement that withstands additional, collective evaluation can often be found in the social sciences.

Other kinds of higher-order defeaters from disagreement are also conceivable. If, in the Restaurant case, the subject's opponent makes her calculation only once because she is permanently distracted afterwards, while the subject herself can quickly re-calculate in her head (e.g. during re-evaluation), the subject is in a simple case and suffers only fleeting higher-order defeat: All she has to do is re-evaluate.

Disagreement-based cases of infectious higher-order defeat are much more exotic and unrealistic. A possible case would be a Restaurant-style case where both parties re-evaluate equally often on the basis of the same data, consistently come to conflicting conclusions and are both immediately informed of the other's verdict (say, there is a screen behind each that shows their conclusions to the other in real time). So, by and large, the relevant peer-disagreement cases are cases of persistent higher-order defeat.

The general lesson from this chapter is this: What one is to do in a case of peer-disagreement highly depends on the details of the case. One needs to pay attention to the extent to which the input is shared between the disagreeing parties in combination with their relative competence, as well as to whether the input is re-usable by the parties during re-evaluation and whether the re-evaluation is itself undermined. The framework developed here will give a verdict on any given case, as soon as the values of these variables are determined. That said, we have seen that a powerful theoretical argument from the structure of defeat in combination with the analysis of cases exemplifying source-sensitivity of support and defeat can be given that supports Strong Conciliationism, at least for the Restaurant-style case type of shared-evidence peer-disagreement central to much of the current debate. Given that such cases feature higher-order defeaters, Christensen is thus right in thinking that they require the disagreeing parties to "bracket" the shared input. This can also be seen from the detailed analysis of higher-order defeat that the Rebasing Account allows. Nevertheless, cases of peer-disagreement where the input is not or only partially shared should be sufficiently common to make the analytic tools provided by Weak Conciliationism very fruitful. This is because such cases will, at least in part, feature rebutting defeat, which does not engender bracketing.

# Conclusion

The most important result of this book is the development of the Rebasing Account of Defeat. It can be shown to be one of the few, if not the only, theory that fits the requirements extrapolated from the case-data. Furthermore, it is easily accommodated with almost any theory of justification, ranging from staunchly internalist to staunchly externalist views, and it efficiently supplements discussions in applied epistemology, such as the one surrounding disagreement. That said, it should be clear that the Rebasing Account does not come out of this discussion unrivaled. One may well think that what I have said about the relationship between causal and non-causal accounts is not enough to prefer causal accounts and that more must be said on the subject. If so, at least a modified version of Loughrist's reasons-based theory of defeat can be defended as a relevant alternative. The relevant modifications and motivations for rejecting causal accounts must be left to future work.

Leaving these theoretical positionings aside, the characteristic focus on doxastic justification that goes with the Rebasing Account makes it a powerful analytic tool for the treatment of a number of issues in epistemology. First, there are topics within social epistemology that profit from its application. This has already been done for the epistemology of disagreement, but there are other discussions where this would be fruitful. The theory's ability to explain the bracketing effect of higher-order defeat is, for example, potentially helpful in analyzing the idea of the verdict of an epistemic authority "preempting" the view of a layperson (Zagzebski 2012, p. 102ff). Preemption is supposed to have the effect of rendering a set of input rationally unusable (Constantin and Grundmann 2020; Grundmann 2019) and, as was seen, this can be explained in terms of re-evaluation.

Second, the developed account of defeat has bearing on more general issues in epistemology. For example, we can likely find points of contact between the connection between rational usability of input and aspects of doxastic justification that go beyond a causal relation between supportive input and the relevant attitude. John Turri (2010) convincingly argues that some sort of competence-related or dispositional aspect must be part of the concept of doxastic justification since accidental basing on the right kind of input seems to be incompatible with it. Clearly, this fits well with the idea that, in certain scenarios, we rely on our own past competence and, more specifically, that there are defeaters that target one's competence, rather than the causal or evidential relationship between input and attitude. Accordingly, the conception of doxastic justification employed in this book could be expanded and the conception of higher-order defeaters more generally applied to it.

Another interesting question that has only been brushed in chapter 5 is the question how Evidentialism should deal with defeaters that make evidence unusable, where the kind of defeater that can be said to do this depends on the relevant conception of the Connector that is accepted. Specifically, while it seems that a certain tension between the postulation of higher-order defeaters and Evidentialism is being discussed, the tension between the postulation of *undercutting* defeaters and moderate versions of Evidentialism appears to have remained undetected. Given the much broader acceptance of undercutting defeat, compared to higher-order defeat, this should make a difference with respect to the plausibility of Evidentialist constraints on justification and rationality. Similarly, while a proposal for a Reliabilist accommodation of defeat has been made in chapter 5, the sketched discussion leaves plenty of room for a range of theoretical decision on the side of the Reliabilist and for different conceptions of the relationship between descriptive theories of justification and normative defeaters.

Of course, the development of the Rebasing Account and its application is still rough around the edges and, at times, in need of further scaffolding and testing. For example, I have relied on a number of assumptions about higher-order material surrounding a justified doxastic attitude, like conceptions of typical ways to form attitudes and about the psychological and epistemic significance of doxastic incompatibility. Also, while I have provided accounts of the process of re-evaluation and its normative structure, I have not argued that these accounts are the only ways to model the phenomena. Here, one may well come up with more economic or psychologically adequate conceptions that can be incorporated in the general project.

Similarly, I have not conclusively established that rebutting and undercutting defeat are the only basic categories of defeat. There may be other kinds of defeaters that function in a systematically different way (possible additional types can be found in Pryor 2004; Kotzen 2008). Whether there are such kinds and how these can be given a treatment in keeping with the Rebasing Account must be left open for future work.

Finally, I have not added much to the question what it means that knowledge is defeasible or how defeaters must be treated under certain frameworks like knowledge-first epistemology (as developed in Williamson 2000). This, too, will be left to more committed proponents of the relevant views, admitting to the possibility that results from such projects may have further theoretical bearing on what I have said in this book.

The development of the Rebasing Account has brought with it the discussion of a number of issues and frameworks that are interesting but rarely discussed on their own, such as rebasing, re-evaluation, the difference between committed and uncommitted suspension of judgment or the indistinctness of the line between normative and doxastic defeaters. In spite of all these caveats and potential topics for future work, I hope to have provided a comprehensive and, most importantly, theoretically independent and explanatorily basic account of epistemic defeat. In the end, I stand by the thesis that epistemic defeat is worthwhile to investigate, not just as the flipside of epistemic justification or as a theoretical tool for avoiding problems in the analysis of knowledge. When we are trying to understand what it means to be justified in believing something, we are often just trying to provide theoretical underpinnings of a ubiquitous epistemic phenomenon. In general, it is plausible that we can quickly, more or less automatically and successfully form justified beliefs. Indeed, sometimes, we cannot help ourselves when it comes to this. But when we investigate under what circumstances our beliefs lose their justification status and must be given up, the issue becomes more normatively tinged. Giving up belief in the face of new information in a rational and justification-*preserving* way is less obviously something which we just naturally do successfully. Finding out what it means to properly treat defeaters is more than just finding a description of what we already do. It has a more pronounced potential to teach us better epistemic practice.

# Bibliography

Alexander, David. 2013. "The Problem of Respecting Higher-Order Doubt." *Philosophers' Imprint* 13. http://hdl.handle.net/2027/spo.3521354.0013.018

Alexander, David. 2017. "Unjustified Defeaters." *Erkenntnis* 82 (4), pp. 891–912. https://doi.org/10.1007/s10670-016-9849-z

Alston, William P. 1985. "Concepts of Epistemic Justification." *The Monist* 68 (1), pp. 57–89. https://doi.org/10.5840/monist198568116

Alston, William P. 1986. "Internalism and Externalism in Epistemology." *Philosophical Topics* 14 (1), pp. 179–221. https://doi.org/10.5840/philtopics198614118

Alston, William P. (1988): "The Deontological Conception of Epistemic Justification." In *Philosophical Perspectives* 2, pp. 257–299. https://doi.org/10.2307/2214077

Alston, William P. 1989. *Epistemic Justification. Essays in the Theory of Knowledge.* New York: Cornell University Press.

Alston, William P. 1995. "How to Think about Reliability." *Philosophical Topics* 23 (1), pp. 1–29. https://doi.org/10.5840/philtopics199523122.

Alston, William P. 2002. "Plantinga, Naturalism and Defeat." In *Naturalism Defeated? Essays on Plantinga's Evolutionary Argument against Naturalism* [with a response by Alvin Plantinga], edited by James Beilby, pp. 176–203. New York: Cornell University Press.

Axtell, Guy. 2011. "From Internalist Evidentialism to Virtue Responsibilism". In *Evidentialism and its Discontents*, edited by Trent Dougherty, pp. 71–88. Oxford: Oxford University Press.

Bach, Kent. 1985. "A Rationale for Reliabilism." *The Monist* 68 (2), pp. 246–263. https://doi.org/10.5840/monist198568224.

Baehr, Jason. 2009. "Evidentialism, Vice, and Virtue." *Philosophy and Phenomenological Research* 78 (3), pp. 545–567. https://doi.org/10.1111/j.1933-1592.2009.00255.x.

Baker-Hytch, Max; Benton, Matthew A. 2015. "Defeatism Defeated." *Philosophical Perspectives* 29 (1), pp. 40–66. https://doi.org/10.1111/phpe.12056.

Ballantyne, Nathan; Coffman, E. J. 2011. "Uniqueness, Evidence, and Rationality." *Philosophers' Imprint* 18. http://hdl.handle.net/2027/spo.3521354.0011.018.

Beddor, Bob. 2015. "Process Reliabilism's Troubles with Defeat." *The Philosophical Quarterly* 65 (259), pp. 145–159. https://doi.org/10.1093/pq/pqu075.

Beilby, James, ed. 2002. *Naturalism Defeated? Essays on Plantinga's Evolutionary Argument against Naturalism*; [with a response by Alvin Plantinga]. New York: Cornell University Press.

Bergmann, Michael. 2005. "Defeaters and Higher-Level Requirements." *Philosophical Quarterly* 55 (220), pp. 419–436. https://doi.org/10.1111/j.0031-8094.2005.00408.x.

Bergmann, Michael. 2006. *Justification without Awareness.* Oxford: Oxford University Press.

Bergmann, Michael (2009): Rational Disagreement after Full Disclosure. In *Episteme* 6 (3), pp. 336–353.

Betz, Gregor. 2013. "Degrees of Justification, Bayes' Rule, and Rationality." In *Bayesian Argumentation. The Practical Side of Probability*, edited by Frank Zenker, pp. 135–146. Dordrecht: Springer (Synthese library, 362).

Boghossian, Paul. 2003. "Blind Reasoning." *Aristotelian Society Supplementary Volume* 77 (1), pp. 225–248. https://doi.org/10.1111/1467-8349.00110.

BonJour, Laurence. 2010. "The Myth of Knowledge." *Philosophical Perspectives* 24 (1), pp. 57–83. https://doi.org/10.1111/j.1520-8583.2010.00185.x.
Bratman, Michael. 1981. "Intention and Means-End Reasoning." *The Philosophical Review* 90 (2), pp. 252–265. https://doi.org/10.2307/2184441.
Burge, Tyler. 2003. "Perceptual Entitlement." *Philosophy and Phenomenological Research* 67 (3), pp. 503–548. https://doi.org/10.1111/j.1933-1592.2003.tb00307.x.
Casullo, Albert. 2003. *A Priori Justification*. Oxford: Oxford University Press.
Casullo, Albert. 2016. "Pollock and Sturgeon on Defeaters." *Synthese*, pp. 1–10. https://doi.org/10.1007/s11229-016-1073-5.
Cath, Yuri. 2011. "Knowing How Without Knowing That." In *Knowing How. Essays on Knowledge, Mind, and Action*, edited by John Bengson and Marc A. Moffett, pp. 113–135. Oxford: Oxford University Press.
Chandler, Jake. 2013. "Defeat reconsidered." *Analysis* 73 (1), pp. 49–51. https://doi.org/10.1093/analys/ans129.
Choi, Sungho; Fara, Michael. 2018. "Dispositions." In *Stanford Encyclopedia of Philosophy*, edited by Edward N. Zalta. https://plato.stanford.edu/archives/fall2018/entries/dispositions/, visited on 07/09/2018.
Christensen, David. 2004. *Putting Logic in its Place: Formal Constraints on Rational Belief*. Oxford: Oxford University Press.
Christensen, David. 2007. "Epistemology of Disagreement: The Good News." *Philosophical Review* 116 (2), pp. 187–217. https://doi.org/10.1215/00318108-2006-035.
Christensen, David. 2009. "Disagreement as Evidence. The Epistemology of Controversy." *Philosophy Compass* 4 (5), pp. 756–767. https://doi.org/10.1111/j.1747-9991.2009.00237.x.
Christensen, David. 2010a. "Higher-Order Evidence." *Philosophy and Phenomenological Research* 81 (1), pp. 185–215. https://doi.org/10.1111/j.1933-1592.2010.00366.x.
Christensen, David. 2010b. "Rational Reflection." *Philosophical Perspectives* 24 (1), pp. 121–140. https://doi.org/10.1111/j.1520-8583.2010.00187.x.
Christensen, David. 2011. "Disagreement, Question-Begging, and Epistemic Self-Criticism." *Philosophers' Imprint* 11. http://hdl.handle.net/2027/spo.3521354.0011.006, visited on 01/31/2017.
Christensen, David. 2016. "Disagreement, Drugs, etc. From Accuracy to Akrasia." *Episteme* 13 (04), pp. 397–422. https://doi.org/10.1017/epi.2016.20.
Cloos, Christopher Michael. 2015. "Responsibilist Evidentialism." *Philosophical Studies* 172 (11), pp. 2999–3016. https://doi.org/10.1007/s11098-015-0454-9.
Comesaña, Juan. 2010. "Evidentialist Reliabilism." *Noûs* 44 (4), pp. 571–600. https://doi.org/10.1111/j.1468-0068.2010.00748.x.
Comesaña, Juan; Tal, Eyal. 2015a. "Evidence of Evidence is Evidence (trivially)." *Analysis* 75 (4), pp. 557–559. https://doi.org/10.1093/analys/anv072.
Comesaña, Juan; Tal, Eyal. 2015b. "Is Evidence of Evidence Evidence?" *Noûs* 51 (1), pp. 95–112. https://doi.org/10.1111/nous.12101.
Conee, Earl. 2004. "Heeding Misleading Evidence." In *Evidentialism*, edited by Earl Conee and Richard Feldman, pp. 259–276. Oxford: Oxford University Press.
Conee, Earl; Feldman, Richard. 1985. "Evidentialism." *Philosophical Studies* 48 (1), pp. 15–34. https://doi.org/10.1007/BF00372404.

Conee, Earl; Feldman, Richard. 1998. "The Generality Problem for Reliabilism." *Philosophical Studies* 89 (1), pp. 1–29. https://doi.org/10.1023/A:1004243308503.

Conee, Earl; Feldman, Richard. 2004a. "Internalism Defended." In *Evidentialism*, edited by Earl Conee and Richard Feldman, pp. 53–82. Oxford: Oxford University Press.

Conee, Earl; Feldman, Richard. 2008. "Evidence." In *Epistemology*, edited by Quentin Smith, pp. 83–105. Oxford: Oxford University.

Conee, Earl; Feldman, Richard. 2011. "Replies." In *Evidentialism and its Discontents*, edited by Trent Dougherty, pp. 221–323. Oxford: Oxford University Press.

Conee, Earl Brink; Feldman, Richard. 2004b. *Evidentialism. Essays in Epistemology.* Oxford: Clarendon Press.

Constantin, Jan. 2020. "Replacement and Reasoning: A Reliabilist Account of Epistemic Defeat." *Synthese* 197 (8), pp. 3437–3457. https://doi.org/10.1007/s11229-018-01895-y.

Constantin, Jan; Grundmann, Thomas. 2020. "Epistemic Authority: Preemption through Source Sensitive Defeat." *Synthese* 197 (9), pp. 4109–4130. https://doi.org/10.1007/s11229-018-01923-x.

DiPaolo, Joshua. Forthcoming. "Higher-Order Defeat is Object-Independent." *Pacific Philosophical Quarterly*.

Egan, Andy; Elga, Adam. 2005. "I Can't Believe I'm Stupid." *Philosophical Perspectives* 19 (1), pp. 77–93. https://doi.org/10.1111/j.1520-8583.2005.00054.x.

Elga, Adam. 2007. "Reflection and Disagreement." *Noûs* 41 (3), pp. 478–502. https://doi.org/10.1111/j.1468-0068.2007.00656.x.

Elga, Adam. 2013. "The Puzzle of the Unmarked Clock and the New Rational Reflection Principle." *Philosophical Studies* 164 (1), pp. 127–139. https://doi.org/10.1007/s11098-013-0091-0.

Enoch, David. 2010. "Not Just a Truthometer: Taking Oneself Seriously (but not Too Seriously) in Cases of Peer Disagreement." In *Mind* 119 (476), pp. 953–997. https://doi.org/10.1093/mind/fzq070.

Ewing, Alfred. C. 1953. *Ethics.* London: English Universities Press.

Feldman, Richard. 2001. "Voluntary Belief and Epistemic Evaluation." In *Knowledge, Truth, and Duty*, edited by Matthias Steup, pp. 77–92. Oxford: Oxford University Press.

Feldman, Richard. 2002a. "Epistemological Duties." In *The Oxford Handbook of Epistemology*, edited by Paul K. Moser, pp. 362–384. New York: Oxford University Press.

Feldman, Richard. 2002b. *Epistemology.* Upper Saddle River, NJ: Prentice Hall (Prentice Hall Foundations of philosophy series).

Feldman, Richard. 2004. "Having Evidence." In *Evidentialism*, edited by Earl Conee and Richard Feldman, pp. 219–241. Oxford: Oxford University Press.

Feldman, Richard. 2005. "Respecting the Evidence." *Philosophical Perspectives* 19 (1), pp. 95–119. https://doi.org/10.1111/j.1520-8583.2005.00055.x.

Feldman, Richard. 2007. "Reasonable Religious Disagreements." In *Philosophers Without Gods: Meditations on Atheism and the Secular.* Edited by Louise Antony, pp. 194–214. New York: Oxford University Press.

Feldman, Richard. 2014. "Evidence of Evidence is Evidence." In *The Ethics of Belief: Individual and Social*, edited by Jonathan Matheson & Rico Vitz, pp. 284–300. Oxford: Oxford University Press.

Festinger, Leon. 1957. *A Theory of Cognitive Dissonance.* Stanford: Stanford University Press.

Fitelson, Branden. 2012. "Evidence of Evidence is not (necessarily) Evidence." *Analysis* 72 (1), pp. 85–88. https://doi.org/10.1093/analys/anr126.

Frances, Bryan. 2008. "Live Skeptical Hypotheses." In *The Oxford Handbook of Skepticism*, edited by John Greco, pp. 225–245. Oxford: Oxford University Press.

Friedman, Jane. 2013a. "Rational Agnosticism and Degrees of Belief*." In *Oxford Studies in Epistemology*, vol. 4, edited by Tamar Szabó Gendler, John Hawthorne, pp. 57–81. Oxford: Oxford University Press.

Friedman, Jane. 2013b. "Suspended Judgment." *Philosophical Studies* 162 (2), pp. 165–181. https://doi.org/10.1007/s11098-011-9753-y.

Friedman, Jane. 2015. "Why Suspend Judging?" *Noûs* 50 (4), 1–25. https://doi.org/10.1111/nous.12137.

Frise, Matthew. 2018. "The Reliability Problem for Reliabilism." *Philosophical Studies* 175 (4), pp. 923–945. https://doi.org/10.1007/s11098-017-0899-0.

Gelfert, Axel. 2011. "Who is an Epistemic Peer?." *Logos & Episteme* 2 (4), pp. 507–514. https://doi.org/10.5840/logos-episteme2011242.

Gibbons, John. 2006. "Access Externalism." *Mind* 115 (457), pp. 19–39. https://doi.org/10.1093/mind/fzl019.

Gibbons, John. 2013. *The Norm of Belief*. Oxford: Oxford University Press.

Goldberg, Sanford. 2013. "Disagreement, Defeat, and Assertion 1." In *The Epistemology of Disagreement: New Essays*, edited by David Christensen & Jennifer Lackey, p. 167–189. Oxford: Oxford University Press. http://www.oxfordscholarship.com/view/10.1093/acprof:oso/9780199698370.001.0001/acprof-9780199698370-chapter-8, visited on 01/26/2017.

Goldberg, Sanford. 2016. "On the Epistemic Significance of Evidence you should have had." *Episteme* 13 (4), pp. 449–470. https://doi.org/10.1017/epi.2016.24.

Goldberg, Sanford. 2017a. "Should have Known." *Synthese* 194 (8), pp. 2863–2894. https://doi.org/10.1007/s11229-015-0662-z.

Goldberg, Sanford. 2017b. "The Asymmetry Thesis and the Doctrine of Normative Defeat." *American Philosophical Quarterly* 54 (4), pp. 339–352.

Goldberg, Sanford. 2018. *To the Best of our Knowledge: Social Expectations and Epistemic Normativity*. Oxford: Oxford University Press.

Goldman, Alvin I. 2009. "Replies to Discussants." *Grazer Philosophische Studien* 79 (1), pp. 245–288. https://doi.org/10.1163/18756735-90000866.

Goldman, Alvin I. 2012. "What is Justified Belief?" In *Reliabilism and Contemporary Epistemology. Essays*, edited by Alvin I. Goldman, pp. 29–48. New York: Oxford University Press.

Goldman, Alvin I.; Beddor, Bob. 2016. "Reliabilist Epistemology." In *The Stanford Encyclopedia of Philosophy*, edited by Edward N. Zalta. https://plato.stanford.edu/archives/win2016/entries/reliabilism/, visited on 01/31/2017.

Greco, John. 1990. "Internalism and Epistemically Responsible Belief." *Synthese* 85 (2), pp. 245–277. https://doi.org/10.1007/BF00484794.

Grundmann, Thomas. 2009a. "Introspective Self-Knowledge and Reasoning. An Externalist Guide." *Erkenntnis* 71 (1), pp. 89–105. https://doi.org/10.1007/s10670-009-9169-7.

Grundmann, Thomas. 2009b. "Reliabilism and the Problem of Defeaters." *Grazer Philosophische Studien* 79 (1), pp. 65–76. https://doi.org/10.1163/18756735-90000857.

Grundmann, Thomas. 2011. "Defeasibility Theories." In *The Routledge Companion to Epistemology*, edited by Sven Bernecker & Duncan Pritchard, pp. 156–166. London: Routledge (Routledge philosophy companions).

Grundmann, Thomas. 2013. "Doubts about Philosophy? The Alleged Challenge from Disagreement." In *Knowledge, Virtue, and Action: Putting Epistemic Virtues to Work*, edited by Tim Henning & David P. Schweikard, pp. 72–98. New York: Routledge (Routledge Studies in in Contemporary Philosophy).

Grundmann, Thomas. 2019. "How to Respond Rationally to Peer Disagreement: The Preemption View." *Philosophical Issues* 29 (1), pp. 129–142. https://doi.org/10.1111/phis.12144.

Harman, Gilbert. 1968. "Knowledge, Inference, and Explanation." *American Philosophical Quarterly* 5 (3), pp. 164–173.

Harman, Gilbert. 1973. *Thought*. Princeton and London: Princeton University Press.

Harman, Gilbert. 1980. "Reasoning and Evidence One Does Not Possess." In *Midwest Studies in Philosophy* 5 (1), pp. 163–182. http://dx.doi.org/10.1111/j.1475-4975.1980.tb00403.x.

Horwich, Paul. 2016. *Probability and Evidence*. Cambridge: Cambridge University Press.

Huemer, Michael. 2001. *Skepticism and the Veil of Perception*. Lanham: Rowman & Littlefield.

Huemer, Michael. 2007. "Compassionate Phenomenal Conservatism." *Philosophy and Phenomenological Research* 74 (1), pp. 30–55. https://doi.org/10.1111/j.1933-1592.2007.00002.x.

Huttegger, Simon M. 2017. *The Probabilistic Foundations of Rational Learning*. Cambridge: Cambridge University Press.

Jäger, Christoph. 2005. "Warrant, Defeaters, and the Epistemic Basis of Religious Belief." In *Scientific Explanation and Religious Belief. Science and Religion in Philosophical and Public Discourse*, vol. 17, edited by Michael G. Parker, pp. 81–98. Tübingen: Mohr Siebeck (Religion in philosophy and theology, 17).

Janvid, Mikael. 2017. "Defeater Goes External." *Philosophia* 45 (2), pp. 701–715. https://doi.org/10.1007/s11406-016-9803-y.

Jeffrey, Richard. 1992. *Probability and the Art of Judgment*. Cambridge: Cambridge University Press.

Jeffrey, Richard. 2004. *Subjective Probability: The Real Thing*. Cambridge: Cambridge University Press.

Kelly, Thomas. 2005. "The Epistemic Significance of Disagreement." In *Oxford Studies in Epistemology*, Volume 1, edited by Tamar Szabó Gendler, John Hawthorne, pp. 167–196. Oxford: Oxford University Press.

Kelly, Thomas. 2010. "Peer Disagreement and Higher-Order Evidence." In *Social Epistemology: Essential Readings*, edited by Alvin I. Goldman & Dennis Whitcomb, pp. 183–217. Oxford: Oxford University Press.

Kelly, Thomas. 2011. "Peer Disagreement and Higher-Order Evidence." In *Social Epistemology. Essential Readings*, edited by Alvin I. Goldman, pp. 183–217. Oxford: Oxford University Press.

Kelly, Thomas. 2013. "Disagreement and the Burdens of Judgment." In *The Epistemology of Disagreement: New Essays*, edited by David Phiroze Christensen & Jennifer Lackey. Oxford: Oxford University Press.

Kelly, Thomas. 2016. "Evidence." In *The Stanford Encyclopedia of Philosophy*, edited by Edward N. Zalta. https://plato.stanford.edu/archives/win2016/entries/evidence/, visited on 01/31/2017.

Kiesewetter, Benjamin. 2017. *The Normativity of Rationality*. Oxford: Oxford Scholarship Online.

Klein, Peter. 2005. "Infinitism is the Solution to the Epistemic Regress Problem." In *Contemporary Debates in Epistemology*, edited by Matthias Steup & Ernes Sosa. Malden Mass: Blackwell (Contemporary debates in philosophy, 3).

Klein, Ralf-Thomas. 2014. "Where there are Internal Defeaters, there are "Confirmers"". *Synthese* 191 (12), pp. 2715–2728. https://doi.org/10.1007/s11229-014-0415-4.

Kölbel, Max. 2014. "Agreement and Communication." *Erkenntnis* 79 (1), pp. 101–120. https://doi.org/10.1007/s10670-013-9447-2.

Korcz, Keith Allen. 1997. "Recent Work on the Basing Relation." *American Philosophical Quarterly* 34 (2), pp. 171–191.

Korcz, Keith Allen. 2000. "The Causal-Doxastic Theory of the Basing Relation." *Canadian Journal of Philosophy* 30 (4), pp. 525–550. https://doi.org/10.1080/00455091.2000.10717542.

Kornblith, Hilary. 1983. "Justified Belief and Epistemically Responsible Action." *The Philosophical Review* 92 (1), p. 33. https://doi.org/10.2307/2184520.

Kornblith, Hilary. 2012. *On Reflection*. Oxford: Oxford University Press.

Kotzen, Matthew. 2008. *Evidence, Entailment, and Defeat*. Dissertation. New York University, New York.

Kvanvig, Jonathan. 1996. "Plantinga's Proper Function Account of Warrant." In *Warrant in Contemporary Epistemology. Essays in Honor of Plantinga's Theory of Knowledge. With assistance of Alvin Plantinga*, edited by Jonathan L. Kvanvig. Lanham, Md.: Rowman & Littlefield (Studies in epistemology and cognitive theory).

Kvanvig, Jonathan. 2003. "Propositionalism and the Perspectival Character of Justification." *American Philosophical Quarterly* 40 (1), pp. 3–18.

Kvanvig, Jonathan. 2007. "Two Approaches to Epistemic Defeat." In *Alvin Plantinga*, edited by Deane-Peter Baker, pp. 107–124. Cambridge: Cambridge University Press (Contemporary philosophy in focus).

Lackey, Jennifer. 1999. "Testimonial Knowledge and Transmission." *The Philosophical Quarterly* 49 (197), pp. 471–490. https://doi.org/10.1111/1467-9213.00154.

Lackey, Jennifer. 2000. *Rationality, Defeaters, and Testimony*. PhD Dissertation. Brown University, Providence.

Lackey, Jennifer. 2005. "Memory as a Generative Epistemic Source." *Philosophy and Phenomenological Research* 70 (3), pp. 636–658. https://doi.org/10.1111/j.1933-1592.2005.tb00418.x.

Lackey, Jennifer. 2008. *Learning from Words. Testimony as a Source of Knowledge*. Oxford: Oxford University Press.

Lackey, Jennifer. 2010. "A Justificationist View of Disagreement's Epistemic Significance." In *Social Epistemology*, edited by Adrian Haddock, Alan Millar, Duncan Pritchard, pp. 145–154. Oxford: Oxford University Press.

Lackey, Jennifer. 2014. "Socially Extended Knowledge." *Philosophical Issues* 24 (1), pp. 282–298. https://doi.org/10.1111/phis.12034.

Lam, Barry. 2012. "Justified Believing is Tracking your Evidential Commitments." *Logos & Episteme* 3 (4), pp. 545–564. https://doi.org/10.5840/logos-episteme2012342.

Lasonen-Aarnio, Maria. 2014. "Higher-Order Evidence and the Limits of Defeat." *Philosophy and Phenomenological Research* 88 (2), pp. 314–345. https://doi.org/10.1111/phpr.12090.

Lehrer, Keith. 2000. *Theory of Knowledge*. Boulder, CO: Westview Press (Dimensions of philosophy series).

Lehrer, Keith; Paxson, Thomas. 1969. "Knowledge. Undefeated Justified True Belief." *The Journal of Philosophy* 66 (8), p. 225. https://doi.org/10.2307/2024435.

Leplin, Jarrett. 2009. *A Theory of Epistemic Justification*. Dordrecht: Springer (Philosophical studies series, 112).

Lewis, David. 1973. *Counterfactuals*. Malden Mass: Blackwell.

Lewis, David. 2000. "Causation as Influence." *Journal of Philosophy* 97 (4), pp. 182–197.

Lord, Errol. 2015. "Acting for the Right Reasons, Abilities, and Obligation." In *Oxford Studies in Metaethics. Volume 10*, edited by Russ Shafer-Landau, pp. 26–52. Oxford: Oxford University Press.

Loughrist, Timothy. 2015. *Reasons against Belief. A Theory of Epistemic Defeat*. PhD Dissertation. University of Nebraska, Lincoln.

Lynch, Michael P. 2013. "Epistemic Commitments, Epistemic Agency and Practical Reasons." *Philosophical Issues* 23 (1), pp. 343–362. https://doi.org/10.1111/phis.12018.

MacFarlane, John (2014): *Assessment Sensitivity: Relative Truth and its Application*. Oxford: Oxford University Press.

Marques, Teresa. 2014. "Doxastic Disagreement." *Erkenntnis* 79 (S1), pp. 121–142. https://doi.org/10.1007/s10670-013-9448-1.

Matheson, Jonathan. 2009. "Conciliatory Views of Disagreement and Higher-Order Evidence." *Episteme* 6 (3), pp. 269–279. https://doi.org/10.3366/E1742360009000707.

Matheson, Jonathan. 2015a. "Disagreement and Epistemic Peers." In *Oxford Handbooks Online*. https://doi.org/10.1093/oxfordhb/9780199935314.013.13, visited on 02/21/2021.

Matheson, Jonathan. 2015b. *The Epistemic Significance of Disagreement*. Houndmills: Palgrave Macmillan (Palgrave Innovations in Philosophy).

McCain, Kevin. 2014. *Evidentialism and Epistemic Justification*. New York: Routledge.

McFarlane, John. 2007. "Relativism and Disagreement." *Philosophical Studies* 132 (1), pp. 17–31. https://doi.org/10.1007/s11098-006-9049-9.

Meeker, Kevin. 2004. "Justification and the Social Nature of Knowledge." *Philosophical and Phenomenological Research* 69 (1), pp. 156–172. https://doi.org/10.1111/j.1933-1592.2004.tb00388.x.

Melis, Giacomo. 2014. "Understanding Undermining Defeat." *Philosophical Studies* 170 (3), pp. 433–442. https://doi.org/10.1007/s11098-013-0238-z.

Melis, Giacomo. 2016. "Undermining Defeat and Propositional Justification." *Argumenta* 1 (2), pp. 271–280.

Merricks, Trenton. 2002. "Conditional Probability and Defeat." In *Naturalism Defeated? Essays on Plantinga's Evolutionary Argument against Naturalism; [with a response by Alvin Plantinga]*, edited by James Beilby, pp. 165–175. New York: Cornell University Press.

Mittag, Daniel M. "Evidentialism" In *The Internet Encyclopedia of Philosophy*. ISSN 2161–0002, https://www.iep.utm.edu/; visited on 13/02/2021.

Moser, Paul K. 1991. *Knowledge and Evidence.* Cambridge: Cambridge University Press (Cambridge studies in philosophy).
Nelson, Mark T. 2010. "We Have No Positive Epistemic Duties." *Mind* 119 (473), pp. 83–102. https://doi.org/10.1093/mind/fzp148.
Nottelmann, Nikolaj. 2010. *Blameworthy Belief. A study in Epistemic Deontologism.* Dordrecht: Springer (Synthese library, 338).
Palmira, Michele. 2013. "A Puzzle About the Agnostic Response to Peer Disagreement." *Philosophia* 41 (4), pp. 1253–1261. https://doi.org/10.1007/s11406-013-9453-2.
Pappas, George. 2017. "Internalist vs. Externalist Conceptions of Epistemic Justification." In The Stanford Encyclopedia of Philosophy, edited by Edward N. Zalta. https://plato.stanford.edu/archives/fall2017/entries/justep-intext/, visited on 02/21/2021.
Plantinga, Alvin. 1986. "Epistemic Justification." *Noûs* 20 (1), pp. 3–18. https://doi.org/10.2307/2215273.
Plantinga, Alvin. 1993a. *Warrant. The Current Debate.* New York: Oxford University Press.
Plantinga, Alvin. 1993b. *Warrant and Proper Function.* New York: Oxford University Press.
Plantinga, Alvin. 1994. "Naturalism Defeated." http://static1.1.sqspcdn.com/static/f/38692/383655/1263300179793/Naturalism+Defeated.pdf?token=skqA3gfcDvUI1Sx0vlJA43%2FXQEs%3D, visited on 02/21/2021.
Plantinga, Alvin. 2000. *Warranted Christian Belief.* New York: Oxford University Press.
Plantinga, Alvin. 2002. "Reply to Beilby's Cohorts." In *Naturalism Defeated? Essays on Plantinga's Evolutionary Argument against Naturalism*; [with a response by Alvin Plantinga], edited by James Beilby, pp. 204–276. New York: Cornell University Press.
Pollock, John L. 1974. *Knowledge and Justification.* Princeton: Princeton University Press (Princeton Legacy Library).
Pollock, John L. 1987. "Defeasible Reasoning." *Cognitive Science* 11 (4), pp. 481–518. https://doi.org/10.1207/s15516709cog1104_4.
Pollock, John L. 2001a. "Defeasible Reasoning with Variable Degrees of Justification." *Artificial Intelligence* 133, pp. 233–282. https://doi.org/10.1016/S0004-3702(01)00145-X.
Pollock, John L. 2001b. "Nondoxastic Foundationalism." In *Resurrecting Old-fashioned Foundationalism*, edited by Michael R. DePaul, pp. 41–59. Lanham MD: Rowman & Littlefield (Studies in epistemology and cognitive theory).
Pollock, John L. 2010. "Defeasible Reasoning and Degrees of Justification." *Argument and Computation* 1 (1), pp. 7–22. https://doi.org/10.1080/19462161003728921.
Pollock, John L.; Cruz, Joseph. 1999. *Contemporary Theories of Knowledge.* Lanham Md.: Rowman & Littlefield (Studies in epistemology and cognitive theory).
Priest, Graham. 2006. *In Contradiction: A Study of the Transconsistent.* Oxford: Clarendon Press.
Priest, Graham. 2008. *An Introduction to Non-classical Logic. From If to Is.* Cambridge: Cambridge University Press (Cambridge introductions to philosophy).
Pritchard, Duncan. 2018. "Anti-luck Virtue Epistemology and Epistemic Defeat." *Synthese* 195 (7), pp. 3065–3077. https://doi.org/10.1007/s11229-016-1074-4.
Pritchard, Duncan; Turri, John. 2014. "The Value of Knowledge." In *The Stanford Encyclopedia of Philosophy*, edited by Edward N. Zalta. https://plato.stanford.edu/entries/knowledge-value/#WeaStrConKno, visited on 2/13/2017.
Pryor, James. 2004. "What's Wrong with Moore's Argument?" *Philosophical Issues* 14 (1), pp. 349–378. https://doi.org/10.1111/j.1533-6077.2004.00034.x.

Pryor, James. 2018. "The Merits of Incoherence." *Analytic Philosophy* 59 (1), pp. 112–141. https://doi.org/10.1111/phib.12118.

Quinn, Philip. 1985. "On Finding the Foundations of Theism." *Faith and Philosophy* 2 (4), pp. 469–486. https://doi.org/10.5840/faithphil19863325.

Reed, Baron. 2006. "Epistemic Circularity Squared? Skepticism about Common Sense." *Philosophy and Phenomenological Research* 73 (1), pp. 186–197. https://doi.org/10.1111/j.1933-1592.2006.tb00610.x.

Robitzsch, Andrea. "What are Epistemic Duties." https://www.academia.edu/2629151/What_are_Epistemic_Duties, visited on 02/21/21.

Roche, William. 2014. "Evidence of Evidence is Evidence under Screening-off." *Episteme* 11 (1), pp. 119–124. https://doi.org/10.1017/epi.2013.40.

Rosen, Gideon. 2001. "Nominalism, Naturalism, Epistemic Relativism." *Philosophical Perspectives* 15, pp. 60–91.

Rothschild, Daniel; Spectre, Levi. 2018. "At the Threshold of Knowledge." *Philosophical Studies* 175 (2), pp. 449–460. https://doi.org/10.1007/s11098-017-0876-7.

Schechter, Joshua. 2013. "Rational Self-Doubt and the Failure of Closure." *Philosophical Studies* 163 (2), pp. 428–452. https://doi.org/10.1007/s11098-011-9823-1.

Schoenfield, Miriam. 2015. "A Dilemma for Calibrationism." *Philosophy and Philosophical Research* 91 (2), pp. 425–455. https://doi.org/10.1111/phpr.12125.

Shope, Robert. 1978. "The Conditional Fallacy in Contemporary Philosophy." *Journal of Philosophy* 75 (8), pp. 397–413. https://doi.org/10.2307/2025564.

Shpall, Sam. 2013. "Wide and Narrow Scope." *Philosophical Studies* 163 (3), pp. 717–736. https://doi.org/10.1007/s11098-011-9841-z.

Shpall, Sam. 2014. "Moral and Rational Commitment." *Philosophy and Phenomenological Research* 88 (1), pp. 146–172. https://doi.org/10.1111/j.1933-1592.2012.00618.x.

Silva, Paul. 2017. "How Doxastic Justification Helps Us Solve the Puzzle of Misleading Higher-Order Evidence." *Pacific Philosophical Quarterly* 98, pp. 308–328. https://doi.org/10.1111/papq.12173.

Sliwa, Paulina; Horowitz, Sophie. 2015. "Respecting all the Evidence." *Philosophical Studies* 172, pp. 2835–2858. https://doi.org/10.1007/s11098-015-0446-9.

Smith, Martin. 2016. *Between Probability and Certainty. What Justifies Belief.* Oxford: Oxford University Press.

Sosa, Ernest. 2002. "Tracking, Competence, and Knowledge." In *The Oxford Handbook of Epistemology*, edited by Paul K. Moser, pp. 265–284. New York: Oxford University Press.

Sosa, Ernest. 2010. "The Epistemology of Disagreement." In *Social Epistemology*, Adrian Haddock, Alan Millar, Duncan Pritchard, pp. 278–297. Oxford: Oxford University Press.

Steup, Matthias. 2017. "Epistemology." In *The Stanford Encyclopedia of Philosophy*, edited by Edward N. Zalta. https://plato.stanford.edu/archives/fall2017/entries/epistemology/, visited on 2/13/2017.

Sturgeon, Scott. 2014. "Pollock on Defeasible Reasons." *Philosophical Studies* 169 (1), pp. 105–118. https://doi.org/10.1007/s11098-012-9891-x.

Sudduth, Michael. 2008. "Defeaters in Epistemology" in *The Internet Encyclopedia of Philosophy*. ISSN 2161–0002, https://www.iep.utm.edu/, visited on 1/28/2019.

Swain, Marshall. 1985. "Justification, Reasons, and Reliability." *Synthese* 64 (1), pp. 69–92. https://doi.org/10.1007/BF00485712.

Talbott, W. J. 2002. "The Illusion of Defeat." In *Naturalism Defeated? Essays on Plantinga's Evolutionary Argument against Naturalism*; [with a response by Alvin Plantinga], edited by James Beilby, pp. 153–164. New York: Cornell University Press.

Thune, Michael. 2010. "'Partial Defeaters' and the Epistemology of Disagreement." *Philosophical Quarterly* 60 (239), pp. 355–372. https://doi.org/10.1111/j.1467-9213.2009.611.x.

Titelbaum, Michael G. 2015. "Rationality's Fixed Point (or In Defense of Right Reason)." In *Oxford Studies in Epistemology, Volume 5*, edited by Tamar Szabó Gendler, John Hawthorne, pp. 253–294. Oxford: Oxford University Press.

Turri, John. 2010. "On the Relationship between Propositional and Doxastic Justification." *Philosophy and Phenomenological Research* 80 (2), pp. 312–326. https://doi.org/10.1111/j.1933-1592.2010.00331.x.

van Inwagen, Peter. 1996. "It Is Wrong, Everywhere, Always, for Anyone, to Believe Anything upon Insufficient Evidence." In *Faith, Freedom, and Rationality: Philosophy of Religion Today*, edited by Howard-Snyder, Jeff Jordan, pp. 137–154. London: Rowman & Littlefield.

Wheeler, Gregory. 2014. "Defeat Reconsidered and Repaired." *The Reasoner* 8 (2), pp. 12–15.

White, Roger. 2005. "Epistemic Permissiveness." *Philosophical Perspectives* 19 (1), pp. 445–459. https://doi.org/10.1111/j.1520-8583.2005.00069.x.

White, Roger. 2009. "On Treating Oneself and Others as Thermometers." *Episteme* 6 (3), pp. 233–250. https://doi.org/10.3366/E1742360009000689.

Willaschek, Marcus. 2007. "Contextualism about Knowledge and Justification by default." *Grazer Philosophische Studien* 74 (1), pp. 251–272. https://doi.org/10.1163/9789401204651_014.

Williams, Michael. 2001. *Problems of Knowledge. A Critical Introduction to Epistemology.* Oxford: Oxford University Press.

Williamson, Timothy. 2000. *Knowledge and its Limits.* Oxford: Oxford University Press.

Wright, Crispin. 2004. "Warrant for Nothing (and Foundations for Free)." *Aristotelian Society Supplementary Volume* 78 (1), pp. 167–212. https://doi.org/10.1111/j.0309-7013.2004.00121.x.

Zagzebski, Linda Trinkaus. 2012. *Epistemic Authority. A Theory of Trust, Authority, and Autonomy in Belief.* Oxford: Oxford University Press.

# Index – Definitions and Examples

Basing
    Terminology   11
C-based Undercut
    *Definitions:* Alternative Accounts   96
C-J Link
    *Definitions:* Alternative Accounts   97
Competent Reevaluation
    *Definitions:* Supplementary   181
Def
    *Definitions:* Defeat (final)   165
Def-1
    *Definitions:* Defeat   24
Def-2
    *Definitions:* Defeat   30
Def-3
    *Definitions:* Defeat   41
Def-4
    *Definitions:* Defeat   82
Def-5
    *Definitions:* Defeat   90
Def-6
    *Definitions:* Defeat   123
Def-7
    *Definitions:* Defeat   155
Deontological Justification (DJ)
    *Definitions:* Justification   172
DEVICE
    *Examples:* Rebutting Defeat   88
Disagreement
    *Definitions:* Disagreement   235
DOUBLE-AGENT
    *Examples:* Counterexamples   153
Doxastic Base
    Terminology   12
FEEBLE
    *Examples:* Undercutting Defeat   162
FLIGHT
    *Examples:* Higher-Order Defeat   259
FRIDGE
    *Examples:* Normative Defeat   216
Generic Attitude-Formation Process
    *Definitions:* Justification   197

Generic Evidence
    *Definitions:* Justification   183
Generic Evidentialism
    *Definitions:* Justification   183
Generic Reliabilism
    *Definitions:* Justification   196
Generic Reliability
    *Definitions:* Justification   198
Generic Support 1
    *Definitions:* Justification   186
Generic Support 2
    *Definitions:* Justification   186
Generic Well-Foundedness
    *Definitions:* Justification   186
HOUD
    *Definitions:* Alternative Accounts   68
HYPOXIA
    *Examples:* Higher-Order Defeat   260
HYPOXIA-C
    *Examples:* Higher-Order Defeat   262
HYPOXIA-I
    *Examples:* Higher-Order Defeat   267
HYPOXIA-S
    *Examples:* Higher-Order Defeat   265
IDLE DEFEATER
    *Examples:* Rebutting Defeat   149
IDLE EVIDENCE
    *Examples:* Supplementary   156
Input
    Terminology   9
Justifier
    Terminology   12
LAW
    *Examples:* Reason-Defeating Defeat   14
LEAVE
    *Examples:* Rebutting Defeat   14
LEAVE-ENOUGH
    *Examples:* Rebutting Defeat   39
LEAVE-FULL
    *Examples:* Rebutting Defeat   32
LEAVE-PART
    *Examples:* Rebutting Defeat   32

LEAVE-PERFECT
   *Examples:* Rebutting Defeat   32
LEAVE-WISH
   *Examples:* Counterexamples   45
MICRO
   *Examples:* Undercutting Defeat   84
MILK
   *Examples:* Undercutting Defeat   65
N-Def
   *Definitions:* Supplementary   242
Negative Updating Obligation
   *Definitions:* Justification   175
NEWSPAPER
   *Examples:* Normative Defeat   218
NEWSPAPER-2
   *Examples:* Normative Defeat   222
No-Conflict Obligation
   *Definitions:* Justification   174
No-Defeater Obligation
   *Definitions:* Justification   173
Partial Rebuttal
   *Definitions:* Supplementary   36
Peerhood
   *Definitions:* Disagreement   236
Perfect Rebuttal
   *Definitions:* Supplementary   37
RB (Rebasing)
   *Definitions:* Supplementary   109
Rebasing/Re-evaluation and Defeat
   *Definitions:* Supplementary   149
Rebasing/Re-evaluation and Undercutting
   *Definitions:* Supplementary   130
Rebut
   *Definitions:* Rebutting Defeat (final)   166
Rebut-1
   *Definitions:* Rebutting Defeat   25
Rebut-2
   *Definitions:* Rebutting Defeat   31
Rebut-3
   *Definitions:* Rebutting Defeat   41
Rebut-4
   *Definitions:* Rebutting Defeat   90
Rebut-5
   *Definitions:* Rebutting Defeat   148
Rebut[i]
   *Definitions:* Supplementary   170

RECALCITRANT
   *Examples:* Counterexamples   49
RED-FALSE
   *Examples:* Undercutting Defeat   192
RESTAURANT
   *Examples:* Disagreement   235
SCHOOL
   *Examples:* Undercutting Defeat   14
S-Def
   *Definitions:* Supplementary   239
SND
   *Examples:* Supplementary   245
SNS
   *Examples:* Supplementary   244
SSD
   *Examples:* Supplementary   246
SSS
   *Examples:* Supplementary   244
STAKES
   *Examples:* Normative Defeat   219
Successful Rebuttal
   *Definitions:* Supplementary   37
The Demandingness Trilemma
   *Definitions:* Supplementary   106
The Exclusive Thesis
   *Definitions:* Supplementary   54
The Inclusive Thesis
   *Definitions:* Supplementary   49
The Revised Epistemic Reasons-Against-Belief Theory
   *Definitions:* Alternative Accounts   161
THE UNREFLECTIVE COGNIZER
   *Examples:* Counterexamples   73
THEORY
   *Examples:* Counterexamples   85
Type 2, the First
   *Definitions:* Supplementary   177
Type 2, the Second
   *Definitions:* Supplementary   179
Type 2, the Third
   *Definitions:* Supplementary   180
Type 2, the Fourth
   *Definitions:* Supplementary   181
UNASSUMER
   *Examples:* Counterexamples   140

Undercut'
  *Definitions:* Undercutting Defeat (final) *166*
Undercut-1
  *Definitions:* Undercutting Defeat   *25*
Undercut-2
  *Definitions:* Undercutting Defeat   *82*
Undercut-3
  *Definitions:* Undercutting Defeat   *124*
Undercut-3'
  *Definitions:* Undercutting Defeat   *129*

Undercut$^i$
  *Definitions:* Supplementary   *170*
VIRUS-DIFFERENT
  *Examples:* Disagreement   *247*
VIRUS-SAME
  *Examples:* Disagreement   *248*
VIRUS-SAME*
  *Examples:* Disagreement   *254*
VISION
  *Examples:* Counterexamples   *136*

# Index – Names

Alexander, David   54–57
Alston, William Payne   46–47, 52, 54–56
Bergmann, Michael   17–18, 22, 24–26, 52–54, 55–57, 85–86, 158
Casullo, Albert   23–24, 29, 38–40, 65, 68, 71–74, 107, 136–139
Christensen, David   193, 235, 238–240, 258, 260–261, 267, 269
Conee, Earl   9, 11, 151–152, 183–186
Cruz, Joseph   17, 25, 48, 61–76, 227
Elga, Adam   235, 237, 238, 260
Feldman, Richard   9, 11, 151–152, 172, 183–186, 250, 257
Friedman, Jane   77–79, 82, 91
Gibbons, John   47, 184, 216, 222
Goldberg, Sanford   214, 222, 224, 226–228
Goldman, Alvin   9, 196–202
Grundmann, Thomas   35, 113, 142, 200, 215, 237, 243, 247, 257
Harman, Gilbert   227
Kelly, Thomas   237, 240–242, 253
Kvanvig, Jonathan   17, 157, 159

Lam, Barry   94, 97–99, 101
Lackey, Jennifer   48, 143–144, 214–215, 222–223
Lasonen-Aarnio, Maria   77, 258, 261
Lehrer, Keith   11, 151, 215
Loughrist, Timothy   17, 50, 153–165
McFarlane, John   60, 82, 235
Melis, Giacomo   23, 24, 60–61, 67, 93, 95, 96, 102–104
Meeker, Kevin   227
Plantinga, Alvin   3, 9, 17, 37, 38, 46–52, 56, 78, 81, 157
Pollock, John Leslie   17, 21, 22, 24, 30, 33, 45, 48, 61–76, 80, 93–95, 133–134, 227
Pryor, James   45, 49, 51–52
Shpall, Sam   97–99
Sturgeon, Scott   30, 61, 63–67, 69, 71–72, 74–76, 93–96, 103–104, 134–135
Thune, Michael   32, 40
Turri, John   11, 13, 34, 271

www.ingramcontent.com/pod-product-compliance
Lightning Source LLC
Chambersburg PA
CBHW031423150426
43191CB00006B/368